INSIDERS' GUIDE® SE W9-AZA-632

INSIDERS' GUIDE® TO

INDIANAPOLIS

FIRST EDITION

JACKIE SHECKLER FINCH

INSIDERS' GUIDE

GUILFORD, CONNECTICUT
AN IMPRINT OF GLOBE PEQUOT PRESS

To buy books in quantity for corporate use or incentives, call **(800) 962–0973** or e-mail **premiums@GlobePequot.com**.

INSIDERS' GUIDE ®

Copyright © 2010 by Morris Book Publishing, LLC

Editor: Amy Lyons
Project Editor: Lynn Zelem
Layout Artist: Kevin Mak
Text design: Sheryl Kober
Maps: Nick Trotter. © Morris Book Publishing, LLC

Library of Congress Cataloging-in-Publication Data is available on file.
ISBN 978-0-7627-5673-5

Printed in the United States of America
10 9 8 7 6 5 4 3 2 1

CONTENTS

Directory of Maps

ACKNOWLEDGMENTS

Many thanks to Kimberly Harms, one of the hardest-working people in the tourism industry, for answering my endless questions about our marvelous Hoosier home. As associate director of media relations for the Indianapolis Convention & Visitors Association, Kim is an excellent ambassador for the city. My appreciation also to the excellent team of area public relations officials who helped me write this book and to the Indianapolis residents, volunteers, and business owners who took the time to share what makes Indy special. Gratitude to my Globe Pequot editor, Amy Lyons, who saw that Indianapolis is a treasure-filled place ready for an Insiders' Guide and to project editors Ellen Urban and Lynn Zelem for their keen attention to detail.

This book is dedicated to my family—Kelly Rose, Mike Peters, Sean Rose and Devin, Stefanie Rose and Will, Logan Peters, and Miranda and Trey Scott.

A special remembrance to my husband, Bill Finch, whose spirit goes with me every mile and step of the way through life's journey.

—Jackie Sheckler Finch

ABOUT THE AUTHOR

An award-winning journalist, Jackie Sheckler Finch has covered a wide array of topics—from birth to death with all the joy and sorrow in between. She has written for many publications and was named the Mark Twain Travel Writer of the Year by Midwest Travel Writers in 1998, 2001, 2003, and 2006. She is also the author of *Insiders' Guide to Nashville* and *Tennessee Off the Beaten Path* (both published by Globe Pequot Press). She lives in Bloomington, Indiana.

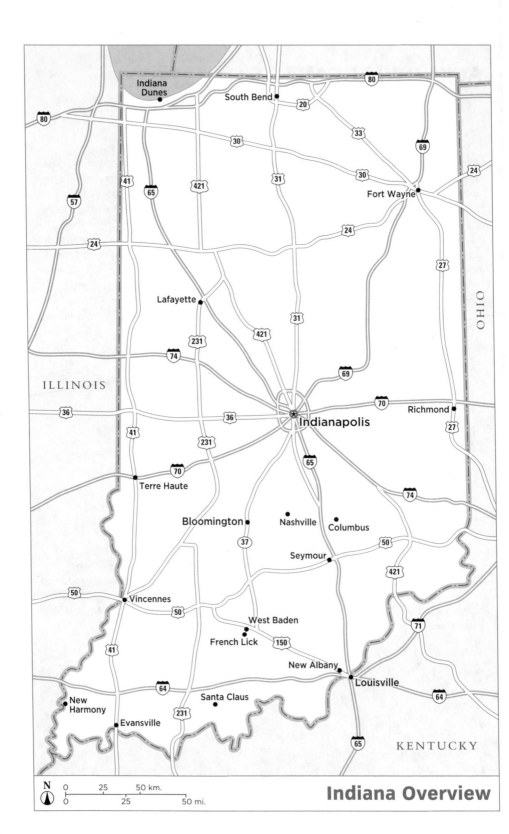

Indiana Overview

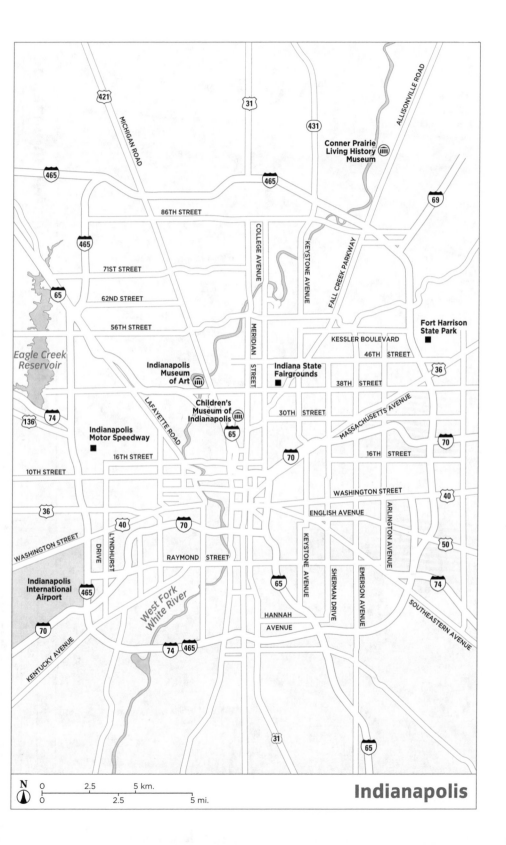

Indianapolis

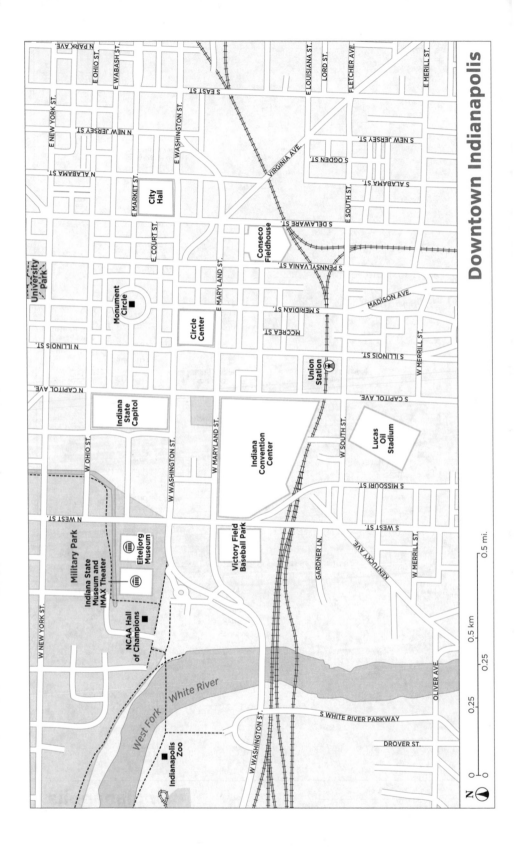

Downtown Indianapolis

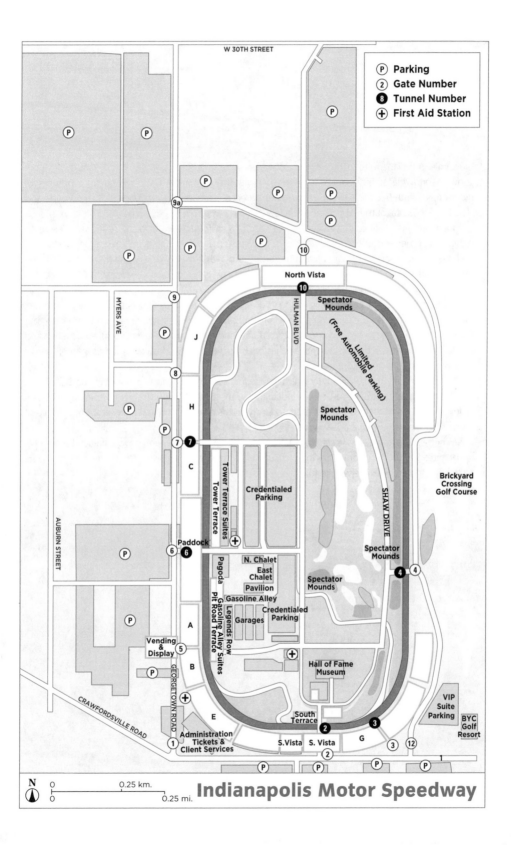

Indianapolis Motor Speedway

PREFACE

Welcome to Indianapolis! In the almost 200 years since its founding in 1821, the community now known worldwide as Indianapolis has earned fame and prestige. It's also picked up a number of nicknames—"Indy," "Circle City," "Crossroads of America," "Amateur Sports Capital of the World," and "The Racing Capital of the World" are just a few.

Interestingly, Indianapolis also was once called "Nap Town"—a slur because it was considered behind the times and boring. As you'll see in this book, that title certainly isn't true. Many people on their first visit to Indianapolis are pleasantly surprised by what they find. And the more they look, the more people seem to discover about Indy.

You might say that Indianapolis is the embodiment of Hoosier hospitality. People smile and speak to you on the street and are generally willing to give you the time of day or directions if you need them. Indianapolis is a laid-back, easygoing place where you can relax and listen to great music, cheer on your favorite team, indulge in outstanding eclectic cuisine, and enjoy countless museums, art galleries, and outdoor recreational activities. Indianapolis has become a top tourist destination among Americans as well as visitors from other countries.

This is a place where, fortunately, quality of life and cost of living don't go hand in hand.

According to the *Wall Street Journal*, Indianapolis ranked No. 1 in the nation in the Value for Money Index in 2008. Compared to the rest of the country, Indy's cost of living in 2009 was about 25 percent lower than the national average.

Whether you're here on vacation, are planning to make a home here, or you already live in Indy, you'll find a wealth of opportunities in practically any area that interests you. No matter why you come to the city, Indianapolis is a wonderful place to restart your engines.

HOW TO USE THIS BOOK

We Hoosiers are friendly people and I hope this book reflects that friendliness. We are proud of where we live and like to share it with others. Writing this book was a labor of love, as though I were talking with good friends about what makes us special and what shouldn't be missed, whether you live here or are just visiting.

Indianapolis is the heart of Indiana, the seat of state government, the 12th largest city in the nation and a mighty fine place to visit or to live. *Insiders' Guide to Indianapolis* is meant to be used and used often. Keep it in the car so you'll have it handy when choosing a place to dine, a shop to visit, an attraction to see, or for any other question that might come up. That said, here are a few suggestions that can help you make the most of this book, so you will soon feel like an insider yourself.

Insiders' Guide to Indianapolis is designed to be self-contained. That means that each chapter essentially stands on its own, so wherever you start reading, you'll find information you need to enjoy that aspect of Indianapolis life. If this is your first visit to Indy and you've just bought the book, a good restaurant might top your list of needs at the moment. The Restaurant chapter is chock-full of places you might want to try. It's certainly not a list of every restaurant in Indy. Nor will you find every lodging in the area in the Accommodations chapter—we are discerning in our choices.

There are plenty of cross-references to be sure you catch all the information. Watch for the Insiders' Tips with interesting little tidbits. The Close-Ups feature stuff that was so fascinating I pulled it out of the regular text and put a little spotlight on it.

Don't hesitate to personalize this book. Make it your own. Scribble notes in the margins, circle places you have visited, underline points of interest. Add your point of view to an attraction or lodging or accommodation so you'll remember next time what you liked or didn't like. Write your own brief restaurant review next to a site, telling what you particularly enjoyed and might want to recommend or order again. That is also a good way to plan itineraries when friends and family come to visit. You will know the best that Indy has to offer.

Many of the chapters, such as Accommodations and Parks, are divided into geographic areas or neighborhoods that are popular with locals and visitors alike. Other chapters, like Restaurants, are organized by subject so you can find what you want to see quickly and easily. The Annual Events chapter, of course, is organized chronologically.

The Accommodations, Restaurants, and Attractions chapters include pricing guides to help give you an idea of how much each choice will end up costing you. Luckily, many of Indianapolis's attractions are free, and when this is the case it's been noted.

Please remember that in a rapidly changing world, things are bound to change. By the time you read this book, there will be new places to visit and experiences to savor. Unfortunately, some old favorites may have bid farewell. Menus will be revised and schedules altered. It's always a good idea to call before visiting an attraction or restaurant. And please feel free to share your experiences with me. If you find a new restaurant, B&B, shop or some other favorite, let me know so it can be in the next edition. We want to keep *Insiders' Guide to Indianapolis* as accurate and up to date as possible.

It's an honor that, whether you're a visitor, a newcomer, or perhaps even a longtime resident wanting to see whether you've been missing anything, you have chosen this book to be your companion in Indianapolis. I sincerely hope I can help make your Indy experience a memorable one.

AREA OVERVIEW

When I moved to Indiana more than 20 years ago, my friends and coworkers in Massachusetts usually mentioned their two first impressions about my new home—Larry Bird and the Indy 500.

That was first and foremost what the state of Indiana brought to their minds. It is true that the great Bird (a former Boston Celtic, now the Indiana Pacers' president) and the world-famous auto race are a big part of what makes Indianapolis special. But there is so much more. I am still discovering little gems about the place I now call home.

Of course, Indy is a great sports mecca, has wonderful memorials, monuments, and museums, and is home to one of America's loveliest urban spaces—White River State Park. Then there are the award-winning restaurants, shops galore, trendy and tried-and-true nightspots, and top-notch professional performance venues.

Indy is also winning praise for reinventing the bicycle and pedestrian experience downtown with the Indianapolis Cultural Trail, the first of its kind. The 7.5-mile path allows users to pass by and though many destinations that make Indianapolis a recognized leader in the arts community. Since 2007 the trail has been completed in phases and is scheduled for final completion in 2011.

The Glick Peace Walk, scheduled for completion in 2010, is already drawing accolades. The walk will offer 12 distinctive sculptural gardens that celebrate the lives and accomplishments of "luminaries"—Susan B. Anthony, Andrew Carnegie, Thomas Edison, Albert Einstein, Benjamin Franklin, Martin Luther King Jr., Abraham Lincoln, Franklin D. and Eleanor Roosevelt, Jonas Salk, Mark Twain, Booker T. Washington, and the Wright brothers. The gardens will feature granite terrazzo plazas depicting the individuals' contributions to society and a timeline noting significant events that helped shape their lives. Signs will tell their stories through text and images. The centerpieces of the gardens will be 12-foot stainless-steel and glass "luminaries" featuring lighted glass etchings of the individuals. Ten of the luminary gardens will be located on the Indianapolis Cultural Trail along a median to be constructed on Walnut Street between Meridian Street and Capitol Avenue.

One of the biggest assets of the capital city is its friendly people. Hoosier hospitality is not just a catch phrase. It actually exists here. I learned that firsthand when moving from New England. And that friendly, helpful nature was demonstrated time and again when I was working on this book. People went out of their way to help me and were very excited about their city having an *Insiders' Guide*.

Founded on the banks of the shallow White River in 1821, the capital city is a major transportation hub known as the "Crossroads of America." The 12th largest city in the United States, Metropolitan Indianapolis includes nine counties—Marion County/Indianapolis, Hamilton County, Madison County, Hancock County, Shelby County, Johnson County, Morgan County, Hendricks County, and Boone County. It also has several suburban towns with interesting attractions of their own.

Once you've visited Indianapolis proper, try branching out and seeing what else Metropolitan Indianapolis has to offer. This chapter will help you understand the lay of the land and give you some information about the Greater Indianapolis area.

Vital Statistics

Founded: 1821; Established as state capital of Indiana: 1825

Population: Indianapolis—795,458 (2009); Indianapolis Metropolitan Statistical Area—1,666,032

Area: Marion County—403 square miles; Indianapolis Metropolitan Statistical Area—3,863 square miles

Government: Mayor Greg Ballard

Average temperatures: April: 63 high, 41 low
July: 86 high, 65 low
September: 77 high, 55 low
December: 39 high, 23 low

Average precipitation: 41 inches

Average snowfall: 27 inches

Elevation: 715 feet

Public transportation: IndyGo—$1.75 single ride

Highways: Indianapolis is intersected by I-69, I-70, I-74, I-65, and I-465. Fifty percent of the nation's population lives within a day's drive of Indianapolis.

Tax: Indiana's statewide sales tax is 7 percent.

Time Zone: Eastern, Daylight Saving Time

MONUMENT CIRCLE
(800) 323-4639
www.visitindy.com

Every city has one—a famous landmark that serves as a symbol for the city. In Indy, it's historic Monument Circle, the site that the Goodyear blimp broadcasts during football games and postcards promote with their colorfully perfect renditions. The Circle (as locals call it) is a favorite gathering spot. It's a great place to enjoy lunch or sit on the steps on a sunny day and watch people. It's where free concerts are performed and the annual Christmas tree lighting is observed the day after Thanksgiving.

The geographic heart of Indianapolis, Monument Circle is the large circular plaza at the union of Meridian and Market Streets. At the center of the Circle is the Soldiers and Sailors Monument. The four city blocks that front the Circle are bounded by Ohio Street to the north, Pennsylvania Street to the east, Washington Street to the south, and Illinois Street to the west.

Today, the busy plaza is surrounded by small shops, radio station studios, the Hilbert Circle Theatre, financial institutions, the Columbia Club (one of the oldest social clubs in Indianapolis), and the historic Christ Church Cathedral. Take time to admire the architecture of Circle Tower. Built eight years after the discovery of King Tut's tomb in 1922, the tower displays "hieroglyphics" above its Market Street door, a reflection of the Egyptian craze of the day. The tallest building directly on Monument Circle, each level above floor 10 features a setback, designed to reduce the amount of shadow cast on the Circle in the morning hours.

i On June 26, 1977, Elvis Presley stepped upon the stage at Market Square Arena in Indianapolis for what would be the last concert of his career. More than 18,000 concertgoers listened to Elvis croon his last song, "Can't Help Falling in Love." Less than two months later on August 16, Elvis was dead at his Memphis home. He was 42 years old.

3

DOWNTOWN INDIANAPOLIS
(317) 237-2222
www.indydt.com
A thriving success story and model for revitalization, downtown Indianapolis is a dynamic and growing area. The Regional Center of downtown Indianapolis covers 6.5 square miles in an area bounded by 16th Street to the north, I-65 and I-70 to the east, I-70 to the south, and Belt Railroad to the west.

Downtown Indianapolis is home to almost 20,000 residents and more than 210 shops, 300 restaurants and bars, 18 museums and historic sites, 24 memorials and parks, 8 major sports venues, countless performing arts, theaters, entertainment, and recreation options, numerous art galleries, and many other interesting attractions.

Even during a tough economy, downtown Indianapolis has seen strong demand and numerous new construction. Currently, there are 77 new projects worth more than $2 billion to be completed by 2015. Of these 77, there are 32 residential projects with 2,327 units, worth nearly $390 million.

BEECH GROVE
(317) 788-4977
www.beechgrove.com
Incorporated in 1906, Beech Grove is located in the southeast portion of Marion County and is part of the Greater Indianapolis Metropolitan Area. Beech Grove elected not to participate in Indianapolis's Unigov initiative, which consolidated the city and county governments in 1970. With nearly 15,000 residents, Beech Grove has its own independent government with a mayor, city council, and clerk-treasurer, although its residents do vote for the mayor of Indianapolis, who serves as the county executive.

Mainly a residential community, Beech Grove covers 4.3 square miles and is bordered by I-465 and the Conrail line and by Southern and Perkins Avenues.

i Best-known as a longtime broadcaster for NBC's *The Today Show,* Jane Pauley was born in 1950 in Indianapolis, where she had her first broadcasting job on WISH-TV in 1972. She is married to Doonesbury cartoonist Garry Trudeau.

LAWRENCE
(317) 549-8670
www.cityoflawrence.org
First platted in 1849 with just 16 lots, Lawrence is located minutes north of downtown Indianapolis and now covers 20 square miles with a population of about 41,000. In 1960 Lawrence became a city and nine years later annexed Fort Benjamin Harrison. Lawrence offers easy access to major interstate highways, including I-69, I-70, I-65, and I-74.

Lawrence is one of the "excluded cities" allowed to retain its city government when the rest of Marion County adopted the unified government structure known as Unigov. But Lawrence does vote for the mayor of Indianapolis as county executive and maintains representation on the Indianapolis/Marion County City-County Council.

Lawrence was named in honor of Captain James Lawrence, naval hero of the War of 1812, who is best remembered for the command "Don't give up the ship!"

SOUTHPORT
(317) 786-3585
www.cityofsouthport.org
A small city at the south end of Marion County, Southport was established in 1832 and offers easy access for commuters working in Indy. Situated east of Madison Avenue along Southport Road, Southport has a population of about 1,850.

Although it is landlocked and not a true port, Southport got its name because it was used as a place for loading and unloading by teamsters driving goods north to Indianapolis. Southport elected not to be a part of Unigov and has its own mayor, clerk-treasurer, and common council.

Close-up

What's a Hoosier?

That's the question often asked by Indiana visitors. No one seems to know exactly where the word *Hoosier* came from, but there are plenty of stories on its origin. Here are some of the more popular theories:

- When a visitor hailed a pioneer cabin in Indiana or knocked on its door, the settler would respond, "Who's yere?" Over time, the words of this frequent response became slurred and Indiana became known as the Hoosier state.

- Kentucky contractor Samuel Hoosier hired Indiana workers to build the Portland canal at Louisville. Those superior laborers became known as "Hoosier's men" or "Hoosiers" and carried the nickname back north with them. History, unfortunately, doesn't show that a Mr. Hoosier ever existed.

- Indiana poet James Whitcomb Riley said the origin of the word came from the pugnacious habits of the early settlers. "They were vicious fighters . . . [and] frequently bit off noses and ears. This happened so often that a settler coming into the barroom after a fight would see an ear on the floor and ask, 'Whose ear?'"

- Brawls were common during frontier days and Indiana river men became so skilled at trouncing or "hushing" their opponents that they were called "hushers" and eventually Hoosiers.

Today, the word is used to denote an Indiana native or resident—or a member of Indiana University's sports teams. Although the origin is uncertain, *Hoosier* and *hospitality* go hand in hand, and folks from Indiana wear the name proudly.

SPEEDWAY

(317) 241-2566

www.townofspeedway.org

Officially incorporated in 1926, Speedway chose to keep its individuality when Unigov came into existence. A separate government unit within Indianapolis, Speedway has its own town council, police department, fire department, street department, parks and recreation department, water and wastewater utilities, school system, and public library.

Covering 4.8 square miles, Speedway has a population of about 13,000. Located about 6 miles from downtown Indianapolis, Speedway is bounded by 10th and 30th Streets and by I-465 and the Indianapolis Motor Speedway.

The town gets its name from the Indianapolis Motor Speedway, which is located entirely within the town limits. Hundreds of thousands of people converge on Speedway in May for the Indy 500 and later for the Brickyard 400—two of the largest single-day sporting events in the United States. Developed as a city of the future, Speedway was meant to be a testing ground much like its famed namesake. Speedway was designed to be car friendly. Unlike many other Indianapolis streets that were often narrow brick, Speedway streets were paved and graced with homes featuring garages for cars.

Mostly a quiet place—except for the big races, of course—Speedway has well-maintained homes, plus numerous parks and golf courses, including the popular Brickyard Crossing championship golf course, located inside the speedway.

i Richard Gatling, an Indianapolis physician, invented the world's first rapid-firing machine gun in 1862. An early model fired 200 shots a minute. By 1898, the Gatling gun could fire 3,000 rounds a minute. Dr. Gatling envisioned his gun as a weapon so terrible that it would end war forever.

BOONE COUNTY
(765) 482-1320
www.boonechamber.org
Located 20 minutes from downtown Indianapolis, Boone County covers 423 square miles with a population of 55,027. One of the largest towns in Boone County, Zionsville has a population of about 13,000 and covers 25 square miles. But all that will change in Jan 2010, when Zionsville will increase to 52 square miles and boost its population thanks to a reorganization plan adopted by Zionsville and two surrounding townships. The plan will increase the opportunity for new business development.

One of the few towns in the United States that has preserved its brick main street, Zionsville draws visitors with more than 50 shops, plus restaurants and cafes. Surrounding the village is a mosaic of preserved historic homes, many dating back to the 19th century. The city is known for its peaceful, tree-lined streets, parks system, and nature center.

i Indianapolis and Oklahoma City are the only state capitals with the name of the state in the name of the city.

HAMILTON COUNTY
(800) 776-8687
www.hccvb.org
Located in the north central section of Metropolitan Indianapolis, Hamilton County was named in honor of Alexander Hamilton, the first U.S. secretary of the Treasury. One of the fastest growing counties in the nation, Hamilton County was ranked as the "No. 1 County in America to Raise a Family" by *Forbes* magazine.

Hamilton County covers 320.2 square miles and has a population of about 270,000. Carmel is one of the largest suburbs within Metropolitan Indianapolis, with a population of 68,653. Located immediately north of Indianapolis on SR 431, Carmel covers about 50 square miles and has been nationally recognized for its careful community planning and excellent city design. Carmel boasts over 800 acres of parkland and has been designated a "Bicycle Friendly City" for its extensive trail and path system.

The Arts & Design District of Carmel offers wonderful dining and shopping. Currently under construction, City Center will be home to the Regional Performing Arts Center. The project will include a 1,600-seat Concert Hall and 500-seat multipurpose theater, as well as retail, restaurant, office, and residential space.

HANCOCK COUNTY
(317) 477-TOUR
www.hcvb.org
Situated just east of Indy, Hancock County was named for John Hancock, the first signer of the Declaration of Independence. From 1990 to 2000, Hancock County was one of the fastest growing counties in Indiana. Covering 306.1 square miles, the county has a population of about 68,000.

As the county seat of Hancock County, Greenfield is known for its gracious Victorian homes. Restored to their former grandeur, many of the homes date to the days of the "gas boom"—the period between 1887 and 1907 when natural gas was found near Greenfield, prompting growth of the community.

HENDRICKS COUNTY
(317) 718-8750
www.tourhendrickscounty.com
Just minutes west of Indianapolis, Hendricks County covers 408.4 square miles with a population of 137,240. The largest town in Hendricks County, Plainfield boasts 25,739 people on close to 40 square miles.

Incorporated in 1839, Plainfield got its name from the early Friends (Quakers) who settled around the area and established several meetinghouses throughout the county. The Friends were "plain" people and thus the name Plainfield. The high school continues to honor the Quakers, using the name for the school's mascot.

Plainfield has long been associated with the National Road, US 40, which goes through town as Main Street. In 1842 the nation's spotlight was turned on Plainfield when President Martin Van Buren was deliberately dumped from his stagecoach into the thick mud of the highway. The practical joke was in response to Van Buren's veto of a bill from Congress to improve the highway. Western setters were angered by the vote and showed their displeasure when Van Buren came through Plainfield to gather votes for the 1844 election. The roots of an elm tree caused the incident and later became known as the Van Buren Elm. Van Buren Elementary School is located near the site.

JOHNSON COUNTY
(317) 881-8527
www.franklin-in.gov
Located immediately south of Indianapolis along I-65, Johnson County was formed in 1822 and named after Indiana Supreme Court judge John Johnson. The second fastest growing county in Indiana, Johnson County covers 320.2 square miles and has a population of about 140,000. The county is home to Hoosier Horse Park and the Greenwood Mall.

Named after Benjamin Franklin, the county seat of Franklin has about 11.3 square miles and a population of 20,000. Franklin College is located here and gives the town much of its charm. Downtown Franklin is known for its well-maintained older homes.

i The late Bernard Vonnegut, an Indianapolis native, was an internationally renowned atmospheric scientist who discovered how to make it snow or rain by seeding clouds with silver iodide. His younger brother, novelist Kurt Vonnegut Jr., once said that Bernard knew "more about tornadoes than any man alive."

MADISON COUNTY
(800) 533-6569
www.mccog.net
Formed in 1823, Madison County was named for James Madison, fourth president of the United States. Located in the east central part of Indiana, Madison County covers 452.1 square miles with a population of about 132,000.

The ninth largest city in Indiana, with a population of almost 58,000, Anderson serves as

county seat and attracts residents with a low cost of living and pleasant quality of life.

Anderson also has Hoosier Park Racing & Casino and Mounds State Park. Although it is Indiana's second smallest state park, Mounds has some of the best-preserved mounds in the state built by prehistoric Adena and Hopewell people.

MORGAN COUNTY
(317) 831-6509
www.mooresvillechamber.com
Founded in 1822, Morgan County is a fast-growing neighbor on the south side of Indianapolis. Covering 450 square miles, the county has a population of about 71,000. The county was named for General Daniel Morgan, who defeated the British at the Battle of Cowpens in the Revolutionary War.

Just 15 minutes southwest of Indianapolis, Mooresville is one of the hot growth areas for Indy. The city was founded in 1824 by North Carolina Quaker Samuel Moore and named for its founder. With a population that has doubled since 1990, Mooresville works to maintain its small town atmosphere. Brick sidewalks characterize Mooresville's downtown area.

SHELBY COUNTY
(317) 398-6624
www.cityofshelbyvillein.com
Located immediately southeast of Indianapolis on I-74, Shelby County serves as a "bedroom community" for folks who want to live in a smaller town while working in Indy. Covering 412.6 square miles, Shelby County has a population of 44,186. The county was named for General Isaac Shelby, who defeated the British at the Battle of Kings Mountain in the Revolutionary War. Shelby then became the first governor of Kentucky. During the War of 1812, Shelby led the Army of Kentucky into Canada and defeated the British at the decisive Battle of the Thames in 1813.

In the heart of Shelby County, the county seat of Shelbyville is 26 miles southeast of Indianapolis. Incorporated in 1850, Shelbyville has a population of about 18,000 on 9 square miles.

GETTING HERE, GETTING AROUND

With my trusty Garmin hooked on the car dashboard, I have navigated through cities that used to seem a maze to me. What did I do before the GPS? Get lost a lot. Indianapolis, on the other hand, is a fairly straightforward place to get around—even for someone who admits to not being born with a natural compass. Once you understand the lay of the land, it is easy to figure out the city.

Founded on the banks of the shallow White River, Indianapolis has a network of wide boulevards ranging outward from the center. Architect Alexander Ralston, who had worked with Pierre L'Enfant in designing Washington, D.C., used an easy navigation system of a mile-square grid to lay out Indianapolis. With a circle (now Monument Circle) at its center, Ralston used four diagonal spoke-like streets. To make it even simpler, the four streets are named North, South, East, and West.

Monument Circle is bisected by Meridian Street, the city's primary north-south street. A block south of the Circle, Washington Street is the primary east-west street. Four diagonal avenues lead out from the square and are named in honor of states—Massachusetts, Indiana, Virginia, and Kentucky. All east-west streets have names for 9 blocks north of the Circle. After that, they have numbers, starting with Ninth Street. One of the most well-traveled is 16th Street, home of the Indianapolis Motor Speedway.

Known as the "Crossroads of America," Indianapolis is intersected by: I-69, I-70, I-74, I-65, I-465, I-865, US 40, and State Roads 37, 67, 36, 136, 421, 135, 31, 431, and 52. Indianapolis International Airport is easily accessible from I-70 and I-465 on the city's southwest side. The beltway, I-465, encloses the city and provides direct access to all main avenues and all parts of Indianapolis.

As a transportation hub, Indy had the nation's first union rail depot at Union Station. With the development of the National Road, a steady stream of settlers poured into Indianapolis. Today the National Road is US 40, known in Indianapolis as Washington Street.

Indianapolis has several one-way streets, and during rush hour many left turns are prohibited. Speed limits generally run from 25 to 45 mph. If you're looking for a place to park, downtown Indy has more than 70,000 parking spaces, including about 4,000 parking meters. Metered parking is 25 cents for 20 minutes. The meters are free after 6 p.m. on weekdays and all day Saturday, Sunday, and holidays (New Year's Day, Dr. Martin Luther King Day, Presidents' Day, Memorial Day, Independence Day, Labor Day, Thanksgiving Day, and Christmas Day). Metered parking is limited around special event areas, so plan your route ahead of time.

Indy has many parking lots and garages, as do most hotels and many attractions. Lots and garages charge from $1.50 for three hours to $18.00 per day. When the Colts are playing in town, those rates go up considerably. For example, the popular Circle Centre Mall in downtown Indy has three handy parking garages, accessible at Washington, Maryland, Georgia, and Illinois Streets. Regular fees are $1.50 for three hours, but during Colts game days or other big downtown events, the garage may charge a $20.00 event rate.

Indy could be called a 30-minute city since you can get just about anywhere within a half hour drive. The city is easily accessible from a wide variety of locations. Not only that, but half the nation's population is within a day's drive, which makes traveling to Indy by car an attractive option for many. If flying is more your speed, the new Indianapolis International Airport offers travel on 11 airlines and nonstop and direct flights to 43 destinations. And, it's only a short 15-minute drive to the heart of downtown.

Of course, if you prefer, you can leave the driving to somebody else. Indianapolis has a number of transportation alternatives that are detailed in this chapter. No matter what mode of transportation you choose, if you happen to make a few wrong turns along the way, don't worry. You might discover a real treasure that you didn't expect to see. If you need assistance in finding your way, don't hesitate to ask someone for help. Hoosiers are known for their friendliness and will be glad to give you directions and welcome you to our city.

GETTING HERE

By Air

INDIANAPOLIS INTERNATIONAL AIRPORT
7800 Col. H. Weir Cook Memorial Dr.
(317) 487-7243
www.indianapolisairport.com
One of the most convenient airports in the nation (it's only 15 minutes from downtown Indianapolis), the new $1.1 billion Indianapolis International Airport opened November 12, 2008. One of the first U.S. airports built and opened since 9/11, the terminal building is 1.2 million square feet, with 500 feet of terminal frontage on a 1,000-foot, two-level drive.

More than 30 years in the making, the airport was built with no local or state tax dollars. One of the nation's fastest growing cargo airports, it is home to the world's second-largest Federal Express operation. Indianapolis International is served by 11 airlines and offers approximately 188 daily departures to 43 destinations. Competitive airfare combined with easy access brings more than 8.25 million passengers a year to the new airport. The terminal offers streamlined check-in and security screening areas, 96 ticket counters, 10 moving sidewalks, and a 5,900-space parking garage.

Built for maximum convenience and safety, Indianapolis International is also a beauty. Architecturally, it has an aerodynamic profile pointed skyways as if the airport itself were about to take off. The passenger terminal features soaring architecture with 80-foot-high glass walls in the main hall and abundant natural light, spacious security checkpoints, great shopping and dining, and free Wi-Fi throughout.

> **i** Top destinations from Indianapolis International Airport include: Orlando, Tampa, Las Vegas, Washington/Baltimore, Atlanta, Miami, Phoenix, New York, and Dallas.

Along with guest services, the airport offers a barbershop, shoeshine stations, currency exchange, USO room, travel spa, and post-security amenity centers with Internet access and pay phones. To give the airport a personal Hoosier touch, local restaurants offer great choices like Patachou on the Fly, King David Dogs, Shapiro's Delicatessen, 96th Street Steakburgers, Giorgio's Pizza, South Bend Chocolate Company, and Harry & Izzy's, along with national chains.

Shopping also is pure Indy. The first-ever Indianapolis 500 Grill is a sit-down restaurant accompanied by Brickyard Authentics, an auto-racing apparel and collectibles store. Cultural Crossroads offers merchandise and displays from eight leading Indianapolis museums and cultural institutions.

The terminal offers nearly $4 million in original art created by 15 artists, including many with Hoosier ties. The art represents an array of artistic forms and mediums. The abstract glass murals in each concourse are my favorite, featuring original poetry written by Indiana artists to evoke thoughts of travel, flying home, and Indiana history. Even the parking garage has neat art—local

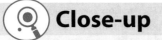

Close-up

Aviation Pioneer Honored at New Airport

The road leading into Indianapolis International Airport is called Col. H. Weir Cook Memorial Drive. The main terminal is named H. Weir Cook Terminal. So who is Harvey Weir Cook?

Born June 30, 1893, in Wilkinson, Indiana, Cook saw the beginning of aviation and was a hero who fought in two wars and gave his life for his country. Cook also was instrumental in bringing an airport to Indianapolis.

Cook's airplane career began when the aviation industry was young and dangerous. Cook often flew alongside other aviation pioneers in the early days of aviaiton. World War I flying ace Eddie Rickenbacker, Charles Lindbergh, Amelia Earhart, and fellow Hoosier daredevil pilot Roscoe Turner were among his good friends. Cook's 1926 racing pilot license was signed by friend and cohort Orville Wright.

During World War I, Cook flew with the famed 94th Aero Squadron—Rickenbacker's legendary Hat in the Ring troops, some of the most daring pilots of the time. Battling fierce air attacks over European skies, Cook brought down seven enemy aircraft and was twice awarded the Distinguished Service Cross.

After the war, Cook became active in several World Peace Missions and helped pioneer the first transcontinental airmail service. After a hurricane hit Miami in September 1926, Cook chartered a plane to rush desperately needed vaccine to residents hard hit by the storm. He became the first aviator in the nation to fly critical serum and medical supplies to families in need around the United States.

Cook worked to advance technical and safety standards in aviation and in the 1930s hosted a network radio program for children. As an officer with the Indianapolis Chamber of Commerce, Cook helped select the site for the Indianapolis airport, which opened in 1931. He also suggested the construction and development of concrete airstrips, radio devices to aid in landing during fog, and lighting racks on runways to allow for night landing. His technical and safety advances were quickly and readily adopted by airports through the world.

When the Japanese bombed Pearl Harbor on December 7, 1941, Cook recognized the importance of air power and again stepped up to serve his county. Quickly back in duty, Cook trained young pilots. Learning that his old friend Eddie Rickenbacker and others had crashed at sea during a secret raid near Japan, Cook helped rescue Rickenbacker and others after they had been lost at sea for weeks. On March 24, 1943, Cook was killed while flying in action over New Zealand.

artist Greg Hull's *Breath* fills an atrium with red bags that expand and contract.

i Indianapolis outshines other midwestern airports in regard to low fares, according to a U.S. Department of Transportation report in the first quarter of 2009. In fact, of the top 100 airports in the nation, only 21 have lower fares than Indy, which averaged fares of $276.

Whether you are saying hello or goodbye to Indy, many travelers stop to catch a clear view of downtown Indianapolis through the curved wall of glass in the airport's Civic Plaza.

Airlines Serving Indianapolis

Air Canada: (800) 247-2262; www.aircanada .com; Concourse B

Air Tran: (800) 825-8538; www.airtran.com; Concourse B

American Airlines: (800) 433-7300; www.aa
.com; Concourse B
Continental Airlines: (800) 523-3273; www
.continental.com; Concourse A
Delta Airlines: (800) 221-1212; www.delta.com;
Concourse A
Frontier Airlines: (800) 432-1359; www
.frontierairlines.com; Concourse B
Midwest Airlines: (800) 452-2022; www
.midwestairlines.com; Concourse B
Northwest Airlines: (800) 225-2525; www.nwa
.com; Concourse A
Southwest Airlines: (800) 435-9792; www
.southwest.com; Concourse B
United Airlines: (800) 864-8331; www.united
.com; Concourse B
U.S. Airways: (800) 428-4322; www.usairways
.com; Concourse B

i To remember where you parked at the
Indianapolis International Airport,
write the parking shelter number and the
parking row on your ticket and keep it in
a safe place such as your wallet or purse.
If you parked in the Economy Parking Lot,
your ticket will be blue; if you parked in
the Long-Term Parking Lot, your ticket will
be orange.

Parking at the Airport

Indianapolis International Airport offers parking
for 18,000 vehicles. Long-term parking is $12,
economy parking is $9, and the parking garage
is $2 for 30 minutes or a maximum of $18 for 24
hours. The airport also offers two types of valet
service. Express valet guarantees your vehicle is
safely parked under cover for the duration of your
stay, at $10 for four hours or $18 daily. Rooftop
valet guarantees your vehicle is safely parked on
the top floor of the garage for $15 a day. When
you return, attendants bring your vehicle to you,
including complimentary snow and ice removal
in the winter.

i A Cell Phone Lot at Indianapolis
International Airport allows visitors
to park and wait for free until passengers
have landed and claimed their baggage.
Travelers can then call on a cell phone and
alert their ride that they have arrived.
The lot contains 49 first-come, first-served
spaces.

Ground Transportation from the Airport

Various taxi services and other forms of transportation are available at the airport's Ground
Transportation Center on Level 1 of the parking
garage. A handy one-stop location, the center
provides rental cars, taxi and limousine service,
commercial bus and shuttle service, public transportation via IndyGo, and hotel courtesy vehicles.

If you're staying downtown, many hotels
operate free shuttles for their guests. Ask when
you make your reservations, or try the courtesy
telephones in the airport baggage claim areas.
Here are some other choices:

INDYGO

The cheapest way to get downtown is public transportation via IndyGo. Take Route 8 via
Washington Street and pay $1.75. For $7, take the
GreenLine Airport Downtown Express Shuttle via
IndyGo and travel nonstop. Green Line service
runs daily from 5 a.m. to 9 p.m. The cost is $7 per
trip. Call IndyGo at (317) 635- 3344 or visit www
.indygo.net.

LIMOUSINE

Pay $11 for a Share-A-Ride Limousine with Carey
Indiana, (317) 241-6700.

i Need to mail a letter at the airport? A
U.S. mailbox is located in the ticketing hall near the top of the escalators and
in the baggage claim area behind the escalators at Indianapolis International Airport.
Stamps may be purchased at guest services.

i Smoking is not permitted on any of the property at Indianapolis International Airport—that includes any airport building, structure, facility, or vehicle.

TAXI

For about $15, catch a cab. There is a $15 minimum charge for all fares from the airport, regardless of distance.

RENTAL CARS

If you'd prefer to captain your own ship, on-site rental car agencies include:

Alamo: (800) 327-9633; www.alamo.com
Avis: (800) 230-4898; www.avis.com
Budget: (800) 572-0700; www.budget.com
Dollar Car Rental: (800) 800-3665; www.dollar .com
Enterprise: (800) 736-8222; www.enterprise.com
Hertz: (800) 654-3131; www.hertz.com
National: (800) 227-7368; www.nationalcar.com
Thrifty Car Rental: (800) 847-4389; www.thrifty .com

i Indianapolis built its first passenger terminal in 1931 at a cost of $150,000. In comparison, the second terminal, which was built in 1956, cost $1.9 million. The new airport complex which opened in 2008 off I-70 cost $1.1 billion and was the largest civic development in the city's history.

By Train

Although Indianapolis was once one of the largest passenger railway centers in the nation, the city now has very limited train service. Amtrak's Hoosier State, which departs from Union Station at 350 S. Illinois St., runs daily between Chicago and Indianapolis. Amtrak's Cardinal operates between New York and Chicago, with stops in Indianapolis,

Call Amtrak at (800) 872-7245 or check the Web site at www.amtrak.com.

By Bus

Greyhound bus connections can be made at 127 N. Capitol Ave. Call (800) 231-2222 or see the Web site at www.greyhound.com.

GETTING AROUND

By Taxi

Unlike in other cities, taxis don't usually cruise Indy streets in search of fares. The best places to hail a cab are in front of major downtown stores or at downtown taxi stands. Otherwise, call a cab and it will come find you. The average fare is $3 per pickup and $2 per mile. The major cab company in Indianapolis is Yellow Cab, (317) 487-7777, www.ycindy.com.

By Public Transportation

Nicknamed IndyGo, the public transit system for the city of Indianapolis is, naturally, the Indianapolis Public Transportation Corporation. Now you know why we just say IndyGo. Its history started in 1953 when the city's streetcar system was converted to bus routes. Most of the buses followed the same routes as the streetcars.

The city of Indianapolis took over public transportation in 1975 and originally operated buses under the name Metro Bus. The IndyGo name came aboard in 1996. Not surprisingly, IndyGo is now seeing an increase in ridership as folks try to save money on gasoline and parking. In the fall of 2007, IndyGo reinstated express routes, including one to Indianapolis International Airport.

IndyGo operates 34 city bus routes serving downtown and most of Marion County. The fare is $1.75; 85 cents for ages 65 and older, children under 18, and people with disabilities. Riders may apply for an IndyGo Half Fare ID card at the customer service center. The half-fare cards must be presented when boarding. Children age five and under may ride free with a paying passenger (limit two children). A day pass is $4; $2 for half fare. Exact fare is required. Transfers are free. Contact IndyGo at (317) 635-3344 or www .indygo.net. The IndyGo Customer Service Center is located in the Indianapolis City Market, 222 E. Market St.

By Carriage

The clip-clop of horses' hooves and the gentle rhythm of a carriage will transport you back to another era in a downtown carriage ride. Reservations are recommended but the carriages are often waiting for fares outside downtown spots if you would like a last-minute romantic ride.

Two main carriage companies provide rides year round, weather permitting. A half-hour ride costs about $50. For more information contact Yellow Rose Carriages, (317) 634-3400, www .indycarriage.com; or Blue Ribbon Carriage Company, (317) 631-4169, www.blueribboncarriages .com.

By Gondola

Sit back and let your imagination take you to the canals of Venice. Actually, it's Indianapolis but the romance of Old Italy is alive with gondola rides on the Indy canal.

Old World Gondoliers offer 15-minute rides for $15 for each adult, Tues through Sat from 6:30 to 10:30 p.m., weather permitting. Rides leave from 337 W. 11th St. You also can order a picnic basket to savor while on the water. Each ride features three songs sung in Italian. Call (317) 340-2489 or visit the Web site at www.4gondola.com.

HISTORY

Transportation was the major reason Indianapolis was founded. Little did the city's founding fathers know that their tiny settlement would one day grow up to become a transportation giant known as the "Racing Capital of the World" and the "Crossroads of America."

Back then, folks were just looking for a place to settle along a river. Indy certainly can boast of the White River but, then as now, the White River is too shallow and sandy most of the year for big boats to navigate. From the beginning, Indianapolis was landlocked. In fact, famed writer Kurt Vonnegut once noted that his Indianapolis birthplace is the world's largest city not located on a navigable waterway. However, that didn't stop Indy from becoming a gem of the Midwest.

Although it didn't have a river for transportation, Indianapolis did have a big advantage—it was located in the heart of the nation. When roads and highways, railways, and air routes were laid out, Indianapolis became an important meeting place for east-west, north-south traffic.

But that is getting ahead of our story. Here is how it all began.

PREHISTORY

When the last glaciers retreated 13,500 years ago, humans didn't even live in Indiana. As a reminder of the Ice Age visit, glaciers left behind a landscape rich with fertile soil and flowing with abundant water. Dense hardwood forests soon flourished and animals roamed the wilderness.

Long before European Americans claimed the land, the marshy site at the confluence of the White River and Fall Creek was home to mound building cultures. Prehistoric tribes traded, hunted, and lived here. For some reason, those tribes had disappeared by the mid-15th century. For the most part, historians don't know what happened in Indiana between the end of the Mississippian culture and the arrival of the first white men in the 17th century.

When the French explorer Robert de La Salle entered Indiana in 1679, there were maybe a dozen Native American tribes in Indiana. Living in the Indianapolis area were mostly the Miami and Potawatomi. The tribes first had contact with French fur trappers in the early 1700s. Those interlopers didn't seem to pose a threat to the native inhabitants. In fact, the French learned native ways and often married native women.

TREATY OF 1818

Negotiated by William Henry Harrison, former governor of the Indiana Territory, the Treaty of 1818 was the turning point for the settlement of Indiana. In the New Purchase, or Treaty of St. Mary's, several tribes ceded the central portion of the state. The Delawares agreed to removal west of the Mississippi. Two tribes, the Miami and the Potawatomi, were the only major tribes to remain in Indiana after 1820. They then "traded" land needed for construction of the Michigan Road and the Wabash and Erie Canal in 1826.

It was a bad deal for the Indians. In exchange for money—which was seldom paid—and tokens, the Indians gave up their homeland and agreed to live wherever the federal government sent them. The Indian Removal Act of 1830 allowed the Indiana General Assembly to remove the remaining Native inhabitants from the state. Members of the tribe who objected were forcibly removed. More than 800 were "escorted" to Kansas by an armed militia company in a disorganized and tragic march known as the "Trail of Death."

> **i** Ninety percent of the world's popcorn is grown in Indiana.

14

The Treaty of 1840 required that the last Indian tribe in Indiana—the Miami—also would move to Kansas. That migration took place in 1846, although several chiefs and their families were given individual land near Fort Wayne.

Once the Indians were safely out of the way, settlers began heading for the new territory. While the Indians were cheated out of their land by the treaties, Indiana came out a winner. Made a state in 1820, Indiana more than doubled in size. Ironically, the heritage of those early Native Americans is memorialized in the state's name— Indiana, "land of Indians."

The first European settlers of Indianapolis were John, James, and Samuel McCormick. John and his brother built a log cabin on the east bank of the White River in 1820. He lived there with his wife and eight children. John was one of three of the first county commissioners of Marion County—named for Revolutionary War general Francis Marion, nicknamed the "Swamp Fox." It was in McCormick's home that Indianapolis was chosen as Indiana's state capital. The engineer who laid out the plans for Indianapolis stayed with McCormick to do his work. John McCormick died in 1824 but his descendants still call Indiana home today. On the east bank of the White River in White River State Park is McCormick's Rock, a memorial that commemorates the site of McCormick's cabin.

> **i** The city's first luxury apartment building, Blacherne Apartments, was built by Civil War general Lew Wallace from the proceeds of his novel, *Ben-Hur*.

CREATING A STATE CAPITAL

In June of 1820, state representatives appointed commissioners to select a site for Indiana's capital city. At the time, the town of Corydon was serving as capital. But Corydon, located in the southeast part of Indiana, was no longer the center of the state. Instead, the area around John McCormick's cabin was picked. Now the state legislature had to choose a name for the new capital. That honor went to Judge Jeremiah Sullivan, who invented

the name by joining *Indiana* with *polis,* the Greek word for city.

Now came the hard work of making the small settlement into a fitting state capital. Not everyone was sure it would actually happen. The new capital was a scraggly village. Its only cleared street was full of tree stumps. The houses were scattered about the deep woods of the mile square and could be reached only by cow paths. With the final decision to bring the capital here, Indianapolis began to show signs of permanency.

Alexander Ralston, who had helped Charles L'Enfant design Washington, D.C., was chosen to bring order to the heavily wooded site. He designed a city modeled after Washington. He laid out Indianapolis in a circular pattern based on a square mile because that was as large as he thought the struggling city would ever become. Ralston's 1821 plan called for four diagonal streets radiating out from the center like spokes on a wagon wheel.

At the center, on a wooded knoll circled by a wide street, would sit the governor's mansion. Completed in 1827, the mansion cost $6,500 during the term of Governor James B. Ray, but the governor's wife refused to move into the home because of its lack of privacy. Having the first family's dirty laundry hung out for all to see on the public square was not a happy prospect. No governor ever lived in the mansion and it was eventually demolished in 1857. Later, Governor's Circle became known as Monument Circle, when the magnificent Soldiers and Sailors Monument was completed on the site in 1901.

At first it seemed as though doubters might be proven right. A malaria outbreak, caused by mosquito infestation around Pogue's Run and White River, hit the settlement in 1821 and again in 1822, claiming many lives. But by the end of 1822, the town had a gristmill, two sawmills, three groceries, two mercantile houses, several small workshops, and seven taverns.

The arduous task of moving the state capital from Corydon started in November of 1824. State treasurer Samuel Merrill loaded up the state's silver and archives along with his family and headed north in four wagons. No roads existed

Notable Events in Indianapolis History

January 6, 1821: New settlement site was named Indianapolis.

1830: The National Road, now US 40, was routed through Indianapolis.

1902: The 284-foot-tall Soldiers and Sailors Monument, the first monument in the nation to honor the common soldier, was dedicated.

1909: Indianapolis Motor Speedway was built.

1911: First Indianapolis 500-Mile Race was held on the 2.5-mile oval racetrack at the Indianapolis Motor Speedway.

1926: The Children's Museum of Indianapolis, the largest of its kind in the world, opened.

1970: Indianapolis merged with surrounding Marion County to form a consolidated government structure called Unigov.

1971: The first Indiana Black Expo Summer Celebration was held at the Indiana State Fairgrounds. The event is now the largest and longest running exposition of its kind in the nation celebrating African-American culture and heritage.

1984: The NFL Colts moved to Indianapolis from Baltimore, Maryland.

1984: Circle Theatre, a 1916 movie palace, was renovated and became the permanent home of the Indianapolis Symphony Orchestra, now called the Hilbert Circle Theatre.

1987: The 10th Pan American Games were held, bringing 4,453 athletes from 38 countries to Indianapolis.

1987: The regatta course at Eagle Creek Park was built, one of only two courses in the U.S. sanctioned for international competitions.

1988: The $64 million Indianapolis Zoo opened in White River State Park.

1988: The $10.9 million restoration of the Indiana Statehouse was completed.

1988: Conner Prairie, an interactive history park, opened a $10 million museum center.

and a path for the wagons had to be cut through the dense forests during the winter trip. The 160-mile journey covered about 12 miles a day. By the end of November, the seat of government had been relocated to Indianapolis. The first session of the General Assembly convened there in January 1825.

TRANSPORTATION CENTER

Although the White River never lived up to expectations from Indy's founders as a major transportation route, the city soon found other ways to become a commerce center. The National Road (US 40) spurred growth when it came through in 1834. From 1827 to 1834, workers completed the

156-mile route across Indiana to join the Northwest Territory to the eastern United States.

Michigan Road (US 421) started at the Ohio River and ran north toward Lake Michigan. At the center of these two important roads, of course, was Indianapolis, and therein rested the city's future. With all their possessions lodged onto wagons, pioneer families could hope to make five to 10 miles a day on these early roads.

The ultimate transportation dream was the creation of the Central Canal project to link the landlocked Indianapolis with a system of canals that would connect to major waterways and open avenues of commerce and trade. The 1825 success of the Erie Canal in New York spawned

1989: The Eiteljorg Museum of American Indians and Western Art opened.

1989: American Cabaret Theatre moved to Indianapolis from New York.

1991: Indianapolis hosted the NCAA Division 1 Men's Basketball Championships (the Final Four), the PGA Championship, and the World Gymnastics Championships.

1994: Brickyard Crossing, a Pete Dye–designed championship golf course, opened to the public at the Indianapolis Motor Speedway.

1995: The $319.5 million Circle Centre mall opened. About 12 million people visited the mall during its first year of operation.

1995: A permanent memorial to the USS *Indianapolis,* the legendary World War II flagship that was sunk by a Japanese torpedo two weeks before the war ended, was dedicated.

1996: The $18 million, 13,500-seat Victory Field opened in White River State Park downtown as home to the AAA Indianapolis Indians.

1996: A $10 million IMAX 3D theater opened in White River State Park.

1999: White River Gardens, a sister institution to the Indianapolis Zoo, opened. The $15 million project contains 3.3 acres of botanical and water gardens, plus a five-story conservatory.

1999: The $183 million Conseco Fieldhouse opened as home to the Indiana Pacers and its sister team, the Indiana Fever.

2002: After being housed in the old Indianapolis City Hall for more than 33 years, the $105 million Indiana State Museum opened.

2007: The Indianapolis Colts won Super Bowl XLI.

2008: NFL team owners voted to award the bid for the 2012 Super Bowl to Indianapolis.

2008: Lucas Oil Stadium, the $17 million permanent home of the Indianapolis Colts, opened on August 16.

2008: The $1.1 billion Indianapolis International Airport opened.

"Canal Fever" in midwestern states, including Indiana. By 1827 the state began longing for a system of canals that would connect Indianapolis with the Wabash and Erie Canal. The city's Central Canal was part of the Mammoth Internal Improvements Act signed into law in 1836 with a hefty $10 million price tag. Its single largest project was the Central Canal, the longest of the canals planned for Indiana.

Unfortunately, very little canal was actually constructed and then watered, ultimately bankrupting the state. A distance of 24 miles was dug from Broad Ripple to Port Royal. Sadly, a severe depression and financial panic gripped the nation from 1837 to 1839. By 1841, Indiana could not even pay the interest on its internal improvement debt, much less the principal. The delinquent interest was increasing by half a million dollars a year.

The bankruptcy of the state created by the failure of internal improvements was one of the principal reasons that a new state constitution was created in 1851. This constitution prohibits the state from going into debt, and it still guides the State of Indiana to this day.

With the arrival of the railroad in 1847, manufacturing gained new speed in Indianapolis. The nation's first Union Station was built in 1853, and by 1855 Indianapolis had eight rail lines. Indianapolis was well on its way to being the Crossroads of America.

BIRTH OF A CITY

Incorporated as a town in 1832, Indianapolis didn't officially become a city until 1847. The city's first mayor, Whig Party candidate Samuel Henderson, was elected on April 24. The city council's first order of business was to improve city streets. With a population of almost 6,000, Indianapolis still boasted one major street—Washington, which was clogged with many tree stumps.

Although many early setters were from bordering states, European immigrants soon came looking for a new life in the young city. By mid-century, immigration—especially from Ireland and Germany—had increased the city's population to 18,611. In 1863, Kingan and Company, a meatpacking company that originated in Belfast, Ireland, located a plant on the banks of the White River. The company enticed workers from Ireland to Indy, and by 1880 Kingan was the third largest pork-packing center in the world, ranking behind Chicago and Cincinnati.

German immigrants flocked to Indianapolis from the 1820s through the 1890s. The majority of immigrants came to the United States after the failed revolution of 1848 and became known as "Forty-Eighters." Bringing with them the idea of "club" life, the new Americans were eager to form social, political and religious groups. Formed in 1854, the Indianapolis Maennerchor is the oldest men's choir in America, preserving the tradition of German choral music. The choir was created by a group of German immigrants homesick for their native homeland.

Neighborhoods such as Germantown and Irish Hill sprang up. So did churches. The Irish celebrated their first Catholic Mass in 1837 at a tavern on West Washington Street. They founded what would become St. John Catholic Church in 1840. Worship buildings of all denominations soon joined the religious roster. A new city cemetery was constructed in the 1860s. Unlike the tidy rows of small pioneer cemeteries with their often handmade markers, Crown Hill Cemetery was large and picturesque. Its massive stone gates and Romanesque Revival waiting station gave the cemetery an imposing monumental quality. The individual stones and mausoleums for those buried there provide an interesting collection of sculptural work.

In 1850, African Americans made up only about 5 percent of the city's population and it was a subject of debate as to who was the first black Indianapolis resident. Some local historians say it was Aaron Wallace. Others believe it was Cheney Lively. The difference of opinion is rooted in how long each person was here.

Wallace arrived in the early 1820s as a servant of Gen. John Tipton, the military hero who had helped select Indy to replace Corydon as the state capital. Shortly after the site was picked, Tipton left town and took his slave with him.

A housekeeper, Cheney Lively was brought to Indianapolis by Alexander Ralston, the man who laid out downtown Indy's Mile Square. After Ralston died, Lively stayed in Indianapolis, living in a Maryland Street home that she owned. In the 1830 census, Lively was listed as the only female black head of household. She changed that in 1836 by marrying John Britton, a former slave from Ohio and local leader of the nationwide Negro Convention Movement, which sought to improve conditions for African Americans.

Barred both by law and prejudice from participating in much community life, African Americans developed their own community. By 1836, an African American settlement called "Colored Town" had grown up along the banks of the waterway now known as the Indianapolis Water Co. Canal. Barred from public schools, denied jobs and the right to vote, African Americans were hit with another barrier to equality in 1851. Indiana enacted a law prohibiting African Americans from entering the state. Article 13 also levied fines against anyone who hired African Americans.

As a result, some African Americans left Indiana. Some migrated to Canada. A few moved to Africa. But most black Hoosiers refused to be run out of Indiana and fugitive slaves increasingly found refuge in and around Indianapolis. The nation was on the verge of a Civil War.

CIVIL WAR

As a major railroad hub, Indianapolis was a major base of pro-Union activity. The governor of Indiana, Oliver Morton, was a big supporter of Abraham Lincoln and he quickly turned Indy into a staging point for Northern troops eager to invade Southern states.

Indiana was the first state in what was then considered the American Northwest to join in the fighting of the Civil War. When news of the attack on Fort Sumter, which began the war, reached Indiana on April 12, 1861, mass meetings were held to decide the state's position. Indiana chose to remain in the Union and to quickly send troops to help suppress the rebellion. Keeping Indiana in the Union was important because the state's rich agricultural products would become increasingly valuable to the Union after the lush farmland of the South was lost.

On April 14, Gov. Morton issued a call to arms. Lincoln had initially asked that Indiana send 7,500 men. On the first day, 500 men assembled, and within three weeks more than 22,000 had volunteered—so many that thousands were turned away. Before the war ended, Indiana had contributed a total of 208,367 men, 15 percent of the state's total population, to serve in the Union Army and 2,130 to serve in the Union Navy.

Men from around the state poured into Indianapolis to train for the war at Camp Morton (named for you-know-who). Located on the northeastern edge of the Mile Square, Camp Morton was later converted into a prison camp for Confederate soldiers. Another of Gov. Morton's schemes was to create an arsenal to be sure Indiana troops were well supplied. Originally located on the State House grounds, the well-stocked arsenal and munitions manufacturing plant was moved to a 76-acre site just east of the Mile Square. The site later became home to Arsenal Technical High School, which is today one of Indy's best-known public schools.

On the east side of town, Hiram Bacon's dairy farm operated as a stop on the Underground Railroad as runaway slaves made their daring escape from Confederate states north to freedom. Bacon's farm included a rare and ancient peat bog, a swampy hiding place that was perfect for runaway slaves. Sometimes the slaves and their guides would sprinkle red pepper in their footsteps to confound the sneezing bloodhounds. Bacon, his wife, and 10 children also hid slaves in their home or under bales of hay in the barn.

By the end of the war, 46 general officers in the Union army had resided in Indiana at some point in their lives. More than 35 percent of the Hoosiers who entered the Union Army—a total of 24,415—gave their lives. More than 50,000 were wounded. The impressive Solders and Sailors Monument that now dominates the Circle was erected in their honor.

POST–CIVIL WAR GROWTH

When the war ended, Indianapolis was in prime condition for industrial growth. As a railway center, the city enjoyed significant progress, boosted even more when Mayor John Craven decided in 1876 to encircle the city with a system of railroad tracks to connect with all the rail lines already in place. Known as the Belt Line, the track system gave all freight trains access to a series of factories, warehouses, and stockyards along the tracks.

A returning Civil War veteran started a business that same year that would make him wealthy and spotlight Indianapolis as home to one of the top pharmaceutical companies in the world. Eli Lilly enlisted in the Union Army during the Civil War and recruited a company of men to serve with him in an artillery battery. He was later promoted to colonel. Captured near the end of the war, Lilly was held as a prisoner until its conclusion. After the war, Lilly worked in several pharmacies with partners. He then opened his own business in 1876 and had plans to manufacture drugs and market them wholesale to pharmacies.

Among Lilly's early advances were the creation of gelatin capsules to hold medicine and the addition of fruit flavoring to liquid medicines. Lilly shared his wealth in numerous philanthropic pursuits, including the creation of the city's children hospital, which was later expanded to become Riley's Children Hospital. Today, Eli

Lilly and Company is an international corporation and one of the major employers in Indianapolis. The Lilly Endowment remains one of the largest charitable benefactors in the world. Lilly is buried in the city's Crown Hill Cemetery.

In addition to pharmaceutical and agricultural industries, Indianapolis was home to publishing companies, manufacturers, foundries, carriage and wagon makers, bicycle builders, machine shops, and much more. By 1900 about 150 passenger trains a day passed through the Indianapolis station. In 1910 the number peaked at around 200 passenger trains a day. The railroad tracks, still at grade level and declared dangerous to pedestrians and motorists, were elevated between 1915 and 1919.

i Wonder Bread was created at the Taggart Baking Company in Indianapolis in the 1920s, following the invention of the bread-slicing machine.

The early 20th century was a golden age for Indianapolis. The city's population nearly doubled from 169,164 to 314,194 between 1900 and 1920. The city's industrial base expanded. Businesses such as auto parts makers, furniture builders, grain processors, pork packers, railroad repair shops and others drew thousands of rural Midwest families, as well as workers from overseas. Streetcar lines made it easier for people to live in the suburbs and commute to work. The city began to sprawl outward with large neighborhoods of single-family homes, a source of pride for Indianapolis residents who weren't clustered in crowded neighborhoods that blighted so many other cities.

By the turn of the 20th century, Indianapolis had become a sophisticated city with sidewalks, streetlights, streetcars, churches, schools and universities, and musical and literary organizations.

i During the Great Depression of the 1930s, the Public Works Administration oversaw the construction of Lockfield Gardens, one of the nation's first public housing developments.

AUTO INDUSTRY

In 1894, Indiana rumbled into the auto age when Elwood Haynes of nearby Kokomo motored down a country road in his home-engineered gasoline-powered carriage. Indianapolis carriage makers soon were tinkering with their own light carriage designs, devising ways of adding internal combustion engines to them.

When the automobile industry took to the nation's streets, Indianapolis was ready for the new industry. Entrepreneurs set up factories to produce automobiles. Carriage and bicycle manufacturers turned their skills to making cars. In the early days of the automobile industry, Indianapolis rivaled Detroit as the car capital of the world.

By 1910, Indianapolis was a city of over 233,000 and already had 17 automobile plants or auto parts manufacturers, making it the fourth in the nation for auto production. It is estimated that over 90 makes of automobiles were manufactured in Indianapolis.

By the teens, Ford and the Detroit factories had outpaced Indianapolis but local makers found another niche—the luxury auto. Cole, Stutz, Dusenberg, and Marmon were brands known internationally.

Auto magnate Carl Fisher and a group of fellow auto industrialists built the Indianapolis Motor Speedway in 1909. The 2.5-mile oval was originally intended to be a test facility for automobile engineering and safety. Grueling competition would serve as the test. In 1911, Fisher and business partner James Allison established the first 500 Mile Race. Ray Harroun, driving a locally made Marmom Wasp, won the first race with a breakneck average speed of 74.59 mph.

Allison and Fisher also planned the industrial suburb of Speedway, just south of the track. Many residents of Speedway worked in the auto industries there, including Fisher's plant for Prest-O-Lite auto headlights and batteries. Allison was also interested in aircraft engines, and workers at his Allison Experimental Company produced the Liberty engine during World War I. Allison Experiment became the Allison Division of General Motors.

In the 1920s and '30s, plant engineers invented the V-1710 engine, which, with improvements, powered the Tomahawk, Lightning, and Air Cobra flights during World War II. The P-40 Tomahawk, with its Indianapolis-made piston engine, could cruise at about 300 mph, approximately the speed Indy Cars reach on the front stretch of the Indianapolis Motor Speedway. In the late 1940s and 1950s, the Allison firm continued to make history with new jet engines. In 1995, Allison merged with Rolls Royce, and Rolls Royce/Allison powered aircraft are still zooming through the air.

The city of Indianapolis changed to accommodate the burgeoning public love affair with the auto. Carl Fisher promoted the idea of a "Dixie Highway," now known as US 31, to connect north and south. The 1925 Test Building brought about another change—a built-in parking garage.

Indianapolis lost the race to become the country's auto manufacturing center. Lack of capital, and the fact that Indianapolis was not located on a navigable waterway, slanted the odds in favor of Detroit. But it won another kind of race—the Indy 500. A Memorial Day tradition, the Indianapolis 500 has become the largest single-day sporting event in the world. See the Motorsports chapter for more on the history of the Indianapolis Motor Speedway.

i Actor Clark Gable drove the pace car at the 1950 Indy 500.

CITY PARKS

The city's park system is monumental by any measure—3,400 acres of the system are listed in the National Register of Historic Places. When Alexander Ralston mapped out the Mile Square design of Indianapolis in 1821, however, he did not include parks. Residents began to show an interest in planned open spaces in the late 19th century. Indianapolis was growing rapidly and the city needed more parks for its citizens.

However, at the turn of the century, the city's parks future didn't look good. Residents were fussing over where the parks would be located—

everyone wanted them in their own backyard—and legal problems and increasing land values were threatening the whole parks program.

i More than 100 species of trees are native to Indiana. Before the pioneers' arrival, more than 80 percent of Indiana was covered with forest. Now only 17 percent of the state is considered forested.

Then George Edward Kessler came to town. One of the preeminent landscape architects in the United States, Kessler was born in Germany in 1862 and moved to the United States as a child. With beautiful parks in Cincinnati, St. Louis, and Kansas City on his résumé, Kessler was selected in 1908 to develop a plan for Indy. The plan he created is now among the best known of his city park systems.

After a year's worth of research, Kessler presented his plan to city officials and it was adopted. Along with major regional parks on every side of town, the plan had a comprehensive parkway system, which combined parks with green space and boulevards in a network of transportation and recreation corridors.

Even park planning was affected by the auto age. Kessler planned for auto pleasure drives following the meandering creeks of central Indiana to connect all parts of the city. Drivers today enjoy that lovely park and boulevard system.

Kessler bestowed a different character for each of the major parks. Ellenberger Park would feature its old tree stands and natural paths. Garfield Park would have formal sunken gardens with spray fountains. For the heart of the city, Kessler redesigned University Park with formal paths and paths for a central fountain. University Park is part of the World War Memorial Plaza and doubles as an art gallery with its large bronzes by artists such as Henry Hering, Loredo Taft, and Alexander Calder.

Kessler guided the city park commission for six years until 1915. He was hired once again in the 1920s and was in the city supervising construction of a new belt road when he died in 1923. The new belt road was named Kessler Boulevard in his honor.

(Q) Close-up

Indianapolis Fire Department Has Long History

Soon after Indianapolis was cut from the heart of a thick forest, settlers realized they needed a defense against fire. Village fathers came together and took measures to protect their log cabins and rough-board houses from the ever-present danger of fire. In June of 1821 the settlement's first fire department was organized. The company operated with buckets being passed from hand to hand and ladders. It was not until 1835 that better protection came with a hand engine that could be pulled by men to the site of a fire and pumped by hand.

In 1863 the city placed a tower on a three-story building as a lookout point for fire. The tower was staffed by a watchman whose duty it was to look over the city and give alarm if a fire broke out. At the time, Indianapolis was divided into nine sparsely settled wards, and the watchman would ring a bell designating the number of the ward where the fire was located. Indianapolis firemen were not uniformed until 1874. Before that, men working fires were ordered to wear leather hats, both as a means of protection for their heads and faces and as a distinguishing mark to identify firefighters.

To learn more about Indianapolis firefighters, visit the Firefighters Museum at 748 Massachusetts Ave. The free museum contains several antique pieces of equipment, including a 1775 manual hand pumper, turn-of-the-century steam pumper, 1921 Stutz ladder truck, and much more. Call for current hours at (317) 262-5161.

KU KLUX KLAN

The Roaring 20s were a time of jubilation for many. But in Indiana and Indianapolis, it was the beginning of a dark period when the Ku Klux Klan ruled supreme. For a time, the automotive industry attracted African Americans from the south and European immigrants, but their arrival was not always warmly greeted. To already settled residents, those outsiders meant increasing competition for low wage jobs. In the aftermath of a world war, people were suspicious of anything foreign and worried about changes sweeping the nation. After all, Indianapolis prided itself on being an All-American city.

Along came the Klan with its hate-filled, warped message of white supremacy. The first Ku Klux Klan was an organization that thrived in the South during the Reconstruction period following the Civil War. Mostly vigilantes and terrorists, the group took its name from the Greek word kyklos, meaning circle. The second development of the Klan occurred when it rose to prominence in Indiana politics and society after World War I.

Primarily in response to Indianapolis job competition, the state of Indiana quickly registered the most KKK members in the nation.

Founded in 1920, the Indiana chapter of the Klan became the most powerful Klan organization in the United States. When David Curtiss Stephenson was appointed the Klan Grand Dragon in 1922, he immediately moved the Indiana Klan's headquarters to Indianapolis. Stephenson was in charge of Indiana and 22 other states. From 1921 to 1928, the KKK was the most powerful political and social organization in the city.

The Klan's power seemed to peak in the 1924 election of Edward Jackson for governor, along with a Klan-backed slate of candidates that swept state elections. The Klan seized control of the Indiana General Assembly. To celebrate, an estimated 25,000 Klansmen, women, and children gathered at the Indiana State Fairgrounds in Indianapolis. Later, some 6,500 Klansmen and their supporters paraded through downtown while a crowd of almost 100,000 lined the streets.

The goal of the Klan was to eventually gain control of Congress and the White House. But that plan fell apart when Stephenson kidnapped a young Indianapolis woman and raped her. Madge Oberholzter, a teacher, swallowed poison to kill herself and escape from her captor. She lived long enough to identify Stephenson and tell what he had done. Despite boasting that he was above the law, Stephenson was convicted by a jury of second-degree murder and sentenced to life in prison on November 16, 1925.

With Stephenson out of power, the Klan suffered a tremendous setback. When Gov. Edward Jackson refused to pardon him, Stephenson had no problem getting even by exposing all the corruption going on in the governor's office and other political top spots. Indicted on charges of bribery, Jackson was acquitted in 1928 because the statute of limitations had run out, but he finished out his term in disgrace. The mayor of Indianapolis and several other officials were convicted of bribery and jailed. The Klan had lost its base of power in Indiana and around the nation. The national organization officially disbanded in 1944.

TOOLMAKER TO THE NATION

When World War II hit, Indianapolis was once again needed for its rail system and central location. Workers were in demand and factories ran 24 hours a day, seven days a week, to crank out necessary parts and equipment for the war effort. More companies moved in—RCA, Western Electric, Ford, and Chrysler. Indy was a manufacturing boomtown.

Then the war ended and Americans began to take to the road instead of riding the rails. Airplanes became a faster way to travel, and railroad traffic began to decline. In the 1970s the central business district saw decreased economic activity, racial tension, and flight to growing suburbs. As a result, downtown Indianapolis saw little new construction.

The city of Indianapolis set about to address these issues by developing plans in the 1980s to redefine the city's downtown. Neighborhoods near the city center were redeveloped. A series of modern skyscrapers was constructed, including what is currently the tallest building in the state, the Chase Tower.

Forced to rethink its future after the decline of heavy industry, Indianapolis began looking at ways to reinvent itself. The city's love affair with sports became one of those avenues. Combined with an aggressive downtown revitalizing campaign, Indianapolis was ready for the next stage of its life.

i Endangered Species Chocolate (ESC) is a rare company, and one that calls Indianapolis home. Founded in 1993, the company is firmly committed to the idea that all life is precious, including that of animals. The company states that its organically grown chocolate is ethically traded, and part of its profits go toward the preservation of species and habitats. ESC has also donated time and money to sponsor schools and water pumps in Nigeria.

UNIGOV

In 1969, Indianapolis became one of the first municipalities to experiment with consolidating city and county government.

Since 1970, Indianapolis and Marion County have functioned under a consolidated city-county government called Unigov. The Unigov system contains three branches. The first is executive, led by the mayor of Indianapolis, who serves as the chief executive officer of the city and the county. The second is legislative, which is embodied in the 29-seat city-county council. The third branch is judicial, consisting of a Circuit Court and Superior Court, with civil, criminal, probate, juvenile, and small claims divisions.

Most city and county functions have been consolidated under Unigov, with the exception of school districts and fire departments. Four cities within Marion County chose not to join the Unigov system—Beech Grove, Lawrence, Speedway, and Southport. Although not part of Unigov, these residents do pay county taxes and vote in mayoral and council elections.

In 2005 the city-county council approved a merger of the Indianapolis Police Department and the Marion County Sheriff's Department, creating the Indianapolis Metropolitan Police Department. In 2008 the council gave the mayor authority over the police department.

> **ℹ** On April 4, 1968, the day of the assassination of Martin Luther King Jr., presidential campaigner Robert F. Kennedy delivered an impromptu speech on race reconciliation to a mostly African-American crowd in a poor inner-city Indianapolis neighborhood. Indianapolis was the only major city in which rioting did not occur following King's death. Many credit the speech by Kennedy for helping calm the tensions.

INDIANAPOLIS TODAY

Indianapolis today is a cosmopolitan blend of arts, education, culture, and sports, a city with a clear vision for its future. Building on momentum gained in the last decade of the 20th century, the city is in the midst of a cultural and quality of life resurgence.

What's new? The list is quite long and diverse.

In 2005 the new Indianapolis Museum of Art opened following a $74 million expansion and renovation, including additional gallery space, new events, an entrance pavilion, and a restaurant. That same year, the Eiteljorg Museum of American Indians and Western Art completed a 47,000-square-foot expansion with a new wing that expands the exhibit space by 50 percent and includes three new galleries and a sculpture court.

The new Dolphin Adventure opened at the Indianapolis Zoo in 2005. A fully submerged dome allows visitors a 360-degree view of the mammals. The Zoo also began offering an in-water experience, taking participants waist deep in the water and face to face with the dolphins.

In March 2006, Conrad Indianapolis celebrated its grand opening and addition to the city's skyline. The luxurious hotel is the fourth Conrad property to debut in the United States and the first to be built from the ground up. Funding for a $900 million expansion of the Indiana Convention Center and a new multiuse stadium venue was approved. The expanded Indiana Convention Center is scheduled to be completed in 2010.

The $719 million Lucas Oil Stadium, home of the Indianapolis Colts, as well as a venue for conventions, trade shows, concerts, and other special events, opened in August 2008. Also in 2008, groundbreaking took place for a new $425 million JW Marriott Indianapolis, located in the heart of downtown. When completed in its entirety in 2011, the complex will feature four new hotel properties with more than 1,600 rooms.

In November 2008, the new $1.1 billion Indianapolis International Airport opened. More than 30 years in the making, the airport is one of the first U.S airports built and opened since the tragic events of 9/11.

Those are just a few of the many projects bringing new life to the Hoosier city. Offering world-class sports and a diverse economy, Indianapolis nurtures numerous businesses for a healthy economy as it rolls into the 21st century.

ACCOMMODATIONS

Company's coming. And Indianapolis is ready with its famed Hoosier hospitality. There's a style of lodging to suit every preference, from penthouse suites with personal staff to budget-friendly places with free breakfasts. You can even sleep in a refurbished Pullman train car or feel like a celebrity at a hotel with a top-secret private entrance.

Most likely your biggest problem will be choosing from among the city's numerous and varied lodging options. Seven downtown hotels with more than 2,800 rooms are connected via a skywalk and located only a short distance from area attractions. Branch out from downtown Indy and find even more hotels. With the city's interstate system, it is easy to get around to most destinations. There are so many hotels and motels in Indianapolis, I have chosen just a small representative portion of the properties. If you have a favorite trustworthy chain and don't see one of its properties listed here, call the chain's central reservation number to find out if there is a location in Indianapolis.

When choosing your accommodations, keep in mind that May is a very busy month in India-napolis. The Indy 500 draws some 400,000 spectators with activities throughout May, culminat-ing in the big automobile race each Memorial Day weekend at Indianapolis Motor Speedway. Because Indy welcomes so many guests, it is a very good idea to secure your accommodations well in advance.

Then there's the party Indy will be hosting in February 2012 when the Super Bowl comes to town. From what I've heard, folks started making reservations for places to stay as soon as the bid announcement was made. Get a room as soon as possible or find some long-lost friend or family member you suddenly remembered lives in the Indianapolis area.

In the following list, I've provided a price guide to help you choose a hotel. The rate infor-mation was provided by each property. Most have more than one rate, and in some cases rates span a wide range—from hundreds to even thousands of dollars per night. The price code is based on the "rack rate"—what one night's stay, double occupancy, midweek in peak season would cost you if you walked in off the street. Often you will pay less than that, however. Many properties offer lower rates on weekends, and most offer a few discounts. AAA and AARP mem-bers, for example, get discounts at many hotels. There are a lot of other discount programs, so be sure to inquire about them when you make your reservation. Always ask for the best rate—you can often enjoy significant savings by doing so.

This chapter is divided into geographic categories. That's to help you quickly locate a suit-able property in your preferred area. I have also listed a variety of properties in all price ranges.

All the hotels in this chapter accept major credit cards, and most offer free local telephone calls. Amenities vary widely. Some places offer little more than a bed and a bath, while others pamper you with lovely luxuries. In general, Indianapolis hotels have wheelchair-accessible rooms. Many offer smoking rooms but more and more are becoming smoke-free properties. Be sure to check ahead if you are a smoker. Most hotels do not accept pets, and the ones that do often require a nonrefundable deposit.

Price Code

The following price code represents the average cost of a double-occupancy room during peak season. Prices do not include occupancy tax or sales tax.

$..................Less than $90
$$ ....$91 to $125
$$$ ....$126 to $175
$$$$ ....$176 and more

DOWNTOWN

ALL NATIONS BED & BREAKFAST $$$
2164 N. Capitol Ave.
(317) 923-2622
www.allnationsbnb.us

Travel around the world without a passport at All Nations Bed & Breakfast. Offering four guest rooms with different national decors, All Nations is based on locations the owner, Tressa Mazhandu, has visited. Tressa spent four weeks touring China and brought a piece of the Orient home with her. The China Room is complete with silk bedding, a Chinese terra-cotta statue, Chinese tea, and a full-size bed. The Zimbabwe Room has an African safari feel, with mosquito netting over the queen-size bed. Welcoming with hues of green, the Ireland Room has an Irish prayer on the wall and offers a full-size bed. With a queen-size bed and full-size pullout sofa, the New Zealand Room has a full-length sheepskin on the floor and a New Zealand flag on the wall. Each guest room features a TV and DVD player. Wi-Fi is also provided.

For dining, the brightly painted terra-cotta and ocean-blue breakfast room features the flavors of Mexico combined with international dishes. With its Caribbean theme, the family room is a great place to relax. All Nations Bed & Breakfast also has a sunny backyard and a porch where breakfast can be served. The home is within walking distance of downtown Indianapolis and is 9 blocks from the Indianapolis Children's Museum.

CANTERBURY HOTEL $$$$
123 S. Illinois St.
(800) 538-8186
www.canterburyhotel.com

With a lineage dating back to the 1850s, the beautiful Canterbury Hotel is listed in the National Register of Historic Places. In 1983 the hotel was renovated to create an intimate upscale hotel with European tradition and ambience, reflecting the charm and historical quality of Canterbury, England—hence the name the Canterbury Hotel. Featuring 99 luxurious rooms and suites, the hotel has a private entrance to Circle Centre Mall and the Indiana Convention Center via skywalks. Each room offers Chippendale four-poster beds, plush linens, marble vanities, comfy terry-cloth bathrobes, goose-down and nonallergenic foam pillows, and gold-plated fixtures. Twice daily housekeeping service includes an evening turndown with chocolate truffles left on your pillow.

COLUMBIA CLUB $$$$
121 Monument Circle
(800) 635-1361
www.columbia-club.org

Located in a beautiful 10-story clubhouse built in 1925, the Columbia Club is a private city club originally established in 1889. Listed in the National Register of Historic Places, it features polished marble floors and an unusual two-story fireplace in the Grand Lobby. The Club also has dark wood paneling, Tiffany windows, 96 guest rooms, fine and casual dining, and a complete fitness center. Conveniently located in the heart of downtown on Monument Circle, Columbia Club offers excellent views of the Circle. This is the place to stay, particularly at Christmas time when the Circle is illuminated with holiday lights. Reciprocal club members are honored.

COMFORT SUITES INDIANAPOLIS
CITY CENTRE $$$
515 S. West St.
(317) 631-9000
www.dorahotels.com

Conveniently located near Lucas Oil Stadium and within walking distance of downtown dining, shopping, and attractions, this new hotel features 130 guest suites. Comfort Suites offers complimentary hot breakfast, indoor pool with whirlpool, and a large fitness center. The all-suite hotel includes extra spacious guest suites with a sitting area, refrigerator, microwave, flat-panel high-definition TV, and work desk with complimentary high-speed Internet.

CONRAD INDIANAPOLIS $$$$
50 W. Washington St.
(317) 713-5000
http://conradhotels1.hilton.com

Ideally located at the most prominent downtown intersection, Conrad Indianapolis offers a pampered experience. A sky bridge provides an uninterrupted path from the Conrad to downtown attractions. Conrad's 23-story tower boasts 241 guest rooms with upscale amenities such as 42-inch flat-screen high-definition plasma TVs, in-room safes sized to fit a laptop computer, bathrobes and slippers, custom-made Italian hardwood furniture, and luxurious 500-thread-count bed linens. The Conrad also includes a world-class spa, large indoor pool, state-of-the-art fitness facility, 24-hour in-room dining, the Tastings wine bar, and the Capital Grille.

i The expansion of the Indiana Convention Center, to be completed in 2010, will be complemented by the opening of a new 1,005-room JW Marriott Hotel. The property will be located adjacent to the Indiana Convention Center and connected via skywalk. The $425 million JW Marriott Complex will include Indy's largest full-service convention hotel and a total of 1,623 rooms including: 1,005 rooms in the JW Marriott Tower, 294 rooms in the Courtyard by Mariott, 168 rooms in the Fairfield Inn & Suites by Marriott, and 156 rooms in the SpringHill Suites by Marriott. Additionally, the JW Marriott Complex will contain 105,000 square feet of meeting and event space, including a 40,500-square-foot grand ballroom—the largest ballroom in the state of Indiana and the largest hotel ballroom in the Midwest.

i Opened in 1888, Union Station in Indy was the nation's first union railway depot. A young Thomas Edison worked there as a Western Union telegraph operator. Today, Union Station is home to the Crowne Plaza, where you can sleep in real Pullman train cars.

COURTYARD BY MARRIOTT AT THE CAPITOL $$$
320 N. Senate Ave.
(800) 321-2211
www.marriott.com

Conveniently located in the heart of downtown Indy, the Courtyard by Marriott at the Capitol offers easy access to local attractions and companies. Enjoy jogging or a leisurely stroll along the historic Canal Walk adjacent to the hotel. The Courtyard also offers a business center, exercise room, indoor pool, and whirlpool, along with an outdoor sun patio. The Courtyard features 124 rooms. Rooms have a shower and bath separate from a vanity dressing area, plus a large desk with an ergonomic chair for comfort and free high-speed Internet. A complete breakfast menu includes a full hot buffet with eggs cooked to order.

COURTYARD INDIANAPOLIS DOWNTOWN $$$
601 W. Washington St.
(317) 573-6536
www.jwindy.com

Scheduled to open Feb 2011, this 297-room hotel will be part of the $425 million JW Marriott Indianapolis complex. Once completed, the hotel will be connected to the JW Marriott Downtown Indianapolis, which has more than 104,000 square feet of meeting, banquet, and exhibit space and one of Marriott's largest hotel ballrooms in the world, totaling 40,500 square feet. This landmark hotel development will serve as an anchor for central Indiana's convention and tourism industry. Located on a seven-acre site overlooking White River State Park, the hotel is steps away from a thriving downtown with numerous attractions, and an easy 15-minute commute from the new Indianapolis International Airport.

CROWNE PLAZA AT HISTORIC
UNION STATION $$$
123 W. Louisiana St.
(317) 631-2221
www.ichotelsgroup.com

Located in the midst of downtown Indianapolis, the Crowne Plaza is housed within America's first Union Station. Steps away from major attractions, dining, nightlife, and shopping, the hotel is connected to the Indiana Convention Center and Lucas Oil Stadium and a block from Circle Centre Mall. Listed in the National Register of Historic Places, the Crowne Plaza offers 273 rooms, including 26 authentic Pullman sleeper train cars resting on their original track. The Pullman train cars are named and decorated in honor of prominent personalities from the early 1900s, such as Charlie Chaplin, Louis Armstrong, and Greta Garbo. Another popular feature of the hotel is the white fiberglass ghost travelers dressed in period clothing and still lovingly haunting the premises. The Romanesque Revival–style hotel is still an active train station, which enhances its authenticity and ambience. The hotel features a restaurant and lounge, indoor swimming pool, and business center.

DEWOLF-ALLERDICE HOUSE $$$
1224 N. Park Ave.
(317) 822-4299
www.dewolf-allerdicehouse.com

Turn back the hands of time and stay in an 1870s home in historic Old Northside Indianapolis. The DeWolf-Allerdice House is close to attractions but far away from the city's hustle and bustle. The three-story Italianate Inn features a country estate–like setting, yet is minutes away from major attractions, downtown Indy, and the Indianapolis International Airport. The inn offers three guest rooms on the second floor and an executive suite encompassing the entire third floor. All rooms are furnished in an eclectic mix of Victorian and modern-day decor.

Caroline DeWolf was the original owner who designed and built the home around 1871. A Scottish immigrant, Joseph Allerdice, bought the house in 1891, and his family lived there until 1923. Joseph and a partner established the Indianapolis Abbatoir Company, which dealt in hides, wool, pelts, fur, and tallow. Joseph eventually became president of the firm, a role he held until 1921 when illness forced early retirement. At that time, the business had about 600 employees and was the largest of its kind in the country.

The inn's guest rooms reflect its heritage. Joseph's Room is the master bedroom and offers a queen-size sleigh bed, sitting area, private bathroom with a claw-foot tub, and shower. Caroline's Room welcomes guests with a full-size antique four-poster bed, writing desk, sitting area, and shared bathroom with claw-foot tub and shower. Named for one of Joseph's nine children, Ruth's Room has a queen-size four-poster bed, sitting area, and shared bathroom with claw-foot tub and shower. The Ovid Butler Suite on the third floor has a private bathroom with queen-size and full-size beds, a small meeting area, two daybeds in the lounge area, and a private bathroom with tub and shower.

The DeWolf-Allerdice House also features a parlor with fireplace and TV, keeping room, veranda, dining room, and English-style gardens. A European-style breakfast buffet is offered during the business week, with leisurely family-style breakfasts served on the weekends.

EMBASSY SUITES HOTEL DOWNTOWN $$$
110 W. Washington St.
(317) 236-1800
www.embassysuites1/hilton.com

Renovated in 2009, Embassy Suites is connected via skywalk to Circle Centre Mall and the Indianapolis Artsgarden. Spacious suites feature two rooms, two TVs, microwave, refrigerator, and pullout sleeper sofa in a separate living room. Free coffee and tea are available in the lobby. A full cooked-to-order breakfast and evening manager's reception with complimentary beverages are featured. An indoor pool, sauna, whirlpool, and exercise room are available. The hotel is 2 blocks from the Indiana Convention Center and Lucas Oil Stadium.

FAIRFIELD INN & SUITES BY MARRIOTT DOWNTOWN INDIANAPOLIS $$$

501 W. Washington St.
(317) 573-6536
www.jwindy.com

Scheduled to open in Feb 2010, the 168-room Fairfield Inn & Suites by Marriott is part of the grand $425 million Marriott Place Indianapolis. Once completed, the hotel will be connected to the JW Marriott Downtown Indianapolis and help serve as an anchor for central Indiana's convention and tourism industry. Located on a seven-acre site overlooking White River State Park, the hotel will put guests only steps away from numerous attractions. The hotel features a complimentary continental breakfast, gift shop, business center, and restaurant on-site.

i The city's three major professional sports teams—Indianapolis Colts (NFL), Indiana Pacers (NBA), and Indiana Fever (WNBA)—play in facilities within easy walking distance of each other and a brief stroll from many downtown hotels.

FOUNTAINVIEW INN $$$

1105 Prospect St.
(866) 363-0303
www.fountainsquareindy.com

Located in the historic Fountain Square Theatre Building, the Fountainview Inn is on the third floor, with keyed elevator access available for guests only. One-bedroom and studio suites are individually decorated and have a king- or queen-size bed, sitting area, TV, kitchenette, and tiled bath. The inn offers free wireless Internet. Three restaurants are located on the premises, and several other restaurants are within easy walking distance.

Only a mile and a half from downtown Indianapolis, Fountain Square was the first commercial historic district in Indiana. The existing buildings span more than a century of development, beginning in 1871. The Fountain Square Building opened in 1928 as a place for entertainment, shopping, and professional offices. In the late 1960s the project began to decline. In 1993 renovations began and the building now houses entertainment and events at the Fountain Square Theatre, duckpin bowling in either of two vintage alleys, three restaurants, and the Fountainview Inn.

HAMPTON INN DOWNTOWN $$$

105 S. Meridian St.
(317) 261-1200
www.schahethotels.com

Housed in the beautifully restored, nine-story historic Chesapeake Building, Hampton Inn Downtown is located across the street from Circle Centre Mall and a short walk from the Indianapolis Convention Center, Lucas Oil Stadium, Conseco Fieldhouse, and several popular restaurants. The hotel features 180 rooms and offers a complimentary continental breakfast bar every morning with more than 45 delicious items. The property also has 24 suites and three meeting rooms. All rooms have free high-speed Internet and a "lap desk" for guests to comfortably move around and work. Rooms feature new Cloud Nine beds, with your choice of feather or foam pillows, high-quality soft sheets, plush down-like comforter, crisp white duvets, and comfy pillowtop mattress, all arranged on top of a raised bed.

HILTON GARDEN INN DOWNTOWN $$$$

10 E. Market St.
(317) 955-9700
www.hiltongardenindianapolis.com

Located in the renovated Fletcher Trust Building, the 180-room Hilton Garden Inn overlooks Monument Circle and is close to major Indy attractions. The building itself has an interesting history. Constructed in 1915, the 16-story building was considered a skyscraper at the time. Designed by the architectural team of Arthur Bohn and Kurt Vonnegut Sr. (father of famed author Kurt Vonnegut), the Fletcher Trust Building is an outstanding example of the Neoclassical style, featuring limestone and granite facades, a marble floor in the main lobby, brass elevator doors on the first floor, and marble and ironwork on the first three floors. Features include a full-service restaurant, salon and spa, business center, heated indoor pool, and exercise room. Listed in the National

Register of Historic Places, the building has operated as the Hilton Garden Inn since Dec 2003, with special attention to historic preservation.

HILTON INDIANAPOLIS $$$$
120 W. Market St.
(317) 872-0600
www1.hilton.com

A luxury hotel in a prime location, the Hilton Indianapolis features some of the largest suites in the city. The hotel has 332 spacious rooms, with 30 of them being 1,100 square feet. Each hotel room has two phone lines, data ports, high-speed Internet, large work desks, and WebTV. Other features include a gift shop, indoor pool and Jacuzzi, and two restaurants on the premises—120 West Market Fresh Grill and McCormick & Schmick's Seafood Restaurant. A Precor fitness center is available 24 hours a day.

HOLIDAY INN EXPRESS HOTEL & SUITES
INDIANAPOLIS CITY CENTRE $$
410 S. Missouri St.
(317) 822-6400
www.dorahotels.com

Conveniently located just 1 block south of the Indiana Convention Center and Lucas Oil Stadium, this six-story hotel features 108 guest rooms, including suites and kitchenettes and some whirlpool rooms. A shuttle service is available for the immediate downtown area. On-site amenities include an indoor pool, whirlpool, and fitness center. Complimentary hot breakfast is provided.

HOMEWOOD SUITES BY HILTON
INDIANAPOLIS-DOWNTOWN $$$
211 S. Meridian St.
http://homewoodsuites1.hilton.com

Enjoy the comforts of home at Homewood Suites, featuring a fully equipped kitchen with full-size refrigerator, microwave, and two TVs. The 92 suites also offer sitting areas. On-site amenities include an indoor pool and spa, fitness center, business center, meeting rooms, complimentary laundry facilities, and 24-hour shop for snacks and sundries. Homewood Suites offers a com-

plimentary hot breakfast buffet daily, with eggs, bacon, sausage, fruits, cereals, and homemade Belgian waffles. Mon through Thurs evenings feature a complimentary Welcome Home reception, where guests can enjoy a light meal, salad bar, and beverages, including beer and wine.

i Extended-stay hotels have single-night rooms available, especially on weekends, and offer upscale amenities at bargain prices.

HYATT REGENCY INDIANAPOLIS $$$$
One S. Capitol Ave.
(800) 233-1234
www.indianapolis.hyatt.com

Located in the heart of downtown Indy and connected by skywalk, the Hyatt Regency Indianapolis offers easy access to Circle Centre Mall, the Indiana Convention Center, and other attractions. A dramatic 21-story lobby atrium welcomes guests to the newly renovated hotel, which features 497 lovely guest rooms. Amenities include iPod docking stations, a generous work desk with executive chair, and the comfy Hyatt Grand bed. Guests can work out any time of day in the 24-hour state-of-the-art gym or take a dip in the indoor pool. Restaurant choices include fine dining at the rotating Eagle's Nest above the Hyatt, the only revolving restaurant in Indiana. Or try the hotel's newest dining spot, One South.

INDIANAPOLIS MARRIOTT
DOWNTOWN $$$$
350 W. Maryland St.
(877) 640-7666
www.marriott.com

Indy's largest hotel, the Marriott Downtown recently completed a $9.5 million renovation for a stylish new look. The 622 guest rooms include luxurious bed linens, a rolling desk with ergonomic chair, and a 37-inch flat-screen TV with Marriott's new plug-and-play connectivity (plug-in iPod and a split screen). Contemporary art with a classical modern design adds to the decor. The hotel is connected via skywalk to the Indiana Convention Center and Circle Centre Mall and is just steps from Lucas Oil Stadium, White River State Park, Conseco Fieldhouse, and other attractions. Located inside the hotel are Circle City Bar & Grille, Starbucks Coffee, and Champions Sports Bar. Other features include an exercise room, gift shop, hot tub, indoor swimming pool, and business center. The Marriott is a smoke-free facility.

JW MARRIOTT DOWNTOWN
INDIANAPOLIS $$$$
10 S. West St.
(317) 573-6536
www.jwindy.com

Scheduled to open in Feb 2011, the JW Marriott Downtown Indianapolis is part of the spectacular $425 million Marriott Place Indianapolis and will feature 1,005 rooms. The rooms will feature sumptuous Revive bedding with crisp cotton sheets and plush duvets.

The JW Marriott will be the city's largest full-service convention hotel, with a 40,500-square-foot Grand Ballroom and more than 104,000 square feet of meeting, banquet, and exhibit space. Located on a seven-acre site overlooking White River State Park, the hotel will host guests just steps away from popular downtown attractions. The 34-story hotel will be conveniently connected via skywalk to the newly expanded Convention Center and open directly onto White River State Park. Hotel features include a gift shop, fitness room, hot tub, and indoor swimming pool. The JW Marriott will feature three different dining options—High Velocity, a high-tech sports bar; Tuscan bistro, a fine Italian dining restaurant; and Coffee, a gourmet European-style cafe. J.W. Marriott is a smoke-free facility.

THE LOOKING GLASS INN $$$
1319 N. New Jersey St.
(317) 639-9550
www.stonesoupinn.com

A Free Classic–style mansion, the Looking Glass Inn was built in 1905 by Elizabeth Gates, the widow of a wholesale grocery merchant. The inn is located in the heart of the city's Old Northside, an area that was home for principal leaders of Indianapolis at the turn of the century. Opened to guests in Feb 1999, the inn offers six rooms with Victorian charm. The home also has two sister properties within blocks of The Looking Glass—Stone Soup Inn and The Villa Inn.

NESTLE INN BED & BREAKFAST $$
637 N. East St.
(877) 339-5200
www.nestleindy.com

Located in historic Chatham Arch, the Nestle Inn Bed & Breakfast is within walking distance of popular Mass Ave (Massachusetts Avenue) with its dining, nightlife, and art galleries. Sports fans are also minutes away from the Pacers, Colts, and Indians. The inn offers four guest rooms and one suite. All have private baths, TV, phone, and wireless Internet. Common areas include a parlor, library, lobby, and a second-floor seating area. A snack bar, microwave, and refrigerator are also for guest use. Guests enjoy a delicious full breakfast in the 1896 Victorian home.

OLD NORTHSIDE INN $$$
340 N. Alabama Street
(800) 635-9127
www.oldnorthsideinn.com

Built in 1885, this lovely brick residence is considered one of the best examples of Romanesque Revival architecture in the city. It was constructed by Herman C. DeWenter, a German immigrant who became a prominent Indiana industrialist. The carefully renovated home features slat floors, hand-carved cherry and mahogany woodwork, and hand-painted murals on the walls and ceilings. All six rooms at the Old Northside Inn offer private baths with whirlpool tubs, cable TV, VCRs, and high-speed Internet.

The Bridal Room features a massive canopy bed with a custom-made fireplace and lovely pastel colors. The largest and only guest room on the main floor, the Tiffany Room, has a stained glass window along with king-size bed, separate shower, fireplace, and art deco pictures on the wall. In the Hollywood Room, glamour photos of stars like Clark Gable, Errol Flynn, Marilyn Monroe, Frank Sinatra, Ava Gardner, James Cagney, and Katharine Hepburn set the tone. A decoupage of genuine World War I sheet music decorates walls, along with other memorabilia from those times. Star lights on a dressing table make any guest feel like a celebrity. The room also features a small library of books on theater, Hollywood, and the arts.

The Literary Room is a salute to the literary greats of Indiana, including James Whitcomb Riley, Booth Tarkington, Lew Wallace, George Ade, George Meredith, and others. The room is decorated in turn-of-the-20th-century decor, along with an antique slate fireplace and books by the authors. Named for the man who built the mansion, the DeWenter Room has original woodwork, a brick wall—reminding guests that this is the only brick structure in a neighborhood of frame houses, a fireplace, and a queen-size bed. Century-old photographs of the family and house adorn the walls. The Library/Wedding Suite features faux-painted walls, antiques, a library of books, and a gas fireplace. The suite, which is the newest and largest guest accommodation in the mansion, has a bathroom with two gold sinks and a glass shower, along with a double whirlpool tub.

Each morning, a complete breakfast is served in the formal dining room. Guests are welcome to help themselves to snacks and drinks in the Butler's Pantry.

OMNI SEVERIN HOTEL $$$$
40 W. Jackson Place
(317) 634-6664
www.omnihotels.com

One of Indy's premier hotels, the 424-room historic Omni Severin Hotel has played host to some of the city's biggest names. Located in the heart of the downtown Wholesale District, the Omni Severin is connected via skywalk to Nordstrom, Circle Centre Mall, and the Convention Center. The 1913 hotel offers a lovely Edwardian-style decor with elegant cherry veneer furniture. Amenities include plush robes, triple-sheeted beds, a minibar, and sitting area. On site are 40 West Coffee Cafe, Olives martini bar, and the Severin Bar and Grille, which offers breakfast, lunch and dinner. Also available are children's activities,

an exercise/fitness room, gift shop, and indoor swimming pool.

Room choices include penthouse accommodations with vaulted ceilings, oversize windows for maximum natural lighting, and furnished patios with magnificent views of the city. The Penthouse Lilly Suite is a treat, featuring a parlor room with a dining table that seats up to eight, French doors, marble bath, and a furnished patio with fantastic views. For the ultimate, the Penthouse Presidential Suite is a 1,344-square-foot bi-level suite that includes a lovely foyer with marble floors leading to a living room and separate dining room. A handy powder room completes the lower level of the suite. A spiral staircase leads to two bedrooms, each with its own full bathroom and a private balcony with views of the exciting Wholesale District. For the health conscious, the Get Fit guest rooms feature a motorized portable treadmill, Get Fit Kit, and healthy snacks in the refreshment center.

RESIDENCE INN BY MARRIOTT DOWNTOWN ON THE CANAL $$$
350 W. New York St.
(800) 331-3131
www.marriott.com

Offering the comforts of home to travelers, the Residence Inn by Marriott Downtown on the Canal features 134 suites on five floors. As the name notes, the inn is located on the downtown canal. Suites are spacious, with a full kitchen and separate areas for sleeping and working. The hotel is a smoke-free facility. A complimentary buffet breakfast is a welcome way to start the day, and a manager's reception allows guests to relax. The inn offers an indoor swimming pool, Jacuzzi, exercise room, and recreation/game room.

SHERATON INDIANAPOLIS CITY CENTRE HOTEL $$$
31 W. Ohio St.
(888) 627-8186

This 378-room hotel on historic Monument Circle offers great downtown views and is within easy walking distance of the Convention Center, Lucas Oil Stadium, Conseco Fieldhouse, and Circle Centre Mall. Amenities include the Sheraton Sweet Sleeper bed, ergonomic desk chairs, work desk, and flat-screen TVs. On site are an outdoor pool and exercise room, as well a Starbucks Coffee Shop, Churchill's Bar & Grill, and Ethan's, known for its popular weekday Monumental Pasta Bar, where diners can create their own pasta favorites. The hotel is a smoke-free facility.

i If you are a smoker, be sure to ask for smoking rooms. Indianapolis is becoming more and more a smoke-free city.

SPRINGHILL SUITES BY MARRIOTT
DOWNTOWN INDIANAPOLIS $$$
607 W. Washington St.
(317) 573-6536
www.jwindy.com
Part of the massive $425 million Marriott Place Indianapolis project, SpringHill Suites by Marriott Downtown Indianapolis will feature 156 rooms. Once completed, the hotel will be connected to the JW Marriott Downtown Indianapolis, which will serve as a downtown tourism anchor. Scheduled to open in Feb 2010, the hotel will offer complimentary continental breakfast, an exercise/fitness room, gift shop, indoor swimming pool, and business center. Located on a seven-acre site overlooking White River State Park, the hotel will be handy to many major attractions.

STAYBRIDGE SUITES INDIANAPOLIS CITY
CENTRE $$
535 S. West St.
(317) 536-7500
www.dorahotels.com
Located adjacent to Lucas Oil Stadium (home of the Indianapolis Colts), this extended stay hotel features 113 suites with fully equipped kitchens, living rooms with sleeper sofas, plus a flat-screen TV and DVD player. On site are a 24-hour exercise/fitness room, gift shop, indoor swimming pool, hot tub, guest lending library, and business center. Guests can enjoy complimentary hot breakfasts as well as evening receptions.

STONE SOUP INN $$$
1304 N. Central Ave.
(317) 639-9550
www.stonesoupinn.com
Located in Indy's premier historic district—the Old Northside—Stone Soup Inn was built in 1901. Featuring Mission-style and Victorian-era antiques, the inn's nine rooms offer individual decor. The Lily Room is the most popular, featuring a sleigh bed, carved teak wood, a two-person whirlpool tub and shower, and a large bay window overlooking a lily pond. The Blue Room has a beautifully carved 6-foot-high-headboard, steam shower, and decorative fireplace. The innkeeper's favorite, the Craftsman Room, is completely furnished with Mission-style antiques, Arts and Crafts stenciling, and a welcoming bay window seat. It has a queen-size bed and shared bath. The Victorian Room features two twin beds or a king-size bed (meaning the two twin beds are pushed together) and shared bath, lace curtains, and a decorative fireplace.

Stone Soup Inn also has four lofts with additional amenities such as small kitchens, dining areas, lounges, and private bathrooms. The Carriage House is a fully furnished apartment with large sleeping loft overlooking a comfortable common area. The room includes laundry facilities and a full kitchen. The inn's Butler's Pantry is stocked with complimentary snacks and beverages.

UNIVERSITY PLACE CONFERENCE CENTER
AND HOTEL $$$
850 W. Michigan St.
(800) 627-2700
www.universityplace.iupui.edu
University Place is located right where its name says—on the campus of a university, Indiana University-Purdue University Indianapolis to be exact. The 278-room upscale hotel features a 30,000-square-foot high-tech conference center, 28 meeting rooms, exhibition hall, and parking garage. The property also includes restaurants, lounge, food court, and gift shop. Complimentary shuttle service is offered to downtown attractions, which are about five minutes away, and

to the airport, about 15 minutes away. A skywalk connects the hotel to the IUPUI Sports Complex, including the IU Natatorium pools, and the IU Medical Center.

THE VILLA INN, RESTAURANT, SPA $$$$
1456 N. Delaware St.
(317) 916-8500
www.thevillainn.com

With its Italian theme, The Villa Inn offers six guest rooms with two-person whirlpool tubs and king- or queen-size beds. Known as *stanzas*, the rooms offer TV, DVD players, and high-speed Internet. Workout facilities and a Butler's Pantry with complimentary snacks and beverages are offered. The Villa Inn also has an Italian restaurant and spa on-site. Spa services are also offered in the suites.

Stanza One has a massive hand-carved four-poster bed, an oversize chair for two, and a bistro table and chairs. Located steps from the rooftop terrace, Stanza Two has a queen-size palm frond canopy bed, pewter and rattan armchairs, and a wooden inlaid desk. With saffron and crimson decor, Stanza Three has a queen-size bed and rattan and cherrywood furnishings. The most deluxe accommodation, Stanza Four, offers a sitting room with fireplace and bedroom with king-size bed. Decorated in a Japanese style and tucked away in the Carriage House, Stanza Five has a queen-size bed, full kitchen, and dining nook. Featuring art deco flair, Stanza Six is located in the Carriage House and has a queen-size bed.

THE WESTIN INDIANAPOLIS $$$
50 S. Capitol Ave.
(317) 262-8100
www.starwoodhotels.com

Connected by skywalk to the Indiana Convention Center, the 573-room Westin offers spacious guestrooms with modern decor and Westin's signature Heavenly Beds. Amenities include terry-cloth bathrobes and a large desktop workspace. The Westin offers an indoor pool, business center, nearby fitness center, in-room spa services, whirlpool, Westin Kids Club, and gift shop. On the second level is Shula's Steak House, named one of America's best for steak.

i For help finding an Indianapolis B&B, contact the Indianapolis Convention and Visitors Association at (800) 323-4639 or click on the Web site at www.visitindy .com.

YELLOW ROSE INN $$$$
1441 N. Delaware St.
(317) 636-7673
www.yellowroseinn.com

Constructed at the turn of the 20th century, Yellow Rose Inn is located in the historic Old Northside. The 8,000-square-foot brick Georgian Revival colonial was built by Harry J. Milligan, an Indianapolis attorney and Indiana land baron. The home was his treasure until his death in 1913. Today, Yellow Rose Inn continues its tradition of welcoming guests to enjoy its hospitality and architectural antiques. The inn boasts five fireplace mantels from different periods, stained and beveled glass, an early 1870s Gothic Revival stairs, gas chandeliers, and other fine furnishings.

Yellow Rose Inn offers four suites, each with its own decor. As the master suite of the house, the Wedgwood Suite features a gas log fireplace, sitting room, and bathroom with two-person whirlpool tub, two porcelain sinks, and a solid marble shower. A stained-glass window separates the bathroom from the outer hallway. The Oak Suite features a white-oak ceiling canopy opposite a Queen Anne oak fireplace mantel with working gas log. A large bathroom has a massive porcelain tub and a modern shower. The Emerald Suite features a sitting room with queen-size hide-away bed, as well as a bedroom. The bathroom is shared by these two rooms. One of Indiana's largest guest suites, the Ballroom Suite features 1,800 square feet of white-oak flooring with brand new oak and ceramic kitchen, a raised king-size sleeping pavilion, a rare 1873 Brunswick Monarch pool table, two-person whirlpool tub, separate bedroom with queen-size bed, lounge area with leather couch, and a 32-inch TV.

All suites enjoy access to the 1,200-square-foot roof deck and six-person hot tub overlooking the downtown skyline. The gardens are great for a stroll or to relax in the pavilion. Massage therapies can be arranged, and bicycles are available for a spin. A gourmet breakfast starts the day.

NORTHWEST

BEST WESTERN COUNTRY SUITES NORTHWEST $$$
3871 W. 92nd St.
(317) 879-1700
www.bwcountrysuites.com

An all-suite hotel located about 15 minutes from downtown Indianapolis, Best Western Country Suites was completely renovated in 2007. The 40 guest suites offer a king bed, sleeper sofa in the living room area with a microwave oven and refrigerator, wet bar, and two televisions with cable channels. With a traditional style decor, Best Western has an exercise/fitness room, business center, and free parking. With easy interstate access, the hotel is close to local dining, shopping, and entertainment, including Crooked Stick Golf Club, Butler University, and Castleton Square shopping mall. A complimentary hot/cold breakfast buffet is offered each morning.

CANDLEWOOD SUITES INDIANAPOLIS NORTHWEST $$$
7451 Woodland Dr.
(800) 225-1237
www.ichotelsgroup.com

Less than 10 miles from the Indianapolis Motor Speedway, Lucas Oil Stadium, the Convention Center, and downtown Indianapolis, Candlewood Suites Indianapolis Northwest was opened in 2009. An all-suites property, Candlewood features separate bedroom and living room, full kitchen, and TV with VCR and DVD players. An on-site gym, indoor pool, free laundry facility, video library, snack bar, and business center are also offered. Candlewood is one block east of I-465, with easy access to Indianapolis International Airport.

CLARION HOTEL & CONFERENCE CENTER $$$
2930 Waterfront Parkway West Dr.
(317) 299-8400
www.clarionhotel.com

This 143-room hotel is less than 3 miles from Indianapolis Motor Speedway and 12 miles from downtown Indianapolis. Clarion offers shuttle service to Indianapolis International Airport, which is about 15 miles away. Most rooms have a poolside or lakeside view and many have microwaves and refrigerators. A business center and fitness room are offered on-site, as well as an indoor pool and hot tub located in a tropical setting in the hotel atrium. Clarion also features the cocktail bar Excalibur and a restaurant, Stefan's Restaurant & Pizzeria at the Waterfront, which specializes in Italian cuisine.

> **i** Room prices for area hotels and motels often drop dramatically the farther you travel in any direction from downtown. If you've traveled to Indy by car, it might be worth the extra travel time to check out the rooms a few exits up the highway.

CLARION INN & SUITES NORTHWEST $$
7001 Corporate Dr.
(317) 298-3700
www.clarionhotel.com

Newly renovated, this 67-room hotel is located off I-465, with easy access to major attractions, downtown Indianapolis, and Indianapolis International Airport. Complimentary breakfast, free 24-hour coffee, and free Otis Spunkmeyer cookies are offered. Also available are an indoor pool, exercise room, business center, and conference facility. All guest rooms have pillow top mattresses. Mini-suites come equipped with microwaves, refrigerators and wet bars, and separate sitting areas with sofas. The Presidential Suite features a hot tub.

> **i** If you would like a more complete list of Indianapolis-area hotels, call the Indianapolis Convention & Visitors Association at (800) 323-4639 or log on to its Web site at www.visitindy.com.

COMFORT INN & SUITES AIRPORT WEST $$
5855 Rockville Rd.
(800) 323-2086
www.comfortinnhotel.com

Close-up

Indy-area Campgrounds

If it's a truly down-to-earth experience you're looking for, there are plenty of places to pitch a tent or plug in an RV in the Indianapolis area. Check out the campgrounds in Indianapolis and its immediate area, which have sites for both recreational vehicles and tent campers. Some camping opportunities also are available at nearby state parks.

Although most area campgrounds will be happy, when possible, to accommodate campers who just show up looking for a site, you are strongly encouraged to make reservations. Sites tend to fill up, especially during nice weather and particularly during the month of May for the Indy 500.

Many campgrounds are open year-round for RVs. Amenities vary greatly at the different facilities, so it is best to be sure that a campground offers what you want. Please note that prices are subject to change and that many increase around specific events, such as the Indy 500. Off-season rates may be a little cheaper.

Indiana State Fairgrounds RV Campgrounds
1202 E. 38th St.
(317) 927-7510
www.in.gov/statefair/fairgrounds/general/camping.html

The Indiana State Fairgrounds RV Campgrounds is a great spot to stop and see the sights. Located on the northwest side of the fairgrounds, the campground offers 170 sites, with 80 featuring full seasonal hookups (water, electricity, and sewer) and 90 having electricity and water. Campsites are available year-round. Price is $25 per day with hookups; with no hookups, the cost is $16 per day. Spaces are very limited in August during the Indiana State Fair. The fairgrounds provide 24-hour security, indoor showers and flush toilets, potable water, and sanitary dumping stations.

Indy Lakes
4001 W. Southport Rd.
(317) 888-6006
www.indylakes.com

Located less than 10 miles from downtown Indianapolis, Indy Lakes offers 55 full-service hookups and five primitive campsites. Full service includes water, sewer, and 30- and 50-amp electricity. Primitive campsites have 20-amp electricity. Not all lots accommodate dogs but the campground has a large dog walk bordering the dog-friendly sites. Dogs larger than 20 pounds need preapproval. RV camping is allowed year-round. Primitive camping is permitted only when the on-site store is open 24 hours—early May through Labor Day and weekends from later March through early October. RV campers are required to have full bathroom facilities as part of their campers when the store is not open 24 hours.

Amenities include three fishing lakes on-site for an extra fee, wireless Internet, outside restrooms, and three inside single full bathrooms when the store is open. Showers are $2 each. The property has an automatic security gate with remote control for access, along with more than 25 security cameras. High-definition DIRECTV is available for $2.99 per day, and a satellite signal is free for campers who have their own service. Based on two adults and two children, RV prices start at $21 a day. Camping fees are $8 for the first person and an additional $5 per person for others, with a limit of four people. Owners live on-site.

KOA Indianapolis
5896 W. 200 North, Greenfield
(800) 562-0531
www.indykoa.com

Open March 1 through November 15, KOA Indianapolis is part of the KOA chain, which means you know what to expect—clean facilities, plenty of amenities, and a family-friendly campground close to major attractions. The 240-acre campground is located on the east side of Indiana, about 20 minutes from Indianapolis Motor Speedway and 15 minutes from the Children's Museum, Indianapolis Zoo, and downtown Indy. Family owned and operated, the KOA Indianapolis offers a playground, swimming pool, rental lodges and cabins, deluxe patio sites, free wireless Internet, tiled restrooms with hot showers, bike rentals, group kitchen and gathering room, 24-hour laundry facilities, tent camping with fire rings, dump station, propane, and a store with RV supplies, foodstuffs, ice, and firewood. Security is provided around the clock.

A meandering creek and towering canopy of oak, maple, and sycamore trees add to the campground's country ambience. Miniature horses are a pleasant sight at the corral. This is a popular place to be during area events, particularly the Indy 500, so be sure and reserve in advance. Prices range from $24.89 for a primitive tent site ($36.84 during the Indy 500) and $33.78 for an RV site with water and 30-amp electrical hookup only ($49.87 during the Indy 500) to $39.49 for the deluxe sites with full hookup and a large patio ($67.63 during the Indy 500). Rates are based on two adults; children under 5 stay for free.

Lake Haven Retreat
1951 W. Edgewood Ave.
(317) 783-5267
www.lakehavenretreat.com

Offering 110 full hookup sites and primitive tent camping, Lake Haven Retreat is located 2 miles south of the Indianapolis beltway on SR 37. The campground is less than a 10-minute drive from Indianapolis International Airport, downtown Indianapolis, and the Indianapolis Motor Speedway. The 22-acre campground has a 5-acre stocked lake for catch-and-release fishing, laundry facility, restrooms and showers, recreation hall, and beach area open from Memorial Day through Labor Day. Full hookups feature 30- and 50-amp electricity as well as pull-through sites. Complimentary high-speed wireless Internet and cable TV are available. Based on two adults and three children, prices start at $27 plus tax for RV sites and $19 per day plus tax for tent camping. Many RV owners choose to stay year-round at the campground.

Lidy's Race Parking & Camping
4853 McCray St.
(317) 241-2248
www.indy-raceparking.com

Offering electrical and RV hookup, Lidy's Race Parking & Camping is within walking distance of the Indianapolis Motor Speedway. Water is available. The campground offers trucks to pump RV holding tanks at their locations. Portable toilets also are provided, as well as wireless Internet. Reserve early if you plan to stay here any time in May for the Indy 500. Coffee and muffins are available on racing mornings for guests.

Raceview Family Campground
3380 N. County Rd. 1000 East, Brownsburg
(317) 852-5737
www.raceviewcampground.com

For race fans who want to get close to the action, Raceview Family Campground is the place to be. The campground is located 50 feet from Gate 4P of O'Reilly Raceway Park, home of the National Hot Rod Association's U.S. Nationals as well as many other events. Most campers walk from their sites to Raceway Park. Raceview is also 7 miles west of Indianapolis Motor Speedway and 12 miles from downtown Indianapolis. Located on 70 acres, Raceview features 200 RV sites with electrical hookups, modern restrooms, showers, water, a lighted camping area, and an RV sanitary station, as well as a health board–approved water fill station. Rates vary according to the racing action, ranging from $16 per adult for a camping site without electricity to $30 for a site with electricity. Sites with electrical hookups often sell out quickly, and many campers reserve for the entire racing event, often a week.

A 94-room hotel with spacious rooms and suites, Comfort Inn is conveniently located near sporting venues and Indianapolis International Airport. A popular option for local travelers is the Stay & Fly Package (about $99), which includes a one-night stay, free transportation to and from Indianapolis International Airport, a free Grab & Go breakfast for early departures, and free parking for up to 30 nights. The hotel offers an exercise room, indoor atrium pool, hot tub, meeting room, and game room with a ball pit, slides, and arcade games. A full breakfast and 24-hour airport transportation are complimentary.

COMFORT INN & SUITES NORTH AT THE PYRAMIDS $$
9090 Wesleyan Rd.
(800) 228-5151
www.comfortinnandsuitesnorth.com
Offering 103 guest rooms and 13 suites, Comfort Inn & Suites is about 20 minutes from downtown Indianapolis and a short distance from major interstates. Start the day with a complimentary Sunshine Breakfast. Amenities include Perfect Sleep premium bedding in every room plus a desk and chair, microwave, and refrigerator. Two suites have whirlpools. On site is an outdoor swimming pool and business center. Guests get a pass to Gold's Gym.

COUNTRY INN & SUITES—CARMEL $$
9797 N. Michigan Rd., Carmel
(317) 876-0333
www.countryinns.com
With the look and feel of a bed-and-breakfast, this 66-room inn offers oversized guest rooms and a complimentary continental breakfast. Decorated in a warm country style, the suites have a mini-refrigerator, microwave, and wet bar. Whirlpool suites include a two-person Jacuzzi tub. An indoor swimming pool, hot tub, and exercise/fitness room are available. Guests are greeted with complimentary cookies at check-in. Coffee and cookies are offered 24 hours a day in the lobby. Country Inn & Suites is a smoke-free facility.

DAYS INN & SUITES NORTHWEST $
3910 Payne Branch Rd.
(800) 329-7466
www.daysinn.com
Located at I-465 and US 421, Days Inn features 138 rooms with Jacuzzi Suites available. On site is an indoor pool, fitness center, spa, hot tub, and business center. A complimentary continental breakfast starts the day. The hotel is close to shopping, dining, and major attractions.

FREDERICK-TALBOTT INN $$$
13805 Allisonville Rd., Fishers
(866) 680-6466
www.fredericktalbottinn.com
A restored 1875 two-story brick home, Frederick-Talbott Inn is handy to Indianapolis, Carmel, Fishers, and Noblesville. Sitting on a tranquil two-acre estate, the inn has country gardens, horseshoe pits, and a spacious veranda overlooking the prairie. The deck is a good place to catch the fireworks and summer concerts at nearby Conner Prairie, a living history museum. The inn features 10 rooms, each with private bath, cable TV, and individual decor. Some rooms have whirlpool tubs and fireplaces.

The Hollingsworth, a private dormer room on the second floor, has a king-size bed, oversize garden tub, and separate shower. The Bransfield on the first floor has two queen beds and private patio access. Also on the first floor, the Eastman features a soft-yellow decor and two twin beds. Step onto the first-floor deck from the Frederick, which also features a fireplace, king-size bed, and shower-only bath. The Atkinson is wheelchair accessible and has a queen-size bed, shower-only bath, and access to the first-floor deck. On the second floor, the Talbott has two queen-size beds and a lovely periwinkle-blue color illuminated by four large windows. The Hamilton on the second floor has two double-size beds. The Courtney on the second floor is the smallest of the rooms and has a queen bed. The Caldwell on the second floor has a king-size bed and shower-only bath. Decorated in pale yellows and greens, the second-floor Garrity has a king-size bed and shower-only bath.

A continental breakfast is served weekdays in the dining room. On weekends a full hot buffet breakfast is served. If you have to leave early, the hosts will prepare a muffin basket to take with you.

HOLIDAY INN EXPRESS HOTEL & SUITES $$
1180 Wilson Dr., Greenwood
(317) 881-0600
www.ichotelsgroup.com
Featuring a contemporary design, this new 85-room hotel offers two-room suites, whirlpool tubs, kitchenettes, and 46-inch TVs. Some rooms have refrigerators and microwaves. On site are a 24-hour exercise/fitness room, indoor swimming pool, 24-hour business center, and guest laundry. Located off I-65, the hotel is handy to downtown Indianapolis and Greenwood. A complimentary continental breakfast starts the day, and a manager's reception on weekdays, with a complimentary cocktail, is a nice way to relax in the evening.

MARTEN HOUSE HOTEL & LILLY CONFERENCE CENTER $$$
1801 W. 86th St.
(800) 736-5634
www.martenhousehotel.com
Adjoining the Lilly Conference Center, the Marten House Hotel offers 163 deluxe guest rooms and is known for high-quality and personal service. Rooms are equipped with full- or king-size beds, work areas, and 25-inch TVs. Junior suites offer over 400 square feet, a living area, refrigerator, microwave, wet bar, and double windows overlooking the courtyard. An indoor pool and fitness center are on-site. The new Lilly Conference Center offers 34,000 square feet of state-of-the-art meeting space with a videoconference center and executive boardroom. Located at the hotel, Piccard's Restaurant features a complete menu, as well as daily buffets and room service. Marten House is a smoke-free facility.

RED ROOF INN SPEEDWAY $
6415 Debonair Lane
(317) 293-6881
www.redroof.com

Geared towards race fans, this Red Roof Inn is strategically located between Raceway Park and the Indianapolis Motor Speedway. The inn is seven miles from downtown Indianapolis. The 108-room inn offers many restaurants within walking distance.

SLEEP INN WEST/AIRPORT $
5845 Rockville Rd.
(800) 753-3746
www.sleepinn.com
Located near Indianapolis International Airport, this 63-room economy hotel offers complimentary continental breakfast and a free 24-hour airport shuttle.

WINGATE BY WYNDHAM INDIANAPOLIS AIRPORT $$
5797 Rockville Rd.
(800) 228-1000
www.wingatehotels.com
A free 24-hour airport shuttle and complimentary hot breakfast buffet make this a convenient hotel for travelers. The Wingate's 96 comfortable rooms offer a separate work area as well as top-of-the-line mattresses with plump pillows and fine-quality linens, a refrigerator, a microwave, and a safe. An indoor pool, whirlpool, exercise room, and 24-hour business center are available.

NORTHEAST

BEST WESTERN CASTLETON INN $
8300 Craig St.
(800) 232-5757
www.bestwestern.com
This newly remodeled hotel offers 101 rooms and is conveniently located off I-69, about 15 miles from downtown Indianapolis. A hot breakfast and newspaper are complimentary ways to start the day. A seasonal outdoor pool and business center are on-site. The Best Western is situated in the heart of a popular dining and shopping district.

CANDLEWOOD SUITES INDIANAPOLIS
NORTHEAST $$
8111 Bash St.
(888) 226-3539
www.ichotelsgroup.com
Designed for the corporate traveler's short or extended stays, Candlewood Suites is nestled in the heart of Castleton, minutes from hundreds of restaurants and shopping. The Candlewood is an all-suite hotel that features fully equipped kitchens, desks, recliners, a free lending library, a fitness facility, an indoor pool and hot tub, and a business center. Guests also are invited to use the gazebo with gas grill and free laundry facilities. The Candlewood Cupboard is a 24-hour convenience store with reasonable prices.

i Even with a previously made reservation, whenever you check in it is worth asking about the room rate. Frequently, a desk clerk might quote the "rack rate," which is the highest. Sometimes a reduced rate is available when you make a polite inquiry.

COMFORT SUITES INDIANAPOLIS EAST $$
7035 Western Select Dr.
(800) 537-1133
www.comfortsuites.com
With easy access to I-70, Comfort Suites offers 90 suites with luxurious bedding, a spacious living and work area, recliner, clock radio with MP3 jack, and well-equipped kitchen with microwave, refrigerator, and dining area. A complimentary breakfast is offered each morning, and a Wednesday evening manager's reception features free beer, wine, and a light dinner. The site offers an indoor pool, exercise room, laundry facilities, business center, and an executive meeting room. Guests are invited to relax on the sundeck or enjoy the picnic area and outdoor sports court. Comfort Suites is a smoke-free facility.

DOUBLETREE GUEST SUITES $$
11355 N. Meridian St., Carmel
(317) 844-7994
http://doubletree1.hilton.com
Located about 12 miles north of downtown Indianapolis in the suburb of Carmel, Doubletree Guest Suites provides easy access to attractions, shopping, dining, and Indianapolis International Airport. Newly renovated, the all-suite hotel boasts rooms with a bedroom area with separate living room, and sleeper sofa and two TVs in every two-room suite. All suites offer a refrigerator and microwave. The hotel has a full-service restaurant and lounge on-site as well indoor and outdoor pools with a hot tub.

DRURY INN & SUITES INDIANAPOLIS
NORTHEAST $$
8180 Shadeland Ave.
(800) 378-7946
wwws.druryhotels.com
This beautiful new hotel offers 210 rooms with many amenities. All rooms have microwaves, refrigerators, and flat-panel LCD TVs. On site are indoor and outdoor pools, a whirlpool, a snack pantry, an exercise room, a 24-hour business center, and a guest laundry. Drury's complimentary breakfast includes hot scrambled eggs, Belgian waffles, biscuits and gravy, sausage, fresh fruit, cereal, and much more. The hotel also offers a free soda fountain and fresh popcorn.

HOLIDAY INN EAST $
6990 E. 21st St.
(800) 892-5084
www.indianapolis.com/holiday-inn-east
Located 8 miles from downtown, Holiday Inn East offers 184 guest rooms. Amenities include an indoor pool, whirlpool, guest laundry, and a fitness center. Kids eat free at the hotel. The restaurant on-site is Damon's, known for its barbecue ribs and unique onion loaf.

HOTEL INDIGO FISHERS–INDY'S
UPTOWN $$$
9791 North by Northeast Blvd., Fishers
(317) 558-4100
www.hotelindigo.com
Offering 115 guest rooms on three floors, the upscale Hotel Indigo is located in the Indianapolis suburb of Fishers. With easy access to I-69, the

hotel is convenient to major attractions. Amenities include a 24-hour business center, indoor pool, whirlpool, 24-hour fitness center, guest laundry, and lounge. Hotel Indigo also boasts two dining spots. Phi Bar, a casual yet chic spot to enjoy a cocktail with friends, features a full-service bar with delicious appetizers and outdoor patio seating. The Golden Bean Cafe serves breakfast and includes the Starbuck's Coffee Bar.

STUDIO 6 HOTEL $
8250 North by Northeast Blvd., Fishers
(317) 913-1920
www.staystudio6.com
Boasting "more in your room, less on your bill," Studio 6 has gained a reputation for being a comfortable property with lower prices. The hotel features 124 rooms with fully equipped kitchens, including microwaves, stove tops, coffeemakers, refrigerators, dishes, cooking utensils, and pots and pans. Rooms offer an expanded work area and multichannel TVs with cable channels. A guest laundry is on-site. Studio 6 is located within walking distance of restaurants and shops.

WEST

RENATA'S BED & BREAKFAST $$$
2201 S. Lynhurst Dr.
(317) 486-4577
www.renatasbandb.com
Location is a big plus at Renata's Bed & Breakfast—five minutes from Indianapolis International Airport, 10 minutes from Indianapolis Motor Speedway, and 10 minutes from downtown Indianapolis. Opened in 2006, the B&B was originally built in 1930 as a two-story home. Nestled on one and a half acres, Renata's offers four guest rooms, each with a themed decor—America, Indiana, Romance, and German. The German room is a salute to the owner's heritage. Renata came to America from a small town near Nuremberg, Germany, when she was 18 years old. Each guest room includes a private bath, cable TV, wireless Internet, and snacks. A European breakfast is offered on weekdays. Weekends feature a traditional American country breakfast

with biscuits and gravy, bacon, sausage, eggs, pancakes, and syrup. A lovely Gingerbread House in the backyard can be rented for parties, meetings, reunions, workshops, or other special occasions. Holding 35 people, the Gingerbread House is equipped with a kitchenette and bathroom.

> **i** In true Hoosier hospitality, when bed-and-breakfasts are booked, many of the innkeepers will refer you to one of their "competitors." That's a nice way to spread the goodness around.

SPEEDWAY BED AND BREAKFAST $$$
1829 Cunningham Rd., Speedway
(317) 487-6531
www.speedwaybandb.com
The largest house in the town of Speedway, the home was originally built on 900 acres of land. Over the years, however, the land around the house was sold and the town of Speedway grew up around the big, white plantation-style estate. For almost a decade the home has served as a bed-and-breakfast. Landscaped grounds on over an acre include a gazebo and two ponds with hanging gardens. The inn also offers meeting space, including a boardroom that will accommodate up to 20 people.

Within walking distance of Indianapolis Motor Speedway, the inn offers shuttle service to the track on race days. On the main level of the home, the Getaway Suite and Reading Room has a queen canopy bed, two-person whirlpool tub, and adjoining room with daybed and shower. The two rooms also can be rented separately. The Vintage Room on the second floor offers a king bed or twin beds and private bath. The Trackside Room has a queen bed, plus private shower. Andrew's Room has a daybed or twins, with the bath outside the room. On the third level, the Hideaway Attic Suite has a California king bed and two twin beds. The entire Speedway Bed and Breakfast can be rented, including use of the kitchen, dining room, sitting room, gathering room, and overnight sleeping for 12 to 14 people.

A down-home country breakfast features biscuits and gravy, hash browns, sausage, bacon, coffee, juice, and fruit. For a change of pace, breakfast is sometimes Eggs Benedict and scones. Breakfasts are made to order daily, along with special evening desserts.

SOUTHWEST

ADAM'S MARK INDIANAPOLIS $$$$
2544 Executive Dr.
(800) 790-4109
www.adamsmark.com

Only a quarter mile from Indianapolis International Airport and eight minutes from downtown Indianapolis, Adam's Mark offers easy access to major destinations. The 407-room hotel includes 20 suites and offers amenities such as a swimming pool and health club. The Marker Restaurant features award-winning American cuisine and a lunchtime pasta bar where custom-made pasta dishes are created under the diner's direction. Marker Lounge features refreshments, a big-screen TV, pool table, dartboards, and Wii video game system. Park-and-fly packages are available.

CAMBRIA SUITES INDIANAPOLIS
AIRPORT $$$
6016 Gateway Dr., Plainfield
(317) 279-2394
www.cambriasuites.com

Less than 5 miles from Indianapolis International Airport, Cambria Suites offers easy access to area attractions. A contemporary hotel with 104 rooms, Cambria Suites features a state-of-the-art fitness center, indoor pool, hot tub, barista gourmet coffee bar in the lobby, business center, and a 24-hour sundry shop offering gourmet salads and sandwiches, energy drinks, organic snacks, and much more. A contemporary bistro, Reflect provides breakfast and dinner along with a full-service bar. An open and airy two-story lobby provides club-lounge seating and a big screen media wall. Cambria Suites is a smoke-free facility.

COMFORT INN PLAINFIELD $$
6107 Cambridge Way, Plainfield
(800) 228-5150
www.comfortinn.com

A new hotel, Comfort Inn is less than 10 miles from Indianapolis International Airport and close to local attractions. The 66-room hotel offers free deluxe continental breakfast and coffee. Amenities include an indoor pool, fitness center, and guest laundry. All guest rooms include refrigerators, microwaves, and oversize showers. Whirlpool suites also are available.

COURTYARD BY MARRIOTT AIRPORT $$$
2602 Fortune Circle East
(800) 321-2211
www.marriott.com

Newly renovated, the Courtyard by Marriott Airport offers four floors with 141 rooms and 10 suites. The hotel features a business library in the lobby with free high-speed Internet, a gift shop, guest laundry, and free airport shuttle. Open 24 hours a day, the Market carries fresh sandwiches, salads, snacks, and beverages.

DAYS HOTEL AIRPORT $
5860 Fortune Circle West
(317) 248-0621
www.daysinn.com

Located just outside Indianapolis International Airport and minutes from major attractions, Days Inn is a 240-room full-service hotel. Amenities include a complimentary hot breakfast and complimentary airport shuttle. An outdoor swimming pool and guest laundry are also on-site. P.K.'s Dining & Diversions Restaurant serves regional favorites daily. P.K.'s Lounge offers beer, wine, and other drinks.

i Hotels near Indianapolis International Airport often offer "park-and-fly" packages that can save money and hassle. The prices, some starting at $99, include overnight accommodations, continental breakfast, airport shuttle, and free parking for up to 30 days. That is much cheaper than parking at the airport.

EXTENDED STAY AMERICA AIRPORT $$
2730 Fortune Circle West
(317) 248-0465
www.extendedstayamerica.com
This 107-room hotel offers studios with fully equipped kitchens and plenty of work space with computer data ports. An on-site guest laundry is available.

**HAMPTON INN & SUITES INDIANAPOLIS
AIRPORT** $$$
9020 Hatfield Dr.
(317) 856-1000
www.schahethotels.com
Offering the convenience of being near the Indianapolis International Airport and the comfort of a modern new hotel, the 148-room Hampton Inn & Suites is a winning combination. The hotel has a complimentary 24-hour airport shuttle, fitness facility, business center, indoor pool, and hot tub. For breakfast, enjoy a complimentary hot meal with seven food stations. Free coffee and tea also are available in the lobby around the clock. Rooms feature 32-inch flat-screen TVs, mini refrigerators, and microwaves. Hampton beds offer a choice of feather or foam pillows, high-quality soft sheets, plush down-like comforters, crisp white duvets, and a comfy pillow top mattress on top of a raised bed. Guest rooms offer a "lap desk" for guests to work on their laptop computers, with complimentary high-speed Internet.

**RADISSON HOTEL INDIANAPOLIS
AIRPORT** $$
2500 S. High School Rd.
(800) 333-3333
www.radisson.com
A full-service property, Radisson features such welcome amenities as Sleep Number beds and complimentary 24-hour airport shuttle service. Executive and Parlor Suites also offer microwaves, refrigerators, and wet bars. Other conveniences include a 24-hour Corner Pantry, plus meeting and event space. Guests can enjoy lunch and din-

ner at Austin's Restaurant or relax with a drink and watch a game in the Lobby Lounge.

SOUTHEAST

BAYMONT INN & SUITES $$
1540 Brookville Crossing Way
(317) 322-2000
www.baymontinns.com
Conveniently located at I-465 East, Baymont Inn & Suites is a mid-scale, 75-room hotel within easy distance of restaurants, shopping, and local attractions. Spacious rooms feature 27-inch flat-screen TVs, microwaves, and refrigerators. A complimentary continental breakfast is served every morning. Amenities include a 24-hour indoor pool, whirlpool spa, fitness center, guest laundry, and business center. Whirlpool Suites are also available.

BEST WESTERN CROSSROADS $$
7610 Old Trails Rd.
(317) 353-6966
http://book.bestwestern.com
Located less than 5 miles from downtown Indianapolis, Best Western Crossroads offers a business center, free wireless Internet, outdoor pool, and refrigerator and microwave in each room. Start the day with a complimentary continental breakfast featuring homemade Belgian waffles. The hotel also offers meeting facilities that accommodate up to 60 people.

**SUPER 8 MOTEL—
INDIANAPOLIS/EMERSON AVENUE** $
4530 S. Emerson Ave.
(317) 788-0955
www.super8.com
Just 10 minutes away from downtown Indianapolis, Super 8 Motel is located off I-465. Amenities include a guest laundry, cable TV, and free high-speed Internet. A complimentary SuperStart breakfast is served every morning.

RESTAURANTS

Mention Hoosier cooking and mouths start watering. It's no wonder. Food is both a tradition and a passion here. The capital city of Indianapolis has a huge smorgasbord of good cooks spread across the land like smooth butter on a warm biscuit.

Indianapolis cooks delight in serving up delectable food—from country-style cooking to regional recipes to cosmopolitan cuisine. No matter what you're craving, chances are it can be found somewhere in Indianapolis. It's a virtual paradise for taste buds.

Ask the locals. They'll tell you where to find the tenderest steak, tastiest tenderloin, freshest salmon, smoothest mashed potatoes, flakiest phyllo, tangiest lemon meringue pie, silkiest chocolate mousse, richest cappuccino, spiciest chili, zestiest ziti, and coolest salads. Or just glance inside a bustling eatery or packed parking lot and know you've probably found a rewarding eating spot.

Browse through this chapter and you'll see once and for all that the old joke about Indianapolis having no place good to eat except at home really isn't true. And the choices that I've listed are only part of the delicious dining establishments in Indy. I couldn't include them all or this chapter would probably be about as big as the whole book; plus I haven't had the pleasure of dining in each and every restaurant. New ones are always opening up; beloved ones are adding other locations. So if you run across some great little place that should be included next time, let me know. I'd be happy to check it out.

This chapter is arranged by food category, so your favorite specialties should be easy to find. However, many restaurants serve several different types of cuisine, so if you're craving steak and your guy or gal is all set for shrimp, many places feature both. I tried to give you a general idea of where to find what. I've excluded most chain restaurants because you probably already know about them. Mostly I've concentrated on the places that are unique to Indianapolis. For information on even more dining options, see the Nightlife chapter. That's where I've listed sports bars, microbreweries, coffeehouses, and the like. Many of those places have great food, and they often serve it late into the night. You might want to add them to your list of favorites. See the Kidstuff chapter for some especially kid-friendly restaurants.

Most major restaurants take credit cards and debit cards. Many take reservations but don't require them. Parking is usually available. Indianapolis is such a drivable city with handy parking lots as well as street parking. Being able to get just about anywhere in a half hour or less is a blessing.

Finally, keep in mind that Indy's restaurant scene seems to be constantly growing and changing. Operating hours change, businesses switch hands, chefs play musical chairs, eateries close and reemerge with new names and menus. And new restaurants open up regularly. If you're planning a special meal out, it's a good idea to call first, at least to make sure of the operating hours.

Price Code

Use the following price code as a general guide for the cost of dinner entrees for two, excluding appetizers, alcoholic beverages, desserts, and tip. Keep in mind that drinks, desserts, and extras for two can significantly add to the bill and will often put you in a new price category. The tab for breakfast and lunch will most likely be less expensive.

$....................	$15 or less
$$	$16 to $25
$$$	$26 to $40
$$$$................	$41 to $60
$$$$$...........	$61 and more

AMERICAN/CONTEMPORARY AMERICAN

CAPITAL GRILLE $$$$$
40 W. Washington St.
(317) 423-8790
www.capitalgrille.com

Located in the Conrad Hotel in the heart of downtown, the Capital Grille is a fine-dining restaurant that is both comfy and elegant. Rich African mahogany paneling and soft lighting from one-of-a-kind art deco chandeliers create a warm decor made for relaxing. The Capital features an extensive menu that is a pleasure to read. Take time to savor it before ordering. Just look at two of the appetizers—cold shellfish platter with a one-pound lobster, Gulf Coast jumbo shrimp, and freshly shucked oysters. Or the Wagyu beef carpaccio, premium Japanese beef blended with seven spices, seared, chilled, and sliced razor thin, garnished with fresh arugula. The Capital specializes in dry-aged steaks, fresh seafood that is flown in daily, and some creative side dishes. A favorite is the Parmesan Truffle Fries—golden fries tossed in shredded Grana Padano cheese, kosher salt, and white truffle oil. Or try the Lobster Mac 'N' Cheese—baked campanelle pasta and fresh lobster meat tossed in a mascarpone, Havarti, and Grana Padano cream sauce topped with panko bread crumbs, and grated white cheddar. The restaurant is open for breakfast, lunch, and dinner. Dining is also available in the lounge or outdoor patio. An award-winning wine list offers more than 400 wines.

CIRCLE CITY BAR AND GRILLE $$$
350 W. Maryland St.
(317) 405-6100
www.marriott.com

Located in the Indianapolis Marriott Downtown, this upscale restaurant is a good place to dine even if you're not staying at the hotel. Oversized cushy booths, warm wood tones, and colorful artwork of local scenes create a comfortable, relaxed setting. Regional cuisine is a specialty with Indiana farmed foods from eggs and pork to organic vegetables and wild mushrooms. Favorites are Maple Leaf Farms breast of duck served with sweet orange segments, crunchy hazelnut croquettes, and crisp summer vegetables. A nice wine list and a signature martini menu are pleasant extras. Circle City is open for breakfast, lunch, and dinner.

CREATION CAFE $$$
337 W. 11th St.
(317) 955-2389
www.indycanal.com

A hip, eccentric place, Creation Cafe is located in a renovated church with a premium waterfront location on the north end of the Central Canal. An extensive patio offers a lovely view of the Indianapolis skyline. During the 1970s and 1980s, Buggs Temple—so named for its minister—was not only home to a church congregation but was also the site of some of the best gospel singing in Indy. Fresh local ingredients are the basis for salads, sandwiches, and soups. Menu items have creative names such as the Original Mother Clucker—marinated chicken breast on a brioche bun with lettuce, tomato, red onions, and pesto mayo. Or the Oinker—pulled pork smothered with sweet barbecue sauce. Plus the B Cubed—a spicy vegetarian black bean burger served on brioche bun with lettuce, tomato, and onion. Creation also serves beer, wine, and liquor. Closed on Sunday, the cafe also frequently hosts local musicians.

🔍 Close-up

Re-created Tearoom Serves Tastes of the Past

Once upon a time, little girls dressed up in their Sunday best and went to the L. S. Ayres Tea Room. Boys squirmed in coats and ties while they practiced proper etiquette. It was a place where many children learned manners. And when they were done eating, they could choose a free gift from the Treasure Chest.

A popular downtown Indianapolis landmark, the old tearoom opened in 1905 and soon became an important shopping and dining mecca. Known for its elegant decor, gracious service, and delicious food, the tearoom had diners looking forward to a visit. For many years, a message book was located at the first-floor doorway, where Ayres patrons could leave messages for friends they were meeting to shop or dine in the tearoom.

The chicken velvet soup was very popular. So was the chicken potpie served in a "setting hen" dish. Diners were served on real china, and tables had linen tablecloths and fresh flowers.

After the L. S. Ayres Tea Room closed in 1990, the Indiana State Museum obtained much of its memorabilia and re-created the tearoom—right down to a view outside the make-believe windows. In fact, there are no windows at all in the new tearoom. A blank wall has been creatively designed to feature draped, paned windows looking out on a mural of a landscape that might have been seen decades ago.

The re-created dining room is as accurate as possible for the 1950s–'60s era, including the original wood tables and chairs from the former tearoom. China, teapots, silver, menus, and historical images from the actual tearoom are on display. Reproductions of tearoom wall coverings, drapes, furniture, and chandeliers are included, along with a redesign of the reception desk. Even the traditional Treasure Chest is on display, with tissue-wrapped gifts tied with blue ribbons for boys and red ribbons for girls.

CHICKEN VELVET SOUP

¾ cup butter

¾ cup flour

1 cup warm milk

1 pint hot chicken stock

1 cup warm cream

1 quart chicken stock

1½ cups chopped, cooked chicken

¼ tablespoon salt

Dash of pepper

Combine butter and flour, blending well. Add warm milk, pint of hot chicken stock, and warm cream. After cooking well, add remaining ingredients. Makes two quarts.

EAGLE'S NEST RESTAURANT $$$$$
One S. Capitol Ave.
(317) 616-6170
www.hyatt.com
This restaurant got its name for a good reason.

Perched high atop the Hyatt Regency, Eagle's Nest is the city's only revolving rooftop restaurant. Voted "The Most Romantic Restaurant in Indianapolis," Eagle's Nest offers glorious sunsets and wonderful 360-degree views of the downtown skyline. Take a relaxing glide around the city top while perusing a great menu with so many choices it's wonderfully hard to decide. A favorite is the crab-crusted halibut topped with crabmeat, baked and served on sautéed spinach with roasted fingerling potatoes and lemon-caper velouté. Then again, the grilled Fischer Farms frenched rib eye steak served with truffle butter is a delight as well. Eagle's Nest features an extensive wine list.

ETHAN'S RESTAURANT $$$
31 W. Ohio St.
(317) 635-2000
The Monumental Pasta Bar is the star at Ethan's inside the Sheraton City Centre Hotel. Featured weekdays, the bar offers an amazing number of pasta combinations. Sometimes its fun to see what diners will create before fixing your own.

14 WEST RESTAURANT $$$$
14 W. Maryland St.
(317) 636-1414
www.14west.net
A changing selection of classic American cuisine with a twist has made 14 West a popular dining spot. Combinations are yummy, such as Kobe Mac 'n' Cheese—an eight-ounce Kobe beef filet with lobster macaroni and cheese. Local ingredients are proudly promoted, such as Viking Farms lamb, served with crispy polenta veal jus and tomato jam. The organic Scottish salmon is prepared with red and golden beets, roasted fennel, gnocchi, and yam puree. Attentive servers pamper diners in this posh restaurant.

HARRY AND IZZY'S $$$$
153 S. Illinois St.
(317) 317-635-9594
www.harryandizzys.com
The only offspring of the legendary St. Elmo Steak House, Harry and Izzy's is named in honor of St. Elmo's fathers—Harry Roth and Isadore Rosen. More than a century old, St. Elmo's is one of a kind. And the chip off the old block doesn't try to be like daddy. Although it does feature the famed St. Elmo's shrimp cocktail with its spicy fresh horserad-

ish, Harry and Izzy's has a menu of its own. A light and airy restaurant, Harry and Izzy's offers fare from burgers to deli corned beef to lamb and veal chops and a huge 14-ounce New York strip steak, rolled in cracked peppercorn, pan seared, and served with a hot and sweet orange brandy butter sauce. Better be hungry when ordering that one. The Garbage Salad is a meal in itself with shrimp, Italian meats, cheese, artichoke, hearts of palm, cucumber, and celery. If there isn't a Colts game in town, the Sunday brunch served from noon to 3 p.m. has some great stuff, like the banana chocolate walnut French toast with warm maple syrup. The steak and egg wrap is a favorite with filet mignon, eggs, and queso blanco with house-made cilantro salsa.

HOLLYHOCK HILL $$$
8110 N. College Ave.
(317) 251-2294
www.hollyhockhill.com
Started in 1928 when V. D. Vincent began serving fried chicken dinners to family and friends at his County Cottage on the outskirts of town, this establishment is a family tradition. The name was changed to honor the beautiful hollyhock bushes on the lawn, but the house specialty is still old-fashioned fried chicken. Skillet fried and served with pan gravy, the chicken is accompanied by big bowls of mashed potatoes, green beans, and corn, as well as hot breads with apple butter.

Ownership has changed several times over the years, but the emphasis is still on family-style chicken dinners. A particular favorite on Sundays after church, Hollyhock Hill also serves steak and seafood. Make your own ice-cream sundae for dessert and munch on a brownie while you enjoy the cold treat.

i General dining times are 11:30 a.m. to 2 p.m. for lunch and 5 to 8 p.m. for dinner, although some restaurants often stay open late.

IRON SKILLET $$$
2489 W. 30th St.
(317) 923-6353
www.ironskillet.net

A century-old home is the setting for traditional Hoosier cooking. Family owned and operated since 1956, the Iron Skillet got its name because that was what was used to fry steak and chicken. Generous portions are served in a comfortable setting of soft music, candlelight, fresh flowers, and delicate latticework. Chicken, seafood, and steak come accompanied by big bowls of mashed potatoes, gravy, and homemade baking-powder biscuits. Dessert is make-your-own sundaes. The Iron Skillet also offers a wine list.

THE JAZZ KITCHEN $$$$
5377 N. College Ave.
(317) 253-4900
www.thejazzkitchen.com

Great food and great music are the winning combo that make this a popular restaurant. Featuring culinary creations from around the world, the menu ranges from steaks and seafood to inventive vegetarian and pasta creations. Paella is a Jazz Kitchen specialty, with a blend of shrimp, scallops, fish, mussels, andouille sausage, and chicken in a savory saffron rice. The dish takes at least one hour to cook. Another goodie is the Crescent City Crab Cakes, four handmade crab cakes served with Cajun rice and homemade Creole mayonnaise and cocktail sauce.

OAKLEY'S BISTRO $$$$
1464 W. 86th St.
(317) 824-1231
www.oakleysbistro.com

Opened in Dec 2002, Oakley's has been winning awards and devoted diners. *Bon Appetit's* 2004 restaurant issue named it "one of the hottest restaurants from coast to coast." Using fresh ingredients, chef and owner Steven Oakley creates dishes that are pleasing to the palate and the eye. Savor the lobster waffle as a starter—a basil waffle, lobster, zucchini sauce, mustard cream, and crispy leeks. The wild mushroom soup also is a tasty choice with caramelized onions, wild mushrooms, and herb truffle cream. An unusual entree is the pork loin with root beer barbecue glaze, sweet corn polenta, onion marmalade, bok choy, and spicy corn nuts. Oakley's offers several

seating choices: a table, booth, or banquette in the dining room, on the covered outside patio, or at the "kitchen table," where you get a clear view of the artists in the kitchen preparing the meals. A nice wine list is available.

PULLMAN'S RESTAURANT $$
123 W. Louisiana St.
(317) 236-7465
www.ichotelsgroup.com

Located in the Historic Union Station at the Crowne Plaza, Pullman's is a comfy family restaurant. The daily breakfast buffet is a great way to start the day, with choices from fresh fruit and yogurt to tomatoes and cheese, along with the usual breakfast entrees. At first glance, diners might wonder where the eggs are. They are cooked fresh to your order. A server will take your order and quickly deliver the prepared eggs, including poached if that is your desire. Atmosphere at the Pullman is reminiscent of a railcar and servers are very attentive. The Crowne Plaza is a treat for an overnight stay. It is best known for 26 authentic Pullman train car guest rooms. Children and train buffs will enjoy that. Also look for the "ghost figures," statues of passengers and other people from the past. You might see a statue of an old-time shoe shiner, a paperboy, or lady in a long dress waiting to catch a train.

R BISTRO $$$$
888 Massachusetts Ave.
(317) 423-0312
www.rbistro.com

Located in Indy's Mass Ave arts district, R bistro offers an eclectic, creative cuisine from chef Regina Mehallick. Exhibiting a fusion of global culinary influences, the menu changes weekly and uses fresh local ingredients and seasonal flavors. Proud of its Hoosier offerings, the restaurant offers dishes such as Indiana fried green tomatoes, an Indiana burger, and White Marble Farm pork tenderloin. When summer produce is at its peak, look for the summer vegetable stew over rice. Desserts are tasty and sometimes feature unexpected combinations. Favorites are the cherry apricot upside-down cake and the plum tarte tatin with honey ice cream.

🔍 Close-up

Milan Miracle Memorialized at Indy Restaurant

The score is tied, 30-30. Seconds remain. Bobby Plump crouches, pumps—his right arm thrusts. The ball arcs through the air amid a roar of screaming and crying fans. He scores.

And tiny Milan High School, one of the state's smallest, makes history as the 1954 Indiana state basketball champions. The small town high school with a senior class of 50 has toppled the powerhouse defending champ, Muncie Central High School.

More than half a century later, that ultimate David versus Goliath story—inspiring the movie *Hoosiers*—is still the heartbeat of Hoosier hysteria. Youngsters tossing hoops in barnyards, backyards, and makeshift basketball courts are reared by it. It has put the ordinary town of Milan near the meandering Ohio River on the map and changed the lives of that amazing team forever. It is also the basis for an Indy dining spot known as Plump's Last Shot Bar and Restaurant.

"If I missed that shot, I wouldn't be talking to you now," Plump says. "It had a very positive influence on every player and anybody associated with that team. It put us in the public eye. There's hardly a day goes by but what I am not reminded of it."

Of the 12 Milan Miracle Men, all but two went on to college, and several became coaches. Most still live in Indiana; none live in Milan, but they return often. After graduating from Butler University, Plump played three years for Phillips 66 of the National Industrial Basketball League. Then he began a nearly forty-year career in the life insurance and financial consulting industry. After retiring, Plump opened his restaurant.

Sports Illustrated named the Milan team one of the top 20 teams of the 20th century. Indiana sports writers chose it as the No. 1 sports story in all of Indiana history. But the heart-stopping last-second win that put a quiet rural town at the top may never come again.

Back then, no attendance classifications separated the largest schools from the smallest in the state tournament. In a state where basketball is king, all competed as equals. In 1997 Indiana ditched its one-classification basketball tournament and divided the schools into four classes.

The 1954 celebration motorcade to escort the young heroes home in glory started with five cars in Indianapolis and reached thousands lined bumper to bumper for at least 13 miles along cornfields to Milan. Many say the community is still celebrating, and folks at Plump's Last Shot still like to talk about it with the star himself.

Serving classic American cuisine, Plump's Last Shot, at 6416 Cornell Ave. in Broad Ripple, also has a full bar serving cocktails and beer. Restaurant decor, of course, revolves around sports, with photos and memorabilia everywhere and plenty of televisions showing all the great games. For more information contact Plump's Last Shot at (317) 257-5867.

RAM RESTAURANT AND BIG HORN BREWERY $$$
40 S. Illinois St.
(317) 955-9900
www.theram.com

The Ram offers a huge menu so be prepared to spend some time deciding unless you already know your favorite. You can build your own pasta or order a fresh-made burger, including turkey burgers and veggie burgers. Add a brewery touch and order the Pacific Rock Shrimp Fajitas with Big Horn Buttface Amber Ale–marinated shrimp, pan sautéed with lime cilantro sauce, onion, red pepper, and Anaheim pepper. The fish and chips entree gives you a choice of Alaska Arctic cod or wild sockeye salmon dipped in Big Horn Hefeweizen beer batter and cooked golden. Enjoy a full-service bar and big-screen TV in the lounge.

S.I. RESTAURANT AND LOUNGE $$$$
725 Massachusetts Ave.
(317) 536-0707
www.scholarsinn.com

Opened in 2002, S.I. (Scholar's Inn) Restaurant and Lounge is located in a century-old, two-story building in the historic Mass Ave arts district. Featuring the latest trends in upscale dining, S.I. is open and airy yet private, filled with comfortable custom booths with high, tapestried backs and flowing white curtains that can be closed. Marble tabletops, custom artwork, warm rich colors, lush carpeting, high-tech gadgets (a coffee table that serves as a TV screen), and white-linen-covered tables add to the upscale ambience.

S.I. also features an 18-seat table where solo diners can choose to sit. Constructed of see-through hard plastic, the 21-foot light-infused table has a light switch that changes colors from neon purple and rosy red to lime green and sunshine yellow for a psychedelic atmosphere. The person who sits on the right side of the table can control the lights. Good thing to remember. Meals start with a loaf of warm bread—made by Scholar's Inn Bakery—and seven-herb butter. Descriptions on the menu showcase the delectable choices, such as rainbow trout and toasted couscous with homemade tomato ginger jam, roasted forest mushrooms, sweet onions, spinach, and Saratoga sauce. Another entree is roasted squash lasagna with ricotta squash stuffing, roasted corn cream sauce, and fresh spinach. The Chocolate Oblivion dessert is a decadent flourless cake. The outside patio is a great gathering place, clustered around a massive 17-foot, two-way fireplace. Recipient of the *Wine Spectator* Award of Excellence, Scholar's Inn also features a signature cocktail list. A champagne brunch is offered Sun from 10 a.m. to 2 p.m.

TIE DYE GRILL $$$
1311 N. Shadeland Ave.
(317) 353-9393
www.thetiedyegrill.com

A funky little place opened by Shayne and Jan Dye, the Tie Dye Grill has a menu you have to take time to read and enjoy. It might bring back some memories with '70s names like the Crimson and Clover Tuna, Lava Lamp Wings, Garfunkel French Onion Soup, Yoko's Shrimp Basket, and Bogart Cheese Fries. The names are cute but the food is good and plentiful. Try the Abby Road, fresh homemade chicken or tuna salad on focaccia bread, or the Magic Mushroom Swiss Burger. A wall of fame features pictures of diners in their tie-dyed shirts. Groovy!

BAKERY/CAFE

AH BARISTA CAFE $
201 S. Capitol Ave.
(317) 638-2233
www.ahbarista.com

Located across the street from the Convention Center, Ah Barista is a handy place for breakfast and lunch. The cafe features free Wi-Fi and has indoor and outdoor dining. Check the daily specials like meat loaf panini and milkshake choices. The mango creamsickle milkshake is a favorite. A build-your-own Barista classic sandwich is a nice way to get exactly what you want. Choose the bread, meat, cheese, topping, and sauce from a wide choice. The cafe also features a nice selection of coffees and teas.

CANAL CAFE AND TERRACE AT INDIANA STATE MUSEUM $$
650 W. Washington St.
(317) 232-1637

Dine inside or outside on the terrace overlooking the canal at Canal Cafe and Terrace. See where the place got its name. Located in the Indiana State Museum, the cafeteria-style restau-

i The pork tenderloin sandwich is considered an unofficial "official" Indiana delicacy. Served at fairs across the state, it consists, simply, of a breaded pork tenderloin slapped between two buns. Basic, yet tasty, it's one of the most popular dishes in the state.

⊙ Close-up

Hoosier Cream Pie a State Favorite

It's official. The sweet treat known as sugar cream pie is now Indiana's state pie. The legislature heartily approved the honor on January 23, 2009. Often known as Hoosier cream pie, the recipe has been traced back to 1816, the year Indiana became a state. The pie was often made in Amish and Shaker communities as a staple after the fall harvest, when all the fruit was gone. Sometimes called Desperation Pie, it was made from basic inexpensive ingredients that most households had. In fact, some recipes don't even call for eggs. The pie was often served as a dessert centerpiece for Thanksgiving and Christmas.

In some circles, the pie was known as finger pie because the filling was sometimes stirred with a finger during the baking process to prevent breaking the bottom crust and whipping the cream. People used to skim the thick yellow cream from the top of chilled fresh milk to make this delectable dessert. Family recipes vary but here is a basic one to try:

OLD-FASHIONED HOOSIER PIE

1 cup sugar

9-inch unbaked pie shell

5 tablespoons flour

$1/8$ teaspoon salt

1 cup whipping cream

1 cup half-and-half

2 egg yolks

1 teaspoon vanilla

Ground nutmeg or cinnamon

Preheat oven to 350 degrees. Mix sugar, flour, and salt completely in piecrust. Add the whipping cream (unwhipped) and blend. In a bowl, blend the half-and-half with the egg yolks and stir into the sugar mixture. Add vanilla and stir gently until creamy. Do not beat. Add a fine sprinkle of nutmeg or cinnamon, depending on preference. Bake until filling is set, about one hour.

---

rant offers family dining in a casual atmosphere. Menu items include burgers, pizza, salads, deli sandwiches, and more.

BARBECUE

DICK'S BODACIOUS BAR-B-Q $$
50 N. Pennsylvania St.
(317) 916-9600
www.dicksbbq.com

Born in East Texas and raised on Texas barbecue, Rich "Dick" Allen always wanted to open his own eatery. After moving to Indiana in 1996, Dick

did just that. Opened in 1999, Dick's Bodacious Bar-B-Q features authentic Texas barbecue slow smoked, not grilled, to enhance the meat's natural flavor while adding a succulent smoky flavor. Listed among the best barbecue in Indianapolis by *National Barbeque News* and the best barbecue in Indianapolis by *Dine* magazine, Dick's has no trouble getting and keeping customers. If you have trouble deciding what to order, try the Texas Feast—three ribs, sliced beef brisket, and smoked sausage, served with two sides and white bread to sop up the sauce. Beer is also available.

ℹ️ Indianapolis grocer Gilbert Van Camp discovered his customers enjoyed an old family recipe for pork and beans in tomato sauce. He opened up a canning company and Van Camp's Pork and Beans became an American staple.

SMOKEHOUSE ON SHELBY $$$
1103 Shelby St.
(317) 685-1959
www.fountainsquareindy.com

Located in historic Fountain Square, this casual eatery features hickory-smoked ribs and meats smoked in-house, along with wings, sandwiches, and burgers. Watch sports on the big screens or play a game on two full-size pool tables. Lunch specials, kids' menu, beer, wine, and cocktails, are available. The restaurant serves lunch and dinner.

WEBER GRILL RESTAURANT $$$
10 N. Illinois St.
(317) 636-7600
www.webergrillrestaurant.com

Created by the company that set the standard for outdoor cooking, Weber Grill Restaurant prepares everything on—you guessed it—Weber charcoal kettles. The menu offers grilling favorites: steak, barbeque, seafood, and hamburger. For something different, try the Black Angus meatloaf, three thick slices glazed with Weber Hickory BBQ Sauce; or the Beer Can Chicken, half a chicken roasted with garlic, beer, and Weber Signature Spice Rub. Weber's serves cocktails and wines. The restaurant is no slouch at desserts either. Try the Big G's Warm Dutch Apple Pie with Maker's Mark bourbon caramel sauce and cinnamon ice cream.

BREAKFAST

LE PEEP
www.lepeepindy.com

301 N. Illinois St.
(317) 237-3447

6335 Intech Commons Dr.
(317) 298-7337

12213 N. Meridian St.
(317) 580-9193

8487 Union Chapel Rd.
(317) 259-8344

8255 Craig St.
(317) 576-0433

2258 W. 86th St.
(317) 334-9690

Since opening in 1988, Le Peep has consistently won awards for "Indy's Best Breakfast." Specializing in the art of breakfast, Le Peep's offers its signature Pampered Eggs, skillet dishes, omelets, French toast, and pancakes. A sweet way to start the day, the French toast is made of Vienna bread dipped in rich custard batter and grilled golden. Madagascar vanilla and a pinch of cinnamon create the old-fashioned taste. Dusted with powdered sugar and served with a side of Mom's Sassy Apples or blueberry compote, the toast is heavenly. A steaming pot of hot coffee at each table is a nice touch. Homemade soups and creative sandwiches are popular lunch offerings.

DELI

PATACHOU ON THE PARK
www.cafepatachou.com

225 W. Washington St.
(317) 632-0765

PETITE CHOU BY PATACHOU
14390 Clay Terrace Blvd., Carmel
(317) 566-0765

823 Westfield Blvd.
(317) 259-0765

CAFÉ PATACHOU
4911 N. Pennsylvania St.
(317) 925-2823

8691 River Crossing Blvd.
(317) 815-0765

4733 126th St., Carmel
(317) 569-0965
Civic Plaza, Indianapolis International Airport

Close-up

Royalty of the Hot Dog World

An Indy original, the King David brand of hot dogs was originally developed by the Hene Meat Company in the early 1940s. Created by brothers Paul and William Hene, who left Europe to escape the Holocaust, the hot dog was all beef and weighed a hunky one-quarter pound. The popular hot dog was sold to local groceries and delis until the early 1990s. Then it was gone. In 2006 Brent Joseph, grandson of co-founder William Hene, along with his wife, Hannah, came up with the idea to bring back the original King David hot dog. With the family blessing to use the original recipe, Brent found a manufacturer who could re-create the traditional hot dog. Then he decided to open a place where hot dog lovers could top those special dogs with choices from pickles and peppers to bacon and white chicken chili, jalapeños, and just about anything their minds could come up with.

Picking a great location at 15 North Pennsylvania St., near Monument Circle and Conseco Fieldhouse, Brent opened King David Dogs in 2006. Diners have been happily munching on such specialties as the Three Cheese Dog with nacho, cheddar, and Swiss; the State Fair Dog served on a stick; the BBQ Dog with barbecue sauce, bacon, cheddar cheese, and chopped onions; and the New York Dog with New York–style onion sauce, spicy brown mustard, and sauerkraut. Or you can build your own dog, choosing from a long list of toppings. No dog is complete until it is plopped in a freshly steamed or grilled poppy-seed bun. For travelers who need a quick fix, King David Dogs now has another handy location at the new Indianapolis International Airport, Concourse B.

Since opening in 1989, Patachou has gathered a devoted following and several spin-off restaurants. The secret is award-winning gourmet breakfasts and healthy lunches. The menu emphasizes "ultra-premium," organic, all-white-meat chicken poached in-house and turkey freshly roasted. No processed or deli meats that have added preservatives, coloring agents, and chemicals are used at Patachou. Fruits and vegetables come from certified organic sources when available, and dressings are prepared from scratch. Patachou uses fresh free-range eggs from Indiana farms for its many omelet choices and egg dishes. Patachou proudly presents a bunch of coffees from beans that are often organic and shade-grown, sourced from sustainable farms engaging in fair trade. A family-owned coffee roaster that has been in the business for over a century, along with a water purification system, makes the coffee a favorite.

SHAPIRO'S DELICATESSEN $$
www.shapiros.com

808 S. Meridian St.
(317) 631-4041

SHAPIRO'S CARMEL
918 Rangeline Rd.
(317) 573-3354

SHAPIRO'S INDIANAPOLIS INTERNATIONAL AIRPORT
Next to Gate B14, near United, American, and US Air

The granddaddy of delis, Shapiro's is listed in *USA Today* as one of the 10 great places to nosh on authentic Jewish deli cuisine. Shapiro's offers quick cafeteria-style service and you can choose from original home-cooked recipes mastered over generations. Louis Shapiro started it back in 1905 with a motto that holds true today: "Cook good. Serve generously. Price modestly. People will come." And they certainly do. Enjoy corned beef and pastrami piled high on rye or egg bun, matzo ball and chicken noodle soups, comfort foods such as Swiss steak, baked chicken, meat loaf, macaroni and cheese, and mile-high pies, cakes, and pastries.

SKY CITY CAFÉ $$
500 W. Washington St.
(317) 636-9378
www.eiteljorg.org
Located in the Eiteljorg Museum of American Indians and Western Art, the Sky City Café offers tasty southwestern and Native American inspired cuisine. Dine inside or choose to enjoy the canal view on the scenic terrace. The contemporary 90-seat café offers direct access from Indy's Central Canal. Favorites include the Tatanka Burger—a buffalo burger with guacamole, pico de gallo, shredded lettuce, and jalapeño jack cheese served on toasted onion bread—and the Tularosa Grilled Chicken—grilled chicken, chihuahua cheese, red onion, and garlic lime mayonnaise served on grilled rustic white bread. Sky City is open for lunch and serves beer and wine. Daily special soups are served with fresh baked corn bread.

STANLEY'S DELI $$
8555 N. Ditch Rd.
(317) 254-3354
www.stanleysdeli.com
An authentic New York deli, Stanley's serves the real thing, along with homemade potato chips. Try the Bronx Bomber, corned beef and pastrami with Swiss cheese and yellow mustard piled high on Old World rye; or the Brooklyn Bridge with pastrami, Swiss cheese, homemade coleslaw, and thousand island dressing on pumpernickel bread. The menu also features fresh bagels, salads, meats, cheeses, and fish available by the pound. Flat-screened TVs and some framed New York art set the decor. Nothing fancy here, just a good neighborhood deli.

GERMAN

RATHSKELLER RESTAURANT $$–$$$
401 E. Michigan St.
(317) 636-0396
www.rathskeller.com
Located in the historic 19th-century Athenaeum Building, the Rathskeller is the granddaddy of them all. Established in 1894, the Rathskeller is the city's oldest restaurant still in operation. It routinely is voted the best German restaurant in town. An extensive menu features classic, gourmet German cuisine and contemporary fare. Some of the favorites are sauerbraten—beef roast marinated five days in the Rathskeller's own marinade, then slow roasted and topped with brown gravy accented with currants and ginger—and rouladen—beef roll-up filled with bacon, onions, spicy mustard, and tart pickle wedge slowly cooked for tenderness and topped with homemade brown gravy.

Of course, a huge beer selection is available, and so is wine. The outdoor Biergarten is a fun place from late Apr through Oct, featuring great live bands from acoustic rock to blues to polka music. *Guten appetit!*

GREEK

GREEK ISLANDS RESTAURANT $$$
906 S. Meridian St.
(317) 636-0700
www.greekislandsrestaurant.com
A true family affair, Greek Islands Restaurant is operated by Elias and Fofo Stergiopoulos, along with their children George, Penny, and Angela, the chef. As you can tell from the names, this is authentic Greek cuisine. Hand-rolled phyllo pies and items such as the *taramosalata*—caviar pate with lemon and olive oil—taste straight from the Old Country. The menu does a great job of giving the Greek name and explaining each dish. The *galactobouriko* is a sweet ending to a meal. The phyllo pastry is filled with homemade custard and smothered in light syrup. Greek Islands also has a nice selection of wine and features a belly dancer for entertainment on Fri and Sat.

INDIAN

INDIA GARDEN $$$
www.indiagardenindy.com

207 N. Delaware St.
(317) 634-6060

830 Broad Ripple Ave.
(317) 253-6060
Owned by Darshan Mehra, known as "Tony," India Garden serves chicken, lamb, seafood, and a large selection of vegetarian dishes, plus beer and wine. The menu features authentic northern India entrees using a special charcoal clay oven, known as a tandoor, to produce unique flavors. Take some time to enjoy the extensive menu and make sure you see the dessert choices, such as *kulfi*—an authentic Indian ice cream made with milk and nuts—and *rasmalai*—homemade cheese balls sweetened in milk and flavored with rose water and nuts.

i The India Garden menu features an interesting quote by Bibiji Inderjit Kaur, a cooking teacher and author: "Perhaps the best way to bring the nations of the world into harmony would be to spread a dinner table that spans the globe. It would be a wonderful sight, all those different foods, cooked to perfection, with a rainbow of colors and a myriad of pleasing, tempting aromas, being shared in joy and gratitude by all the people of the world—and no reserved seating."

ITALIAN

IARIA'S ITALIAN RESTAURANT $$$
317 S. College Ave.
(317) 638-7706
Family owned since 1933, Iaria's serves southern Italy–style food featuring homemade sauce and pizza. Now in the fourth generation of family members, Iaria's still cooks spaghetti sauce with Mama Antonia's recipe. Plenty of pasta dinners are offered, along with traditional pizza pies. Served in a hollow lemon, the lemon sorbet is a nice way to end a meal.

MAGGIANO'S LITTLE ITALY $$$
3550 E. 86th St.
(317) 814-0700
www.maggianos.com
Love pasta? This is your place. Baked ziti, lobster ravioli, beef braciole, and many more pasta dishes can tempt an appetite; or go with seafood, veal, chicken, steak, or pork. There are so many menu choices that it might be hard deciding. Maggiano's features classic Old World–style dishes, specializing in grand portions of southern Italian cuisine. The elegant restaurant features a separate banquet facility, martini bar, and an outdoor terrace. Maggiano's has a nice wine list, including Maggiano's first-ever signature wine from the Robert Mondavi Private Selection. Vinetta is a Bourdeaux-inspired red blend of five varietals, giving a wide range of fruity flavors with notes of vanilla, caramel, and mocha. It goes great with pasta. This is the place to have tiramisu, ladyfinger cookies soaked in espresso and coffee liqueur, layered with mascarpone cheese, dusted with cocoa powder, and served with chocolate.

MILANO INN $$$
231 S. College Ave.
(317) 264-3585
www.milanoinn.com
Serving Indy since 1934, Milano Inn is a comfortable family-owned restaurant with traditional Italian favorites. Of course, there is plenty of homemade spaghetti and meatballs and pizza but the menu is chock-full of many other delicious choices as well as mouth-watering desserts. Sip a specialized martini or order wine while you peruse the menu and enjoy the Old World ambience of the Milano Inn. Attention to detail is a given at the restaurant and diners are made to feel welcome.

RESTAURANT AT THE VILLA INN $$$$
1456 N. Delaware St.
(317) 916-8500
www.thevillainn.com
You don't have to be a guest at this lovely 1906 inn to dine on its cuisine, but it is a luxurious treat to stay here and dine. Casual elegance and fine Italian-American cuisine keep guests returning.

Breakfast items include Grand Marnier French toast and a wide selection of teas. Try the "blooming" tea, premium white tea leaves and natural herbal flowers handcrafted and ready to blossom when immersed in hot water. For dinner, the menu features dishes like the Black Angus filet with port-balsamic reduction, gnocchi, spinach, and whole roasted tomatoes; and handmade Italian meatballs in red wine sauce with fresh Parmesan. Save room for what has been voted Indianapolis's best chocolate dessert. Should you feel so inclined, there is also a lovely spa on the premises featuring full spa services.

ℹ️ Opened in 1934, the Milano Inn has a dazzling mural that decorates all four walls of the main dining room. Telling the story of the Allied liberation of Italy during World War II, the mural was created by Sergeant Donald Peters in 1947 at the behest of the Modaffari family, who owned the inn. Upon mustering out of the military, Sgt. Peters had become a student at the Herron School of Art in Indianapolis. The Modaffaris commissioned him to paint a mural capturing a moment in their homeland that was near and dear to their hearts and legacy. In exchange, Peters received free room and board for the summer in one of the apartments above the restaurant. In vivid colors, images, and detail, Peters saw to it that each scene in the mural has a riveting story to tell.

JAPANESE

MIKADO JAPANESE RESTAURANT $$$$
48 S. Illinois St.
(317) 972-4180
www.mikadoindy.com
Opened in 1997, Mikado is the first Japanese restaurant in downtown Indianapolis. The menu features an array of succulent fusion entrees including steak, scallops, lobster, chicken, and lamb, as well as traditional Japanese favorites such as *udon,* tempura, and bento boxes. Large and varied, the menu offers easy descriptions of the dishes. The sushi and sashimi offerings also are extensive. With private rooms and configurable dining areas, Mikado offers considerable privacy. Mikado also features an extensive wine list, full bar, and premium sake selection.

MEXICAN

EL SOL DE TALA $$
2444 E. Washington St.
(317) 636-1250
Serving authentic Mexican food for over three decades, El Sol De Tala has a rustic Mexican décor, some mariachi music in the background, and a popular guacamole bar. It also features almost 100 varieties of tequila. Servings are generous and all dishes include rice and refried beans.

EL TORITO GRILL $$$
8650 Keystone Crossing
(317) 848-5202
www.etgrill.com
Contemporary and native foods of Mexico are the specialty at El Torito Grill. Flour tortillas are handmade throughout the day so they are fresh as can be. Savor them with fresh salsa or the grill's signature honey butter. A wood-fired mesquite grill imparts a smoky southwestern essence to traditional dishes such as sizzling fajitas, grilled chicken, steak, and fish. Margaritas are the real thing at El Torito—hand-shaken and made with premium Jose Cuervo tequila and Orange Curaçao. El Torito also offers an abundant selection of oak-aged reposado, añejo, and 100 percent blue agave tequilas made for sipping with citrus or alone in a snifter. Prepared table-side, the Mexican shrimp cocktail is a joy to see and to taste, with its jumbo shrimp, fresh tomatoes, cucumbers, onions, and Hass avocado with tomato-lime sauce. Served with crisp tostaditas.

MEDITERRANEAN

BOSPHORUS ISTANBUL CAFÉ $$
935 S. East St.
(317) 974-1770
www.bosphoruscafe.com

Close-up

How Bazbeaux Got Its Name

One of Indy's favorite pizza places often gets asked, why the name Bazbeaux? The story goes that Bazbeaux was the name of a court jester in the French court of King Louis XI. When the king died and his 13-year-old son took over, Bazbeaux decided it was time to hit the road. Hard telling what a spoiled child might do, the jester reasoned. Bazbeaux fled to Florence and got a position in the court of Lorenzo de Medici. Knowing that Bazbeaux must have been clever to survive the reign of the tyrannical Louis XI, Lorenzo offered the jester an unusual challenge: Create new dishes to amuse him. Bazbeaux did just that and excelled. When Lorenzo died, Bazbeaux traveled to the New World with Amerigo Vespucci. That's where the story ends. No one knows what happened to the whimsical, creative man.

Like an oasis hidden away in Indianapolis, Bosphorus Istanbul Café is located in the historic Fletcher Place neighborhood near Eli Lilly's headquarters. The restaurant's hand-painted designs on the floor and ceiling create a cozy atmosphere. Indy's first and only Turkish restaurant offers a variety of authentic Turkish appetizers, soups, entrees, and desserts. A favorite to start the meal is the appetizer combo of hummus, stuffed grape leaves, tabouli, baba ghanoush, börek, and eggplant salsa.

i The Bosphorus Istanbul Café, which specializes in Turkish cuisine, is named for the 20-mile-long Bosphorus strait that joins the Sea of Marmara and the Black Sea and separates the continents of Europe and Asia.

SAFFRON CAFÉ $$$
621 Ft. Wayne Ave.
(317) 917-0131
www.saffroncafe-indy.com

Indy's only Moroccan restaurant, Saffron Café features the culinary talents of owner Anas Sentissi and his family's recipes. To create a Moroccan experience, Sentissi brought the chandeliers, table settings, mirrors, and other decor straight from Morocco. On the menu are Moroccan dishes, including traditional *tajines* (Moroccan stews), *kabbabs*, gyros, pasta, paella (seafood, vegetables, chicken, and saffron rice), desserts, and more. Wine is imported from Morocco and fresh seafood is flown in daily. Everything on the menu is homemade from scratch. Enjoy outdoor dining during warmer months and belly-dancing entertainment every Thursday.

PIZZA

BAZBEAUX $$
www.bazbeaux.com

811 E. Westfield Blvd., Broad Ripple
(317) 255-5711

334 Massachusetts Ave.
(317) 636-7662

111 West Main St., Carmel
(317) 848-4488

Opened in Broad Ripple on May 12, 1986, the original Bazbeaux started off in a decrepit old house that was once the home of the town grave digger. Quickly becoming famous for fresh, delectable pizza, the restaurant earned its first honor its first year for "Best Pizza in Indianapolis." Bazbeaux has expanded into a new home—several of them, in fact. With homemade dough and sauces, plus a choice of 52 toppings, the pizza is still a great choice, but the restaurant also offers salads and sandwiches, along with a nice selection of beer and wine.

SEAFOOD

CANAL POINT GRILL $$$
832 E. Westfield Blvd.
(317) 253-5844
www.canalpointgrill.ws

First opened as the Broad Ripple Seafood Shack, Canal Point Grill now has a larger menu and a full liquor license. Daily fresh fish selections are prepared either grilled, blackened, lemon buttered, or pan battered. Or order pasta your way—penne pasta with red or white sauce and either chicken, fish, shrimp, or vegetables, or any two of those options. The menu has a boatload of sandwiches and appetizers. Sit at the neat outside tiki bar area, munch to your heart's content, and make believe you're on an sea-swept beach. Live music is offered on Fri, Sat, and Sun nights.

**KONA JACK'S FISH MARKET AND
SUSHI BAR** $$$
9419 N. Meridian St.
(317) 843-1609
www.konajacksindy.com

Saltwater aquariums with brilliantly colored fish help set the scene for this Hawaiian-styled restaurant. Named Indy's best seafood restaurant by local diners, Kona Jack's is said to offer the widest array of fresh- and saltwater fish, shellfish, clams, oysters, and sushi in the Midwest. The menu certainly seems that way. Enjoy drinks on the outside patio and maybe take in a sunset special—smaller portions of entrees for a smaller price, available Mon through Fri before 6 p.m.

OCEANAIRE SEAFOOD ROOM $$$$
30 S. Meridian St.
(317) 955-2277
www.theoceanaire.com

The sleek decor takes its inspiration from 1930s ocean liners. Fresh seafood is flown in daily from around the world and prepared in a multitude of ways. Servings are huge and side dishes are served for the table to share. Start off with a champagne cocktail in the open bar, enjoy the delicious oyster bar, or slide into a horseshoe booth to leisurely dine on a seafood dinner. If you're in the mood for something else, there's also steak, pork chops, and chicken. Baked Alaska is a nice follow-up to a grand meal.

RICK'S CAFÉ BOATYARD $$$$
4050 Dandy Trail
(317) 290-9300
www.rickscafeboatyard.com

Located on the water at Eagle Creek Reservoir, Rick's specializes in fresh seafood, live jazz, and a great scenic view. Situated across from the Eagle Creek Airport, Rick's is known to host diners who fly in, drive in, and boat in. A massive outside deck and bar offers a great fireplace during the winter. Start off with blue point oysters, chilled on the half shell or prepared as Oysters Rockefeller with Pernod liqueur, creamed spinach, and Parmesan cheese or as an oyster shooter—a chilled rocks glass with an oyster, cocktail sauce, and splash of vodka. An extensive menu offers a treasure chest of seafood, such as steamed Alaskan red king crab legs or a pick-your-own Maine lobster, as well as choice steak. When summer ends, Rick's offers eagerly awaited winter specialties, such as Veal Chateaubriand, a center cut of veal tenderloin encrusted with Dijon fresh herbs and roasted in a wood-burning oven. No matter the season, it's a treat to dine at Rick's and watch Mother Nature at work along the lake.

STEAK

EDDIE MERLOT'S $$$$$
3645 E. 96th St.
(317) 846-8303
www.eddiemerlot.com

So is there a real Eddie Merlot? Well, yes and no. The story goes that Bill Humphries, founder of Eddie Merlot's, is a well-known wine connoisseur. As a board member, it was Bill's responsibility to choose the wine for a worldwide corporation. At one dinner, a new member named Ed asked Bill to surprise him with a great wine. Of course, Ed was mightily impressed when he tasted the wine and asked what wine had been chosen. When Bill revealed it was a merlot, Ed said, "Always order the merlot." Replied Bill, "And from now on, you're Eddie Merlot." So it came to be. Great steak and wine are what have built Eddie Merlot's reputation but the place also serves fine seafood, as well as chicken and chops. For a special finale, order the Bananas Foster. Prepared table-side in flaming glory, the recipe includes Myers's Jamaican dark rum, banana liqueur, brown sugar, cinnamon, bananas, and vanilla bean ice cream.

MO'S A PLACE FOR STEAKS $$$$
47 S. Pennsylvania St.
(317) 624-0720
www.mosaplaceforsteaks.com

Since opening in 2003, Mo's has developed a devoted following. Known for its table-side meat-tray presentation, where servers show you what you can order before it's prepared, Mo's has steak, steak, and more steak. Its signature steak is a whopping 24-ounce bone-in rib eye. Kobe beef also is available in limited supplies. But the menu has more than steak. It offers, pork, veal, chicken, tuna, salmon, lobster, and much more. An extensive wine list and cocktails are available.

RUTH'S CHRIS STEAK HOUSE $$$$$
www.ruthschris.com

9445 Threel Rd.
(317) 844-1155

45 S. Illinois Street
(317) 633-1313

Sure, it's a chain steak house. But it's such a high-quality one that diners often look for Ruth's Chris Steak House wherever they travel. Started by a single woman, Ruth Fertel, almost 50 years ago, Ruth's Chris Steak House can be relied on for a prime steak cooked just the way you like. If you've ever wondered about that awkward name, it came about because Ruth Ertel bought the Chris Steak House in New Orleans in 1965. Eleven years later, a fire destroyed the thriving restaurant. Building a few blocks away, Ruth was faced with a dilemma. Under a contractual agreement with the previous owner, she couldn't name the new restaurant the Chris Steak House. Not wanting to lose the years of great name recognition that she had built up, Ruth just added her own name to it—Ruth's Chris Steak

House. Now they seem to be everywhere, which says something about the place. If it ain't good, it ain't gonna last. Ruth died at age 75 in 2002, but her restaurants are still thriving.

SHULA'S STEAK HOUSE $$$$$
50 S. Capitol Ave.
(317) 231-3900
www.donshula.com

Dubbed "One of America's Best Steak Houses," Shula's serves certified Angus beef, fresh Florida seafood, lamb, and poultry. Also, enjoy the No Name Lounge for a martini and cigar. The restaurant is themed after the 1972 Miami Dolphins' "Perfect Season"—the only team in National Football League history to finish a season undefeated. The menus are hand painted on an official NFL game football. Don Shula, of course, is the former professional football coach for the NFL, best known as coach of the Miami Dolphins, the team he led to two Super Bowl victories and to the NFL's first and only perfect season. Shula currently holds the NFL record for most career wins with 347. At Shula's Steak House, one of the featured entrees is a 48-ounce porterhouse. Those who finish it join Shula's 48-Ounce Club, which currently has more than 26,000 members. Wonder how many of those are football players?

i As of 2006, a smoking ban within Indianapolis prohibits smoking in any restaurant or bar that admits people under 18. Private clubs and cigar bars are not affected by the ban.

ST. ELMO STEAK HOUSE $$$$$
127 S. Illinois St.
(317) 635-0636
www.stelmos.com

An Indianapolis tradition since 1902, St. Elmo's was named after the patron saint of sailors. The turn-of-the-20th-century Chicago saloon decor has changed little. Located in the heart of downtown, St. Elmo's is famed for its shrimp cocktail, steak, impeccable service, and wine list with the largest cellar in Indiana. Seafood, chicken, and chops also are featured. The menu isn't that big

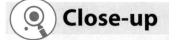

Close-up

The Skinny on Jared

Jared Fogle had no idea the unplanned course his life would take. Born August 23, 1977, in Indianapolis, Jared's father was a doctor and his mother a teacher. He has a brother two years younger and a sister seven years younger. No one in his family had weight problems, Jared recalls. But a gift he received in the third grade changed his future dramatically. The much-prized birthday present was a Nintendo game. "I can trace back my weight gain to that," he says. "That's when it started."

Jared was soon glued to video games. Riding his bike and playing sports no longer interested him. He also developed a love for junk food. "I'd have one hand on the Nintendo and one in a bag of chips," he recalls.

By the time he was in the sixth grade, Jared was bigger than the other children. His parents worried and tried to restrict his video games and fast-food addiction. "But I would find ways to get around it," Jared says.

Telling his parents he was going for a bike ride, Jared would head for the nearest fast-food joint and buy the biggest, fattest meal possible with his allowance. He graduated from North Central High School in Indianapolis in 1995. When he went off to Indiana University in Bloomington, it got even worse. In his dorm room, Jared loaded up on food. By the time he was 20, he was eating enough for five people—sometimes 10,000 calories a day. It wasn't unusual for him to eat a whole large pizza by himself, with extra meat, extra cheese—as a bedtime snack.

Weight was controlling his life. He hurt all over and walking was torture. Taking 20 steps meant he would have to stop and catch his breath. He required two parking spots for his car because unless he could open the driver's door completely he couldn't get out of the vehicle. He couldn't ride in the back seat of an automobile and couldn't fit in an airplane seat. His shirt size zoomed to an XXXXXXL. He developed sleep apnea and would stop breathing often during his sleep because of his enormous weight.

Jared really didn't know what he weighed and was afraid to find out. When he finally stepped on the doctor's scales, he had ballooned to 425 pounds. Terrified, he headed straight to the nearest restaurant. One day in March 1998, Jared was doing what he often did—standing in line to order some food. He didn't have far to walk. Jared's college apartment shared a wall

but most patrons know what they want and find it at St. Elmo's.

SULLIVAN'S STEAKHOUSE $$$$$
3316 E. 86th St.
(317) 580-1280
www.sullivansteakhouse.com

Given the Wine Spectators Award of Excellence in 2009, Sullivan's Steakhouse in Indy features a 1940s-style steak house atmosphere with great beef, seafood, and signature martinis. Try the Knockout martini made with Smirnoff Orange Vodka infused with fresh Hawaiian gold pine-

apple and an orange twist. An extensive menu includes specialties like Kansas City strip and ahi tuna. An upscale bar features live entertainment seven nights a week. For a grand finale, try the classical soufflé with raspberry, chocolate, lemon, and Grand Marnier served with sauce anglaise.

TASTE OF TANGO $$$$
36 E. Washington St.
(317) 636-1122
www.thetasteoftango.com

The Taste of Tango brings some of the great-ness of Argentina to Indianapolis. In Argentina, with a Subway restaurant. A nutritional information brochure touting Subway's "7 sandwiches with 6 grams or less" caught his eye.

Thinking he'd give it a try, Jared ordered a 6-inch turkey with no oil, mayo, condiments, or cheese and a bag of Baked Lay's potato chips. For dinner, he came back for a 12-inch veggie with no condiments or cheese. He ate the same sandwiches every day with diet soft drinks. And the pounds began to melt off. At the end of three months, Jared had lost 94 pounds. And he still enjoyed the taste of the food. Elated, he continued his Subway sandwich diet. Consuming only 1,000 calories a day, he loaded his sandwiches with tons of lettuce, green peppers, banana peppers, jalapeño peppers, and pickles, topped with a bit of spicy mustard.

Once he had gotten down to about 300 pounds, Jared began adding exercise to his diet. Formerly unable to walk across his room without getting winded, he replaced riding the bus with walking to campus. At 250 pounds, he walked everywhere he could. After sticking to his self-prescribed diet for almost a year, Jared had lost a whopping 245 pounds. His size 60 waist had shrunk to a 34. A friend who was an editor at the university newspaper wrote about Jared's feat. Associated Press picked up on it, followed by a health magazine.

Subway officials heard of the tremendous story and came calling. Jared shot a test commercial in the fall of 1999. Slated only for the Midwest, the commercial was a great success in Chicago and led to a national spot in 2000. When Subway sales took off and rose by 19 percent that first year, officials knew they had a surefire winner.

That was a decade ago. Today, Jared has branched out to include other foods in moderation in his normal 2,400 calories a day and maintains a healthy 190 pounds on his 6-foot-2-inch frame. In 2000 he gradated from IU with a degree in management and international business. Jared makes a comfortable living filming Subway commercials, as well as traveling with his 60-inch-waist jeans and telling his story. "Those pants are more famous than I am," he laughs, adding, "I'm still an Indiana kid. I never expected all this to happen. I was just trying to get the weight off."

But the message he is trying to spread is a serious one, Jared adds. "I want to help others so they do not live with the pain and suffering of obesity like I did. It's important to help young people especially develop healthy eating and exercise habits."

steaks are an art form, so expect to savor the steak choices offered here. The menu also offers tempting seafood dishes. Argentine cuisine is heavily influenced by Italian, Spanish, and French gastronomy, and it's fun to see those influences at work here. Taste of Tango features 100 percent natural Angus beef, homemade pastas, and a nice selection of Argentine beer and wine.

Z'S OYSTER BAR AND STEAKHOUSE
6220 Castleway West Dr.
(317) 644-8000
www.zoysterbar.com

"Simply Prepared and Elegantly Served" is the motto of this award-winning dining establishment. Opened in 2007 in Indy, Z's Oyster Bar and Steakhouse doesn't use sauces or seasoning to disguise its food. The true taste of the food is what comes through, which means it definitely is fresh. Talking with the day boat fishermen, the restaurant's chef learns what's been caught and has it shipped that day. A mouth-watering menu includes snails stuffed in silver-dollar mushrooms and served with roasted garlic-herb butter. There's also Maine's Ducktrap River smoked salmon with fresh lemon, olive oil,

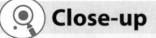 # Close-up

Hoosier Cabinet a Kitchen Helper

Around the turn of the 19th century, Indiana housewives had very little storage space in their kitchens—no cabinets, just some open shelves, storage bins, and a worktable. In the later part of the 1800s, "baker's cabinets" evolved. A one-unit workstation, the cabinets had closed shelves above a bit of work space and flour and sugar bins below. First manufactured in 1898 by Hoosier Manufacturing Co. of New Castle, Indiana, the Hoosier cabinet was a refinement of the baker's cabinets. With its efficient features and lovely looks, the cabinet swept the country and spawned a number of other makers, many in Indiana.

While each had its individual variation, the cabinets became forever linked in the public's mind as Hoosier cabinets. Generally, Hoosier cabinets were 4 feet wide, 6 feet high and 2 feet deep. Open the doors to a Hoosier cabinet and see a cook's paradise. Spice and condiment racks, metal racks for pots and pans, even a built-in flour sifter were there.

Hoosier cabinets consisted of a deep base part containing drawers and one large cabinet. On top of the base was a more shallow top part containing shelves, bins, and cabinets. The two parts were joined by metal channels, which held a slide porcelain counter. Pulling out the counter, the lady of the house could roll her morning biscuits, make a piecrust, and do much of her food fixing. My grandmother would sketch on hers with a pencil to entertain us youngsters—works of art with horses, dogs, old-time ladies, and flowers, which she would quickly wipe off with the corner of her apron as if embarrassed at such prideful frivolity.

When the cooking was done, the counter could be washed off and pushed back in its space. The doors would be closed and all the organized clutter was out of sight. Around the 1930s, however, wall cabinets and countertops became common and the Hoosier cabinet fell out of favor. Most manufacturers went out of business shortly thereafter.

The original Hoosier cabinets are now sought after as antiques. If you are lucky enough to have one, cherish it.

capers, shallots, and lemon zest. And that's just for starters. Entrees include steaks, duck, veal, pork, lamb, and more. For a side dish, try Z's signature Cheese Browns, hash browns topped with cheddar cheese. The wine cellar holds more than 450 different varieties of wine. Start the evening with a cocktail or glass of wine on the 6,000-sqaure-foot patio and watch the sunset.

TAPAS

BARCELONA TAPAS　　　　　　　$$$
01 N. Delaware St.
(317) 638-8272
www.barcelonatapas.com
Serrano hams and dried *bacalaos* hang in BARcelona Tapas, much as they would in a Spanish tapas bar. The authentic traditional atmosphere lets you know this is the real thing. The word "tapa" literally means "lid," and the origin of the tapas custom most probably lies in the placing of a small plate or lid over a glass of wine when served.

It is also said that a centuries-old decree insisted that all bars and roadhouses serve food as an accompaniment to wine, in an attempt to ensure at least a modicum of sobriety among the nation's coach drivers. It's fun to read a large tapas menu and decide what to order. Favorites are the Spanish meatballs in tomato sauce with Manchego cheese and the grilled beef tenderloin with blue cheese, spinach, and a Rioja reduction sauce. A full cocktail menu and Spanish wine list are available. When it comes time for dessert, you might not want to share. The *tres leches*, or Spanish three-milk cake topped with cream and caramel, is delightful.

ZING   **$$$**
543 Indiana Ave.
(317) 636-7775
www.zingrestaurant.com

A charming eclectic restaurant, ZING offers a small-plate dining experience. Rather than individual starters and main courses, ZING serves dishes that are designed for sharing among friends. The food is brought to your table steadily and continuously throughout the meal. Try the *apocollo*—air-dried, seasoned pork shoulder ham—or the pan-seared jumbo sea scallops with sweet-pea nage, blackberry habanera butter, and smoked paprika, or the pineapple tamale with sautéed shrimp and spicy chipotle spinach Alfredo. In fact, you can enjoy all these and more since you are sharing. At ZING you will find daily drink specials and a wide selection of martinis, wines, lagers, and ales. Enjoy Indy's skyline in ZING's relaxed and comfortable atmosphere inside or out on the balcony. ZING offers easy access to hotels, the canal, White River State Park, museums, Circle Centre mall, IU Medical Complex, IUPUI, and various entertainment venues and spectator sports.

NIGHTLIFE

When the sun goes down, Indianapolis lights up with a wealth of nightlife options. In fact, there are probably more after-dark diversions and destinations than you ever imagined. Just take a glance at this chapter, keeping in mind that this is only a small sampling of what Indy has to offer. I'd probably still be typing and we'd need another book if I tried to include every nightlife venue.

You can dance the night away, catch a game with the gang at the neighborhood sports bar, watch a movie, grab a bite to eat with friends in a cozy pub, laugh at a comedy club, or savor a drink while people-watching in some bustling tavern. If you don't find what you're looking for here or if you have discovered some great spot that I haven't spotlighted, let me know. I'll try to feature it in the next update.

Three things to remember:

1. If you're going to drink, do it in moderation.
2. The drinking age is 21.
3. A designated driver is a good thing—if you don't have one, don't drink.

The Indianapolis night scene is ever-changing, with new venues coming and going regularly, so give a place a call if you really have your heart set on going there. Otherwise, there are so many nightspots in party areas that you can easily change gears to slip into another nearby place that may turn out to be a treasure. Unless otherwise noted, the following establishments do not require a cover charge. This chapter is divided into areas of Indianapolis. But no matter what part of the city you are in, you're never far from a sports bar. Indianapolis is one sports-crazed town—with good reason—and you can always find a place to watch a game or talk sports.

DOWNTOWN

CHATTERBOX JAZZ CLUB
435 Massachusetts Ave.
(317) 636-0584
www.chatterboxjazz.com

For almost three decades, the Chatterbox has been offering live jazz from some of the area's best musicians. A tiny hole-in-the-wall dive in the Mass Ave arts district, the Chatterbox can get quite loud, crowded, and smoky, but that's how many folks like their jazz. Bring money for the tip hat when it's passed around and $5 for the cover charge when a live group is playing. If you get there early, you might get a better seat. If you get there late, you might catch sight and sounds from musicians who like to drop by and sit in after their evening gigs are done.

ℹ️ Take time to look at the historic touches in the Chatterbox Jazz Club on Mass Ave. The dark interior is covered with posters and signatures scrawled everywhere. An unintelligible scrawl on the side of the fridge on the way to the bathrooms is said to bear the name of Mick Jagger, who jammed in the place when the Rolling Stones were in town. Someone said Keith Richards also left his signature, but it's hard to tell. You won't doubt that the jazz is the real thing.

CLADDAGH IRISH PUB
234 S. Meridian St.
(317) 822-6274
www.claddaghirishpubs.com

Located in the heart of downtown Indy, the Claddagh Irish Pub is a handy spot for food, drink, and frivolity. Patterned after the Irish pubs—coming from the phrase *public house*—Claddagh has a long list of traditional Irish fare, including the time-honored classic of corned beef and cabbage. Fish and chips is one of the favorites, as is the Irish Monte Cristo—sourdough bread dipped in egg batter and fried in a griddle, then filled with cheese, rasher bacon, and turkey and sprinkled with powdered sugar. The homemade shepherd's pie and Guinness beef stew are surefire warmer-uppers on a chilly day. Claddagh offers plenty of Jameson Irish Whiskey and Guinness in 20-ounce pints. Live music is often featured, but call ahead to be sure someone is playing if that is one of your main reasons for stopping by.

i There's a story behind the vibrant painted door of the Claddagh Irish Pub. When Queen Victoria's husband died, a royal decree was sent through the United Kingdom, which included Ireland at the time. The decree stipulated that all the doors in the city must be painted black to mourn the late Prince Albert. Being a rebellious lot, the Irish ignored the order and painted their doors every color but black. To this day, the doors of Ireland remain a colorful reminder of their disobedience.

CRACKERS COMEDY CLUB
247 S. Meridian St.
(317) 631-3536
www.crackerscomedy.com
Located 1 block south of Circle Centre, Crackers has been the place for comedy in Indy since 1980. Offering hilarious stand-up comedy, Crackers boasts quite an alumni list of comedians who have graced the stage—Tim Allen, Drew Carey, Ellen DeGeneres, Jeff Foxworthy, Brad Garrett, Rosie O'Donnell, Jay Leno, Larry the Cable Guy, Dennis Miller, Chris Rock, and Ray Romano.

Crackers, which is wheelchair accessible, accepts reservations even after 4 p.m. Reservations are good for up to 10 minutes before showtime. Crackers does not mail tickets; they are held for you at the club. Specials include

Ladies Night on Wednesday when admission for women is free (reservations required). Thursdays are College ID Night, with $5 admission for college students (reservations required).

Crackers offers a full bar and good appetizer menu. For frozen drinks, consider a Dirty Banana—banana, ice cream, rum, Frangelico, and dark crème de cacao; or a Frozen Alligator—a piña colada with ice cream and Midori Melon Liqueur. For munchies, order Bobeck's BBQ Pork—a sub-size bun filled with tender, tangy shredded pork—or the Louis CK Chicken Dilla—a large tortilla with mozzarella cheese and southwest chicken strips, served with salsa, sour cream, and jalapeños. There is a two-item minimum per person inside the showroom. Open Tues through Sat. Crackers also has another club in Broad Ripple at 6281 N. College Ave.

THE ELBOW ROOM
605 N. Pennsylvania St.
(317) 635-3354
www.elbowroompub.com
An old-time bar, the Elbow Room could probably tell some whopping stories if it could talk. Opened shortly after the repeal of prohibition in 1933, the Elbow Room is located in one of the few historic flatiron buildings remaining in Indy. The building was constructed in 1893 and is situated in the historic St. Joseph's neighborhood. A favorite with the after-work crowd and weekend drinkers, The Elbow Room serves a good one-half pound Elbow Room Burger, complete with Cajun spices, sautéed onions, and hot-pepper cheese on Texas toast. Onion rings are a cut above average and full dinners are also among the choices on a larger-than-usual bar menu. Play pool in the upstairs bar or watch sporting events on the televisions.

FORTY FIVE DEGREES
757 Massachusetts Ave.
(317) 635-4545
www.45indy.com
A restaurant and sushi bar by day, Forty Five sports a different vibe at night. The place features plasma screens with films playing as well as some oldie-but-goodie movies. Of course, most

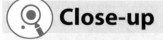 # Close-up

The Slippery Noodle

The oldest continually operating tavern in Indiana, the Slippery Noodle was established in 1850 and is still going strong. Notorious for its booze and blues, the Slippery Noodle has hosted such noted musicians as Clarence "Gatemouth" Brown, Buddy Miles, Jay Giles, Rick Derringer, Albert Collins, John Mayall, Rare Earth, Edgar Winter, James Cotton, and Sugar Blue, to name a few. A long list of celebrities also have found their way into the Slippery Noodle, including Harrison Ford, Jerry Stiller, Neil Diamond, Robert DeNiro, Liza Minelli, Harry Connick Jr., Ernest Borgnine, and many more.

Listed in the National Register of Historic Places, the Slippery Noodle was originally built as the Tremont House, a luxurious roadhouse for railway passengers. Later, it became a brothel and several taverns, and it was linked to the Underground Railroad. Notorious Hoosier criminal John Dillinger reportedly hung around the tavern and used a back inside wall for target practice. You can still see bullets embedded in the brick wall. Legend says that the Slippery Noodle is haunted, perhaps by the ghost of a bordello customer killed in a brawl over a woman, or maybe a woman who used to work the premises. A spectral woman is said to have been seen on a balcony, and numerous reports claim strange noises, whispered voices in the basement, the touch of unseen fingers, and cold spots where there should be none.

Loaded with atmosphere, the Slippery Noodle now features local, regional, and national blues, along with a full-service menu and full bar. The ceiling in the front barroom is made from pressed tin and was installed around 1890. The tiger-oak bar and back bar are well over a century old and believed to be original. The trough at the edge of the bar was used as a cash register in the old days. The "honor" system worked, or else the Colt 45 did. Operating under its current name since 1963, the Noodle is the oldest commercial building left standing in Indianapolis, and the TREMONT HOUSE sign painted on the north side of the building dates back to its birth in the 1850s. The slogan for the Slippery Noodle pretty well describes it—"Dis is it!"

---

of those television channels are turned to sporting events when games are on. DJs spin tunes on Thurs, Fri, and Sat nights. Named for the odd angle at which Massachusetts Avenue meets North College Avenue, Forty Five Degrees has angled walls, odd seating areas and tubular light pendants. Forty Five is nonsmoking. Every Friday is rumba night, with free dance lessons at 10 p.m.

HOWL AT THE MOON
20 E. Georgia St.
(317) 955-0300
www.howatthemoon.com

Two baby grand pianos are the stars of the show, but audience members usually end up being the scene stealers. Piano players take the stage two at a time, but they aren't really dueling. They more or less play along with each other and off each other. At the end of an hour, two more players come out

and the four do a four-way before the new players take over. At the changeover, other instruments are often added—guitars, drums, and sax. Howl servers get in on the act every hour, too, for the raucous Showtime, when servers lead the diverse audience in loud tunes. A popular spot for bachelorette parties and other celebrations, Howl attracts people of all ages. Be prepared to show two forms of ID and arrive early unless you want to wait outside, where it can become quite cold during Indiana winters. The cover charge runs about $10 on the weekend, with no cover on Tues, $3 on Wed, and $5 on Thurs. Thursdays are free with a college ID, so you know a bunch of students turn out for this one. Buckets of booze are a big hit, with huge slurps of hurricanes, mega-margaritas, and the Howlin' Punch, consisting of vodka, Cruzan Pineapple Rum, and citrus juice. A complimentary buffet is offered on Fri from 5 to 7 p.m.

IKE AND JONESY'S
17 W. Jackson Place
(317) 632-4553
www.ikeandjonesys.com
Created by a former waitress and a one-time bartender, Ike and Jonesy's sports the motto "The fun damn place downtown." Opened in 1984, Ike and Jonesy's is named, appropriately enough, after its two creators. The story goes that the two met in college at DePauw University. When the bar where they worked closed for the night, partiers weren't ready to call it quits, so they would head to Ike and Jonesy's secret apartment for more late-night merriment. When Ike and Jonesy graduated, they married and decided to start their own bar—just like they remembered from their college days in that after-hours hideaway. Patronized by drinkers of all ages, the place features a live band on Tues and Wed and a DJ on Fri and Sat spinning dance tunes from the '60s through today. Cover charge on Fri and Sat is $5. Ike and Jonesy's is also open during Colts Sunday home games. The menu features a larger-than-usual choice of bar food plus steak and chicken dinners and a bunch of beer.

LEVEL ONE AT THE HYATT REGENCY
One S. Capitol Ave.
(317) 632-1234
www.indianapolis.hyatt.com
A perfect place to mix business with pleasure, Level One is has a great location in the downtown Hyatt Regency. Slide into a comfy seat in front of a huge video wall with more than a dozen plasma televisions and savor a signature martini. Classic cocktails and a tasty bar menu with specialties such as seared ahi tuna and mini-meatball subs make this a popular place. Stop by Level One for happy hour Thurs from 5:30 to 8:30 p.m. Listen to live music and enjoy discounted drinks and appetizers. Take time to stroll through the light-filled atrium lobby of the hotel with its soaring 21 stories, cascading greenery, and waterfall.

NICKY BLAINE'S
20 N. Meridian St.
(317) 638-5588
www.nickyblaines.com

A blast from the past, Nicky Blaine's would make Frank Sinatra and the rest of the Rat Pack feel right at home. The atmosphere is dark with wood-paneled walls, luxurious carpeting, wingback chairs, a long, wide bar and comfy plush sofas. It's also smoky and sometimes loud. After all, this is a cigar bar. If you don't like cigars or the smell of such, you won't like it here. Nicky's carries a wide, eclectic selection of cigars and cigarettes. Two built-in wall humidors and a large walk-in humidor are filled with smokes from the Dominican Republic to Nicaragua, the Bahamas, and India.

Specializing in martinis, Nicky's full bar offers a world-class choice of wine, port, grappa, single malt scotches, and vodkas. Sip on a Dean Martini, a classic with Bombay Sapphire, dry vermouth, and a single olive; the Cagney, a savory libation with Effen Vodka, dry vermouth, and a squeeze of lemon served up with a rosemary sprig and gorgonzola olives; or the Citizen Kane, Hendrick's cucumber-infused gin garnished with a caper berry and fresh rosemary.

Nicky's menu has surprisingly good appetizers. The kitchen is open every night until 2 a.m., so this is a good place to get a late-night snack downtown or to savor an after dinner port or coffee with a sweet dessert or plate of cheese. Favorite appetizers are the Seafood Dip, herbed crabmeat and shrimp mixed with fresh garlic, olive oil, and Romano cheese, then baked in a massive sourdough bread bowl, served with garlic butter and crackers; and the Vesuvius Sub—Genoa salami, ham, and provolone cheese, served hot on a toasted baguette with lettuce, red onion, tomato, banana peppers, and pickle spear. The weekend cover charge is $5; no cover during the week.

NO NAME LOUNGE AT THE WESTIN INDIANAPOLIS
50 S. Capitol Ave.
(317) 262-8100
Relaxed, comfortable, and quiet, the No Name Lounge is not pretentious or a trendy hangout for the hip-hop crowd. It's a great upscale setting for unwinding with a martini or glass of wine. It also

offers one of the best menus in town because it is located right next to Shula's Steak House at the Westin and shares the Shula menu. Dubbed "one of America's best steak houses," Shula's is named after Don Shula, former pro football coach for the NFL, best known for guiding the Miami Dolphins to the NFL's first and only perfect season. Shula's serves certified Angus beef, fresh Florida seafood, lamb, and poultry. As might be expected, bar service at No Name Lounge is very good.

i Many Indy nightspots have a dress code that they enforce. If you have any doubts about what to wear, give an establishment a call to be sure you can enter. Most of the dress codes are along these lines—no athletic wear, no sleeveless shirts, no work boots, no baggy clothing, no bandanas, skull caps, or stocking caps, no chains hanging out, no recognized gang attire, and no flip-flops.

OLIVES MARTINI AND CIGAR BAR
Omni Severin Hotel
40 W. Jackson Place
(317) 396-3626
Located in the elegant Omni Severin Hotel, Olives is a popular place for a before- or after-dinner drink. It's also the only area in the Omni where people can smoke, so the air can get a bit hazy. If you don't like cigar or cigarette smoke, go somewhere else. True to its name, Olives makes some top-notch martinis, including the signature Key Lime Pie Martini.

Many of the patrons are business and leisure travelers staying at the Omni. When the Colts or the Pacers are in town, however, the atmosphere changes considerably. Since Olives is situated between Lucas Oil Stadium and Conseco Fieldhouse, it's a handy place to grab a drink before heading to a game or to enjoy a cold one while watching the action on the bar's big-screen televisions. Oversized leather chairs and comfy couches help set the upscale atmosphere. Almost 40 premium cigars are showcased in the fully stocked humidor.

ROCK BOTTOM BREWERY
10 W. Washington St.
(317) 681-8180
www.rockbottom.com
A sprawling two-story entertainment center built around a working brewery, Rock Bottom has plenty of room for everyone. The first floor is home to the main bar and restaurant. Large plasma-screen televisions make sure no one misses the action in this sports-crazy city. The second level of Rock Bottom is in the basement with 3,500 feet of action, including five pool tables, Nintendo Wii, Mega Touch Bar Top Trivia, two big-screen televisions, and six more television screens. Produced on-site, the beer is fresh and seasonal. The food menu features plenty of choices, like the favorite jambalaya with Red Ale rice—shrimp, chicken, and andouille sausage in a spicy tomato and poblano sauce, served over Red Ale rice.

SCOTTY'S BREWHOUSE
1 Virginia Ave.
(317) 571-0808
www.scottysbrewhouse.com
If you want to catch every minute of the game, this is the place to be. There are flat-screen televisions everywhere—including one at every booth and even above the urinals in the men's room. Featuring a pub atmosphere with old gas burning lanterns, solid brick interior, long bar, stools, tables, and booths, Scotty's serves plenty of ice-cold beer and a big choice of bar food. Some folks like them and some don't, but the "minnies" are an interesting option. According to the menu notes, the minnies are a throwback to Scotty's school days. Served on cafeteria lunch trays—those alone can quickly turn someone off or maybe even bring back good memories—all trays come with a choice of minnie, potatoes, coleslaw, cinnamon applesauce, and a mini-dessert. The minnie sandwiches come in burgers, grilled tenderloin, pulled pork, grilled chicken, turkey hoagie, or Cuban-style roasted pork. If you don't want a minnie on your tray, you can opt for a slice of the classic school cheese pizza. Some dining memories might be better left in the past.

TALBOTT STREET DISCO-CABARET
2145 N. Talbott St.
(317) 931-1343
www.talbottstreet.com

High-energy and raucous, Talbott Street is a disco and cabaret that really comes to life late at night. Open until the wee hours on the weekends, Talbott Street features enthusiastic disc jockeys and has one of the state's largest dance floors, along with a massive copper bar. A popular part of the gay scene, Talbott Street has an adjacent cabaret show bar named Legends that features the best of area female impersonators with the Ladies of Legends and their guests. The Sky Bar offers a cool-white heavenly perch overlooking people dancing below. The cover fee is $5 on Sat; no cover fee for Fri or Sun.

TASTINGS
50 W. Washington St.
(317) 713-5000
http://conradhotels1.hilton.com

Opened in Oct 2009, Tastings is a unique wine bar and bistro concept where guests can try over 100 wines from around the world by the taste, glass, or bottle. You don't have to be a wine snob to enjoy Tastings. In fact, this would be a good place to learn more about wine with the help of a friendly sommelier. Located in the Conrad Indianapolis, Tastings is on the ground level of the hotel at the corner of Washington and Illinois streets. The wine is sold at retail price and can be opened in the shop or taken home to enjoy. Tastings also displays progressive wine technologies including Enomatic tasting stations that work to dispense oxygen with nitrogen to preserve the wine in a vacuum-like seal.

Artisanal cheese platters, flatbread pizza, gourmet sandwiches, tapas, bistro plates, and delicious desserts are also available. In addition to wine, the bar offers premium beer and spirits, sparkling wines, and flights. Outdoor table and lounge seating is available overlooking the beautiful Artsgarden.

TIKI BOB'S CANTINA
231 S. Meridian St.
(317) 974-0954
www.tikibobsindy.com

With its spring break theme—think floor-to-ceiling artificial palm trees, plastic tiki gods, and fishing nets strung across the walls—Tiki Bob's is a fun place. Often crowded and noisy, Tiki Bob's is regularly voted the best dance spot in Indy. Boasting one of the largest dance floors in the city, Tiki Bob's also has a state-of-the-art sound system, plus 20 televisions playing non-stop sports and favorite movies. Opened since 2000, the place offers tons of drink specials and requires two pieces of ID for people under 25.

WILD BEAVER SALOON
20 E. Maryland St.
(317) 423-3080
www.wildbeaversaloon.com

Mostly for the 20-something crowd, this rowdy bar looks like a cross between a mountain lodge and an Old West saloon. Women bartenders in skimpy cutoff jeans slide down a fireman's pole and dance on the bar. Drinks are reasonably priced and the shells of complimentary peanut litter the floor. This bar doesn't mind if you shout out a drink order. In fact, you probably will have to shout in order to be heard. Party-hearty folks who love it come time and again.

i Both downtown Indy and the Broad Ripple area are good places to experience the city's nightlife. You can walk in the areas, but to get from one district to the other, you will need to drive or phone for a taxi.

BROAD RIPPLE

AVERAGE JOE'S
816 Broad Ripple Ave.
(317) 253-5844
www.averagejoes.ws

MINESHAFT SALOON
812 Broad Ripple Ave.
(317) 253-5844
www.mineshaftsaloon.ws

ROCK LOBSTER
820 Broad Ripple Ave.
(317) 253-5844
www.rocklobster.ws

Known as "Broad Ripple's Party Trifecta," these three clubs are usually going strong with those who like to dance and drink and find a late-night pickup. Owners Fred Treadway and Rob Sabatini opened the establishments one at a time. The Mineshaft Saloon came first in June of 1992. Dark and loud, the Mineshaft plays a mix of retro and today's hottest dance mixes.

Next came the Rock Lobster in April 1993, named after the popular B-52's song of the early 1980s. Although it started as an '80s bar, the Rock Lobster later expanded to offer a more diverse music format. The Rock has a larger dance floor with an elevated area where everyone seems to want to dance, flat-screen televisions, and an outdoor patio open year-round.

Opened in April 1995, Average Joe's was the third and features sports bar decor. Big-screen televisions make it possible to watch the game action from almost anyplace in the bar. Even in the bathroom. It's interesting to browse around the sports memorabilia, most of which was donated by staff, friends, and customers. Racing stars such as Helio Castroneves, Arie Luyendyk, Robby Gordon, Tony Stewart, and Jimmy Vasser have been known to cruise in to Average Joe's. Of course, it might help that co-owner Fred Treadway's Treadway Racing team finished first and second in the 1997 Indy 500. Pictures of that winning season are displayed around the bar, along with some pieces of not-so-lucky cars from past racing seasons. Domestic and imported beer is abundant, and fans crave the spicy chicken wings.

CASBA
6319 Guilford Ave.
(317) 251-3138
www.casbaindy.com

Follow the neon arrow into the "underground" for a place that has been a destination for night crawlers for more than 30 years. Broad Ripple's oldest basement bar, the Casba is dark and sometimes frenetic on the weekends, with a frat party feel. On Sunday nights, the Casba is transformed into a reggae bar, a favorite for more than a decade. The bar hosts bands and DJs playing almost every genre of music. Upstairs is the Usual Suspects, a chic restaurant with a great menu.

THE JAZZ KITCHEN
5377 N. College Ave.
(317) 253-4900
www.thejazzkitchen.com

This is the place for hot jazz, great ethnic cuisine, and a casual atmosphere. Intimate tables are arranged around a dance floor while deck seating is a plus during warm months. The Jazz Kitchen hosts an array of local, regional, and national jazz along with other shows including a long-running Thursday night Latin Dance Party. Check the calendar online to see what's coming. Open Mon through Sat at 5 p.m. for dinner, the Jazz Kitchen is smoke-free in the main dining and listening room and for all national shows as well as the Thursday-night Latin Dance Party. Smoking is permitted in the lounge area for nonnational shows. Cover charge sometimes, depending on who is playing. Since music is the main reason most folks come to the Jazz Kitchen, talking is kept to a minimum so listeners don't miss a beat. If you want a rowdy party night, don't come here for the jazz performers. Along with the jazz, the Jazz Kitchen serves some delicious dishes that keep diners returning. The paella is tops, with a delicate blend of shrimp, scallops, calamari, fish, mussels, pork, and chicken in a savory saffron rice. Another favorite is the Crescent City Crab Cakes, with homemade crab cakes, Creole mayonnaise, and tomato horseradish cocktail sauce.

LANDSHARKS
810 Broad Ripple Ave.
(317) 254-8157
www.land-sharks.com

With its beach-party atmosphere, Landsharks

seems like a spring break type of club—plenty of dancing, reasonably priced drinks, and people having fun. There's very limited seating at Landsharks, but people don't seem to mind. They are there to dance or chat with friends. The place is packed most weekends after midnight. The cover charge is usually $3 to $5. DJs, bartenders, and spotlight dancers are the stars here. Landsharks features theme nights and drink specials. Check out the Web site to see what's going on.

i On the last Friday of the month, Jazz on the Avenue is a refreshing after-hours gathering for the entire family from 6 to 10 p.m. in the Grand Casino Ballroom on the fourth floor of the historic Madame Walker Building, 617 Indiana Ave. The evening's atmosphere is filled with jazzy sounds and lots of southern-style food. Admission is $10 and an additional $10 for the buffet.

UNION JACK PUB
924 Broad Ripple Ave.
(317) 243-3300
www.unionjackpub-broadripple.com
What a breath of fresh air! The Union Jack Pub is a nonsmoking facility that has been a Broad Ripple landmark since 1979. It's an English pub with a decidedly American twist. You won't miss any of the sports action with the pub's 11 high-definition televisions, plus free Wi-Fi. The full bar features over 100 beers and nightly drink specials. The Pub Grub menu is creative and delicious. Try the breaded asparagus—fresh asparagus coated with the Union Jack's own breading, then deep-fried and served with the pub's honey jalapeño dressing. The Union Jack's pizza has won numerous awards and is worth sampling. Choose from Chicago style pizza, regular, New York thin crust, or stuffed crust. Save room for dessert, which is better than any pub fare has a right to be—key lime pie, strawberry shortcake, tiramisu, molten chocolate cake, or an old-fashioned root beer float. The place even offers breakfast on Sat and Sun mornings from 9 a.m. to noon.

USUAL SUSPECTS
6319 Guilford Ave.
(317) 251-3138
www.usualsuspectsindy.com
Located above the Casba, these two places are as different as night and day. Usual Suspects is light and airy with a great menu. The Casba is a dark basement bar. Usual Suspects has a more-subdued atmosphere without being boring. This is a good spot to linger over a delicious meal or after-dinner drink. Allow time to peruse the menu. Some really good choices, like the osso bucco—pancetta-wrapped pork shanks lightly flour dusted, browned and braised slowly in red wine with carrots, onion, celery, garlic, and wild mushrooms atop truffled risotto. Or try the unusual mac and cheese—ditalini pasta with fresh mozzarella, Parmesan, provolone, and butter-cream sauce, with a choice of grilled chicken, ground beef, bacon, shrimp, or broccoli.

Usual Suspects kicks off the first Wednesday of every month in style with the Little Black Dress Night, offering $20 bottles of Prosecco and complimentary appetizers from 7 to 10 p.m. Usual Suspects makes its cocktails with freshly squeezed juices, making for quite a taste difference. The full bar also has specialty drinks like Banana Bread and Blueberry Hill.

THE VOGUE
6259 N. College Ave.
(317) 259-7029
www.thevogue.ws
Since it opened Dec 31, 1977, The Vogue has been a major draw for music, dancing, and drinking. Big names have performed here, including Bo Diddley, Willie Nelson, John Hiatt, Johnny Cash, Bonnie Raitt, The White Stripes, Cheap Trick, the Dave Matthews Band, Todd Rundgren, Tori Amos, George Clinton, Buckwheat Zydeco, and many more. Once a movie theater in the 1930s—and even an X-rated theater in the early '70s where cult favorite *Deep Throat* was shown—the Vogue also features local musicians. With a capacity of about 600, the Vogue is often crowded (with people bumping into each other, spilling drinks), loud, and smoky. If you don't

like any of that, stay away. If it is your scene, you can see some great musicians here. The Vogue regularly wins awards for best dance club and best live music. When live music isn't offered, DJs play dance music. Food is limited to popcorn, pizza, and chips. Seats are limited and there is no reserved seating, so arrive early unless you want to stand the whole evening. Check out the Web site to see who is playing. Cover charges vary, so check first or carry an extra $5 just in case.

NORTHWEST INDIANAPOLIS

THE EXCALIBUR LOUNGE
Clarion Hotel & Conference Center
2930 Waterfront Parkway West Dr.
(317) 295-8343
Savor a glass of wine or cold beer at this waterfront lounge, which caters to both smokers and nonsmokers. In a nice arrangement, the Excalibur has no smoking inside the facility but a comfortable place with tables and seats outside. Both have excellent lake views. Smokers can also enjoy food and drinks at the outside area. The lounge offers billiards and darts and a large-screen television for sporting events. Karaoke is a hoot on Fri and Sat nights, and occasional live music is featured. The popular lawn game of cornhole is offered outside the lounge. If you haven't played the Midwest favorite, this would be a good place to give it a try. The lounge features a full bar and if you're hungry, you can order from Stefano's Restaurant and Pizzeria, which is also located in the hotel, and eat in the lounge. Stefano's specializes in tasty Italian cuisine. Decorated with a large bar, tables and chairs, and oversize leather couches and chairs, Excalibur also has the benefit of being in the Clarion Hotel. Watch some of the exciting Indy sports, hoist some drinks in the lounge, and head for your room afterwards instead of driving.

INDY SPORTS GRILLE
Holiday Inn North at the Pyramids
3850 DePauw Blvd.
(317) 872-9790
Formerly Benchwarmers Sports Bar & Grille, this Holiday Inn was recently renovated to be more like a sports-themed restaurant with a bar. Now known as Indy Sports Grille, it is still a great place to watch a sporting event on the 10 large flat-screen televisions. In the remodeling, the Grille was made brighter and more open than the dark Benchwarmers. Most of the sports memorabilia was removed, but some sports trophies and a locker setup behind the bar still evoke the old Benchwarmers. Indy Sports Grille offers a full bar and nice menu in a casual atmosphere. A popular choice is the pork tenderloin sandwich with homemade chips.

NORTHEAST INDIANAPOLIS

APRÈS JACK'S
9419 N. Meridian St.
(317) 843-1609
www.konajacksindy.com
If you like Daddy Jack's and Kona Jack's, you should love Après Jack's. They are all part of the same family. French for "After Jack's," Après Jack's is a neat place to stop after work, after play, or after dinner. This upscale hangout features a full bar, fine cigars, and a delicious menu with sushi, fresh seafood, burgers, barbecued pork, tenderloin, and much more. Sushi favorites include the California roll with snow crab, cucumber, and avocado; and the sesame ahi tuna, seared in spicy sesame seeds and topped with teriyaki plum wine sauce. The blackened steak medallions also earn raves—beef tenderloin medallions, lightly blackened and topped with grilled onions and mushrooms, served over white rice. Just like Daddy Jack's and Kona Jack's, Après Jack's has a legendary tale behind it. Supposedly, Daddy Jack felt something was missing from his life—a warm comfortable place where he could relax and reflect on his good fortune, so he decided to create such a place. Sketching out this plan on a cocktail napkin, Daddy Jack designed a private sanctuary den with rich mahogany walls, plush leather chairs, a game table, gleaming brass, and top-shelf refreshments. That is how Après Jack's came to be, so the story goes. Guests are now invited to enjoy a cozy spot by the fireplace, sip a drink, and listen to live music Tues through Sat.

INDY CIGAR BAR
3357 E. 86th St.
(317) 292-0720
www.indycigarbar.com
Turn back the hands of time to visit this nostalgic place where cigar lovers can savor the finest in high-end cigars and premium liquors. Indiana's only Diamond Crown cigar lounge, the Indy Cigar Bar is serious about what it offers. A room-size humidor keeps flavored cigars fresh in separate cases. Indy Cigar Bar boasts almost 20 bourbons, 25 single-malt scotches, and more than 300 types of cigars. Located across from the Fashion Mall, Indy Cigar Bar is a great place to stop in for a cigar and drink on the way home. But be aware that it is not a late-night bar spot. It is open Mon through Sat from 11 a.m. to 9:30 p.m. and Sun from noon to 5 p.m. Those are the posted hours, but don't be surprised if the bar is closed by 8 p.m. on a weeknight. Call ahead before making the drive. If you happen to get hungry, Indy Cigar Bar offers a nice sandwich but this is not a restaurant. A large bar, black leather chairs, and big-screen television add to the retro decor, as does a huge photo of Indy from the past dominating one wall.

MOVIE THEATERS

Indianapolis isn't lacking in movie theaters. Large multiplexes can be found in every part of town. Here are a few to get you started. For more, look at the entertainment pages of the daily or alternative newspapers.

AMC CASTLETON SQUARE
6020 E. 82nd St.
(317) 849-3471

AMC GREENWOOD PARK
461 S. Greenwood Park Dr., Greenwood
(317) 884-0903

CINEMARK WASHINGTON MARKET
10455 E. Washington St.
(317) 898-1086

CIRCLE CENTRE
49 W. Maryland St.
(317) 237-6490

EAGLE HIGHLANDS
4015 Shore Dr.
(317) 298-2091

IMAX THEATER
Indiana State Museum
650 W. Washington St.
(317) 232-1637

KERASOTES SHOWPLACE
4325 S. Meridian St.
(317) 784-0989

KERASOTES SHOWPLACE
6102 Rural Dr.
(317) 475-0899

KERASOTES SHOWPLACE
10280 E. Washington St.
(317) 536-6815

KERASOTES SHOWPLACE—TRADER'S POINT
5920 W. 86th St.
(800) 326-3264

KEY CINEMAS
4044 S. Keystone Ave.
(317) 784-7454

LANDMARK KEYSTONE ART
8702 Keystone Crossing
(317) 579-3009

UA GALAXY STADIUM
8105 E. 96th Ave.
(317) 570-5678

TIBBS DRIVE-IN
480 S. Tibbs Ave.
(317) 243-6666

THE ARTS

Attend a world-class opera or ballet. Listen to a symphony under the stars. Watch Miley Cyrus thrill teenyboppers. Marvel at the wonders of King Tut. Try to figure out whodunit in a stage mystery. Ponder an Indian work of art. Admire a finely crafted contemporary vase. Indianapolis has it all . . . and more. Art lovers can rejoice in a wide variety of offerings around the city. The arts have a significant impact on Indianapolis and the quality of life offered to Hoosiers. A flourishing performing arts culture in the city generates a whopping $468 million annually for the local economy.

Music and the arts have long been an important part of Indianapolis. Not surprisingly, the first musical performances in the newborn city took place in churches by church choirs.

History also recalls fiddlers playing for social gatherings in the early log cabins of 1821. In 1824 the Society for the Cultivation of Church Music became the first voluntary organization to promote the arts in Indianapolis.

While still a struggling settlement, the city had both a music school and an orchestra. Both of those cultural organizations were first established in a church. During the pastorate of the Rev. Henry Ward Beecher (1839–1847) at the Second Presbyterian Church, the first music school and the first orchestra were both organized in the church. The orchestra was a string and flute ensemble composed of 15 members.

When it comes to the arts today, Indianapolis offers plenty to see, hear, and do. Live concert performances are an almost weekly occurrence, and dance is alive and well here. During the summer, when night falls, the stars come out in Indy's open-air stages. Spread a blanket and enjoy big-name and local acts on the Lawn At White River State Park. A tradition since 1982, Symphony on the Prairie brings music to the rolling hills of Conner Prairie. Art museums and galleries are spread around the city. Live theater options continue to expand in Indianapolis.

In 2001 the city launched the Cultural Tourism Initiative to promote and showcase local hubs of activity that stand out for their cultural and artistic offerings. These six designated cultural districts represent and reflect the character and diversity of the community, offering fun and flavor in convenient settings to residents and visitors alike.

This chapter spotlights those six cultural districts, along with a sampling of some of the city's major performing arts groups and facilities.

INDIANAPOLIS CULTURAL DISTRICTS

Broad Ripple Village

About 20 minutes from downtown, this north-side neighborhood features eclectic shops and vintage boutiques, a variety of restaurants—many with alfresco dining—artists and art galleries, bars and taverns with live entertainment, and parks connected by the nationally recognized Monon Trail. While known for its nightlife and music scene, Broad Ripple offers even more. Visitors of all ages can stroll through the neighborhood, experience the unique architecture, and enjoy a day of leisure and entertainment. Take a scenic walk, run or bike ride down the historic Monon Trail, and stop to check out the Indianapolis Art Center—one of the premier community art centers in the Midwest.

Close-up

Trail to Put Art and Culture on the Map

Scheduled to be completed in 2011, the Indianapolis Cultural Trail: A Legacy of Gene and Marilyn Glick is a world-class urban bike and pedestrian path that will connect neighborhoods, cultural districts, and entertainment amenities. The trail will also serve as the hub for the entire greenway trail system. The five downtown cultural districts connected by the Indianapolis Cultural Trail include Fountain Square, Indiana Avenue, Mass Ave, White River State Park, and the Wholesale District.

Upon completion, the Cultural Trail will connect with the 15-mile Monon Trail, allowing visitors easy access to the sixth cultural district, Broad Ripple Village, from downtown. Construction is being done in six corridor stages with early sections already completed.

The brick trail will include benches, bike racks, lighting, signage, and bike rentals and dropoffs along the way. It also will feature local artwork. Currently over $2 million has been spent on public art for the project. The 8-mile path will allow users to pass by and through many destinations that make Indy a recognized leader in the arts community. The trail is being funded by a large public and private collaboration led by Central Indiana Community Foundation, the City of Indianapolis, and several not-for-profit organizations devoted to building a better city. Most of the funding, about $35 million of the $50 million budget, will come from charitable contributions. The trail will use $15 million in federal transportation funds but no local funding. The trail is named for Gene and Marilyn Glick, who gave $15 million in 2006 to help launch the project into reality.

Canal and White River State Park

The Canal and White River State Park feature some of the city's most popular attractions presented in a fresh urban setting. Take a stroll along the 3-mile Central Canal, where paved walkways lined with antique streetlamps and lush greenery provide easy access to arts, recreation, and entertainment, all showcased along a restored urban waterway. There are pedal boats and a wide variety of bikes for rent. You can also go on a gondola ride complete with singing gondolier. White River State Park, as the cultural anchor of the Central Canal, offers a unique urban green space and growing collection of public art and gardens. You can spend days browsing through such cultural venues as the Indianapolis Zoo and White River Gardens, Indiana State Museum, IMAX Theater, Eiteljorg Museum of American Indians and Western Art, Victory Field, NCAA Hall of Champions, and the Indiana History Center.

Fountain Square

This historic commercial district, just a few blocks southeast of downtown, represents more than 200 antique dealers in specialty stores and art galleries. It boasts a great collection of attractions, all located in an eclectic setting of architecturally interesting buildings, including the refurbished Fountain Square Theater Building. Pedestrians can spend a day shopping, dining, viewing art, hearing live music, or watching a play without ever getting back into their vehicle. A trip to Fountain Square takes you back to a simpler time, with attractions such as a '50s-style diner and soda fountain and duckpin bowling. Bistros, gourmet delis, and several ethnic restaurants offer mouth-watering dining options throughout the area.

Indiana Avenue

Historically, "the Avenue" was the center of African-American social life. During the 1920s and into the 1950s, it was home to successful African-American businesses and a spirited club scene, often referred to as the "Broadway of Indianapolis." Many of the era's greatest jazz musicians honed their art here. Today, Indiana Avenue stands as a symbol of African-American culture and pride. Visitors can tour historic buildings such as the Madame Walker Theatre Center and Crispus Attucks Museum and dine in unique restaurants. Vibrant festivals are held annually for the whole family to enjoy.

Mass Ave

The five-block downtown area, known simply as "Mass Ave," is putting a whole new angle on excitement. Known as an arts and theater district, five performing arts theaters are situated along Mass Ave, as well as a collection of top-notch art galleries, locally owned restaurants, and fun and funky boutiques. While visiting Mass Ave, take time to stop and admire the outdoor public art, innovative architecture, and historic neighborhood vibe.

Wholesale District

The Wholesale District is, for many, synonymous with downtown. The District contains or is adjacent to such regional venues as Lucas Oil Stadium, Circle Centre mall, and Conseco Fieldhouse. Unique retailers, along with premier national and local independent restaurants, make the Wholesale District an ideal place to shop, relax, and have fun. Combined with Monument Circle and Washington Street, the district offers countless theaters, museums, historical resources, and other arts and cultural opportunities.

ARTS ORGANIZATIONS

AMERICAN PIANISTS ASSOCIATION
4603 Clarendon Rd., Suite 30
(317) 940-9945
www.americanpianists.org
Founded in New York in 1979 as the Beethoven Foundation, the American Pianists Association (APA) relocated to Indianapolis in 1982. A not-for-profit organization, APA's mission is to support the careers of America's rising young classical and jazz pianists between the ages of 18 and 30. The APA identifies as "fellows" those it supports through annual competitions held in alternate years in classical music and jazz. Fellows are supported through cash prizes, engagements, and career guidance for two years—contributions valued at more than $50,000. APA also organizes and presents the annual Indy Jazz Fest.

ARTS COUNCIL OF INDIANAPOLIS
20 N. Meridian St., Suite 500
(317) 631-3301
www.indyarts.org
Incorporated in 1987, the Arts Council of Indianapolis assists the city's 150-plus arts organizations with grants, programs, and technical-assistance services. The not-for-profit organization oversees the distribution of federal, state, and city funds to artists and arts organizations and serves as a facilitator between arts organizations and the business community. The Arts Council owns and operates the Indianapolis Artsgarden, a glass-domed rotunda that serves as a performance, exhibition, and marketing space for the Indianapolis arts community.

BANDS OF AMERICA/MUSIC FOR ALL, INC.
39 W. Jackson Place, Suite 150
(800) 8480-2263
www.musicforall.org
Founded in 1975, Bands of America (BOA) is a not-for-profit organization and the nation's largest producer of educational events for high school music programs. The organization's mission is to create and provide positive experiences through music for students, teachers, parents, and communities. More than 90,000 students participate in BOA events each year, while 270,000 teens, family members, and band enthusiasts attend them. In 2006 BOA and its Orchestra America division merged with the Music for All Foundation, one of the largest and most influential national music education organizations in support of active music making.

ℹ️ The world's first transistor radio was made in Indianapolis in 1954 by the Regency Division of Industrial Development Engineering Associates.

INTERNATIONAL VIOLIN COMPETITION OF INDIANAPOLIS
30 E. Washington St., Suite 1320
(317) 637-4574
www.violin.org

The International Violin Competition of Indianapolis produces a quadrennial international violin competition to enhance the great tradition of classical music and to heighten the cultural profile of Indiana internationally. The competition is open to premier violinists ages 16 to 29 and offers the richest prize package in the musical world—$30,000, a Carnegie Hall debut, a recording contract, dozens of bookings around the world, and use of a rare 1683 Stradivarius violin for four years. The organization also sponsors the Suzuki & Friends and Ronen Chamber Ensemble professional chamber music series, as well as numerous other events designed to encourage the careers of musical and visual artists.

DANCE

DANCE KALEIDOSCOPE
4603 Clarendon Rd.
(317) 940-6555
www.dancekal.org

Dance Kaleidoscope, Indiana's contemporary dance ensemble, is a nationally acclaimed company of professional dancers trained in classical ballet and Graham Technique. The company has an internationally renowned artistic staff. From Oct through Apr, Dance Kaleidoscope offers four public performances and collaborates with a number of other arts organizations, including the Indianapolis Symphony Orchestra, Indianapolis Museum of Art, Indianapolis Civic Theatre, American Cabaret Theatre, Indianapolis Men's Chorus, and American Pianists Association.

GALLERIES

INDIANAPOLIS ART CENTER
820 E. 67th St.
(317) 255-2464
www.indplsartcenter.org

The fine arts facility, located in Broad Ripple Village, invites visitors to explore more than 50 exhibitions a year. The Frank M. Basile Studio Shop has original works to take home, all made by regional or local artists. Visit ARTSPARK, a 12-acre outdoor sculpture park.

IU HERRON SCHOOL OF ART AND DESIGN & GALLERY AT IUPUI
735 W. New York St.
(317) 278-9418
www.herron.iupui.edu

Throughout the year, visitors to the Herron School of Art and Design at IUPUI can enjoy artistic works of local and internally acclaimed artists. Explore the Herron Gallery and see contemporary works of innovative painters, sculptors, graphic artists, and other artists.

MUSEUMS

EITELJORG MUSEUM OF AMERICAN INDIANS AND WESTERN ART
500 W. Washington St.
(317) 636-9378
www.eiteljorg.org

Through exhibitions, performances, festivals, special events and hands-on workshops with artists, the Eiteljorg immerses visitors in the many cultures of the American West and Native America. It's the only museum in the Midwest to offer this combination. The award-winning museum store sells gallery-quality gifts, and lunch is served at the Sky City Café.

INDIANAPOLIS ARTSGARDEN/VISITOR CENTER
100 W. Washington St.
(317) 624-2563
www.indyarts.org

Owned and operated by the Arts Council of

Indianapolis, this glass structure suspended over a downtown street offers free performances and exhibits and ticketing assistance for major events around the city. Elevated walkways link it to Circle Centre, hotels, offices, shops, and restaurants. The Artsgarden is also an official visitor center with an attendant on duty to answer questions every day.

INDIANAPOLIS MUSEUM OF ART
4000 N. Michigan Rd.
(317) 923-2332
www.imamuseum.org
The IMA is among the largest general art museums in the United States. Situated on 152 acres that incorporate the historic Oldfields estate, as well as breathtaking gardens and grounds, the newly expanded IMA features significant collections of African, American, Asian, European, contemporary, and decorative art, including drawings, sculpture, prints, photographs, textiles, and costumes.

i The Indianapolis Museum of Art was ranked by *USA Today* as one of the top 10 locations for marriage proposals—in front of the famous *LOVE* statue.

INDIANAPOLIS MUSEUM OF CONTEMPORARY ART
340 N. Senate Ave.
(317) 634-6622
www.indymoca.org
Conveniently located in two overlapping Indianapolis cultural districts (Indiana Avenue, and The Canal and White River State Park), Indiana Museum of Contemporary Art is an arts organization with ideas, forms, and creations of our time. Exhibits range from paintings to graffiti to video art.

NATIONAL ART MUSEUM OF SPORT
850 W. Michigan St.
(317) 274-3627
www.namos.iupui.edu
The museum features the nation's largest collection of art depicting sport. Holdings include works by Winslow Homer, George Bellows, LeRoy

Neiman, and Ogden Pleissner. The museum features special exhibits in addition to its permanent collection.

MUSIC

INDIANAPOLIS CHILDREN'S CHOIR
4600 Sunset Ave.
(317) 940-9640
www.icchoir.org
Having grown to more than 1,500 singers in 16 choirs, the Indianapolis Children's Choir continues to be one of the largest and most accomplished children's choral programs in the nation. Singers come from 17 counties, which embrace the urban environment of Indianapolis, the suburbs surrounding the city, and many small rural communities. In addition to its own concert series, the choir performs regularly with professional symphony orchestras, including the Indianapolis Orchestra, and has also performed with the Chieftains and Celine Dion. The Choir has performed several times at Carnegie Hall and regularly tours nationally and internationally.

INDIANAPOLIS OPERA
250 E. 38th St.
(317) 283-3531
www.indyopera.org
The Indianapolis Opera is Indiana's professional regional opera company. The opera presents four productions each season at Clowes Memorial Hall. All performances feature renowned singers and the Indianapolis Symphony Orchestra or the Indianapolis Chamber Orchestra, along with the Indianapolis Opera Chorus. Indianapolis Opera also has a multifaceted educational program that reaches more than 50,000 students across the Midwest.

INDIANAPOLIS SYMPHONY ORCHESTRA
Hilbert Circle Theatre
45 Monument Circle
(800) 366-8457
www.indianapolissymphony.org
Founded in 1930, the Indianapolis Symphony Orchestra (ISO) is firmly established as one of

America's most skilled musical ensembles. The 87-member orchestra is made up of resident artists from all parts of the world and is one of only 18 orchestras that perform a year-round schedule of classical, pop, holiday, and summer concerts. The ISO owns and maintains its downtown concert hall, Hilbert Circle Theatre. Built in 1916 as a classic movie palace, Hilbert Circle Theatre was renovated in the 1980s as an acoustically superb concert hall. The orchestra performs outreach concerts in churches, parks, and communities across Indiana.

i The Philharmonic Orchestra of Indianapolis and Indy Parks have collaborated for more than 40 years to present free pops concerts during the month of June. Concerts include a mix of patriotic songs, jazz, light classical, movie themes, and operetta. Concerts begin at 7 p.m., and parking is free at each location. For more information see www.philharmonicindy.org.

RHYTHM DISCOVERY CENTER
110 W. Washington St., Room A
(317) 974-4488
www.rhythmdiscoverycenter.org
Opened in 2009, Rhythm Discovery Center is located in the heart of downtown Indianapolis, directly adjacent to the Artsgarden. The attraction interprets the role of rhythm and percussion in music and culture through dynamic educational experiences. Interactive exhibits, participatory opportunities, and a hands-on area illustrate rhythm, its role in society, and its connections to daily life. The 15,000-square-foot facility houses three galleries, a hands-on area that allows visitors to play a variety of drums and percussion instruments—including a 96-inch drum—and a gift shop.

VENUES

CLOWES MEMORIAL HALL
4602 Sunset Ave.
(317) 940-6444
www.cloweshall.org

Since opening its doors in 1962, Clowes Memorial Hall of Butler University has brought the finest international, cultural, and artistically diverse entertainment to its patrons. This 2,100-seat venue hosts a performing arts series, the Indianapolis Opera, the Indianapolis Chamber Orchestra, and half of the Broadway in Indianapolis series shows. Clowes Hall is also home to many of the Jordan College of Fine Arts performances, including the Butler Ballet, Butler Symphony Orchestra, and Butler Wind Ensemble.

CHRISTEL DEHAAN FINE ARTS CENTER
1400 E. Hanna Ave.
(800) 232-8634
www.arts.uindy.edu
The $10.2 million Christel DeHaan Fine Arts Center at the University of Indianapolis opened in 1994 and features visiting performing and visual artists. The 59,000-square-foot facility houses an imitation Viennese-style performance hall that hosts an array of performances and art exhibitions for the community.

CONSECO FIELDHOUSE
125 S. Pennsylvania St.
(317) 917-2500
Opened in 1999, Conseco Fieldhouse is a popular venue for performing artists, as well as the home of the Indiana Pacers and its sister team, the Indiana Fever. The Fieldhouse has hosted such major performers as Pavarotti, Bruce Springsteen, Boston Pops, John Mellencamp, Tim McGraw, Faith Hill, Britney Spears, Kid Rock, Miley Cyrus, and many more.

HILBERT CIRCLE THEATRE
45 Monument Circle
(317) 262-1100
www.indianapolissymphony.org
Home of the Indianapolis Symphony Orchestra, Hilbert Circle Theatre is the second-oldest building on Monument Circle. Originally built in 1916, it was the city's first movie theater. When it closed in 1981, the historic facility seemed in danger of destruction. The Indianapolis Symphony Orchestra bought it as a permanent home, after an

intensive renovation project. In 1984 the orchestra performed its first concert in the beautiful and acoustically superior auditorium.

IMAX THEATER
Indiana State Museum
650 W. Washington St.
(317) 233-4629
www.imax.com/indy
The state's first IMAX Theater delivers 2-D and 3-D films to a six-and-a-half-story screen. Hollywood movies and filmed rock concert shows also are featured occasionally, along with traditional IMAX productions projected with the largest film frame in motion-picture history.

LAWN AT WHITE RIVER STATE PARK
801 W. Washington St.
(800) 665-9056
www.in.gov/whiteriver
Since opening in Aug 2003, the Lawn at White River State Park has offered top entertainers to thousands of concertgoers. For the last thee years, the Lawn has been named one of the top 100 outdoor concert venues in the world by *Pollstar* magazine. Complete with a waterfront bandstand, the area can accommodate up to 5,000 people and has been used for concerts, festivals, and other community events. The 2009 lineup was the longest and most diverse of any of the seasons, featuring Bonnie Raitt, Taj Mahal, Moody Blues, Ziggy Marley, Fray, Incubus, Crosby Stills and Nash, Branford Marsalis, and many more.

i A perfect way to experience some of the world's greatest music in an informal outdoor setting, Indianapolis Opera in the Park features familiar opera hits and the best of Broadway, as well as music highlights of Indianapolis Opera's upcoming seasons. Guests are invited to bring their blankets and picnic baskets to enjoy the entertainment. Two events are held every month from June to September. All shows are free and held in the outdoor Celebration Amphitheater at White River State Park. Check for shows at www.in.gov/whiteriver.

LUCAS OIL STADIUM
7001 W. 56th St.
(317) 297-7000
www.lucasoilstadium.com
Opened in Aug 2008, the $719 million Lucas Oil Stadium is home to the Indianapolis Colts, as well as a venue for concerts and other events.

MADAME WALKER THEATRE CENTER
617 Indiana Ave.
(317) 236-2009
www.walkertheatre.com
For decades, the Madame Walker Theatre Center has been the heart of the Indiana Avenue cultural district. Walker Theatre was constructed in 1927 as the home of Walker Manufacturing, founded by the country's first female self-made millionaire, Madame C. J. Walker. The 950-seat theater was placed on the National Register of Historic Places in 1980 and was designated a National Historic Landmark in 1991. The center now serves as an educational and cultural resource center for the community, with particular focus on African-American culture. The center hosts about 150 performances a year.

MURAT CENTRE
502 N. New Jersey St.
(317) 231-0000
www.murat.com
Downtown Indy's historic Murat Centre provides a variety of entertainment options. Originally known as the Murat Shrine Temple, the facility was renamed following an $11 million renovation in 1996. The Murat Centre is now the host facility for some of the city's premier entertainment and special events. The historic beauty and intimate setting of the Murat Theatre make it a wonderful venue for the hottest Broadway shows and finest contemporary entertainers.

PIKE PERFORMING ARTS CENTER
6701 Zionsville Rd.
(317) 216-5455
www.pikepac.org
The Pike Performing Arts Center houses a 1,449-seat, state-of-the-art auditorium and the 150-seat

Studio Theatre. The facility presents a season of professional touring performances, including dance, concerts, musical theater, Shakespearean plays, and one-man shows from Sept through Apr.

i Indiana Avenue, on the northwest side of downtown Indy, became a jazz incubator during the years between World War II and the mid-1960s. Many musicians, including guitarist Wes Montgomery, honed their skills there.

VERIZON WIRELESS MUSIC CENTER
12880 E. 146th St.
(317) 239-5151
www.verizonwirelessmusiccenter.com
Situated on 228 acres of land, Verizon Wireless Music Center provides a diverse array of music through its many concerts and performances. Between 40 and 60 concerts are held from May to Sept. A covered pavilion seats 6,200 patrons, while another 18,000 people can stretch out on the lawn. A high-tech sound system includes a lawn speaker relay delay to assure a clear and echo-free sound, while large video screens provide a close-up view of performances.

WARREN PERFORMING ARTS CENTER
9500 E. 16th St.
(317) 532-6280
www.warrenpac.com
The Warren Performing Arts Center represents state-of-the-art theater design and technology. The facility features a grand stage auditorium that seats more than 1,000 people, a 250-seat studio theater, a dance theater, and several combination rehearsal/recital halls for choral, band, and orchestral groups.

THEATER

ACTORS THEATRE OF INDIANA
716 Stockbridge Dr., Westfield
(317) 669-7983
www.actorstheatreofindiana.org

Actors Theatre of Indiana is a professional equity theater company presenting musical productions with top-notch Indianapolis and New York talent. Enjoy an evening of song and dance and leave the theater humming a tune from singers and songwriters such as Frank Sinatra and Cole Porter.

AMERICAN CABARET THEATRE
401 Michigan St.
(317) 631-0334
www.thecabaret.org
The American Cabaret Theatre relocated to Indianapolis from New York and opened its first season in 1990. The professional theater company produces original musical revues and Broadway shows. For its original revues, the theater incorporates an interesting blend of music, song, dance, and visuals.

ASANTE CHILDREN'S THEATRE
502 N. Tremont St.
(317) 635-7211
www.asantechildrenstheatre.org
The Asante Children's Theatre is a professional theater organization committed to preserving the tradition of African and African-American performing arts. Through annual citywide auditions, children ages 12 to 21 are selected as members of the theater group. The Sept through June season includes performances at the Madame Walker Theatre Center and the Indiana Historical Society, as well as several presentations throughout the state.

BEEF & BOARDS DINNER THEATRE
9301 N. Michigan Rd.
(317) 872-9664
www.beefandboards.com
Beef & Boards Dinner Theatre is Indy's only year-round Equity theatre. The 500-seat theater presents seven Broadway shows each season, as well as its annual "A Beef & Boards Christmas" and national concert acts. Beef & Boards produces all of its shows, recruiting actors locally, as well as from Chicago and New York.

INDIANA REPERTORY THEATRE
140 W. Washington St.
(317) 635-5252
www.irtlive.com
Indiana Repertory Theatre is Indiana's professional, resident, and not-for-profit theater. Established in 1972, IRT was named the state's "theater laureate" by the General Assembly in 1991. IRT presents classic and contemporary theater, including comedy and drama, during its Oct through May season. Since 1908, IRT has been housed in the Indiana Theatre building, an opulent, renovated 1927 movie palace that features distinctive Spanish Baroque architecture. The building boasts a three-theater complex—the 607-seat main stage, 314-seat upper stage, and the 150-seat cabaret—as well as complete production and administrative facilities.

INDIANAPOLIS CIVIC THEATRE
3200 Cold Spring Rd.
(317) 924-6770
www.civictheatre.org
The nation's oldest continuously operating community theater, Indianapolis Civic Theatre has been a vital part of Indianapolis since 1914. Each season, the theater entertains nearly 50,000 patrons during its six main stage productions, while simultaneously serving as a community resource for local theater artists, technicians, volunteers, and aspiring students of the performing arts.

MYSTERY CAFE
838 Greer St.
(317) 684-6668
www.themysterycafeindy.com

At the Mystery Cafe, each play unfolds in four acts, with a dinner course served after each one. Upon arrival, guests are met at the door by the evening's characters and given their new identity. Members of the audience may participate as much as or as little as they like in the mystery, collecting clues along the way. Fifteen to 20 guests have lines to read or songs to sing during the play. At evening's end, a prize is given to the person who best solves the mystery.

PHOENIX THEATRE
749 Park Ave.
(317) 635-7529
www.phoenixtheatre.org
Phoenix Theatre is Indiana's contemporary theater, producing 12 cutting-edge, off-Broadway-style shows each season, using both the main stage and underground stage venue. The Phoenix produces issue-oriented contemporary works and strives to challenge audiences with plays that examine people's responsibilities to society.

THEATRE ON THE SQUARE
627 Massachusetts Ave.
(317) 685-8687
www.tots.org
Theatre on the Square explores popular to lesser-known plays and musicals in an intimate setting. Each show is different in the issues approached and the audience targeted. The theater rates each program and informs prospective ticket buyers whether the play is suitable for families or a mature audience. The theater produces 13 shows each year.

ATTRACTIONS

Once nicknamed "Naptown," Indianapolis has grown to become a vibrant city filled with a diverse array of surprising and world-class attractions. Sure, it's home to the spectacular Indy 500 and boasts more than its fair share of spectator sporting events (see the Motorsports and Spectator Sports chapters for more on that) but Indianapolis has a tremendous amount to offer. Indy is the kind of place you love to show off to visitors, a treasure-filled city that invariably leads to comments like, "Wow, I didn't know Indianapolis had that!" Yep, we certainly do and so much more.

With a commitment to green, Indianapolis is home to some of America's great urban spaces. The fact that White River State Park exists in the heart of a city with more than three quarters of a million people is a big clue that this is not your traditional state park. Campsites? Nope. Park admission? Nope. In fact, the city and the 250-acre park mingle so naturally that visitors might saunter into the park without being aware they have done so. Enjoy the splash of fountains and whisper of ornamental grasses along the city's Canal Walk, a ribbon of water that flows through White River State Park and provides a peaceful respite.

A patriotic city, the Hoosier capital has more memorials and monuments with more acreage devoted to honoring veterans than any other U.S. city except Washington, D.C.

Scattered throughout downtown are statues immortalizing the likes of a young Abe Lincoln (he lived in Indiana from ages 7 to 21), explorer George Rogers Clark, and Miss Victory herself atop the Soldiers and Sailors Monument.

In fact, we have so many great places to visit and so many fun things to do that we can't possibly list them all here. We've highlighted some that we recommend and know that you will find even more. That is part of the thrill of exploring Indianapolis. Put on your walking shoes, head off with a map, and you might be surprised at what treasures you will find. Indy is a great walking city, or you can get a pleasant overview by touring in style in a horse-drawn carriage. If you've never been to Indianapolis before, welcome. This could be the start of a lovely lasting relationship.

Price Code

Use the following as a guide to the cost of admission for one adult. Keep in mind that children's admission prices are generally lower (usually about half the cost of adult admissions) and very young children are admitted free to most attractions. Discounts for senior citizens, students, and groups are usually available.

$	$1 to $5
$$	$6 to $10
$$$	$11 to $15
$$$$	$16 and more

GENERAL ATTRACTIONS

CITY MARKET
222 E Market St.
(317) 634-9266
www.indycom.com
Established in 1886, City Market is listed in the National Register of Historic Places. In an Old World atmosphere, vendors offer fresh produce, meats and fish, imported coffees, and baked goods. Specialty stands include gifts, flowers, candy, alterations, and shoe and leather repair. Cart vendors ranging from portrait artists to various craft and jewelry designers add an

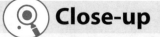 **Close-up**

Hoosier Poet's Home Gives Glimpse into Past

His top hat and cane rest on his bed. A portrait of his beloved white poodle hangs on the wall. His writing desk waits for him to pen another masterpiece. And a calling card stand is an elegant reminder of the guests who once came to call. The James Whitcomb Riley Museum Home at 528 Lockerbie St. seems untouched by time, as though its most famous resident had just stepped out for a stroll and will soon return. Surprisingly, Riley was never an owner of the lovely home where he lived for 23 years. Instead, he was a houseguest, living with the owners as part of their family. When the last owner of the home died, the house was locked up and kept as it was.

A wealthy and renowned poet, Riley could have bought an expensive home of his own. He was like a rock star of his time. He would travel around the country giving talks. His talks sold out in 15 minutes and hundreds would be turned away. In fact, Riley did buy his childhood home, where he let his brother live. But Riley fell in love with the Lockerbie Street house and its quiet neighborhood. He enjoyed the place and its occupants so much that he visited quite often. In 1893 he moved in as a paying boarder and became a member of the family. He died in his bedroom in the house on July 22, 1916. When the last family member in the house passed away later that same year, a group of Riley's friends had the foresight to buy the house and the household goods for a museum.

Born Oct. 7, 1848, in Greenfield, Riley was the son of a lawyer father and a homemaker mother who had a knack for writing verse and frequently contributed to the local papers. The baby was named after an Indiana governor, James Whitcomb. When Riley was 11, his father marched off to fight in the Civil War. It was a difficult time for the family—both emotionally and financially. When Riley's father came home from the war, the family was nearly broke and had to sell their home. They moved into "a cheerless house in the edge of a cornfield," Riley later wrote. Although his family had their hearts set on his becoming a lawyer, young Riley had other thoughts. He joined a traveling medicine show in which he recited stories, played guitar, sang, and did impressions. He also penned his own verse.

ever-changing flavor to the market. Lunchtime patrons can choose from a variety of menus, enjoy outdoor dining on one of the two plazas, listen to performances by local musicians, and experience the Original Farmers' Market every Wed, June through Oct. (See the Shopping chapter for more information.)

CONSECO FIELDHOUSE
125 S. Pennsylvania St.
(317) 917-2500
www.consecofieldhouse.com
The $183 million Conseco Fieldhouse opened in 1999 and stands as a monument to Indiana's rich basketball tradition. This state-of-the-art facility combines the nostalgic feelings of the past with the benefits of the future. The Fieldhouse is home

to the NBA's Indiana Pacers and the WNBA's Indiana Fever, as well as being a venue for hockey, concerts, and other events. It occupies 750,000 square feet with a seating capacity of approximately 18,500, including 69 suites and 2,500 club seats. (See the Spectator Sports chapter for more information.) Conseco Fieldhouse is one of Indianapolis's major tourist attractions, a must-see for every visitor. All 750,000 square feet pay tribute to Indiana's rich basketball history through its retro-style and traditional Indiana Basketball Fieldhouse design.

GARFIELD PARK CONSERVATORY AND
SUNKEN GARDEN $
2450 S. Shelby St.
(317) 327-7183
www.garfieldgardensconvervatory.org

Becoming a newspaperman, Riley continued to write and recite. In 1883, Riley published his first book, *The Old Swimmin' Hole and 'Leven more Poems*. Written in Hoosier dialect—the way people talked at the time—the book was an immediate sensation. Writing in traditional language as well, Riley wrote about 1,400 poems and made about $3 million, a great deal of money, more than almost any other American poet at the time.

Meanwhile, a prosperous cracker baker, John Nickum, and his wife moved with their daughter, Magdalena, and her husband, Major Charles Holstein, into the stylish Italianate home at 528 Lockerbie St. That was in 1873. Later, one of their frequent visitors was the much-revered "Hoosier poet." At the time, Riley lived in a boarding house on Pennsylvania Street. Riley said he loved children and always wanted a wife and a family but it just never worked out. After Riley's death from complications of a stroke, an estimated 35,000 mourners passed by his body as it lay in state under the dome of the State Capitol building. Riley was buried on the highest hill in Indianapolis in Crown Hill Cemetery. His legacy includes the James Whitcomb Riley Hospital for Children, which opened in 1924.

Not a restoration, the Riley Museum Home maintains original carpets, wallpaper, gas fixtures, hand-painted ceilings, native Indiana butternut woodwork, and furniture that has never been removed. Opened to the public in 1923, the James Whitcomb Riley Museum is the only late-Victorian preservation home in the nation open to the public.

Visitors can see such treasures as Riley's last poem written with his left hand after a stroke damaged his right side. Look for an interesting orange cup on a dining room table. Oranges were a treat in those days, and the slanted fruit dish was used for an individual serving. The orange would be cut in half and put in the tipped dish and eaten with a spoon. The juice would be left in the cup and a spoon would be used to drink the juice.

A beautiful ruby window at the top of the staircase landing also had a special use. It was an early caller ID system. You could look out this window and see who was outside the front door without the visitor seeing you. Then you could decide if you wanted to open the door or not. Contact the museum at (317) 631-5885.

Located within the 136-acre Garfield Park on Indianapolis's near south side, the Conservatory is open to the public and offers workshops, gardening demonstrations, youth education, and guest lecturers on horticulture and landscaping. A pleasant place any time of year, the Conservatory features a large variety of plants representing the tropical and subtropical regions of the world, with changing floral displays throughout the year. The Sunken Garden is a lovely representation of the European-style formal gardening with a historic fountain display.

INDIANAPOLIS ART CENTER
820 E. 67th St.
(317) 255-2464
www.indplsartcenter.org

Located in Broad Ripple Village, the Indianapolis Art Center offers a treasure house of things to see, buy, and do. The center features more than 50 exhibitions a year plus classes in many different areas to bring out the artist in you. The Frank M. Basile Studio Shop has original works for sale from regional and local artists. Spend some time in ARTSPARK, a 12-acre outdoor sculpture park. Free admission.

INDIANAPOLIS ARTSGARDEN/VISITOR CENTER
100 W. Washington St.
(317) 624-2563
Owned and operated by the Arts Council of Indianapolis, this seven-story-tall glass enclosed structure is a great place to start a visit to Indy.

Built in 1995, the facility offers a spectacular view of the city and is also a wonderful resource to find out what's going on in Indy. An attendant on duty at the official visitor center is available to answer questions about the city. Located at the corner of Illinois and Washington Streets, the Artsgarden is suspended over downtown streets. It offers free performances and exhibits along with ticketing assistance for major exhibits around the city. Elevated walkways link it to Circle Centre, hotels, offices, shops, and restaurants.

INDIANAPOLIS MUSEUM OF CONTEMPORARY ART
340 N. Senate Ave.
(317) 634-6622
www.indymoca.org
An emerging arts organization, the Indianapolis Museum of Contemporary Art has a handy location in two overlapping Indianapolis cultural districts—Indiana Avenue, and The Canal and White River State Park. Exhibits ranging from paintings to graffiti to video art never fail to be interesting. The museum shop is a great place to buy a gift for yourself or someone else. Admission is free.

i Indianapolis is called the "Circle City," a little boy said, because cars at the Indy 500 drive in circles for hours. A cute story but the nickname really came from Alexander Ralston's 19th-century street layout based on concentric circles. At the very center is Monument Circle around the 284-foot-tall Soldiers and Sailors Monument.

INDIANAPOLIS MOTOR SPEEDWAY
4790 W. 16th St.
(800) 822-4639
www.indianapolismotorspeedway.com
Built in 1909, Indianapolis Motor Speedway (IMS) is home to the Indy Racing League's famed Indianapolis 500 and the Brickyard 400 NASCAR race. These events make up the two largest single-day sporting events in the world. The track is the center of activity during the month of May for the Indianapolis 500 and is used for high-speed tire testing throughout most of the year. In 1994

the IMS hosted its first Allstate 400 at the Brickyard NASCAR Sprint Cup Series race. The 160-lap race was the first major racing event other than the "Indy 500" to be held at the Speedway since 1911. In Sept 2008, motorcycle racing returned to the IMS for the first time in nearly a century for MotoGP's Red Bull Indianapolis GP, the world's premier motorcycle road-racing series. The inaugural Red Bull Indianapolis GP race took place on the new 16-turn, 2.601-mile (4.186-kilometer) motorcycle road course at the Speedway. (See the Motorsports chapter for more information. The Speedway also has a museum, which is listed under this chapter's Museums heading.)

INDIANAPOLIS ZOO AND WHITE RIVER GARDENS $$$
1200 W. Washington St.
(317) 630-2001
www.indyzoo.com
The Indianapolis Zoo is the nation's only accredited combined zoo, aquarium, and botanical garden. Located on 64 acres in White River State Park, the "cageless" zoo features 350 different animal species in simulated natural habitats and nearly 18,000 plant specimens. The Zoo is divided into biomes, or natural settings, that replicate African and Australian plains, forests, and deserts of the world and several different water habitats. Its facilities also include the world's first fully submerged underwater Dolphin Adventure, where two tunnels lead to a 12-foot high, 30-foot diameter dome that allows for a 360-degree view of the dolphins. Above water is the world's second-largest, fully enclosed, environmentally controlled dolphin pavilion and the state's largest aquarium. The Zoo's In-Water Dolphin Adventure allows guests to join the trainers waist-deep in the water and come face to face with the dolphins. Other highlights include the new Oceans exhibit featuring a huge shark touch tank, African elephant preserve, and a unique domed desert habitat with free-flying birds. This family-oriented attraction features a variety of seasonal rides, including the city's only roller coaster, a 4-D simulator, and a wet/dry playground. White River Gardens at the Indianapolis Zoo is the site of a

3.3-acre botanical garden with seasonal botanical shows, theme demonstration gardens, and wedding gardens. The gardens also feature a gift shop, restaurant overlooking the downtown skyline, and the 5,000-square-foot Hilbert Conservatory filled with tropical plants. (See the Kidstuff chapter for more details.)

> ℹ️ Smoking is not permitted in the new Lucas Oil Stadium per city-county ordinance that went into effect March 1, 2006. The law prohibits smoking in any enclosed public space. The ban includes the exterior balconies of Lucas Oil Stadium. Smoking is permitted outside, up to the exterior ticketing checkpoints. A pass to go outside and return may be required for some events.

LUCAS OIL STADIUM
500 S. Capitol Ave.
(317) 262-8600
www.lucasoilstadium.com
The new, state-of-the-art, 63,000-seat stadium is the permanent home of the Indianapolis Colts, as well as a venue for future NCAA Division I Men's and Women's Final Fours. Lucas Oil Stadium will also play host to the 2012 Super Bowl. The almost $20 million facility had its grand opening on Aug 14, 2008. Lucas Oil Stadium also is a major site for conventions, exhibitions, trade shows, concerts, and other events. The unique retractable roof makes it exceptionally flexible for both indoor and outdoor events. The roof can be opened or closed in about nine minutes. The seven-level facility covers 1.8 million square feet and features 137 corporate suites, two club lounges, meeting rooms, and two exhibit halls.

MUSEUMS

AMERICAN LEGION HEADQUARTERS AND MUSEUM
700 N. Pennsylvania St.
(317) 630-1200
The home base of the American Legion, the facility also houses a museum and library. Founded in 1919, the American Legion is the largest veterans' organization in the world, with more than 2.8 million members in posts in 50 states and at least 28 foreign countries.

The organization involves itself in the areas of Americanism, children and youth, veterans' affairs, national security, and foreign relations. Free admission.

THE CHILDREN'S MUSEUM OF INDIANAPOLIS $$$
3000 N. Meridian St.
(800) 820-6214
www.childrensmuseum.org
Whether measured by size, number of artifacts, or number of visitors, the Children's Museum of Indianapolis is the world's largest of its kind. Attracting more than a million children and adults each year, the museum has been identified by the American Association of Museums as one of the 20 most visited museums of any kind in the nation. The five-story museum houses 110,000 artifacts in 11 major galleries that explore the physical and natural sciences, history, world cultures, and the arts. Take a ride on a turn-of-the-20th-century carousel, climb a limestone rock wall, dig for fossils, or get a view of the stars at the SpaceQuest Planetarium. In Story Avenue: African-American Voices that Teach Us All, visitors can stop by the city's first permanent African-American exhibit and "eavesdrop" on a family having Sunday dinner or hear a bedtime story. Dinosphere, a multisensory exhibit allowing kids of all ages to get up close and personal with 65 million-year-old animals, is one of the largest displays of real juvenile dinosaurs in the United States. The museum's newest permanent exhibit is "Power of Children," which takes visitors on a journey through the lives of three children, Anne Frank, Ryan White, and Ruby Bridges, who faced profound trials and emerged as heroes of the 20th century. (See the Kidstuff chapter for more details.)

COL. ELI LILLY CIVIL WAR MUSEUM
1 Monument Circle
(317) 232-7615
The Col. Eli Lilly Civil War Museum, located in the lower level of the Soldiers and Sailors Monument,

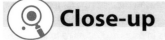 # Close-up

On Her Own Ground: Madame Walker Theatre Center

"I am a woman who came from the cotton fields of the South. From there I was promoted to the washtub. From there I was promoted to the cook kitchen. And from there I promoted myself into the business of manufacturing hair goods and preparations. I have built my own factory on my own ground."

—Madame C. J. Walker

Plagued by a scalp problem, the young mother was losing her hair. Embarrassed by her balding, the woman began to experiment with a variety of homemade remedies. She came up with a product that helped her hair, something that was quickly noticeable at her church. Other churchgoers decided they wanted whatever she was using. From that humble beginning, Madame C. J. Walker became America's first self-made woman millionaire. When she died in 1919, the daughter of former slaves—herself a cotton field worker, laundress, and cook—was worth an estimated $7 million in today's money.

A hard worker, Walker would travel around the country demonstrating her products. As her business grew, Walker knew that she needed a larger factory. That's what brought her to Indianapolis, the crossroads of America, because it was an excellent place to ship her products. She moved her company headquarters here in 1910.

Born into poverty on December 23, 1867, in Delta, Louisiana, Sarah Breedlove was orphaned at 7 when her parents died during a yellow fever epidemic. Sarah and her sister moved across the river to Vicksburg to obtain work as maids. At 14, Sarah married Moses McWilliams to escape her sister's abusive husband. They had a daughter, Lelia. When Lelia was only 2 years old, McWilliams died. Mother and daughter moved to St. Louis, where her brothers had a barbershop. There, the widow worked as a laundry woman. She later moved to Denver and married Charles Joseph Walker—thus the name Madame C. J. Walker. At one point, her thriving empire employed over 3,000 people. The couple divorced around 1910 at the height of her financial success.

An active member of the Indianapolis black community, as well as a social activist and philanthropist, Walker enjoyed music and movies in her free time. But even the successful businesswoman couldn't escape racism. In 1914, Walker went to a movie at the Isis Theatre in

honors the sacrifices made by Indiana citizens who lived, fought, and died during the Civil War. Artifacts, letters, and personal diaries written by Hoosiers during the war are the foundation for the exhibits. The museum takes you on a trip back in time as it follows an Indiana recruit from training to the battlefield and back. The museum is named in honor of Eli Lilly (July 8, 1838–June 6, 1898), an American soldier, pharmaceutical chemist, industrialist, entrepreneur, and founder of the Eli Lilly and Company pharmaceutical corporation, located in Indianapolis. Lilly enlisted in the Union Army during the Civil War and recruited a company of men to serve with him in an artillery battery. He was

later promoted to colonel. Lilly was captured near the end of the way and held as a prisoner until its conclusion. After the war, Lilly worked in several pharmacies with partners before opening his own business in 1876 with plans to manufacture drugs and market them wholesale to pharmacies. Two of the early advances he pioneered were creating gelatin capsules to hold medicine and fruit flavoring for liquid medicines. Lilly became wealthy from the success of his company and engaged in numerous philanthropic pursuits. He personally funded the creation of the city's children's hospital, which was later expanded to become Riley Children's Hospital. The Lilly Endowment remains one of the largest downtown Indianapolis. The ticket seller tried to charge her several times the price of admission to keep her out. Refusing to pay the increased price, Walker returned to her office. She also made a vow: "One day, I will have a theater on my own ground."

Walker didn't live to see that day. She died at age 51 on Sunday, May 25, 1919, from complications of high blood pressure. But eight years after her death, her daughter built a theater on the Indiana Avenue property that Walker had purchased shortly after the Isis Theatre incident. On the triangular-shaped ground, a four-story, block-long flatiron building became home to the corporate offices and factory of the Madame C. J. Walker Manufacturing Company. When it opened its doors in December 1927, the facility also was a forerunner of today's shopping malls, with a drugstore, beauty salon, beauty school, restaurant, professional offices, ballroom, and 1,500-seat theater.

With its African and Egyptian motif, the Walker Theatre was a piece of art. Terra-cotta sculptures of Egyptian sphinxes, brightly painted friezes, decorative 20-foot bamboo spears, elephants holding up the ceiling, and life-size monkey statues posted as sentinels above the stage were part of the African-inspired art deco. The theater showed movies and presented vaudeville acts, including some of the top names in entertainment. Duke Ellington, Count Basie, Lena Horne, the Whitman Sisters, the Blackbirds, and many more graced the Walker Theatre stage. The Walker Theatre was part of the "chitlin' circuit," the name given to a string of performance venues that were safe for black entertainers to perform during the age of racial segregation.

By the 1950s, however, Indiana Avenue, where the Walker Theatre was located, began a gradual decline. People began moving out of the city and didn't come to the Avenue as they used to shop or eat or go to the theater. Finally the theater closed. By the late 1970s, the Walker Building had lost most of its tenants and seemed destined for demolition. But a group of people got together to save the old theater and bring it back to its former grandeur. That wasn't an easy job. After extensive restoration and renovation, the Walker Theatre reopened in October 1988 with a gala featuring the Jimmy Coe Orchestra, actor Roscoe Lee Brown, Rosalind Cash, Isaac Hayes, and Gregory Hines, and *Roots* author Alex Haley. Today, the Madame Walker Theatre Center has a popular performing arts season as well as educational programs, movies, and community activities. Contact the Madame Walker Theatre Center at (317) 236-2099.

charitable benefactors in the world. Lilly is buried in Crown Hill Cemetery. The museum is free.

CONNER PRAIRIE   **$$$**
13400 Allisonville Rd., Fishers
(800) 966-1836
www.connerprairie.org
At this 19th-century living-history museum, Indiana's past becomes the present. Buildings, furnishings, costumes, and even the actors' speech and conversations are thoroughly researched and re-created. Visitors experience many authentic frontier activities, including a camp meeting, a wedding celebration, and a historic baseball game. Discover the Lenape Indian Camp & Trading Post, Blacksmith Studio, 19th-Century Flatboat, 1836 Prairietown, and Liberty Corner, a re-created 1886 town complete with a working farm. Special seasonal programs include Follow the North Star, Symphony on the Prairie, Glorious Fourth, Country Fair, Headless Horseman, and Conner Prairie by Candlelight. (See the Kidstuff chapter for more details.)

CRISPUS ATTUCKS MUSEUM   **$**
1140 Dr. Martin Luther King Jr. St.
(317) 226-2430
Located on the newly renovated campus of the

historic Crispus Attucks Medical Magnet High School, the Crispus Attucks Museum houses memorabilia from the first all-black high school in the state of Indiana. The history-making African American community produced such legends as basketball great Oscar "The Big O" Robinson, jazz sensation Freddie Hubbard, and opera star Angela Brown. The museum's archival collection contains yearbooks dating back to the turn of the 20th century, along with a vast collection of city and state items.

EITELJORG MUSEUM OF AMERICAN
INDIANS AND WESTERN ART $$
500 W. Washington St.
(317) 636-9378
www.eiteljorg.org

The Eiteljorg Museum of American Indians and Western Art opened in 1989 and is located in downtown's White River State Park. The adobe-style museum elicits images of the desert Southwest with its distinctive blend of earth tones. A recent $20 million expansion of the Eiteljorg Museum added the 45,000-square-foot Mel and Joan Perelman Wing. The new wing doubled the museum's exhibit space, including three new galleries, a sculpture court, library, technology center, cafe, and gardens.

Considered one of the finest of its kind in the country, the museum's collection originated with Indianapolis businessman Harrison Eiteljorg, who ventured west looking for coal. While there, he fell in love with the land, the people, and the art. Visitors to the Eiteljorg will experience how the tribes that once lived in what is now Indiana have maintained traditions while adopting new ways of life. The premier event at the museum is Indian Market, which takes place each summer. (See the Kidstuff chapter for more details)

INDIANA HISTORICAL SOCIETY
450 W. Ohio St.
(800) 447-1830
www.indianahistory.org

After closing its exhibits in 2009 for major renovation, the Indiana Historical Society launched a new feature in 2010. In addition to bringing back the popular 1945 grocery, the new Indiana Experience uses super technology to immerse guests in stories of the state's past. Established in 1830, the Indiana Historical Society serves to collect, preserve, and interpret Indiana history. These treasures are housed at the Indiana Historical Society's striking 165,000-square-foot, four-story building situated on downtown Indianapolis's Central Canal, known as the Indiana History Center. There are numerous attractions and programs at the Indiana Historical Society that invite visitors to relive moments from Indiana's rich past. The society boasts an acoustically balanced theater, exhibition gallery, and Great Hall to host interactive exhibits, concerts, plays, workshops and special events. Visitors can listen to the sounds of Hoosier composers and musicians from a Wurlitzer reproduction jukebox or browse through the society's extensive library collection. A gift shop and café complement the list of amenities for visitors to enjoy. A new admission price hadn't been set yet for the renovated facility.

i Frozen in time, the Indiana Medical History Museum represents the beginning of scientific psychiatry and modern medicine. The building itself is the oldest surviving pathology facility in the nation and is listed in the National Register of Historic Places. Make sure to see the 1896 teaching amphitheater, where it is said that students fainted from their chairs during the autopsies.

INDIANA MEDICAL HISTORY MUSEUM $
3045 W. Vermont St.
(317) 635-7329
www.imhm.org

The museum is housed in the historic Pathology Building of the former Central State Hospital. When it opened in 1896, the structure was a medical research and teaching center. Listed in the National Register of Historic Places, it is the oldest surviving pathology laboratories in the United States. The museum features X-ray machines, ophthalmoscopes, old stethoscopes, lab equipment, and other medical artifacts. It may seem barbaric today, but in its time the facility provided physicians in the late 1800s and early 1900s with state-of-the art resources to study mental and nervous disorders. The fascinating collection of 15,000 artifacts educates visitors about the developments that made today's advanced medical treatments possible. The auditorium classroom, labs, and specimens are authentically preserved. The Medicinal Garden is an interesting place with about 90 species of plants.

i The original collection of the Indiana State Museum was started in 1862 during the Civil War when State Librarian R. Deloss Brown began collecting minerals and other curiosities, which he kept in a cabinet. On May 22, 2002, the Indiana State Museum opened its doors at a gigantic new facility in White River State Park.

INDIANA STATE MUSEUM $$
650 W. Washington St.
(317) 232-1637
www.in.gov/ism/

Located in downtown's White River State Park, the Indiana State Museum is easy to find. Just look for the giant prehistoric creatures and listen for the musical strains of "Back Home Again in Indiana." Two giant mastodons were erected outside the museum alongside the canal in 2004. A 17-foot–tall steam clock graces the sidewalk along the canal on the north side of the museum. The clock sounds a few notes of "Back Home Again in Indiana" every 15 minutes, with a more complete version played at the top of every hour. Mike Runyan of the Indianapolis Symphony Orchestra arranged the music to be played on the clock's eight brass whistles.

After you've enjoyed the outside of the museum, plan to spend a long time inside. It is chock-full of fascinating things, including permanent and changing exhibits, two restaurants, a two-story gift shop, and an IMAX Theater. Among the favorites are a re-created Wabash and Erie Canal lock, a hands-on science lab, a working seismograph, and a large pendulum demonstrating the rotation of the Earth. The history of Indiana is

traced through exhibits about pioneer life, Native Americans, and prominent Hoosiers. As if all that weren't enough, in 2010 the museum will debut a Library of Congress exhibition of rare Abraham Lincoln artifacts. The exhibit will include items from a Lincoln Financial Foundation collection that was donated to the State of Indiana. Valued at more than $20 million, the treasured gift is the world's largest private collection of memorabilia from Lincoln's personal and presidential life. Now housed at the museum, the collection includes signed copies of the Emancipation Proclamation and the Thirteenth Amendment, along with Lincoln's wallet and a chair he sat in for some of his most famous photographs. (See the Kidstuff chapter for more details.)

INDIANAPOLIS MOTOR SPEEDWAY HALL OF FAME MUSEUM $
4790 W. 16th St.
(317) 492-6784
www.indianapolismotorspeedway.com

With the most comprehensive collection of historic race cars and automobile memorabilia in the world, the Indianapolis Motor Speedway Hall of Fame Museum is a must-see. The museum allows visitors to get up close with the world of automobiles and auto racing. What is on display is only part of the museum's collection. Items are rotated but some things are on display all the time, like the Marmon Wasp that won the race in 1911.

Started in 1956 in a small building on a corner of the grounds outside the track, the museum opened with six vintage cars from late Speedway owner Tony Hulman. The collection got so big that a new museum was opened in 1976. About a third of the nearly 250,000 visitors who tour the museum each year come in May, when the 2½-mile track hosts the annual Indianapolis 500. About 75 cars are on display at any time. A sleek 1954 Formula One Mercedes-Benz is one of the most valuable cars in the museum. A few years ago, one like it sold in England for about $10 million. Other artifacts on display from Indianapolis 500 winners include trophies, photographs, helmets, and uniforms. Bus rides around the track

(Q) Close-up

Around the State in 92 Sculptures

The 92-County Walk at the Indiana State Museum tells the state's story through original art-work. Sculptures, one for each Indiana county, are designed to depict each region's heritage in a creative way. For example, the sculpture for Adams County (established in 1835 and named for John Quincy Adams) has a lovely greenery design because naturalist/author Gene Stratton-Porter wrote more than 22 books and magazine articles about her experiences at Limberlost Swamp. The swamp encompassed more than 13,000 acres of Adams and adjacent counties before being drained for farming. The sculpture for Spencer County (established in 1818 and named for Spier Spencer) features the face of Abraham Lincoln because the future president spend his youth, from ages 7 to 21, in the county. Referring to the rolling hills and shady forest of what is now Lincoln State Park, the great emancipator reminisced, "Here I grew up." Memorials in the Spencer County include the Lincoln cabin site and the grave of Abraham Lincoln's mother Nancy.

The 92 sculptures and their explanations are scattered around the exterior of the museum. Most are embedded on the building high and low, while some are more cleverly disguised. Challenge yourself to find them all—or grab a free map inside the museum and discover them the easy way.

are offered for a nominal fee when the track is not in use. (See the Motorsports and Kidstuff chapters for more details.)

INDIANAPOLIS MUSEUM OF ART
4000 N. Michigan Rd.
(317) 923-1331
www.imamuseum.org
Founded in 1883, the Indianapolis Museum of Art (IMA) is one of the oldest art museums in the country. It's also one of the nation's largest general art museums, with permanent collections of African, American, Asian, and European art. The IMA houses the largest collection of watercolors by J. M. W. Turner outside of Great Britain, the 2,000-piece Eiteljorg Collection of African Art, and the famous *LOVE* sculpture by Robert Indiana. Following a $180 million renovation and expansion in 2005, the IMA reopened with three new wings, 50 percent more gallery space, an outdoor garden court, new restaurants operated by Wolfgang Puck Catering, expanded educational and family facilities, and other visitor amenities. The project added 164,000 square feet to the museum and included renovation of 90,000

square feet of existing space. The multifaceted project also included the creation of the 100-acre Virginia B. Fairbanks Art & Nature Park, scheduled to open in the spring of 2010. The museum is located on 152 acres of landscaped grounds that include a historic country estate, formal and informal gardens, a working greenhouse, and garden store and gift shop. Admission, parking, and Wi-Fi are all free. The museum is closed Mondays.

MORRIS-BUTLER HOUSE $
1204 N. Park Ave.
(317) 636-5409
www.historiclandmarks.org
Morris-Butler House is a beautifully restored 1865 Second Empire–style home filled with rare furnishings and elegant decorations reflecting the lifestyle of an upper-class Indianapolis family. Themed events and guided tours of the museum emphasize Victorian-era architecture, home decoration, and 19th-century history. Morris-Butler House, located in downtown's historic Old Northside neighborhood, is listed in the National Register of Historic Places. Rooms are adorned with stenciled ceilings, elaborate wallpaper, and plas-

terwork. In addition to its magnificent architecture, the museum contains a collection of 19th-century sculptures, paintings, and lithographs from all over the world. For a special treat, attend one of the elegant Victorian tea programs with raisin scones, cherry tarts, shortbread cookies, chicken salad sandwiches, fresh fruit, and Earl Grey tea. Follow tea with a tour of the Morris-Butler House. The tea and tour costs $22. (Read more about the teas in the Kidstuff chapter.)

NATIONAL ART MUSEUM OF SPORT
850 W. Michigan St.
(317) 274-3627
www.namos.iupui.edu

Housed in University Place on the campus of Indiana University-Purdue University Indianapolis (IUPUI), the National Art Museum of Sport (NAMOS) is the nation's largest collection of sports art, with more than 1,000 paintings, prints, sculptures, and photographs of 44 sports, including ice yachting, auto racing, tennis, and archery. Among the artists represented in the collection are Winslow Homer, Fletcher Martin, George Bellows, and Alfred Boucher. Founded in 1959 by Connecticut artist-sportsman Germain G. Glidden, NAMOS moved to Indianapolis in 1990. The museum's first home was Madison Square Garden in New York City. In 1979 it moved to the University of New Haven. Since being in Indianapolis, the collection has nearly tripled its size. Free admission.

NCAA HALL OF CHAMPIONS $
700 W. Washington St.
(800) 732-6222
www.ncaahallofchampions.org

From the first track and field championship in 1921 to the pageantry and tradition of today's NCAA (National Collegiate Athletic Association) championships in 23 sports, the NCAA Hall of Champions celebrates the journey of the student-athlete. Experience the defeats and triumphs that have fostered student-athletes to become leaders in athletic competition and in careers beyond the courts and fields for more than 85 years. Two levels of exhibits feature interactive displays and award-winning multimedia presentations reflecting what it means to become a champion, from a student-athlete's first competition to a lifetime achievement. Each of the NCAA's 23 championship sports has its own display featuring graphics, relevant artifacts, or memorabilia, as well as photos, video, and several interactive features. NCAA championship banners seasonally grace the curved back wall of this largest exhibit space in the facility. These banners attract proud alums seeking evidence of their school's ultimate success in one of the 23 NCAA sports and 88 championships. (See more details in the Kidstuff chapter).

LANDMARKS

ATHENAEUM
401 E. Michigan St.
(317) 655-2755
www.athenaeumfoundation.com

Built in 1892 as a cultural, social, and athletic club for the German-speaking population of Indianapolis, the Athenaeum was originally called Das Deutsche Haus. German immigrants settled in the state of Indiana from the 1820s through the 1890s, the majority coming after the failed revolution of 1848. Known as "Forty-Eighters," this group was eager to practice their newfound political, religious, and social freedoms. They brought with them the German concept of "club" life. The various German clubs were united under one roof at the Athenaeum. Listed in the National Register of Historic Places, the German Renaissance Revival–style building was designed by Bernhard Vonnegut, the grandfather of noted author and Indianapolis native Kurt Vonnegut Jr. The club includes the Keller Bar, a band shell, banquet facilities, a branch of the YMCA, the American Cabaret Theatre, and the city's oldest restaurant, the Rathskeller.

i The motto inscribed on the East Tower of the Athenaeum reads *"Frisch, Frei, Stark & Treu,"* which means in German "Vibrant, Free, Strong, and Loyal."

(Q) Close-up

USS *INDIANAPOLIS*

Shortly after midnight on July 30, 1945, the USS *Indianapolis* was torpedoed by a Japanese submarine. The ship sank in just 12 minutes. Of the 1,196 men aboard, about 900 made it into the water before the ship went down. Few life rafts were released. Most men had only the standard life jacket to help them survive. Shark attacks began with sunrise and continued until the remaining men were finally rescued five days later. The ship had delivered components for the atomic bomb that would be dropped on Hiroshima, Japan, on August 6. The USS *Indianapolis* had just delivered its top-secret cargo and was returning to the Philippines when it was hit between Guam and Leyte. Because the ship's mission was secret, no one knew it had gone down. No one was looking for it. It wasn't until August 2, that surviving crew members were spotted by chance by a plane flying on routine patrol. The number of men rescued—316.

Situated on the east bank of the Central Canal, the USS *Indianapolis* memorial was built to recognize those who died on the last American ship to sink in World War II. One of only 26 national memorials in the United States, the gray and black granite monument stands in the shape of the USS *Indianapolis* with the story of the sinking etched on one side and the names of all of those who served on the other. Funded by private donations, , the memorial was erected in 1995. The horrific tragedy of the USS *Indianapolis* was recalled in the movie *Jaws* when the character Quint talks about being a survivor of the ship's sinking and the shark attacks.

CANAL WALK
White River State Park
www.indycanalwalk.org

Winding through the heart of Indianapolis, Canal Walk is a lovely vision with lush greenery, old-time street lamps, limestone walls, wonderful views of the White River and the downtown, and sparking fountains with a 17-foot waterfall. The walk is a popular urban respite for fitness enthusiasts and serenity seekers alike. Rent a bike, surrey, pedal boat, or Segway to enjoy the area or look for a gondola on the canal. The canal was originally engineered in the 1830s as a way to ship goods through the state of Indiana. But the project went bankrupt and the Indiana section of the canal was the only piece that was ever dug. Although the canal was never used for what it was built for, recent restoration and development have helped make it a cultural part of Indy. The "new" version of the Central Canal, now known as the Indianapolis Canal Walk, generally follows the path of the original Central Canal from 11th Street to West Washington Street. It passes by residential complexes, the USS *Indianapolis* Memorial, and through the center of White River State Park.

CHRIST CHURCH CATHEDRAL
125 Monument Circle
(317) 636-4577
www.cccindy.org

Built in 1857 on Monument Circle, this Episcopalian house of worship is the oldest church building in Indianapolis. An excellent example of the English Gothic "country church" style of architecture, it has steep gables, tall windows with pointed arches, a spire, bell tower, and in the interior, wooden trusses and stained glass by Tiffany. Public tours are available, free of charge, on Saturday afternoons and Sundays following the last morning service.

i Actor James Baskett (1904–1948) is buried in Crown Hill Cemetery. He is best known for the role of Uncle Remus in Disney's *Song of the South.*

CROWN HILL CEMETERY
700 W. 38th St.
(800) 809-3366
www.crownhill.org
Established in 1863 just north of downtown Indianapolis, this historic cemetery is the third largest in the country and one of the largest natural areas in Marion County. Notable burials and memorials include President Benjamin Harrison, three vice presidents, Hoosier poet James Whitcomb Riley, and infamous bank robber John Dillinger. Resting in the beautiful cemetery are almost 200,000 people from all walks of life and eras of Indiana history. So popular is the cemetery that Crown Hill offers many tours and events throughout the year. Themes of tours include Skeletons in the Closet, Civil War, Art and Architecture, Women of Crown Hill, Victorian, and, of course, the popular John Dillinger tour. Born in Indiana, the gangster was gunned down by the FBI on the streets of Chicago in 1934. Cemetery admission is free; tours are $5.

i Crown Hill Cemetery is the third largest cemetery in the United States at 555 acres. It contains 25 miles of paved road, over 150 species of trees and plants, and more than 185,000 graves.

HILBERT CIRCLE THEATRE
45 Monument Circle
(317) 231-6798
www.hilbertcircletheatreindy.com
Built in 1916, the Hilbert Circle Theatre was known as the Midwest's best performance house for traveling entertainers, silent movies, world premiere features, classical concerts, and talking motion pictures. After a restoration and preservation of the theater's ornate Greco-Roman architecture in 1982, it became the home of the internationally acclaimed Indianapolis Symphony Orchestra. The theater seats 1,786 and is listed in the National Register of Historic Places.

INDIANA STATEHOUSE
Corner of West Washington Street and
Capitol Avenue
(317) 233-5293
Completed in 1888 and built of Indiana limestone, this Renaissance Revival–style structure has been the center of Indiana government for more than 100 years. Focal points are the stained-glass rotunda, Supreme Court, House and Senate chambers, and the governor's office. The 9-acre Capitol complex is home to all three branches of government. The statehouse is bounded by West Washington Street, Capitol Avenue, Senate Avenue, and Ohio Street. Self-guided tour brochures are available at the information desk or tour office. Guided tours also are offered. Free.

i Dr. John S. Bobbs (1809–1870) is buried in Crown Hill Cemetery. Founder of Indiana Medical College, the doctor in 1867 performed the first gall bladder surgery in the country.

INDIANA STATE LIBRARY
140 N. Senate Ave.
(317) 232-3675
www.in.gov/library
Founded in 1825 and housed in an art deco building, the Indiana State Library has extensive research collections in genealogy and Indiana history, including the most complete collection of Indiana newspapers in the world. The library serves as a depository for state and federal documents and maintains several special programs, including the Indiana Talking Book and Braille Library, the Indiana State Data Center, and the Indiana Center for the Book. Exhibits and public programs are presented regularly. Free.

INDIANA THEATER BUILDING AND INDIANA ROOF BALLROOM
140 W. Washington St.
(317) 635-5277
www.indianaroof.com
Built in 1927, this luxurious one-time movie palace features a terra-cotta auditorium and facade based on 17th-century Spanish architecture. The historic downtown gem was saved from the wrecking ball when the 3,000-seat theater was separated into three stages in 1984 to become the permanent home of the Indiana Repertory Theatre (IRT), the

Close-up

President Benjamin Harrison Home

When Benjamin Harrison ran for president in 1888, he made speeches from the front stoop and side porch of his home at 1230 N. Delaware St. In his "front porch campaign," the Republican spoke about 80 times to almost 300,000 people. He won the presidency but he also learned a sad lesson. People who came to hear his speeches at his home took the pickets from his fence. A newspaper report in November 1888 noted that "every little article about the yard has since disappeared." Even the bricks in his pavement were carted off by relic hunters.

During the campaign, banners, torches, and flags were carried in parades through downtown Indianapolis. People also carried large brooms symbolizing a "Clean Sweep with Harrison." Harrison was also known as the "Log Cabin President"—a direct pitch to the common man. Harrison's grandfather William Henry Harrison had used the log cabin symbol in 1840. Erecting log cabins around the country for campaign headquarters was a device used by both Harrisons. Benjamin Harrison altered his grandfather's famous slogan, "Tippecanoe and Tyler too!" to reflect his vice presidential running mate Levi P. Morton of New York. It became "Tippecanoe and Morton too!" The Tippecanoe Club was formed in 1888 for Benjamin Harrison. It was made up of men who had voted in 1841 for William Henry Harrison and were supporting Benjamin in 1888.

Election trivia abounds at the Harrison home. Visitors can see how campaigning has changed over the years. Early presidential candidates in this country thought it was improper to show any "lust" for winning the office. Election was an honor, not something to be sought. Each candidate published a philosophy of government, and voters were expected to read these so they could make an informed choice. Commemorative pieces were produced, rather than campaign pieces. But the fierce 1828 election between Andrew Jackson and John Quincy Adams signaled the beginning of change for election protocol.

By 1840, "Tippecanoe and Tyler Too!" created a boom of campaign banners, buttons, ribbons, and trinkets. Political rallies larger than ever seen before—"15 acres of men"—parades, songs, marches, speeches, and a multitude of regionally produced campaign souvenirs stirred up the election frenzy. Campaigns became the equivalent of a modern-day sporting event.

state's premier resident professional not-for-profit theater. Visitors can see the grand lobby, the main stage (where the IRT performs its season), the upper stage, and the Cabaret Theatre, displaying a collection of costumes and theater props. Housed in the same building, the Indiana Roof Ballroom is a beautifully restored ballroom designed to resemble the plaza of a Spanish village, featuring a 40-foot domed ceiling of stars and clouds.

LOCKERBIE SQUARE
Bounded by College Avenue and Michigan, East, and New York Streets
(317) 638-9368
www.lockerbiesquare.org

Lockerbie Square, where the James Whitcomb Riley home is located, is a restored 19th-century downtown residential area. The oldest Indianapolis neighborhood to be included in the National Register of Historic Places, Lockerbie is characterized by old-fashioned streetlights, a cobblestone street, and many restored homes, condominiums, and apartment buildings. The neighborhood was described over a century ago by James Whitcomb Riley as being "nestled away from the noise of the city and heat of the day." A free walking tour map can be downloaded from the Lockerbie Square Web site.

On election night in 1888, Benjamin Harrison was at home with his family and friends. A special telegraph wire was installed connecting the Harrison home directly with New York, where the national returns were tabulated. Harrison lost the popular vote by a small margin but he won the Electoral College vote.

Harrison carried all the northern and western states except New Jersey and Connecticut. With Whitelaw Reid as his running mate, Harrison ran for reelection in 1892 against Grover Cleveland. This time, Harrison lost. After Cleveland took office, Harrison returned to Indianapolis, where he lived until his death from complications of pneumonia on March 13, 1901. He is buried in Crown Hill cemetery in Indianapolis.

Today, the Harrison home is a museum. Built in 1874–75, the 16-room Italianate Victorian home was considered a gem in its era. Harrison and his wife, Caroline, choose everything from the interior layout to the Italianate red brick design. Unusual for its day, it featured running water in the kitchen, washroom, and second-floor bathroom, along with a coal-fed furnace and 23 working gaslight fixtures. Harrison became the first U.S. president to use electric light in the White House. Upon returning home, he fitted the gas fixtures with electric wiring. Eighty percent of the furnishings belonged to the family. Above the fireplace in the back parlor is T. C. Steele's 1902 portrait of Harrison, the most popular image of the 23rd president.

One of the most unusual items at the museum is a letter from a little schoolgirl in 1892. Caroline Harrison was sick while she was First Lady, and schoolchildren were asked to write letters to her. One letter in particular was signed by a "little unknown friend." Handwritten in flowing and careful letters, the message asks the ailing First Lady to "let them speak to you in voices soft and low" of the love and regards being sent her way. The letter was written by Helen Keller when she was 12 years old. Although she was blind, Keller had painstakingly written the letter using a form to keep the lines straight. Caroline Harrison died of tuberculosis in the White House in October 1892.

Contact the President Benjamin Harrison Home at (317) 631-1888.

MONUMENT CIRCLE
Meridian and Market Streets

The geographic heart of Indianapolis, Monument Circle is the large circular plaza at the union of Meridian and Market Streets. At the center of the Circle is the Soldiers and Sailors Monument. The 4 city blocks that front the Circle are bounded by Ohio Street to the north, Pennsylvania Street to the east, Washington Street to the south, and Illinois Street to the west. The busy plaza is today surrounded by small shops, radio station studios, the Hilbert Circle Theatre, financial institutions, the Columbia Club (one of the oldest social clubs in Indianapolis), and the historic Christ Church Cathedral. The Circle did not always host a monu-ment. Originally, it was designated Governor's Circle because the governor's residence stood in the center of the brick traffic circle. Every Christmas, the monument is decorated as an enormous Christmas tree. Known as the Circle of Lights, the city tradition has been done every year since 1962. The actual tree-lighting ceremony is held the day after Thanksgiving, and the Circle is packed with revelers.

PAN AMERICAN PLAZA
201 S. Capitol Ave.
(317) 237-5565

American Plaza was built to commemorate the Pan American Games held in Indianapolis in

1987. The structure includes a 12-story office building, two Olympic-size indoor ice-skating rinks, and a brick plaza adorned with fountains and landscaping. The plaza is often used for outdoor festivals and performances

OLD NORTHSIDE NEIGHBORHOOD
www.oldnorthside.org
Located about a mile north and several blocks east of the center of downtown Indianapolis, the area now known as Old Northside was the home, during the second half of the 19th century, of the principal leaders of Indianapolis's social, political, commercial, and industrial life, as well as the location of leading religious and educational institutions. The 190-acre neighborhood features Victorian architecture in restored Queen Anne, Free Classic, and Italianate residences. The President Benjamin Harrison Home is located in the Old Northside neighborhood and is open for tours.

i The Indianapolis Visitors Guide is a free guide produced by the Indianapolis Convention & Visitors Association. Two handy downtown locations to pick up the guide are the Indiana Artsgarden at Illinois and Washington Streets and the White River State Park Visitors Center at 801 W. Washington St. Contact the association at (800) 616-4639.

SCOTTISH RITE CATHEDRAL
650 N. Meridian St.
(800) 489-3579
www.aasr-indy.org
The International Association of Architects designated this downtown Gothic-Tudor structure, containing a 54-bell carillon and a 7,000-pipe organ, as "one of seven architectural wonders of the world" shortly after completion in 1929. Built by the Freemasons, the cathedral features hand-carved woodwork and elaborate stained-glass windows, all adorned with Masonic symbols. Today, the cathedral is a site for special events and performing arts. Free guided tours are given weekdays.

i For the last three years, the Lawn at White River State Park has been named one of the top 100 outdoor concert venues in the world by *Pollstar* magazine.

WHITE RIVER STATE PARK
801 W. Washington St.
(800) 655-9056
Located on 250 acres in downtown Indianapolis, White River State Park is Indiana's only urban state park. A city center for recreation and attractions, White River State Park is home to the Eiteljorg Museum of American Indians and Western Art, the NCAA Headquarters and Hall of Champions, Indiana State Museum, Indianapolis Zoo, Victory Field, the Lawn, and Indianapolis Canal Walk. A public sculpture program that started in 1999 features the work of Hoosier artists on the Washington Street Bridge and in the park's green spaces. Summer is a special treat at the Lawn at White River State Park. On a waterfront stage with seating for 6,000, the Lawn offers first-rate concerts in a beautiful outdoor setting.

MEMORIALS

INDIANA LAW ENFORCEMENT AND FIRE FIGHTERS MEMORIAL
Indiana Statehouse, corner of Government Way and Senate Avenue
Dedicated before the World Police and Fire Games in 2001, this $1 million memorial stands as a tribute to the more than 600 Indiana police and firefighters who have given their lives in the line of duty. Located on the west side of the Indiana Statehouse, the crescent-shaped park features statues inscribed with the names of the fallen heroes.

CONGRESSIONAL MEDAL OF HONOR MEMORIAL
650 W. Washington St.
(317) 261-6646
The only memorial designed to recognize recipients of the nation's highest military honor is in downtown Indianapolis. The memorial gives tribute to 3,440 Medal of Honor recipients, an

award that is given by Congress for military valor. The one-acre memorial is located on the north side of downtown's Central Canal in White River State Park. It represents 15 different conflicts, ranging from the Civil War through Somalia, and is composed of 27 curved walls of glass, each between 7 and 10 feet high. Each day at dusk, the memorial's sound system plays recorded stories of medal winners or of the conflicts in which they fought. The memorial was dedicated on May 28, 1999, the last Memorial Day weekend of the 20th century.

i Although Military Park was a Civil War encampment, the 14-acre green space drew its name not from its past but from its shape—like a military badge.

MILITARY PARK
601 W. New York St.
(317) 846-4979
Bounded by West, New York, and Blackford Streets and the Central Canal, this 14-acre park is the oldest in the city. Over the years, Military Park has had many uses. The city's first recorded Fourth of July celebration was held here in 1822. In 1836, militia gathered here to prepare for the Black Hawk War. The first Indiana State Fair was held at this location in Oct 1852. At the outbreak of the Civil War, the park quickly became a military camp used for the recruitment and training of troops. In recent years, Military Park has been used for gatherings of political groups and for festivals, such as the Indy Jazz Fest, Rib America's Rib Fest, and the Indy Irish Festival.

i Soldiers and Sailors Monument has been decorated for Christmas since 1945. Since 1962, the monument has become a Christmas tree, said to be the largest in the world.

SOLDIERS AND SAILORS MONUMENT
1 Monument Circle
(317) 232-7615

Located at the geographic center of Indianapolis on Monument Circle, this 284-foot-tall limestone monument was dedicated in 1902 and stands as a tribute to the valor of Indiana's soldiers and sailors who served in the Civil and Spanish American Wars. An observation tower, accessible by elevator or 32 flights of stairs, provides a panoramic view of the city skyline. You can climb 333 stairs or pay $1 to ride the elevator. Constructed of Indiana limestone and featuring exterior historical and mythological sculptures, the monument is crowned by "Miss Victory."

WAR MEMORIAL PLAZA AND AMERICAN LEGION MALL
Dominating the picturesque, 5-block setting of War Memorial Plaza in downtown Indianapolis is the Indiana War Memorial. Sitting 210-feet above street level, this mausoleum-style limestone and marble memorial pays homage to Hoosiers killed during World Wars I and II, the Korean War, and the Vietnam War. The Shrine Room, with 24 stained-glass windows, is a magnificent architectural setting for the 17-by-30-foot American flag that is suspended from the center of the room. The main floor houses exhibit space, including a listing of all Hoosiers who participated in World War I and all Hoosiers who were killed or are MIA from World War II, Korea, and Vietnam. A military museum in the basement allows visitors to follow the history of Indiana soldiers from the Battle of Tippecanoe through the most recent conflicts.

North of the memorial is the American Legion Mall, a parklike setting that includes the American Legion State and National Headquarters, as well as the Vietnam, Korean, and World War II memorials. Also located on the grounds are Veterans' Memorial Plaza, where the flags of all 50 states fly, and University Park, which features the Depew fountain and statues of Abraham Lincoln, Benjamin Harrison, and Schuyler Colfax, a former U.S. representative from Indiana and vice president of the United States.

KIDSTUFF

No doubt about it, Indianapolis is a kid-friendly place. If you ask someone why they choose to live in the Hoosier capital, the answer is often that "It's a good place to raise a family." It's also a great place to visit with a family.

That's not an exaggeration either. After all, Indianapolis is home to the world's largest children's museum and one of the biggest city parks in the nation. You'll see whole families heading to local sporting events, concerts, and festivals. For a wonderful holiday tradition, bundle up and watch the annual Circle of Lights in downtown Indy the day after Thanksgiving. It's sure to warm your heart to see all the bright young faces watching Monument Circle come alive with thousands of lights, giant toy soldiers, and old St. Nick himself.

This chapter points out some kid-friendly activities and fun spots. It's only a drop in the bucket of what children love to see and do in Indy. Use this as a start to make your own family memories. It's stuff like this that your children will remember for the rest of their lives.

Price Code

Admission prices can change, but use this price code as a guide.

$.......................$1 to $5
$$ ....$6 to $10
$$$ .... $11 to $15
$$$$ ....$16 and up

ARTSY STUFF

INDIANAPOLIS MUSEUM OF ART   FREE
4000 N. Michigan Rd.
(317) 923-1331
www.imamuseum.org
Kids can create their own art project inspired by works of art in the permanent collection of the Indianapolis Museum of Art. Projects are designed to be accessible and fun for visitors of all ages and levels of experience in making art. The free art sessions are offered Sat from noon to 4 p.m.

Founded in 1883, the Indianapolis Museum of Art (IMA) is one of the oldest art museums in the country. It's also one of the nation's largest general art museums, with permanent collections of African, American, Asian, and European art. The IMA houses the largest collection of watercolors by J. M. W. Turner outside of Great Britain, the 2,000-piece Eiteljorg Collection of African Art and the famous *LOVE* sculpture by Robert Indiana. The museum is located on 152 acres of landscaped grounds that include a historic country estate, formal and informal gardens, a working greenhouse, and garden store and gift shop. Admission, parking, and Wi-Fi are all free. The museum is closed on Monday.

KILN CREATIONS $$
918 Broad Ripple Ave.
(317) 251-2386
www.kilncreations.biz
Kids of all ages are welcome at Kiln Creations, where they can create a piece of pottery or a mosaic. Everything needed is provided, including encouragement. Select a piece of unfinished pottery, create a design; choose from over 40 colors, and paint the piece. The studio will glaze and fire the pottery, and it will be ready for pickup in a week.

i In 1854, the average length of the annual school term in Indiana was just over two and a half months.

CRITTER STUFF

INDIANAPOLIS ZOO AND WHITE RIVER
GARDENS $$$
1200 W. Washington St.
(317) 630-2001
www.indyzoo.com
Come face to face with dolphins, touch a shark, see giraffes munch from leaves on trees, watch elephants socialize by a waterhole, and pet a Shetland pony. At the Indianapolis Zoo, children can do all this and more. The Indianapolis Zoo is the nation's only accredited combined zoo, aquarium, and botanical garden. Located on 64 acres in White River State Park, the "cageless" zoo features 350 different animal species in simulated natural habitats and nearly 18,000 plant specimens.

i During really hot weather, the Indianapolis Zoo has misting stations for visitors in the Forests and Plains Biomes, as well as the Splash Park play area with water features for children. You may wish to bring a change of clothes for the children so they can get wet and cool off.

The Zoo is divided into biomes, or natural settings, that replicate African and Australian plains, forests and deserts of the world, and several different water habitats. Its facilities also include the world's first fully submerged underwater Dolphin Adventure, where two tunnels lead to a 12-foot high, 30-foot diameter dome that allows for a 360-degree view of the dolphins. Above water is the world's second-largest, fully enclosed, environmentally controlled dolphin pavilion and the state's largest aquarium. The Zoo's In-Water Dolphin Adventure allows guests to join the trainers waist-deep in the water and come face to face with the dolphins. Other highlights include the new Oceans exhibit featuring a huge shark touch tank, African elephant preserve, and a unique domed desert habitat with free-flying birds. This family-oriented attraction features a variety of seasonal rides, including the

city's only roller coaster, a 4-D simulator, and a wet/dry playground. White River Gardens at the Indianapolis Zoo is the site of a 3.3-acre botanical garden, with seasonal botanical shows, theme demonstration gardens, and wedding gardens. The gardens also feature a gift shop, restaurant overlooking the downtown skyline, and the 5,000-square-foot Hilbert Conservatory filled with tropical plants.

MUSEUM STUFF

THE CHILDREN'S MUSEUM OF
INDIANAPOLIS $$$
3000 N. Meridian St.
(800) 820-6214
www.childrensmuseum.org
With a quizzical look on his face, the boy stopped in his tracks outside the Children's Museum of Indianapolis. Then the questions started. "What are those dinosaurs doing?" he asked. "Where are they going? Is the big one the mother and the little ones the babies? What's the name of the big dinosaur?"

And so it went. With happy patience, the father provided as many answers as he could as quickly as possible. For many families, that is an important reason for visiting the popular museum, exactly what the folks who created the museum had in mind. Curiosity leads to discovery, and the museum encourages questions and hands-on experiences.

What you won't see are the customary DON'T TOUCH signs. Here kids can find a zillion touchable things in seven zones for playing and learning. For starters, pretend to be an earthworm and crawl through the "dirt" at ScienceWorks in the Dow Science Center. At the Fossil Dig, grab a small trowel and find, collect, identify, chart, and classify fossils representing life from long ago. Beyond this area, a 20-foot artificial stone wall affords three distinct climbing challenges.

Whether measured by size, number of artifacts, or number of visitors, The Children's Museum of Indianapolis is the world's largest of its kind. Attracting more than a million children and adults each year, the museum has been

🔍 Close-up

Zoo Animals Live on Realistic Turf

It's high noon and two lizards are having a stare-down. They coldly eye each other, watching for some signal of aggression. Finally, in a surprise move, one of the lizards turns tail and scurries into a "hide tube." Another showdown has been averted at the Indianapolis Zoo.

Attention to detail in the Deserts exhibit has provided such important extras as escape routes if a lizard finds itself in the middle of a turf battle or is being pursued by a rambunctious young visitor. All these extras have helped the zoo reach its overall goal of immersing visitors in the natural habitats of its animals. The zoo's success in breeding some of the rarest desert reptiles also has given the Hoosier attraction an enviable worldwide reputation.

To reach its goals, the Indianapolis Zoo doesn't mind going to extremes. For the Deserts Biome, the zoo staff spent two weeks in Tucson, Arizona, making rubber molds of actual rocks that decorate its deserts. Every nook, crack, and crevice of the rocks in the biome has a twin in Tucson.

Upon return to Indianapolis, the molds were used to shape fiberglass and then sprayed with concrete. The granite gravel lining the floor of the exhibit was trucked in from Arizona, and the giant rocks were painted to match the color of the gravel.

The rocks are situated to form a canyon and river and to sculpt a walkway through the dome for visitors. Larger animals are glassed into the exhibit areas, but the birds and smaller lizards roam freely throughout the dome. The 80-foot transparent dome allows animals to bask in natural sunlight year-round while heating and air-conditioning vents hidden in the rocks keep the temperature in the 80s. For overcast days, 15 rocks and six mats throughout the dome are heated to 115 degrees to simulate the warmth of sunlight for the cold-blooded reptile and tortoises.

But the Deserts Biome is only one part of the Indianapolis Zoo. Unlike many zoos that organize animals according to taxonomy—such as birds, mammals, reptiles, etc.—the Indianapolis Zoo arranges exhibits according to the biomes in which plants and animals are found. At the 64-acre zoo, visitors can spend hours watching the ever-changing animals and landscapes in the different biomes.

identified by the American Association of Museums as one of the 20 most visited museums of any kind in the nation. The five-story museum houses 110,000 artifacts in 11 major galleries that explore the physical and natural sciences, history, world cultures, and the arts. The museum's newest permanent exhibit is "Power of Children," which takes visitors on a journey through the lives of three children, Anne Frank, Ryan White, and Ruby Bridges, who faced profound trials and emerged as heroes of the 20th century.

The $25 million Dinosphere at the Children's Museum opened in 2004 and draws curious minds galore. Spellbound youngsters journey back 65 million years to when dinosaurs ruled the earth. Along with one of the largest displays of real dinosaur fossils in the nation, Dinosphere also has a functioning Paleo Lab, a hands-on dig, interactive stations and activities, and one of the finest collections of dinosaur art in America. And the museum is easy to find—just look for the huge dinosaurs outside the facility, a sure eye-catcher that lets you know you've arrived.

ℹ️ How does the world's largest children's museum keep track of time? With the largest water clock in North America. Designed by French physicist and artist Bernard Gitton, the clock is 26½ feet tall and uses 70 gallons of a solution of water, methyl alcohol, and food coloring. The alcohol prevents algae and fungus from growing inside the pipes, while the food coloring allows visitors to see the clock's function more clearly. The water clock works on three basic principles of physics: Energy cannot be destroyed, only changed; gravity pulls objects down to the lowest possible level; and water seeks its own level.

CONNER PRAIRIE $$$
13400 Allisonville Rd., Fishers
(800) 966-1836
www.connerprairie.org

At this 19th-century living-history museum, Indiana's past becomes the present. Buildings, furnishings, costumes, and even the actors' speech and conversations are thoroughly researched and re-created. Visitors experience many authentic frontier activities, including a camp meeting, a wedding celebration, and a historical ·baseball game. Discover the Lenape Indian Camp & Trading Post, Blacksmith Studio, 19th-Century Flatboat, 1836 Prairietown, and Liberty Corner, a re-created 1886 town complete with a working farm. Special seasonal programs include Follow the North Star, Symphony on the Prairie, Glorious Fourth, Country Fair, Headless Horseman, and Conner Prairie by Candlelight.

EITELJORG MUSEUM OF AMERICAN
INDIANS AND WESTERN ART $$
500 W. Washington St.
(317) 636-9378
www.eiteljorg.org

A little girl fashioned some dried corn husks into a doll. A boy wrapped fabric around some sticks for a tepee. And two children climbed into a stagecoach for a make-believe ride. At the Eiteljorg Museum, children have more options than "look but don't touch." Helping children have a hands-on experience is a goal of the education center. Discovery Junction on the canal level of the museum is home of the Cheyenne to Deadwood stagecoach, 1876 era clothes to try on, a saddle to straddle, buffalo chips to toss, and a chance for children to create their own cattle brand.

The Eiteljorg Museum of American Indians and Western Art opened in 1989 and is located in downtown's White River State Park. The adobe-style museum elicits images of the desert Southwest with its distinctive blend of earth tones. Considered one of the finest of its kind in the country, the museum's collection originated with Indianapolis businessman Harrison Eiteljorg, who ventured west looking for coal. While there, he fell in love with the land, the people, and the art. Visitors to the Eiteljorg will experience how the tribes that once lived in what is now Indiana have maintained traditions while adopting new ways of life. The premier event at the museum is Indian Market, which takes place each summer. The museum also has a neat place to eat, the Sky Café, which offers a kids' menu with items such as maize (corn) dogs, tacos, chicken fingers, and grilled cheese served with fresh fruit and a child's beverage.

INDIANA STATE MUSEUM $$
650 W. Washington St.
(317) 232-1637
www.in.gov/ism

A group of children are trying their hands at toting water and churning butter—part of the Pioneer Indiana section of the Indiana State Museum. With a big grin on his face, one boy asked his friend to take a super whiff of something in a container at Pioneer Indiana. Bending over, the buddy knew immediately what he is smelling—horse manure, something that would have been plentiful in pioneer Indiana.

Located in downtown's White River State Park, the Indiana State Museum helps make history come alive for youngsters. Just look for the giant prehistoric creatures and listen for the musical strains of "Back Home Again in Indiana." Two giant mastodons were erected outside the museum alongside the canal in 2004. A 17-foot–

tall steam clock graces the sidewalk along the canal on the north side of the museum. The clock sounds a few notes of "Back Home Again in Indiana" every 15 minutes, with a more complete version played at the top of every hour.

After you've enjoyed the outside of the museum, plan to spend a long time inside. It is chock-full of fascinating things, including permanent and changing exhibits, two restaurants, a two-story gift shop, and an IMAX Theater. A naturalist lab is a favorite museum stop, where a special computer program plays the sound of a critter, then asks a youngster to try imitating that sound. The recorded imitation is then played back to peals of laughter.

Discovery Carts are also a great way to get curious minds working as soon as they come in the museum. Located in the lobby, the various carts have themes and artifacts to illustrate various subjects. One of the carts, for instance, has owl pellets that are dissected to show what the owl had for dinner. Another cart features instruments that medics used during the Civil War.

INDIANA TRANSPORTATION MUSEUM $$
Forest Park on SR 19 near downtown
Noblesville
(317) 773-6000
www.itm.org
Railroads are fascinating to kids, and the Indiana Transportation Museum lets them get up close and personal with the transportation giants. Examine steam, diesel, and electric trains and even take a ride on the former Nickel Plate Railroad. A train runs on Saturday from Labor Day through Halloween. A special Polar Express with Santa, Mrs. Claus, and the Polar Bear delights during the Christmas holiday. During the two-hour trip, children hear a train-related story and enjoy goodies. Polar Express tickets cost about $18.

MORRIS-BUTLER HOUSE $$$
1204 N. Park Ave.
(317) 636-5409
www.historiclandmarks.org
Miss Manners would be proud! Children ages 7 to 12 are invited for a tea party and etiquette lesson.

The historic home will serve delicious cinnamon-raisin scones with jam, Victorian Snow Cake, strawberry tarts, cucumber sandwiches, jam sandwiches, and tea cookies in its beautifully restored dining room and library. Children also will learn about manners as they munch, daintily, of course. A tour of the Morris-Butler House will follow the tea so that children can see where Anna, Alice, Florence, and Mary "Brownie" Butler lived. Children also will play some Victorian games and make a craft to take home. The Children's Tea is offered several times a year. Reservations are required. The 1865 Second Empire–style home is filled with rare furnishings and elegant decorations reflecting the lifestyle of an upper-class Indianapolis family. Family fun days also are offered throughout the year and offer children a chance to see what life was like in another century.

OUTDOOR STUFF

CANAL WALK
White River State Park
www.indycanalwalk.org
Rent a bike, pedal boat, or Segway or let a gondolier steer you down this lovely Canal Walk. Winding through the heart of Indianapolis, Canal Walk is a beautiful vision with lush greenery, old-time street lamps, limestone walls, wonderful views of the White River and the downtown, and sparking fountains with a 17-foot waterfall. The walk is a popular urban respite for fitness enthusiasts and serenity seekers alike.

The canal was originally engineered in the 1830s as a way to ship goods through the state of Indiana. But the project went bankrupt and the Indiana section of the canal was the only piece that was ever dug. Although the canal was never used for what it was built for, recent restoration and development have helped make it a cultural part of Indy. The "new" version of the Central Canal, now known as the "Indianapolis Canal Walk," generally follows the path of the original Central Canal from 11th Street to West Washington Street. It passes by residential complexes, the USS *Indianapolis* Memorial, and through the center of White River State Park.

CONNER PRAIRIE $$$$
13400 Allisonville Rd., Fishers
(800) 966-1836
www.connerprairie.org

Children can explore their inner adventurer or budding artist at Conner Prairie summer day camps in June and July. For children ages 5 to 14, Adventure Camp explores from water to land. Conquer the White River by canoe, tube, or pedal boat. Then get down and dirty on the challenge course, hike the backwoods of Conner Prairie, or fish for big-mouth bass in the pond. At Art Camp, children ages 8 to 14 can try weaving, painting, drawing, acting, pottery, crafts, and more. Prices are about $185 for a week of day camp. Conner Prairie offers many other programs and activities. Check out the Web site to see what is happening.

STONYCREEK FARM $
11366 SR 38 East, Noblesville
(317) 773-3344

What started as a small pumpkin patch has grown to become a place where children can have a real farm experience. The 1860s-era farm situated on 50 acres of rolling farmland and woods is now the home of the annual Pumpkin Harvest Festival. The farm was named after Stony Creek, which meanders through the property. The creek was an Indian trade route and site of an old gristmill.

The annual festival runs from the last week in Sept through the end of Oct. Visitors can take a hayride through the woods to a secluded pumpkin patch to pick their own pumpkin. Other attractions include face painting, farm animals, pony rides, and a fishing pond. The parking fee is $5 per car and $1 for the hayride to the pumpkin patch. Other activities have additional charges.

SHOPPING STUFF

KIDS INK CHILDREN'S BOOKSTORE
5619 N. Illinois St.
(317) 255-2598

Find favorite books and toys at this shop, where kids can browse to their hearts' content.

MUDSOCK BOOKS & CURIOSITY SHOPPE
11631 Fishers Station Dr., Fishers
(317) 579-9822

Mudsock Books & Curiosity Shoppe provides a mix of new and used books, family games, puzzles, science kits, and other gift items. If you want to take your time, the shop has a warm cozy atmosphere, comfy chairs, a cup of coffee, and more.

WAYNE'S TRAINS
6742 E. Washington St.
(317) 375-0832
www.waynestrains.biz

Train fans will love this place. Wayne's features a large selection of model railroad supplies and detail parts, books, Thomas the Tank Engine and Friends, die-cast race cars, rockets, and free-flight and die-cast model airplanes.

SLEEPOVER STUFF

CROWNE PLAZA AT HISTORIC UNION STATION
123 W. Louisiana St.
(317) 631-2221
www.ichotelsgroup.com

Kids will get a kick out of sleeping in a real railroad car still resting on its original track. Located in the midst of downtown Indy, the Crowne Plaza is housed within America's first Union Station. Listed in the National Register of Historic Places, the Crowne Plaza offers 273 rooms, including 26 authentic Pullman train car sleepers. The railcars are named and decorated in honor of prominent personalities from the early 1900s, such as Louis Armstrong. Look for the white fiberglass ghost travelers dressed in period clothing and still lovingly haunting the premises. The hotel features an indoor swimming pool and a restaurant with a nice breakfast buffet.

HOLIDAY INN NORTH AT THE PYRAMIDS
3850 DePauw Blvd.
(317) 872-9790
www.holidayinn.com

Spend the night at Holiday Inn North and enjoy

the exciting fun of the Caribbean Cove Indoor Water Park. The attached 50,000-square-foot indoor water park features swimming pools, water and tube slides, a leisure river, and a sports activity pool. The hotel is near I-465, the circular interstate that surrounds the city, so you'll have easy access to everything. Reserve the Caribbean Cove Package at the hotel. You can also grab a bite to eat the Calypso Cafe, then enjoy more fun at Crazy CoCo's Arcade.

SPORTY STUFF

INDIANAPOLIS INDIANS   **$$**
Victory Field 501 W. Maryland St.
(317) 269-3545
www.indyindians.com
Buy the cheap seats, spread a blanket on the lawn, and let the kids enjoy an old-fashioned baseball game. There are a number of fun things for little kids to do if the action on the field slows down. Speed pitch, basketball games, and Rowdie the mascot keep folks entertained. A great family value and entertainment, the Indians also have activities for fans throughout the game—footraces on the field, ball pitches, T-shirt tosses, and much more. Visit on a $1 night and eat cheaper than you can cook.

i Presented by Community Health and WISH-TV, the Indianapolis Indians Knot Hole Kids Club offers kids age 14 and under the opportunity to attend all 72 Indians home games for just $14. In addition, members receive an Indians Knot Hole Kids Club T-shirt and may run the bases after every Sunday home game (weather permitting). Sign up your child online at Indy Indians.com or at the Victory Field Box Office.

INDIANAPOLIS MOTOR SPEEDWAY
HALL OF FAME MUSEUM   **$**
4790 W. 16th St.
(317) 492-6784
www.indianapolismotorspeedway.com
Ever want to climb into an Indy race car to see

what it feels like inside the sleek vehicle? Kids of all ages are invited to do just that at the Indianapolis Motor Speedway Hall of Fame Museum. You might be surprised to find out how little room there is in the small racers. Visitors also can look through double-wide wooden doors into a replica A. J. Foyt garage, see a Pontiac driven by Richard Petty, learn how helmets have changed over the years, and watch a 20-minute film of historic footage and Indy 500 highlights. Visitors also can take a 15-minute lap around the track in a tour van and do a special grounds tour.

Started in 1956 in a small building on a corner of the grounds outside the track, the museum opened with six vintage cars from late Speedway owner Tony Hulman. The collection got so big that a new museum was opened in 1976. About a third of the nearly 250,000 visitors who tour the museum each year come in May, when the 2½-mile track hosts the annual Indianapolis 500. About 75 cars are on display at any time. A sleek 1954 Formula One Mercedes-Benz is one of the most valuable cars in the museum. A few years ago, one like it sold in England for about $10 million. Other artifacts on display from Indianapolis 500 winners include trophies, photographs, helmets, and uniforms.

NCAA HALL OF CHAMPIONS   **$**
700 W. Washington St.
(800) 732-6222
www.ncaahallofchampions.org
When the game of football began, it was literally a deadly sport. The menacing formation known as the "flying wedge," widely used in college football in the early 1900s, caused injuries, death, and widespread concern. In 1905, 18 college football players died from injuries.

So disturbing was the situation that President Teddy Roosevelt called college presidents and gave them an ultimatum. He told them to make the game safer or he would abolish college football. Fearing Roosevelt's threat to do away with college football, college presidents hastened to action. At a meeting, college presidents voted to abolish the flying-wedge formation. That meeting later led to the formation of the National Collegiate Athletic Association in 1906.

Since opening in March of 2000, the NCAA Hall of Champions in White River State Park has hosted thousands of visitors to learn the history of the organization and to enjoy a new definition of what it is to be a champion. The hall is different from many museums. It not only celebrates student athletes, but it also educates and informs the public about the real value in being a student athlete. The NCAA has 23 sports and 360,000 student athletes, and the hall talks about what it takes to be a success.

The Hall of Champions focuses on what it means to be a champion in life, not just in one particular competition. From the first championship in 1921, field and track, to the modern competition of water polo and field hockey, all 23 sports and national championships administered by the NCAA are highlighted.

An eye-catching life-size bronze sculpture of the flying wedge is located at the base of the Hall's giant staircase. In the formation, six players without strong protective gear lined up in a "V" formation and locked arms to protect the ball carrier behind them.

In the Gymnasium, visitors get to experience a bygone era. With the look of a turn-of-the-20th-century gym with its glazed tile walls, hardwood floors, and large grille-covered windows, the gym invites visitors to shoot free throws. Special basketball symbols on the floor indicate the buzzer-beater spots where historic shots were made.

One basketball mark foreshadows the greatness that was to come. In the 1982 NCAA Division I Men's Basketball Championship in New Orleans, it notes, a college freshman made a game-winning basket. Michael Jordan sank a jumper with 17 seconds remaining to lift North Carolina to a national championship over Georgetown.

SOLDIERS AND SAILORS MONUMENT
1 Monument Circle
(317) 232-7615
Kids can burn off energy and get some exercise at the Soldiers and Sailors Monument on Monument Circle. Located at the geographic center of Indianapolis on Monument Circle, this 284-foot-tall limestone monument was dedicated in 1902 and stands as a tribute to the valor of Indiana's soldiers and sailors who served in the Civil and Spanish American Wars. An observation tower, accessible by elevator or 32 flights of stairs, provides a panoramic view of the city skyline. Let older kids climb 333 stairs (parents can pay $1 to ride the elevator or hike along) to the top. Constructed of Indiana limestone and featuring exterior historical and mythological sculptures, the monument is crowned by "Miss Victory."

i Boomer, the Indiana Pacers mascot, has created Boomer's Buddies—a plan to assist parents with children who may wander off during games at Conseco Fieldhouse. Boomer's child identification wristbands are available at Conseco Fieldhouse events. Before attaching these wristbands to a child, the bands are updated with the seat location that appears on the adult's and child's event tickets. Boomer's Buddies Wristband is a free in-house service. To register your child, visit Guest Relations on any level.

YUMMY STUFF

ARNI'S $$
4705 E. 96th St.
(317) 571-0077
www.meetyouatarnis.com
With a long tradition in Indiana, Arni's is known for its pizza and junior salads. The first Arni's was opened in Lafayette in 1965 by Arni Cohen. Through the years, several more Arni's opened around Indiana. Arni's offers a kids' menu with the usual choices but families often opt for the thin crust pizza.

BOOGIE BURGER $$
927 E. Westfield Blvd.
(317) 255-2450
www.boogieburger.com
The name of this place always seems to get a kid's attention. The food is delicious, too. Sandwiches are sometimes so huge that a kid will have a bunch leftover. Order the popular Boogie Burger

with cheese and peanut butter. Don't knock it until you try it. Get a real milkshake and you're set.

FOUNTAIN SQUARE DINER $$
1105 Shelby St.
(317) 685-1959

Kids can climb on a stool at the diner counter and enjoy an ice-cream sundae or malt hand-dipped the old-fashioned way. Originally opened in 1959 inside the Woolworth store, the Fountain Diner is showing kids how it used to be.

MUG-N-BUN DRIVE-IN $$
5211 W. 10th St.
(317) 244-5669

Show your kids a real 1950s dining experience at this drive-in restaurant where carhops still hang trays from car windows. A local institution for decades, Mug-n-Bun serves burgers, onion rings, and homemade root beer floats. Blink your headlights when you're ready to order.

THE OLD SPAGHETTI FACTORY $$
210 S. Meridian St.
(317) 635-6325
www.osf.com

What kid doesn't like spaghetti? A family favorite, the Spaghetti Factory offers good food—lots of it—and low prices. Kids like to eat in the trolley car located in the middle of the restaurant. If you arrive at lunchtime or dinner hour, the place is likely to be crowded and you'll have to wait. Try eating early.

THEATER STUFF

PEEWINKLES PUPPET STUDIO $$
25 E. Henry St.
(317) 283-7144
www.peewinklespuppets.com

This old-world-style, 50-seat puppet theater is just few blocks south of Circle Centre mall in downtown Indianapolis.

PYRAMID PLAYERS AT BEEF & BOARD DINNER THEATRE $$$
9301 N. Michigan Rd
(317) 872-9664
www.beefandboards.com

Enjoy a children's theater production complete with juice and snack. Presented by the Pyramid Players at Beef & Board Dinner Theatre, the productions are an hour in length and presented without intermission. Performances are for all ages but offered particularly for children in preschool through sixth grade. Priced at $12, performances take place at 10 a.m. on Fri and at 10 a.m. and 1 p.m. on Sat. Plays for 2010 include *Aladdin* and *The Little Mermaid*.

SHOPPING

Whether you're searching for Hoosier arts and crafts, small treasures from the past, fresh produce, kiddy toys, a new outfit, a coffee table, or a vintage bottle of wine, Indianapolis has some wonderful shopping experiences.

What sets this city apart? Maybe it's the friendly nature of the folks you meet. Shop owners, many of them artists and craftspeople themselves, display a straightforward hospitality that sometimes seems to be missing elsewhere. And they welcome the chance to talk about their work.

Maybe it's the fine historic buildings that have been given new life as shops in neighborhoods throughout the city. It feels good to buy from hospitable people in an interesting old place that you remember as much for its character as for what you bought.

Except for malls and a few special categories, shopping is grouped in this chapter by location, with a few stores mentioned for each district. The list is by no means complete—just enough to give you a start on a shopping adventure. Indianapolis is a very drivable city. You can get from one side of town to the other in less than 30 minutes, so going from one area to another to check out a shop is not difficult.

Plenty of treasures await all across the city. With shops spread around the region, it's no wonder shoppers return again and again to Indianapolis. Get a paper and pen, make a shopping list of what goes together to make an ideal shopping foray, and it's all here. Slip on some comfy shoes, take your saved-up spending money, and get ready to find what your heart desires. Regardless of what you end up purchasing, memories of those special shopping jaunts are truly priceless.

CITY MARKET
222 E. Market St.
(317) 634-9266
www.indycm.com

Dating back to 1821 when Indianapolis was laid out, City Market started as a small site but continued to grow. A new City Market was constructed in 1886, and the popular shopping destination flourished in the early to mid 1900s. However, the encroachment of suburbia took its toll after World War II. People began shopping closer to home at big neighborhood stores. Many City Market vendors went out of business or moved. Buying fresh food from local farmers and merchants was no longer a way of life.

Throughout the 1950s and 1960s, citizens and government leaders debated what should be done with the old City Market. When Mayor

Richard Lugar took office in 1968, change was in the wind. The community was ready to restore City Market. The Lilly Endowment paid for complete restoration and additional construction. With restoration complete in 1977, City Market was granted new life and began drawing shoppers as it once had.

Now, more than ever, people seem to need the old-time City Market. Downtown development has brought more residents living in the area and they support a place to gather, buy fresh food, and enjoy the bustling activity of years gone by.

In 2004 City Market celebrated the unveiling of its new Market District Stage on Whistler Plaza, where entertainment of all types delights shoppers. In 2007 Lilly Endowment funded another renovation that brought new paint, new floors, new lighting, and a new group of stand owners. Stop by the market to see a hearty blend of Indiana grown fresh produce, fresh-cut flowers, tasty cuisine, and other items. A list below shares some of the shops that now operate at City Market.

ABBY'S MARKET
(317) 223-7693

This handy market offers a variety of standard grocery and convenience items, candy, cigarettes, sort drinks, milk, and eggs.

AL'S SHOE REPAIR
(317) 639-5518

A full-service shoe repair, Al's fixes shoes and purses, as well as offering resole services, key cutting, and more.

AMAZING POTATO CHIP COMPANY
(317) 916-2447

This company prides itself on providing upscale snack foods, particularly chips and caramel corn. It is also home to the famous City Market potato chip, a crunchy treat.

AMEER MIDDLE EASTERN CUISINE
(317) 681-8444

Middle Eastern Food is the specialty here, featuring daily goodies such as stuffed grape leaves and *spanakopita*. The fabulous Friday special is *mojadara*.

ASIANA GARDEN
(847) 208-1590

A combination of Asian specialties—Chinese, Japanese, and sushi are offered at the Asiana Garden. Dishes are low fat and low sodium. Asiana Market also has gift items, Asian foods, and snacks.

CAFE OLIVIA
(317) 385-7839

Bringing a small piece of France to the City Market, Cafe Olivia makes all dishes, soups, and roasted meats fresh on the premises. From fresh fruit to omelets, breakfast is served daily.

CONSTANTINO'S
(317) 624-1500

An Italian market and deli, Constantino's features fresh produce and a great line of paninis and Italian deli specialties.

DOTTIE'S KITCHEN/PRESTIGE CATERING
(317) 635-7478

Serving breakfast and lunch, Dottie's also offers catering.

GRECIAN GARDEN AND MARKET
(317) 634-0191

A full-service restaurant featuring authentic Greek cuisine, Grecian Garden and Market has great gyros and other dishes. The market features olive oil, cheese, and more.

HALEIGH'S HARVEST
(317) 236-8999

Haleigh's offers made-to-order specialty sandwiches and homemade soups.

INDY CONE
(317) 753-1937

Feel like a kid again as you slurp a fresh dipped soft-serve ice-cream cone. Or try a sundae, shake, or malt. The Dr. Smoothie is made from 100 percent real fruit.

JACK'S BARBERSHOP
(317) 423-0550

A classic 1920s barbershop, Jack's is dedicated to providing real haircuts, shaves, and neck and shoulder massages.

i Barbasol shaving cream was created in Indianapolis in 1918 by Frank Shields.

JUMBO'S SANDWICHES, STEWS & SALADS
(317) 683-3965

Serving City Market customers since 1975, Jumbo's offers homemade soup, stew, chili, sandwiches, and more.

JUST COOKIES
(317) 634-4456
Stop by for homemade cookies and sweets. Special orders, catering, party trays, and custom giant celebration cookies are also available.

LAS SENORITA'S
(317) 289-4629
Hankering for some South of the Border cuisine? Las Senorita's serves traditional Mexican dishes.

PHILADELPHIA STEAK & FRIES
(317) 635-1199
Savor a Philly Steak sandwich or Philly Chicken Supreme complete with teriyaki sauce. You can also build your own sandwich here. Bread is baked by them, too. If burgers or steak salads are more your style, this place has them as well.

TOMMY'S DELI
(317) 418-7777
Featuring deli sandwiches, hot foods, and homemade soup, Tommy's is the place to satisfy your hunger. Italian beef sandwiches and Big Club deluxe sandwiches are sure to fill you up.

WHITE SANDS SILVER & BOUTIQUE
(317) 423-2978
Silver jewelry, handbags, jackets, men's and women's hats, and many more items are for sale at this stand.

CULTURAL DISTRICTS

Some of the city's most unique neighborhoods feature hundreds of specialty shops. Among the cultural district shopping you might enjoy are these spots.

i First Friday art openings are a prime time to check out downtown Indy's various cultural districts. The popular and free self-guided gallery hops occur the first Friday of each month year-round. See up to 25 participating galleries while enjoying a nice stroll on a warm summer night or a brisk walk in the winter. Visit www.idada.org to download a gallery map for each month.

Broad Ripple Village

A retro neighborhood about 15 minutes north of downtown Indianapolis, Broad Ripple Village (www.discoverbroadripplevillage.com) offers everything from authentic 1920s flapper dresses to hip trends of today's runway. Wonderful gifts, decorative accessories, and local artisans can be found throughout Broad Ripple in eclectic boutiques and art galleries. While you're out shopping, enjoy a lunch or dinner break at one of the many quaint restaurants, authentic pubs, and ethnic eateries peppered throughout the village. Businesses include:

ARTIFACTS CONTEMPORARY ART
6327 Guilford Ave.
(317) 255-1178
www.artifactsindy.com
Established in 1977 as a showplace for American contemporary crafts, Artifacts features an extensive selection of design by American artists in a wide range of media, including fine art, jewelry, ceramics, art glass, wooden boxes, art furniture, accessories, posters, and gifts.

BIG HAT BOOKS
6510 Cornell Ave.
(317) 202-0203
www.bighatbooks.com
An independent bookstore, Big Hat has a large airy location with tons of books. Plan to spend some time browsing here, looking for old literary friends and discovering new ones. Big Hat also schedules author events, book clubs, workshops, and discussions.

HONEYSUCKLE HOME
920 Broad Ripple Ave.
(317) 202- 4663
www.honeysucklehome.com
Opened in 2004, Honeysuckle Home is a home decor boutique with a European flair. Look for tableware, bed and bath items, stationery, kitchen accessories, tote bags, and much more. The shop also carries environmentally friendly items, such as recycled glassware, stationery, rugs, handbags

linens, organic cotton bedding, natural soaps, and cleaning products.

INDY CD & VINYL
806 Broad Ripple Ave.
(317) 259-1012
www.indycdandvinyl.com

Central Indiana's largest independent record store, Indy CD & Vinyl offers a wide selection of new and used CDs and vinyl. Originally established in Salt Lake City in 1993, the business migrated to Indianapolis in 2001 (owner Rick Zeigler is originally from Muncie, Indiana). The shop provides a varied and deep selection of rock from the '50s onward, indie rock, jazz, electronic, hip-hop, country and alt-country, avant-garde, reggae, folk, world, sound tracks, classical, gospel, blues, and spoken word. Additionally, Indy CD & Vinyl has a huge stock of hip-hop, rock, electronic, and jazz LPs, both new and used, as well as a humongous selection of music DVDs.

JUST POP IN
6302 N. Guilford Ave.
(317) 257-9338
www.justpopinonline.com

Twin sisters Carly and Mandy run this gourmet popcorn shop, where you can get fresh popcorn with irresistible flavors like Cajun, dill pickle, chocolate and marshmallow, and blueberry. The Indy-style favorite is caramel and sharp cheddar cheese. Stop in for a sniff and you won't be able to leave without trying some of the tempting popcorn or other sweet treats.

KILN CREATIONS
918 Broad Ripple Ave.
(317) 251-2386
www.kilncreations.biz

No experience is needed to create your own pottery or mosaic at Kiln Creations. Children also are welcome. You don't have to be an artist either. Just pick a piece of unfinished pottery, create your design (use stencils, stamps, and idea books if you need help getting started), choose from over 40 colors, and paint your piece. They will glaze and fire the pottery, and it is ready to pick

up in a week. For mosaics, select a good base, choose glass tiles and gems to create your own design, glue tiles to the wood piece, and take some grout to finish the piece at home.

The pottery is safe to use for eating and drinking. Paints and glazes used at the shop are lead-free. The paint time for an adult is usually one or two hours, children an hour or less—depending on the size of the piece and level of detail.

MARIGOLD CONTEMPORARY CLOTHING
6512 N. Cornell Ave.
(317) 254-9939
www.marigoldclothing.com

Opened in 1989, Marigold is the dream of owner Linda Shikany, who loved playing store as a child. The shop offers clothing, gifts, and accessories for women of all ages. Marigold's believes in the philosophy of "Lifestyle Dressing"—having a personal approach to style that transcends age and reflects a woman's outlook on life.

RED ROSE VINTAGE CLOTHING
6169 N. College Ave.
(317) 257-5016
www.redrose.scottunes.com

Step through the entrance of this 1979 establishment and see a history of vintage clothing, costume jewelry, collectibles, neckties, shoes, knickknacks, and much more. Whether you're looking for rhinestones, gabardine, Victorian, art deco, Edwardian, WWI, WWII, rock-a-billy, or other era clothing, you most likely will find it here.

Fountain Square

A historic commercial and residential neighborhood located southeast of downtown Indy, Fountain Square (www.discoverfountainsquare .com) blends retro and new art in its architecture and interesting collection of art galleries, independent restaurants, antique shops, and entertainment. Shops include:

ARTHUR'S MUSIC STORE
931 Shelby St.
(317) 638-3524
www.arthursmusic.com

Close-up

The Christmas Cherub

The year was 1946. World War II had ended and thousands of servicemen and women were returning home from military service. Virginia Holmes was one of them. A prize-winning commercial artist, Virginia came back to Indianapolis and began a job in the advertising department at L. S. Ayres, a downtown department store.

When Virginia went to create the 1946 holiday catalog, merchandise was still in short supply because of the war, so the artist sketched whimsical cherubs to fill the empty spaces. Shoppers found the cherubs adorable, and thus began an Indianapolis holiday tradition that continues today.

When the 1947 holiday rolled around, L. S. Ayres brought back the popular cherubs. Since it was the store's 75th anniversary, the business thought it needed something special for that year's holiday celebration. Ayres commissioned nationally recognized Indianapolis sculptor and Herron School of Art instructor David Rubins to create a bronze cherub for the store's landmark clock, located on the outside of the building at the corner of Washington and Meridian Streets.

Legend says that the chubby cherub mysteriously appeared atop the clock on Thanksgiving eve in 1947 to keep a watchful eye on the holiday shoppers until Old St. Nick took over on Christmas Eve. For decades that tradition continued. Shoppers would look forward to seeing the cherub perched atop the clock each holiday season. After the holidays, the cherub would quietly disappear until the next season rolled around.

In 1992, L. S. Ayres was bought by the May Department Stores. In 1992, May moved the cherub to its headquarters in St. Louis. Public outcry was so tremendous when the cherub did not appear that holiday season that the May Company donated the cherub to the city of Indianapolis. In 1994, Indianapolis Downtown Inc. became the cherub's legal guardian.

So, the next time you find yourself on Monument Circle during holiday season, look up at the corner of Washington and Meridian to see the cheerful cherub continuing to keep vigil over the city.

In the same location since 1952 and still owned by the Arthur family, the music store stocks everything musical except pianos, organs, and recording gear. Known for featuring fretted instruments, Arthur's Music has a wide variety from guitars to hammered dulcimers. It is one of the few stores in the Midwest where you can find pedal steel guitars, accordions, and Iris tenor banjos alongside other kinds of guitars, basses, drums, amps, and PA (public address) gear. The store buys, sells, and trades. Arthur's also maintains a file of requests for particular instruments and lets a prospective customer know when those instruments are available.

INDIANAPOLIS DOWNTOWN ANTIQUE MALL
1044 Virginia Ave.
(317) 635-5336
Located 11 blocks southeast of Monument Circle, Indianapolis Downtown Antique Mall features 40 individual shops on two floors with a wide variety of antiques and collectibles, including glassware, furniture, American art pottery, and country and primitive items. The mall features no crafts. It is primarily American antiques.

BOCA LOCA BEADS
1211 Prospect St.
(317) 423-2323
www.bocalocabeadsinc.com
Opened for business in the summer of 1989, Boca Loca Beads helps you design and make your own jewelry. Beads, beads, and more beads are available for one-of-a-kind personal creations.

CLAUS' GERMAN SAUSAGE AND MEATS
1845 Shelby St.
(317) 632-1963
www.clausgermansausageandmeats.com
With a history that dates back to 1913, the family-owned Claus' German Sausage and Meats is a wholesale and retail market offering top cuts of meat and lunch meat. Double-smoked bacon, ground beef, and authentic German sausage are some of the favorites.

DOMONT STUDIO GALLERY
545 S. East St.
(317) 685-9634
www.domontgallery.com
Dedicated to the works of artist John Dormont, this art gallery showcases his contemporary work with an emphasis on the Indiana landscape.

DAYS GONE BY ANTIQUES
1802 Virginia Ave.
(317) 636-1954
Want to dress in the style of the 1950s? Have a yen to turn back the clock for your home decor? This is the place to shop; it features tons of collectibles, vintage clothing, antiques, and much more.

Mass Ave

Bursting with renovated galleries, restaurants, and nightspots, Mass Ave (www.discovermassave.com) is a shopper's delight. And, yes, that is a "Mass" without a period and an "Ave" without a period. This is the place to find high-end clothing, fine jewelry, home decor, old fashioned-collectibles, shoes, and an eclectic array of other items.

THE BEST CHOCOLATE IN TOWN
880 Massachusetts Ave.
(317) 636-2800
www.bestchocolateintown.com
Founded in 1998 by Elizabeth Garber, the shop combines the owner's fine-arts background and love of chocolate. All chocolates are handmade and hand-packed at the Mass Ave shop. Rich whipped chocolate infused with fresh ingredients and flavors is a specialty. Known for their truffles, the shop makes them from rich whipped chocolate infused with fresh ingredients and flavors. A broad range of more than 40 flavors is featured, and flavors change all the time. Favorites are Dark Chocolate Guinness Truffles and Ginger Wasabi Truffles. The chocolate makers pride themselves on coming up with unique flavor combinations, and they make good toffee as well.

GLOBAL GIFTS
446 Massachusetts Ave.
(317) 423-3148
www.globalgiftsindy.com
A not-for-profit business committed to serving impoverished artisans and producers in the developing world, Global Gifts is a fair-trade store. That means the store works with artisans who would not otherwise be able to reach a market for their products. Items are all handmade from artisans spanning the globe and representing over 35 countries, mostly from the developing regions of the world.

SAGE
717 Massachusetts Ave.
(317) 423-2919
A boutique specializing in women's clothing and accessories, Sage offers beautiful choices for women with style.

SILVER IN THE CITY
434 Massachusetts Ave.
(866) 955-9925
shopssilverinthecity.com
Opened in 2000, Silver in the City features sterling silver jewelry, watches, and gifts. In 2001,

Home in the City joined the family to provide well-designed yet reasonably priced home accessories and gifts.

SPLURGE
446 Massachusetts Ave.
(317) 637-3000
Splurge is a great place to find a nifty gift for a special friend or something for yourself. After all, that's what Splurge is—a spot to buy trendy men's and women's clothing and accessories and make yourself feel good about a purchase.

STOUTS SHOES
318 Massachusetts Ave.
(317) 632-7818
www.stoutsfootwear.com
The oldest shoe store in the same location in the country, Stout's also has stayed in the family and been run by four generations of the Stout family. Each customer is still individually measured and fit according to what they are looking for at this high-end quality footwear store. And they have the last operating Baldwin Flyer in the country (a basket delivery system that delivers the shoes from the upstairs storage area to customers downstairs). The business thrived in the 1950s by buying factory-second shoes and repairing them to be sold at a discount to the customer. In addition to the foot X-ray machine, Sidney Stout kept a monkey and a parrot in the store. They have another parrot there today.

Wholesale District

While Circle Centre mall is anchored by Parisian and the state's only Nordstrom, the Wholesale District (www.discoverwholesaledistrict.com) offers hundreds of specialty shops and restaurants. Circle Centre is chock-full of chain stores. If you are looking for a favorite specialty shop, chances are it is here.

The Wholesale District traces is origins to 1863 when two German immigrant brothers, August and Henry Schnull, built the city's first wholesale house on Meridian Street. The brothers' goal was to create an entire wholesale district. Buying residential properties, the Schnulls replaced them with commercial buildings and wholesale warehouses. That prompted others to join them.

The Wholesale District freed shoppers from having to depend on retailers outside Indianapolis and having to pay the middleman. The wholesale warehouses offered goods at wholesale prices. August eventually returned to Germany, but Henry continued to invest in Indianapolis and is known as "the Father of the Wholesale District."

Since 1995, more than $1 billion has been invested to transform the Wholesale District into the city's premier arts, entertainment, and shopping destination. Significant additions include Circle Centre, Conseco Fieldhouse, Conrad Indianapolis, Lucas Oil Stadium, and nearly 100 new businesses, expansions, and renovation projects.

COLTS PRO SHOP
Lucas Oil Stadium
500 S. Capitol Ave.
(317) 262-2700
The Indianapolis Colts store is your place to find Peyton Manning jerseys, Colts authentic and replica jerseys, and women's Colts merchandise. There is also a Colts store at Circle Centre.

DOWNTOWN COMICS
11 E. Market St.
(317) 237-0397
www.downtowncomics.com
Established in 1993 by two Purdue grads who hated their jobs, Downtown Comics features just what you think and more. From a single store operation in downtown Indy, the business has grown to a five-store chain.

KRIEG BROTHERS
119. S. Meridian St.
(317) 638-3416
The oldest church-supply house in Indianapolis, Krieg Brothers also offers a huge selection of nativity scenes from around the world. Plan to spend some time here because it is stuffed with interesting items and books.

LANDWERLEN LEATHER
365 S. Illinois St.
(317) 636-7271
Stop into this specialty store to sniff the fresh leather smell. Then shop for leather, leather craft supplies and tools, and shoemaking and repair supplies. Check out the scrap bin, where you can find unusual pieces of leather for small leather projects.

OUTRÉ
245 S. McCrea St.
(317) 632-3328
www.itstheniche.com
Family owned and operated, Outré offers products made only in Indiana. This custom upholstered furniture studio allows consumers to have a more hands-on approach to designing their own furniture.

PACERS HOME COURT GIFT SHOP
Conseco Fieldhouse
125 S. Pennsylvania St.
(317) 917-2755
www.pacers.com
Show your pride in the Pacers. This clothing and souvenir shop at Conseco Fieldhouse specializes in authentic Indiana Pacers and Indiana Fever merchandise. The Home Court Gift Shop sells Pacers, Fever, and Conseco Fieldhouse merchandise. Items include authentic and replica jerseys, team apparel, jackets, basketballs, hats, Bobble Head dolls, and novelties. There is also a shop at Circle Centre if that is more convenient.

TEAPOTS AND TREASURES
7 E. Market St.
(317) 687-8768
www.teapots4u.com
Founded by an Indianapolis woman, Teapots and Treasures is filled with exactly that—teapots, treasures, and much more. The owner creates signature teas for many businesses and ships it everywhere. Ingredients are real, with no chemicals added. The shop boasts almost 400 different blends of tea. The owner also creates various herbal teas for medicinal purposes. Stop in, sip a

spot of tea that is always brewing, and see what else the shop offers.

WINDSOR JEWELRY
16 N. Meridian St.
(888) 634-6736
www.windsorjewelry.com
Founded by an Indianapolis man in 1919, Windsor Jewelry is a full-service jeweler.

MUSEUM STORES

Indianapolis is home to several unique museums that have charming gift shops, featuring unusual items that aren't carried in most stores. Check out these museums and find the treasures that await in their gift shops.

CHILDREN'S MUSEUM OF INDIANAPOLIS
3000 N. Meridian St.
(800) 820-6214
www.childrensmuseum.org
One of the best toy stores in town, the Children's Museum gift shop has gifts designed to encourage wonder, learning, and joy in youngsters. There, you'll find everything from collectible replicas of dinosaurs to amber jewelry made from fossilized tree sap. Visitors can also choose from Science, Space, Thomas the Train, Puzzle and Games, or Imaginary Play areas. The shop also features souvenirs of that special visit.

i John Gruelle, political cartoonist for the *Indianapolis Star,* created the Raggedy Ann and Andy characters in his children's books, thus giving birth to two of America's favorite dolls.

CONNER PRAIRIE
13400 Allisonville Rd., Fishers
(800) 966-1836
www.connerprairie.org
This nationally acclaimed living-history museum sells such gems as heirloom seeds and gourmet foods, jams, soups, and old-fashioned candy. Enjoy wool skeins and other textiles from the Conner Prairie loom house, as well as popular

Conner Prairie pottery. Unusual jewelry, gifts, and household objects also are stocked. An extensive selection of historical books highlight Indiana history, nature, cooking, pioneers, Native Americans, and African Americans.

EITELJORG MUSEUM OF AMERICAN INDIANS AND WESTERN ART
500 W. Washington St.
(317) 636-9378
www.eitlejorg.org

This is a premier shopping place, with an award-winning store called the White River Trader. Whether it includes blankets and purses from Pendleton, pottery by Jacquie Stevens, books on the West, or reproduction bronzes by Frederic Remington, they have one-of-a-kind wonderful gifts.

INDIANA HISTORICAL SOCIETY
450 W. Ohio St.
(800) 447-1830
www.indianahistory.org

Looking for something uniquely Indiana? The Indiana Historical Society History Market features the best of Indiana literature, art, music, jewelry, pottery, toys, games, and much more.

INDIANAPOLIS ART CENTER
820 E. 67th St.
(317) 255-2464
www.indplsartcenter.org

The Frank M. Basile Studio Shop has original works for sale from regional and local artists.

INDIANAPOLIS MOTOR SPEEDWAY
4790 W. 16th St.
(800) 822-4639
www.indianapolismotorspeedway.com

Make a pit stop at Official Trackside Gift Shop inside the Hall of Fame Museum at the Speedway. You'll find all kinds of exclusive collector items, including bricks from the original track, die-cast cars, flags, buttons, and pictures of your favorite drivers dating all the way back to 1909. There is also a wide variety of T-shirts, key chains, pins, and caps.

INDIANAPOLIS MUSEUM OF ART
4000 N. Michigan Rd.
(317) 923-1331
www.imamuseum.org

Chances are you can't afford a Rembrandt. But after looking at one of his paintings at the Indianapolis Museum of Art, you can visit this gift shop and discover plenty of creations that are within your budget. The choices include everything from hand-loomed scarves and "artsy" winter coats to glassware, custom note cards, puzzles, and jewelry. You never know what you'll find down the road at the IMA's Better than New Shop. Friends of the museum donate china, jewelry, crystal, silver, antiques, furniture, clothing, and books to be sold for charity.

INDIANAPOLIS MUSEUM OF CONTEMPORARY ART
340 N. Senate Ave.
(317) 634-6622
www.indymoca.org

This neat gift shop offers apparel and accessories, gifts, children's items, jewelry, stationery, books, and art.

INDIANA REPERTORY THEATRE
140 W. Washington St.
(317) 635-5252
www.irtlive.com

The Indiana Repertory Theatre provides an entertaining shopping experience with whimsical, theatrical, and intellectual choices. Gift items include unusual decorative items, books, jewelry and accessories, fun toys for all ages, and autographed scripts of the season's plays. All proceeds from the gift shop support the artistic and educational work of the theater, so every gift gives twice.

INDIANA STATE MUSEUM
650 W. Washington St.
(317) 232-1637
www.in.gov/ism

The Indiana State Museum gift shop offers two floors of unique items, many from Indiana artisans and businesses like L. S. Ayres Tea Room cookbooks, Vera Bradley totes and purses, South Bend chocolates, and IMAX films on DVD.

INDIANAPOLIS ZOO AND WHITE RIVER GARDENS
1200 W. Washington St.
(317) 630-2001
www.indyzoo.com

What a deal—two gift shops at one attraction. Really, it is two attractions, the Indianapolis Zoo and White River Gardens, but they are at the same location.

The Indianapolis Zoo Store offers an exciting and constantly changing mixture of merchandise from around the world. From unique stuffed animals to books and educational toys for kids to customized jewelry and home decor items for moms, dads, grandmas, and grandpas, the Indianapolis Zoo Store offers something for everyone in the family. The Zoo store also has great items from Africa, including authentic drums handmade in Kenya and hand-carved statues. Help your favorite little one explore new worlds with a "safari" hat or the latest in educational books and games. There are also plenty of plush animal toys and masks from which to choose.

Most important, every purchase made at the Indianapolis Zoo Store provides critical financial support for the ongoing operations, as well as the educational and conservation initiatives, of the Indianapolis Zoological Society.

The Gardener's Pride Gift Shop is a delightful place with original collections of gifts and accessories for home and garden. The E. Andrew Steffen Gardener's Pride Gift Shop is located just inside the entrance of White River Gardens. Plenty of gardening "toys" and home decor items, as well as a wide variety of fun, garden-themed merchandise and gardening books, are for sale. After all, gardening is among the top leisure activities in the United States. Green thumb or not, the shop's selection of books, stationery, artwork, candles and soaps (bath and body accessories), apparel, children's toys and games, and souvenirs could keep you busy browsing.

JAMES WHITCOMB RILEY MUSEUM HOME
528 Lockerbie St.
(317) 631-5885
www.rileykids.org/museum

Visit the James Whitcomb Riley House Gift Shop for beautifully illustrated reproductions of books of poems by the famed "Hoosier poet." There are also toys and other items from the late-Victorian era in which Riley lived.

NCAA HALL OF CHAMPIONS
700 W. Washington St.
(800) 732-6222
www.ncaahallofchampions.org

Almost every family has a sports fanatic. And the NCAA Hall of Champions Campus Corner Gift Shop is a great place to shop for sports lovers. You'll find officially licensed NCAA merchandise featuring a complete clothing line, specialty gifts, books, videos, and more.

PRESIDENT BENJAMIN HARRISON HOME
1230 N. Delaware St.
(317) 631-1888
www.presidentbenjaminharrison.org

Imagine your guests sitting down to dinner at a table dressed with White House china. The gift shop at the President Benjamin Harrison Home offers 12 presidential china patterns, including designs from the Washington, Jefferson, Lincoln, and Harrison administrations. Each is interesting and has a tale to go with the china. For example, the John Adams cornflower design served as the first presidential china to be used in what would eventually be called the White House. This porcelain dinnerware was originally purchased by President and Mrs. Adams while he served as foreign minister to France in 1780. Pieces may be purchased individually or by the place setting. The shop also offers the Flowers of the First Ladies collection—dessert plates decorated with the floral artwork of the First Ladies—and books on presidential homes.

NOTABLE MALLS

The Greater Indianapolis area boasts malls on all sides of town, and they are easy to find. Park at a mall and spend hours shopping in major department stores and specialty shops. When you're hungry, there are plenty of dining options, from sit-down restaurants to munchies-laden food courts. Want to rest your feet? Catch a movie at one of the many mall theaters.

CASTLETON SQUARE MALL
6020 E. 82nd St.
(317) 849-9993
www.simon.com

Located on the northeast side of Indianapolis, Castleton Square is the largest mall in the state of Indiana, as well as the most dominant. Boasting four major department stores, a food court, play area, and over 130 specialty stores, Castleton Square is a shopping magnet. Shops include L.S. Ayres, Von Maur, Macy's, Dick's Sporting Goods, Victoria's Secret, Structure, The Children's Place, and Build-A-Bear Workshop. Those who are hungry will enjoy the mall's newly expanded food court, with its variety of restaurants and eateries.

CIRCLE CENTRE
49 W. Maryland St.
(317) 681-8000
www.simon.com

Located in downtown Indianapolis, Circle Centre is bounded by Illinois Street on the west, Washington Street on the north, Meridian Street on the east, and Georgia Street on the south. Circle Centre spans 2 full city blocks and is filled with four levels and more than 100 shopping, dining, and entertainment options. Seven hotels are conveniently connected to Circle Centre via covered skywalk. A reasonably priced parking garage is very convenient.

Circle Centre is home to the state's only Nordstrom. Other shops include European discount design store H&M, Parisian, Godiva, Banana Republic, Brookstone, and the Disney Store. Take a break to enjoy the variety of offerings in the food court, a nine-screen movie theater, and

Steven Spielberg's GameWorks Studio (video games, full-size Indy cars, and a simulated roller coaster). Those who want to relax are invited to kick back at the Artsgarden for free afternoon arts performances.

CLAY TERRACE
14390 Clay Terrace Blvd.
(317) 566-0011
www.simon.com

The first lifestyle center in central Indiana, Clay Terrace in Carmel offers an eclectic array of high-end fashion and food retailers. Featuring an old-town Main Street setting, Clay Terrace offers such specialty shops as DSW Shoe Warehouse, Vera Bradley, Pier 1 Imports, Indigo Nation, Jos. A. Bank, Circuit City, and Chico's. More than 70 retailers line the center's broad sidewalks. Vintage storefronts and antique lighting combine with modern amenities and convenience. If relaxation is your goal, book an appointment at David & Mary's Day Spa. Delectable dining waits in Clay Terrace, too. Enjoy casual or fine dining in a variety of full-service restaurants or sidewalk cafés.

THE FASHION MALL AT KEYSTONE AT THE CROSSING
8702 Keystone Crossing
(317) 574-4000
www.simon.com

Located at the intersection of 86th Street and Keystone Avenue, the Fashion Mall is an easy jaunt from I-465 on Indy's north side. The mall boasts the only Saks Fifth Avenue store in the state, as well as one of the first Williams-Sonoma Home stores in the nation. Other stores include Discovery Channel, Sephora, The Body Shop, Parisian, Brooks Brothers, Pottery Barn, Sharper Image, bebe, J. Crew, and Crate & Barrel. Several locally owned shops include Abigail's, The Cheese Shop, Cynde's Shoes, The Game Preserve (selling almost any kind of game you can think of), J. T. Muesing, and Kids Corner. Fashion Mall is home to Landmark Theatres, the nation's largest art-house chain, known for showing first-run independent, and foreign films, restored classics, and nontraditional studio fare.

GREENWOOD PARK MALL
1251 US 31 N, Greenwood
(317) 881-6758
www.simon.com
Just minutes from Indianapolis International Airport, downtown Indianapolis, and Conseco Fieldhouse, Greenwood Park Mall offers more than 120 specialty shops. You'll have a great day of shopping with stores like American Eagle, Ann Taylor Loft, Hollister, Fossil, the Disney Store, Build-a-Bear Workshop, Sephora, Victoria's Secret, and Waldenbooks. Stop by one of the anchor stores like Dick's Sporting Goods, JCPenney, Macy's, Sears, or Von Maur for a great selection of quality merchandise. Ready for a break? Try a pretzel from Auntie Anne's Pretzels or maybe a gourmet cookie from Blondie's. You might want to sit down and relax at Applebee's or Friday's and enjoy great food and a relaxed atmosphere. If you're in a hurry, consider visiting one of your favorite fast-food restaurants located in the food court.

LAFAYETTE SQUARE MALL
Lafayette Road at 38th St.
(317) 291-6391
www.shoplafayettemall.com
Located 7 miles northwest of downtown Indianapolis adjacent to I-65, Lafayette Square Mall is an enclosed mall on 113 acres. Home to more than 90 specialty stores, Lafayette Square is anchored by Burlington Coat Factory, Shoppers World, and Xscape. It's also home to Aéropostale, Bath & Body Works, Kittle's Rooms Express, The Children's Place, Merle Norman Cosmetics Studio, GameStop, Victoria's Secret, The Finish Line, Waldenbooks, and much more. Dining spots include Charley's Steakery, Cinnabon, Fish 'N Wingz, FuJun Café, Pizza di Roma, and State Fair.

WASHINGTON SQUARE MALL
10202 East Washington St.
(317) 899-4567
www.simon.com
Located on Indy's east side, Washington Square Mall includes more than 80 specialty shops and five department stores, including Sears, Target, Burlington Coat Factory, Steve & Barry's University Sportswear, and Dick's Sporting Goods. Take in a movie at Kerasotes ShowPlace 12, a state-of-the-art theater with stadium seating and luxurious Euro-style chairs, digital sound, and curved screens for a maximum viewing experience. Dining choices include Buffalo Wild Wings, Fish 'N Wingz, La Hacienda, Longhorn Steakhouse, Luca Pizza di Roma, MCL Cafeteria, Sakura Japan, and Sui Feng Ju.

PARKS

Daffodils and tulips dance in the spring breeze, fireflies glitter on a warm summer evening, a brilliant blaze of autumn leaves shimmers in the sun, freshly fallen snow softly blankets the landscape. No matter the season, Indianapolis is blessed with Mother Nature's beauty. And Hoosiers spend a lot of time enjoying the great outdoors. Part of what makes Indy special is its excellent park system, one of the largest in the nation. The Indianapolis Department of Parks and Recreation (Indy Parks) maintains 206 parks in Indianapolis and Marion County, including one of the largest city parks in the United States. That huge number of city parks doesn't count the nation's only urban state park—fantastic White River State Park, situated almost smack dab in downtown Indy.

The statistics are impressive. Indy Parks is responsible for the operation and maintenance of more than 11,000 acres of parkland, more than 250,000 street trees and a large inventory of park trees, 22 aquatic facilities, 25 family centers, 13 golf courses, 18 spray grounds, 4 nature centers, 4 disc golf courses, 2 ice-skating rinks, a mountain bike trail, conservatory and sunken garden, arts center, Velodrome, skate park, and BMX complex. Canine companions haven't been neglected either. Indy Parks operates three Bark Parks for four-legged furry friends.

Almost anyplace you go in Indianapolis, a park is nearby. Regional parks are the largest in the Indy Parks system. They are intended to provide an open and natural setting, while also containing other facilities such as cultural or nature centers. Community parks are smaller than regional parks and generally place more emphasis on facilities such as recreation centers than on natural landscapes. Neighborhood parks are the smallest. They are generally three acres or smaller and are intended to serve the immediate surrounding neighborhood with facilities such as basketball courts and playground equipment. Neighborhood parks aren't individually listed in this chapter because there are so many of them.

Park programs range from traditional tennis and swimming classes to such offbeat options as annual garage sales, card games, sewing clubs, square dancing, and Touch a Truck, which gives kids a chance to explore fire trucks, police cruisers, tractors, and rescue vehicles. Programs are designed for all ages, from a baby ballerina program for the very youngest to osteoporosis prevention classes for the young at heart. Learn sign language, use a pottery wheel, create your own comic book, or discover belly dancing and much more in Indy parks. And it's all quite affordable, much of it free. Pick up a complimentary copy of the Indy Parks and Recreation *Fun Guide* at parks or contact the parks department at (317) 327-7275. You can also check out the Web site at www.indyparks.org. The guide lists what's offered every season, with the time, place, and price. So get out there, exercise your body, clear your mind, and enjoy the natural beauty that Indianapolis has preserved for a better quality of life.

STATE PARKS

FORT HARRISON STATE PARK
5753 Glenn Rd.
(317) 591-0904
www.in.gov

Located less than 10 minutes from downtown Indy, Fort Harrison State Park features 1,700 acres chock-full of activities and history. A former Citizen's Military Training Camp, Civilian Conservation Corps camp, and World War II prisoner of war camp is preserved at the park headquarters location. Opened in 1906 by President Theodore Roosevelt, Fort Benjamin Harrison was named in honor of President Benjamin Harrison, who came from Indianapolis. After Fort Harrison was decommissioned in 1991, the government decided to give 1,700 acres for use as a state park in 1995.

Unlike most state parks in Indiana, Fort Harrison is a day-use park; its only overnight facilities are at the inn of the Fort Golf Resort, which used to be the officers' club. The fort's golf course, redesigned by Pete Dye, is a popular golfing spot. The park also offers three hiking trails and a horseback-riding trail with horse rentals available. One of the hiking trails, Harrison Trace Trail, is paved and used by bikers and in-line skaters. Other recreation includes fishing, hayrides, picnicking, and a nature center. Naturalists offer guided walks and hikes.

WHITE RIVER STATE PARK
801 W. Washington St.
(317) 233-2434
www.in.gov/whiteriver
Want to attend a baseball game, stroll along a canal, go to the zoo, hear top entertainers at a lawn concert, or visit a world-class American Indian museum? In most cities, that would mean a lot of driving to get from place to place. In Indy, White River State Park has it all—conveniently and beautifully.

The nation's only urban state park, White River State Park offers an awesome array of attractions and entertainment. The 250-acre park covers both sides of the White River just west of downtown, between Washington and New York Streets. It started as part of a revitalization plan in the 1980s, with the goal of providing first-class entertainment, sporting complexes, gardens, and museums to the downtown area. Although the Indianapolis sports facilities were built elsewhere, the former industrial area has lived up to the goals of the dreamers who envisioned it—and more.

The park serves as an anchor for the Canal Cultural District, one of the city's many cultural districts. The park is home to the Indiana State Museum and IMAX Theater, Indianapolis Zoo and White River Gardens, the Eiteljorg Museum of American Indian and Western Art, NCAA Headquarters and NCAA Hall of Champions, the Congressional Medal of Honor Memorial, Victory Field as home of Indianapolis Indians baseball, Military Park, the Governors Lawn concert venue, historic Pumphouse, restaurants, and much more.

i For the last three years, the Lawn at White River State Park has been named one of the top 100 outdoor concert venues in the world by *Pollstar* magazine.

White River State Park offers many areas for walking, hiking, biking, and in-line skating. At Central Canal, you can walk, jog, or skate along this waterway that runs from the White River through the park. Be serenaded on a gondola ride on the canal or rent one of the pedal boats during the summer. Climb on a Segway to enjoy Indy in a different way. Pedal through the park on your own bike or rent one. You can also share the ride with the whole family in one of Bike Indy's unique surreys. Surreys and bicycles for adults and kids can be rented from a kiosk between the Indiana State Museum and the NCAA Hall of Champions. Maps, helmets, and locks are included in the rental cost.

Restoration on the White River State Park area began in the late 1980s. Originally engineered in the 1830s as a way to ship goods through the state of Indiana, the canal project went bankrupt and the Indianapolis section of the canal was the only section that was ever dug. Although the canal was never used for what it was built for, the restoration and development that has occurred has changed the area and made it a main cultural and recreational center for the city of Indianapolis.

REGIONAL PARKS

EAGLE CREEK PARK
7840 W. 56th St.
(317) 327-7110
www.eaglecreekpark.org
One of the largest municipal parks in the nation,

Eagle Creek Park is only 10 minutes from downtown. Bought by J. K. Lilly of the Lilly pharmaceutical family in 1936 as a nature preserve, the property was given to Purdue University in the late 1950s. When the university could no longer maintain it, the land was sold to the City of Indianapolis. An earthen dam was built to control flooding, and the result is the popular Eagle Creek of today. Located southwest of the city, Eagle Creek Park has 3,900 acres of park and 1,400 acres of water, offering a wealth of recreational opportunities.

A one-acre ecology pond, five-acre Lilly Lake, and skating ponds also are located within the park. Open May to Sept, the Eagle Creek Park Marina is the center of water activities such as sailing, canoeing, and rowboat rentals. Sailing lessons, board sailing, bait, and concessions also are available, along with boat rides on the reservoir.

Open May to Aug, the Eagle Creek Park Beach features a sandy beach and grassy sunbathing area. A volleyball court, lifeguards on duty, concessions, and a clothes-check area are available.

Open year-round from dawn to dusk, Eagle Creek Park features more than 10 miles of trails in a serene setting with wonderful views of the glistening reservoir. Six major trails along with additional trails located at the Nature Center wind throughout the park and are easy to moderate in difficulty. Natural and gravel paths lead through mature woods filled with beech, maple, tulip, white ash, and black cherry trees into open meadow areas and past the reservoir and Lilly Lake. Along the way, walkers will find bridges, steps, and a few steep hills. A fitness trail provides a vigorous hike with 20 exercise stations and a total of 32 exercises. Signs explain each exercise, along with how to monitor your heart rate. A year-round Volksmarch steps off on a scenic 10-kilometer trail, where walkers can earn IVV *(Internationaler Volkssportverband)* credit by completing the walk.

The Eagle Creek Park Nature Center was formerly J. K. Lilly's personal library. The Nature Center Complex also includes Lilly Lodge and a reflecting pool. Offering a variety of outdoor educational programs, the Nature Center includes interpretive walks, live animal programs, and outreach programs. The center contains numerous nature games and displays. Also within the complex are self-guided trails, a 600-year-old Douglas fir log, a beech tree where Daniel Boone etched a bear print, native wildflowers, hummingbird and butterfly gardens, and an aquatic garden.

Eagle Creek houses a variety of woodland animals, 260 species of birds, nearly 400 species of flowering plants, and 101 varieties of trees. Located north of the Nature Center, Lilly Lodge overlooks the reservoir and is used for wildlife and nature art shows.

Additional amenities include shelter and retreat houses, a world-class archery field, shooting range, restaurants, Bark Park, sailboat club, concession stands, fishing areas, picnic areas, boat ramp and slips, pistol and archery range and cross-country skiing when there is enough snow.

GARFIELD PARK
2345 Pagoda Dr.
(317) 327-7220
www.garfieldparkindy.org
Once a horse-racing park, Garfield Park is the oldest park in the city. Bought by a group of local businessmen in 1874 for horse racing, the track failed and the City of Indianapolis bought the land. First named Southern Park, the site was renamed following the assassination of President James A. Garfield in 1881.

The 136-acre Garfield Park still retains some of its Victorian elegance. At the turn of the century, workers added a series of winding drives in the Victorian Romantic fashion. Two of the park's graceful concrete arch bridges date from that period. Observation towers were also a popular feature of parks during the turn of the century. In 1903 the park board built a three-tiered pagoda for sightseers and picnickers. The pagoda still offers good views of downtown Indy, some 2 miles north.

i For a lovely summertime experience, attend a performance of the Bard in Garfield Park, performances of plays by William Shakespeare offered at the Garfield Park Arts Center. Admission is free. To see what's playing, check out the Web site at www.bardatgarfieldpark.com.

In 1912 beautiful sunken gardens were added to Garfield Park. Restored in the 1990s, the sunken gardens feature spray fountains lit by colored lights and tan brick walks lining planting beds. The Garfield Park Conservatory and Sunken Gardens are a wonderful place to visit any time of the year. Seasonal shows include the poinsettia show in mid-Nov to mid-Dec and a bulb show in early spring.

The northwest corner of the park features a silent tribute to Marion County's fallen World War I soldiers. Completed in 1920, the Memorial Grove offers majestic trees and is a peaceful spot for personal reflection.

Other amenities at Garfield Park include an arts center, McAlister Center for the Performing Arts, a seasonal aquatic center, picnic shelters, tennis courts, a softball diamond, walking trail, horseshoe courts, an outdoor basketball court, a gym, weight room, playgrounds, and a sledding hill.

RIVERSIDE PARK
2420 E. Riverside Dr.
(317) 327-7171
www.indyparks.org

Five miles from downtown, Riverside Park got its name because of its location—it sits along the White River. So it was no surprise that the park has been flooded, in 1904 and in 1913. Founded in 1898 as part of land 6 miles in length, Riverside was once home to the city zoo, which closed in the park in 1916. A major renovation in the 1990s added a new aquatic center, a family center with a gymnasium, community room, and banquet facilities. Amenities include 12 tennis courts, two baseball diamonds, seven softball diamonds (three of which are lighted), two playgrounds, a boat launch on the White River, picnic shelters, two outdoor basketball courts, a horseshoe pit, and four football fields (two of which are lighted).

SAHM PARK
6801 E. 91st St.
(317) 915-0336
www.indyparks.org

Opened in 1963 as Northeastway Park, this facil-ity was renamed Sahm Park in 1978. The central focal point of the park is the remodeled aquatic center, boasting a 400,000-gallon pool with a zero-depth area, numerous spray features, three slides, and lap lanes. The park is adjacent to Sahm Golf Course, designed in 1963 by Pete and Alice Dye.

Other amenities include a playground, pavilion, shelters, picnic knoll, four tennis courts, a basketball court, soccer fields, sand volleyball courts, a fitness trail, and disk golf course.

SOUTHEASTWAY PARK
5624 S. Carroll Rd., New Palestine
(317) 861-0506
www.indyparks.org

Founded in 1961, Southeastway Park offers 188 acres of varied terrain with 80 acres of woods. Buck Creek runs through the woods in the western section of the park. Southeastway Park offers a variety of natural habitats, including open fields and meadows, wetland, prairie preserve, and a pond. Amenities include six picnic shelters, three-picnic areas, grills, bike trails, more than 3 miles of hiking trails, an activity and education center, a playground, and a sledding hill.

SOUTHWESTWAY PARK
8400 Mann Rd.
(317) 327-7379
www.indyparks.org

Located about 10 miles south of downtown Indy, Southwestway Park features 587 acres with an interesting history. Quakers originally inhabited the area around the park and founded the town of Spring Valley in 1848. Before it was abandoned in 1884, Spring Valley contained five businesses, a post office, a school, and residences. The land around the present-day park was farmed and used for pasture for decades until it was purchased for a regional park.

Southwestway Park contains some of the most outstanding geological features in Central Indiana. The area is part of a delta complex formed by a glacier, with the most significant formation being Mann Hill. Described as a kame—a hill or mound deposited during the melting of

🔍 Close-up

Indy Bark Parks

Fido can enjoy the freedom of being off leash at several Indianapolis parks. Indy Parks and Recreation currently has three Bark Parks or Canine Companion Zones—at Broad Ripple Park, Eagle Creek Park, and Paul Ruster Park. Four-legged friends are invited to run to their hearts' content without being leashed. The city Bark Parks require a fee for admission—$75 for an annual pass, $10 for a gate access card, or $5 for a daily Pooch Pass. Separate Pooch Passes are required for each Bark Park.

To obtain a Pooch Pass, visit the park office with the dog's vaccination record documenting current inoculations for rabies, parvo, distemper, and bordetella. To keep the doggie parks safe and enjoyable for all visitors, a set of rules and etiquette applies—mostly commonsense precautions like cleaning up after your dog and keeping a close watch on your dog and others. Dogs must be kept on a leash until they are inside the Canine Companion Zone. Pet companions also must keep one leash per dog with them at all times, as well as remaining in the Canine Companion Zone with their dog at all times.

Broad Ripple Bark Park is open dawn to dusk Tuesday through Friday and 8:30 a.m. to dusk Saturday through Monday. Call (317) 327-7161 for more information. Eagle Creek Gordon Gilmer Canine Companion Zone is open daily dawn to dusk. Call (317) 327-7110. Paul Ruster Bark Park is open daily dawn to dusk. Call (317) 327-0143.

---

stagnant glacial ice—Mann Hill is the highest hill in Indianapolis. Located along the White River, the bluff rises about 150 feet above the surrounding land.

Southwestway Park is joined with Winding River Golf Course and Cottonwood Lakes. In 2002 the community along with the Park Foundation bought an additional 101 acres to expand the park. Amenities include three baseball diamonds, a picnic shelter, concession stand, six soccer fields, hiking trails, and a playground.

COMMUNITY PARKS

BETHEL PARK
2850 Bethel Ave.
(317) 327-7480
www.indyparks.org
This neighborhood park features an aquatic center, picnic shelter, a playground, baseball, football, basketball, a paved trail, gym, computer lab, game room, horseshoe pits, and an outdoor swimming pool.

i Most outdoor swimming pools in city parks are open from Memorial Day through Labor Day. Hours are usually daily 8 a.m. to 8 p.m.

BROAD RIPPLE PARK
1550 Broad Ripple Ave.
(317) 327-7161
www.indyparks.org
Bordering the White River, Broad Ripple Park was established in 1946. The site was once home to an amusement park, a carousel (now at the Indianapolis Children's Museum), and a steam locomotive (now at the Transportation Museum in Noblesville). It was also the location of the Olympic tryouts for swimming in 1924 and 1953. The park has a family center, seasonal swimming pool, playground, two picnic shelters, picnic knoll, six tennis courts, baseball diamond, athletic field, viewing platform over the White River, woods, fitness trail, dog park, and boat launch in the White River.

BROOKSIDE PARK
3500 Brookside Parkway South Dr.
(317) 327-7179
www.indyparks.org
Established in 1898, Brookside Park has 108 acres of rolling wooded green space about five minutes from downtown Indy. The heart of Brookside Park is the 20,000-square-foot Family Center. Built in 1928, the center hosts numerous programs and activities for both children and adults. The center is also a popular place for family reunions, wedding receptions and other events. Amenities include three playgrounds, three outdoor basketball courts, four tennis courts, five picnic pavilions, a seasonal pool, 18-hole disk golf course, gym, football field, sledding hill, soccer field, three baseball diamonds, a softball diamond, and 10 horseshoe pits.

i Possession of alcohol is not permitted in Indy parks without a permit from the Park Board for a special use.

CHRISTIAN PARK
4200 English Ave.
(317) 327-7163
www.indyparks.org
Established in 1921, Christian Park is located on the southeast side of Indianapolis. For nearly half a century, the park has been home to the Christian Park Little League. The park offers wonderful green parkways and walking trails. Other amenities include a family center, spray pool, two picnic shelters, a picnic knoll, two playgrounds, five tennis courts, five Pee Wee diamonds, three Little League ball diamonds, a football field, and outdoor basketball court.

DOUGLASS PARK
1616 E. 25th St.
(317) 327-7174
www.indyparks.org
Established in 1921, Douglass Park covers 43 acres and offers a variety of programs. Amenities include a family center, kitchen, swimming pool, playground, two picnic shelters, four tennis courts, baseball diamond, softball diamond, football field,

paved fitness trail, basketball courts, meeting rooms, game room, two billiard tables, foosball, air hockey, ping-pong, and computer lab.

ELLENBERGER PARK
5301 E. St. Clair St.
(317) 327-7176
www.indyparks.org
Established in 1909, Ellenberger Park is located in historic Irvington on the east side of Indianapolis. A lovely park with rolling terrain, Ellenberger features an ice-skating rink, seasonal swimming pool, playground, picnic shelter, eight tennis courts, baseball diamond, softball diamond, football field, paved fitness trail, and trailhead for Pleasant Run Trail.

GLENNS VALLEY NATURE PARK
8015 S. Bluff Rd.
(317) 881-7429
www.indyparks.org
Originally called Bluff Road Estates, Glenns Valley Nature Park got its name when owner James A. Himler deeded the land to the City of Indianapolis in 1992. The former Himler residence was renovated and the three-car garage was converted into a classroom. The park features a natural area with native Indiana plants. Amenities include walking trails, tall grass prairie, hardwood forest, picnic area, playground, and sledding hill.

HOLLIDAY PARK
6383 Spring Mill Rd.
(317) 327-7180
www.indyparks.org
Located along the banks of the White River, the 95-acre Holliday Park is one of the city's oldest. The park features a wooded area with natural springs and wetlands, a pond, long stretch of the White River, beech-maple forest, and more than 400 species of trees, shrubs, and wildflowers. While hiking the 2 miles of trails that wind through the forest, bird watchers have spotted more than 200 species of birds. Deer, fox, beaver, rabbits, squirrel, and other native animals can sometimes been seen in the park's heavily wooded ravines.

Amenities include a nature center with interactive exhibit hall and live animals, playground, picnic tables, 3 miles of hiking trails with access to the White River and an extensive arboretum.

ℹ️ Dogs must be on a leash that is less than 20 feet in length in Indy parks unless in Bark Parks or Canine Companion Zones.

JTV HILL PARK
1806 N. Columbia Ave.
(317) 327-7177
www.indyparks.org
Established in 1921, JTV Hill Park was dedicated to James Thomas Vastine Hill, one of Indy's first African-American lawyers who later served as a Marion County deputy prosecutor. The park features a recreation center, gym, shuffleboard, playground, softball field, soccer field, football field, and outdoor basketball courts.

KRANNERT PARK
605 S. High School Rd.
(317) 327-7375
www.indyparks.org
Once the Krannert YMCA, Krannert Park became a city park in 1972. The park features year-round indoor swimming as well as an outdoor pool. Other amenities include a family center, wooded area, pond, trails, playground, weight room, two picnic shelters, four tennis courts, three softball diamonds, football field, and outdoor basketball court.

MUNICIPAL GARDENS
1831 Lafayette Rd.
(317) 327-7190
www.indyparks.org
Before opening as a public park in 1952, Municipal Gardens was a private canoe and yacht club as well as a popular dance hall. Amenities include a gymnasium, multipurpose rooms, kitchen, spray pool, shelter, playground, and outdoor basketball court.

NORTHWESTWAY PARK
5253 W. 62nd St.
(317) 327-1470
www.indyparks.org
Offering 117 acres of recreational opportunities, Northwestway Park includes a 135,000-gallon outdoor swimming pool with a zero-depth entry and a fan-shaped area with many water play features, including the largest body slide in the park system. The park also has Little Eagle Creek, an open prairie, playground, picnic tables, picnic shelters and grills, basketball court, soccer fields, disk golf course, baseball fields, softball fields, and a fitness trail.

PERRY PARK
451 E. Stop 11 Rd.
(317) 888-0070
www.indyparks.org
Established in 1961, Perry Park hosts one of the two ice and in-line skating rinks in the city park system. Perry also has a seasonal swimming pool, shelters, picnic areas, and a community room.

POST ROAD COMMUNITY PARK
1313 S. Post Rd.
(317) 327-0143
www.indyparks.org
Surrounded by beautiful mature trees, the 40-acre Post Road Community Park features a meeting facility, banquet hall, playground, swings, picnic shelter, two basketball courts, and two sand volleyball courts.

RAYMOND PARK—INDY ISLAND
8575 E. Raymond St.
(317) 862-6876
www.indyparks.org
When the local school district needed more room for a middle school in 1993, properties were merged to create Raymond Park Middle School and Indy Island Aquatic Center. The park offers a wide variety of programs and activities for all ages. Amenities include an indoor pool, wetlands, prairie lands, trail, baseball fields, outdoor basketball courts, community room with kitchenette, concession stand, and locker rooms with showers.

RHODIUS PARK
1720 W. Wilkins St.
(317) 327-7191
www.indyparks.org

A supervised and unsupervised play area, Rhodius Park has served the West Indy community for more than three decades and is popular for its youth programming. A new family center includes a fitness center, youth game room, large community room, dance studio, arts and crafts area, conference room, full kitchen, computer lab, library, and new restrooms. Rhodius Park also has a picnic shelter, playground, baseball field, basketball court, tennis court, trail, weight room, gym, and sledding hill.

i Indy Parks has accommodations of all sizes for a variety of occasions. Picnic shelters, pools, gardens, and facilities are perfect for business outings, family gatherings, birthday parties, weddings, and more. Learn more at www.indyparks.org or call (317) 327-7275.

THATCHER PARK
4649 W. Vermont St.
(317) 327-7390
www.indyparks.org

Located on the near west side of Indianapolis, Thatcher Park offers many programs and activities for all ages. Amenities include a family center, indoor swimming pool, two picnic shelters, two Little League baseball diamonds, softball diamond, adult baseball diamond, playgrounds, athletic field, wood-floor gym with basketball or volleyball courts, and walking trail.

WASHINGTON PARK
3130 E. 30th St.
(317) 327-7473
www.indyparks.org

Nestled on the near east side of Indy, Washington Park features 128 acres with a large amount of lovely green space. Amenities include a family recreation center, Sarge Johnson Boxing Center, outdoor basketball complex, outdoor waterslide station, nature walking trails, pond, playground, and 18-hole disk golf course.

WATKINS PARK
2360 Martin Luther King Jr. St.
(317) 327-7175
www.indyparks.org

Watkins Park offers 21 acres and a wide variety of youth programs and activities. Located just northwest of Indy, the park features nice views of the city's skyline. Amenities include a playground, outdoor basketball courts, four tennis courts, gym, game room, football field, baseball field, softball field, and two horseshoe pits.

WINDSOR VILLAGE PARK
6510 E. 25th St.
(317) 327-7162
www.indyparks.org

Windsor Village Park features an open game room with a pool table, foosball table, and PlayStation video games. During the summer, the park offers an eight-week playground program for neighborhood youth. Amenities include a shelter, playground, basketball court, spray pool, and family center. The Indianapolis Parks Foundation is currently raising funds to build a new family center complete with gym and other amenities.

RECREATION

Lace on your running shoes and take a jog past a canal where you might spy an actual gondolier, perhaps crooning a sweet tune. Rent a bike or bring your own and cruise through some of the nation's finest park paths. Splash through the water in one of Indy's many pools or try your luck at pulling in a record catfish at a local lake. Maybe bird-watching is more your speed. Indianapolis has plenty of warblers to enjoy and nature centers where birds and their watchers can happily connect. Whatever your favorite recreation, chances are Indianapolis has a place to do it.

The typical Hoosier isn't one to sit idly around and let the world go by. Activities abound, many of them free of charge. Bad weather? That's okay. It doesn't have to ruin your day. As you'll discover in this chapter, Indy has plenty of indoor recreational opportunities, as well. So you don't have to climb the walls—although, if you really want to, that's an option as well. (See the Climbing section in this chapter.) You'll also find recreational opportunities in the Golf, Kidstuff, and Parks chapters, as well as in Day Trips and Weekend Getaways. So what are you sitting there for? Get out and see what Indianapolis has to offer.

BIKING

MAJOR TAYLOR VELODROME
3469 Cold Spring Rd.
(317) 327-8356
www.majortaylor.com
The Velodrome is a world-class bicycle-racing track, named after one of the sport's 19th-century greats. It's the site of many national competitions and education programs. Also site of the Lake Sullivan BMX Track, an American Bicycle Association–certified bicycle motocross track. Open riding, weather permitting.

WHEEL FUN RENTALS
424 W. Ohio St.
(317) 767-5072
www.wheelfunrentals.com
Enjoy the miles of bike paths in downtown Indy. Offering a variety of two- and four-wheel bikes from cruisers to surrey carriages, Wheel Fun Rentals is open daily during summer and weekends in spring and fall. Look for the bike kiosk in White River State Park by the Indiana State Museum.

BIRD-WATCHING

HOLLIDAY PARK NATURE CENTER
6363 Spring Mill Rd.
(317) 327-7180
www.hollidaypark.org
This 13,000-square-foot facility has a bird and wildlife observation area with feeding stations and a sound system to allow viewers to hear the birds. An extensive wildflower garden and a wildlife-friendly prairie are nearby. Visitors can also relax on the lawns, hike riverside trails, burn off some energy on the playground, with its big slides and a rock-climbing wall, and take in the Ruins, a sculpture park made from a salvaged New York City skyscraper.

BOATING

OLD WORLD GONDOLIERS, INC.
337 W. 11th St.
(317) 491-4835
www.4gondola.com
Experience the beauty, mystique, and charm of downtown Indianapolis from a Venetian-style gondola, complete with singing gondolier and

spectacular canal views. Reservations begin Apr 15, with rides available from Mother's Day through early Sept. Public rides board at the canal's Ohio Street hub. Private rides board at Buggs Temple at the north end on 11th Street. On-board catered dinners are available.

i Jeff Hutson first launched a gondola on Indianapolis's Central Canal in October 2003. His 27-foot, six-passenger gondola, *Black Swan,* was the first one in the city. The first gondola in the Midwest was in 1893 at the Chicago World's Fair, where a ride cost 50 cents.

WHEEL FUN RENTALS
425 W. Ohio St.
(317) 767-5072
www.wheelfunrentals.com
Enjoy Indy's Central Canal on a pedal boat or kayak. The boat shop is located in the canal at the corner of West and Ohio Streets, beneath Fire Station 13. Rentals are available daily during summer from 10 a.m. to 10 p.m. and on weekends during spring and fall.

BOWLING

EXPO BOWL
5261 Elmwood Dr.
(317) 787-3448
www.royalpin.com
A modern smoke-free (nonsmoking except in the bar area) bowling center, Expo Bowl offer 80 lanes with Brunswick automatic scoring. Expo Bowl also features the Laser Storm game, Glow-in-the-Dark Cosmic Bowling, and the Royal Café with sandwiches and other snacks.

SOUTHERN BOWL
1010 S. US 31
(317) 881-8686
www.royalpin.com
Featuring 40 lanes with Brunswick automatic scoring, Southern Bowl is a nonsmoking center with Glow-in-the-Dark Cosmic Bowling and a snack bar with sandwiches and other goodies.

WESTERN BOWL
6441 W. Washington St.
(317) 247-4426
www.royalpin.com
Featuring Brunswick automatic scoring on 80 lanes, this smoke-free lane offers karaoke nights on Fri and Sat, along with Glow-in-the-Dark Cosmic Bowling and a snack bar.

WOODLAND BOWL
3421 E. 96th St.
(317) 844-4099
www.royalpin.com
With 80 lanes and Brunswick automatic scoring, this smoke-free center is home to 23 professional bowling tournaments and has also conducted four world team challenges. Woodland Bowl features two lounges, including a theater-style sports bar and another with five pool tables. Woodland also offers Pirates Cove Miniature Golf, Glow-in-the-Dark Cosmic Bowling, a full-service pro shop, and the Royal Café for sandwiches and snacks.

i Bowling, which developed from the European sport of ninepins, became popular in Indianapolis in the late 1800s. In the 1890s German immigrants operated four bowling alleys in the Athenaeum on East Michigan Street, when the building was called Das Deutsche Haus.

CLIMBING

CLIMB TIME INDY
8750 Corporation Dr.
(317) 596-3330
www.climbtimeindy.com
This facility offers indoor rock climbing for all ages and 10,000 square feet of climbing space for building strength and confidence.

FISHING

INDY LAKES CAMPGROUND
4001 W. Southport Rd.
(317) 888-8006
www.indylakes.com

Indy Lakes Campground features a full-time bait and tackle shop and Indy's oldest pay lakes, including Lake Le-An-Wa, open since 1951. The lake specializes in big cats and carp contests and frequently stocks farm-raised channel catfish to take home. The holding tanks for the "big ones" are stocked every Sunday in season.

FITNESS

ARTHUR M. GLICK JCC
6701 Hoover Rd.
(317) 251-9467
www.jccindy.org
The facility offers programs and services for all ages to become emotionally, intellectually, and physically healthy. Membership is open to all regardless of race, creed, or religious affiliation. Services include early childhood and school-age programs, sports, fitness, and aquatics programs, a fitness center, comprehensive cultural arts program, senior services, networking events, and educational programs.

THE MONON CENTER—CARMEL CLAY PARKS AND RECREATION
1235 Central Park Dr. East, Carmel
(317) 848-7275
www.carmelclayparks.com
Located in a 161-acre park, this facility features natural wetlands, a lagoon, a boardwalk, and miles of trails. The Monon Center has 114,971 square feet of state-of-the-art amenities, including a fitness center, indoor aquatics center, gymnasium, walking and running track, and outdoor aqua park.

NATIONAL INSTITUTE FOR FITNESS AND SPORT
White River State Park
250 University Blvd.
(317) 274-3432
www.nfs.org
The National Institute for Fitness and Sport is within convenient walking distance from downtown Indy and offers daily, weekly, and monthly passes. Features include a 65,000-square-foot fitness center, NBA-size basketball court, 200-meter rubberized running track, extensive equipment, and the latest group fitness classes, including Les Mills's BodyPump and yoga.

SPORTZONE
6601 Coffman Rd.
(317) 293-2255
www.sportzoneindy.com
A premier, six-acre indoor facility and fitness center, SportZone offers excellent indoor arenas for baseball, softball, basketball, soccer, volleyball, and flag football. SportZone offers many leagues as well as informal games. State-of-the-art fitness equipment is also available.

SKATING

MAJOR TAYLOR SKATE PARK
3649 Cold Spring Rd.
(317) 327-8356
www.indyparks.org/skatepark
The park at Major Taylor Velodrome, an elite bicycle arena, is available for skateboarders, in-line skaters and bikers, with staggered hours for each maintained for safety. Mounds for freestyle biking are adjacent to the skate park.

PEPSI COLISEUM
Indiana State Fairgrounds
1202 E. 38th St.
(317) 927-7622
www.in.gov/statefair
Public ice-skating takes place at the State Fairgrounds from mid-Oct through mid-Mar. Rental figure skates and hockey skates are available.

PERRY ICE RINK
451 E. Stop 11 Rd.
(317) 865-1833
Founded in 1983, Perry Ice Rink is an indoor rink open from Oct to Apr. The rink features public skating sessions, figure skating and ice-skating lessons, adult and youth ice hockey lessons, and clinics and broomball.

YMCA Of Greater Indianapolis

From London, England, in 1844 to Indianapolis, Indiana, in 1854, the YMCA maintains a rich tradition of building strong kids, strong families, and strong communities. Throughout Indianapolis, YMCA branches serve more than 185,000 people from diverse communities—providing over $7 million in scholarships, program subsidies, and underwritten programs in low-income communities. Each Indianapolis branch offers various programs for children and adults. Contact the individual YMCA's for details.

Corporate Office
615 N. Alabama St.
(317) 266-9622
www.indymca.org

Baxter YMCA
7900 S. Shelby St.
(317) 881-9347

Benjamin Harrison YMCA
5736 Lee Rd.
(317) 547-9622

Fishers YMCA
9012 E. 126th St., Fishers
(317) 595-9622

Intercollegiate YMCA
4600 Sunset Ave.
(317) 940-9542

Jordan YMCA
8400 Westfield Blvd.
(317) 253-3206

Pike YMCA
7114 Lakeview Parkway West Dr.
(317) 297-9622

Ransburg YMCA
501 N. Shortridge Rd.
(317) 357-8441

Urban Mission YMCA
615 N. Alabama St.
(317) 266-9622

West District YMCA
7811 W. Morris St.
(317) 484-9622

YMCA at the Athenaeum
401 E. Michigan St.
(317) 685-9705

THE ROLLER CAVE
8734 E. 21st St.
(317) 898-1817
www.rollercave.com
This state-of-the-art facility is themed to cave surroundings. The rink features a large skating surface, full-service snack bar, lighted dance floor, and a huge game room. It is also home of the Bat Cave, featuring Indiana's only slam-dunk basketball facility, indoor baseball, and softball batting caves, plus an 18-hole miniature golf course.

TENNIS

INDIANAPOLIS TENNIS CENTER
IUPUI
150 University Blvd.
(317) 278-2100
www.iupui.edu
Open to visitors and within easy walking distance of downtown hotels, the facility features six Deco-Turf II indoor courts, 14 outdoor hard courts, and four outdoor clay courts. Get in a match or rent a ball machine.

TRACK AND FIELD

IU MICHAEL A. CARROLL TRACK & SOCCER STADIUM
IUPUI
1001 W. New York St.
(317) 274-9749
www.track-soccer.iupui.edu
Check in at the Indiana University Natatorium service desk for access to the stadium's 400-meter, eight-land track with a rubber surface, infield for high jumps, pole vault, discus, shot put, hammer throw, and javelin, and a championship sport field for soccer and other team sports. The facility has hosted the U.S. Soccer Open Cup and U.S.A. Olympic Team Trials for track and field.

WATER PARKS & POOLS

INDIANA UNIVERSITY NATATORIUM
901 W. New York St.
(317) 274-3518
www.iunat.iupui.edu
Open to the public, the facility offers year-round programs including learn-to-swim, daily lap swimming, and several aquatic fitness classes.

The Natatorium contains a 50-meter competition pool, 18-foot diving well, 50-meter instructional pool, and two exercise rooms. The facility has hosted several Olympic Trial competitions as well as the USA Swimming National Championship.

INDY PARKS POOLS/AQUATIC PROGRAMS
Various locations
(317) 327-7412
www.indy.gov
Indy Parks has six indoor pools and more than 15 outdoor pools or swimming options.

THE MONON CENTER—CARMEL CLAY PARKS & RECREATION
1235 Central Park Dr. East, Carmel
(317) 848-7275
www.carmelclayparks.com
The new splashy outdoor Aqua Park features an activity pool, lap pool with six 25-meter lanes, lazy river, waterslides, diving board, plunge slide, and more. The indoor aquatics area offers an activity pool, interactive water features, waterslides, and six 25-meter lanes.

SPECTATOR SPORTS

In Indianapolis, sports are much more than a tradition—they are a passion. From the Colts to the Pacers to the Indians to the Fever and the Ice, along with our many college and high school teams, Hoosiers have plenty to love. If you ever doubt how seriously we take our sports, just try to get tickets to the Indy 500 or to some championship game. Motorsports are so important in Indianapolis that I've devoted an entire chapter to that spectacular sport in this book, as well as a chapter on golf.

Some fans have a big red circle on their calendars around the date of Sunday, February 5, 2012. That's when the Super Bowl will be played at Indy's Lucas Oil Stadium. Better start making arrangements now. That is going to be quite a party. Downtown will be alive with celebrants.

Not only do sports thrive in Indianapolis but the city thrives because of them. Sports are big business. And that's no accident. Back in the mid-1970s, Indianapolis chose to use sports as an economic and community development tool and backed the construction of sports facilities and marketing strategies to attract top sporting events.

This effort has paid off handsomely. The publicity surrounding major athletic events results in national and international name recognition for Indianapolis. Ask a man or woman on the street in some far-flung state about their unseen impression of Indy. Most often the answer is sports related. Yes, many of our homes do have basketball nets—even makeshift ones—in our driveways or backyards or barn lots. And a list of all-time favorite movies for Hoosiers often involves at least one of these—*Hoosiers* (basketball), *Rudy* (football) or *Breaking Away* (bike races).

Sporting events provide opportunities to showcase the city—not only as a sports center but also as a tourist destination, a business center, and a good place to live, work, and invest.

In 1979 the Indiana Sports Corporation (ISC) was formed. A not-for-profit, privately funded organization, ISC was one of the first of its kind to target amateur sports as a growth industry. It attracts national and international sporting events to the city and state, represents Indianapolis in the international sports marketplace, and coordinates events. To date, Indianapolis has hosted more than 400 national and international sporting events, attracted numerous sports organizations, and built or renovated an estimated $400 million worth of facilities. From 1977 through 2009, the direct economic impact of amateur sports in Indianapolis was estimated to be in excess of $3 billion.

The city of Indianapolis has built its reputation as the "Amateur Sports Capital of the World," which is due in large part to the world-class sports facilities within its downtown. Victory Field shares the limelight with the neighboring Lucas Oil Stadium, Conseco Fieldhouse, the Indiana University Natatorium, the Indianapolis Tennis Center, and the Michael E. Carroll Track & Soccer Stadium.

The opening of Victory Field in 1996 was seen by many as the catalyst for a revitalization of downtown Indianapolis. The area has enjoyed over $3 billion in public and private capital investment in the last decade. The thriving downtown now boasts more than 200 eating and drinking establishments as well as more than 300 retail stores, including the Circle Centre Mall. Also within walking distance of Victory Field is the Indiana Convention Center and its nearly 600,000 square feet of exhibit and meeting space. Yet within this critical mass of activity, convenient access has remained a priority, as evidenced by the 6,400 parking spaces available within 3 blocks of the ballpark.

In 1999 the most well-known amateur athletic association in the country—the National Collegiate Athletic Association (NCAA)—moved its headquarters to Indianapolis.

Adjacent to the headquarters is the NCAA Hall of Champions museum that opened in 2000. According to an economic impact study, the NCAA generates more than $63 million annually for Indianapolis and Indiana.

Indianapolis, the Indiana Sports Corporation, and the NCAA also have an agreement that will make the city home to the Men's and Women's Division I Final Four, men's and women's basketball regionals, and the NCAA's Annual Convention on an annual, rotating basis beginning in 2011 and continuing through 2039. Indianapolis also will serve as a backup contingency for future Final Fours should the previously designated city be unable to host.

In late December 2010, Indianapolis is scheduled to have one of the nation's top 20 largest convention center complexes. The combination of the new multipurpose Lucas Oil Stadium and an expanded Indiana Convention Center means Indianapolis will be able to offer 3.4 million square feet of exhibit and meeting space. The combined new space will make the Indiana Convention Center the nation's 16th largest. It currently is 32nd.

i In 1954, Milan High School in Milan (pop. 1,739), with an enrollment of 161 students, won the state championship basketball title against Muncie (pop. 69,058) with a last second shot by Bobby Plump. The 1985 movie *Hoosiers,* starring Gene Hackman, was inspired by the victory.

The Indiana Convention Center will have 566,600 square feet of exhibit space. The new exhibit halls are contiguous with the existing halls. Another 183,000 square feet is in Lucas Oil Stadium, which will be connected to the center via a walkway. The Indiana Convention Center expansion will sit on the old RCA Dome footprint. The RCA Dome closed in April 2008 and has been demolished.

The growth of the facilities is partly driven by location. Indianapolis is within a day's drive of more than half of the nation's population. Its airport is just 15 minutes from downtown. The Convention Center is located in the heart of Indianapolis's revitalized downtown and connected by skywalks to eight hotels, 3,200 rooms, and the Circle Centre shopping and entertainment complex with more than 100 stores, shops, and restaurants. Also located within walking distance of the Convention Center are more than 50 major attractions, 200 restaurants, and, by 2011, 27 hotels with more than 7,100 rooms.

If it's sports you are looking for, Indianapolis is the place. Stroll downtown Indy and see the cathedral-like buildings we have erected in honor of our favorite teams. Amble into a sports bar or casual restaurant and see the walls of big-screen TVs, a way to make sure we don't miss a minute of the action. Sports is the lifeblood of Indianapolis, and you'll discover that the heartbeat of our city is going strong.

BASEBALL

INDIANAPOLIS INDIANS
Victory Field
501 W. Maryland St.
(317) 269-3545
www.indyindians.com

This $20 million open-air, grass stadium is the home of the Triple-A Indianapolis Indians baseball team, an affiliate of the Pittsburgh Pirates. The 12,500 permanent-seat stadium features 29 luxury suites and a grass picnic area with open lawn seating for an additional 2,000 fans. The Indians play home games Apr through Sept.

Victory Field opened its gates July 11, 1996, and takes its name from the city's old ballpark. Victory Field also serves as home base to the annual City, County, and High School Baseball State Championships.

i Victory Field was designated "The Best Minor League Ballpark in America" by both *Baseball America* and *Sports Illustrated*.

Originally opened as Perry Stadium in 1931, that ballpark held the name Victory Field from 1942 to 1967, celebrating the United States' victory in World War II. After being named in honor of former player, manager, and team president Owen J. Bush on Aug. 30, 1967, Bush Stadium closed its gates to professional baseball on July 3, 1996.

Located at the corner of West and Maryland streets in downtown Indianapolis, Victory Field offers a spectacular view of the Indianapolis skyline. The facility boasts many unique features, including an open concourse that offers a great view of the playing field throughout the ballpark, festival-style lawn seating, and angled outfield seats that hug the foul lines. The ballpark can comfortably accommodate crowds of 14,500. Victory Field also features 28 luxury suites, five suite-level party areas, and two large picnic areas.

Victory Field represents the southwest border of White River State Park, an urban park that features numerous cultural, educational, and recreational attractions.

Professional baseball was first played in Indianapolis in 1877. After 15 years of various franchises competing in various leagues—including four years in the National League and one year in the American League—the current Indianapolis Indians franchise was founded as an original member of the American Association in 1902. That year's team won 95 games and the first of 21 pennants.

i Slugger Hank Aaron, who hit 755 home runs during his major league career, signed his first baseball contract in 1952 with the Indianapolis Clowns of the Negro American League.

The Indians franchise has included such famous past players as Grover Cleveland Alexander, Luke Appling, George Foster, Gabby Hartnett, Harmon Killebrew, Randy Johnson, Ken Griffey

Sr., Roger Maris, Nap Lajoie, Al Lopez, Rube Marquard, Joe McCarthy, Bill McKechnie, and Ray Schalk. The Indianapolis Indians are the second-oldest minor league franchise in American professional baseball, behind only the International League's Rochester Red Wings.

Admission to baseball games is $9 to $13, with a $1 discount for children 14 and under.

BASKETBALL

INDIANA PACERS
Conseco Fieldhouse
125 S. Pennsylvania St.
(317) 917-2500
www.consecofieldhouse.com

The $183 million Conseco Fieldhouse stands as a monument to Indiana's rich basketball tradition. Opened in 1999, the Fieldhouse is a surprising blend of cutting edge and nostalgia. It is the first retro-styled facility in the NBA. With 750,000 square feet and 18,345 seats, the Fieldhouse is home to the Indiana Pacers and its sister team, the Indiana Fever, as well as an excellent venue for other major events.

Conseco Fieldhouse has 69 suites, 2,400 club seats, and state-of-the-art amenities. There are plenty of places to grab a hotdog or slice of pizza or sit down for a gourmet meal.

The Ultimate Sports Road Trip ranked Conseco Fieldhouse as "the finest of them all in the four major sports" in 2006. *USA Today* called it "A Cathedral to Basketball."

i Oscar Robertson grew up in Indianapolis and was the star of the first all-black basketball team to win a state championship (Crispus Attucks High School in 1955).

The Fieldhouse has hosted major boxing events, ice shows, swimming championships, and performers such as Pavarotti, Bruce Springsteen, the Boston Pops, John Mellencamp, Tim McGraw, Faith Hill, Britney Spears, Kid Rock, and many more. The Pacers square off against basketball's biggest stars from Nov through Apr.

Close-up

Future Sporting Events in Indianapolis Include:

2010

May 30—Indianapolis 500, Indianapolis Motor Speedway

July 25—Allstate 400 at the Brickyard, Indianapolis Motor Speedway

2011

March 3-6—NCAA Big Ten Women's Tournament, Conseco Fieldhouse

March 10-13—NCAA Big Ten Men's Tournament, Conseco Fieldhouse

April 3 and 5—NCAA Division I Women's Final Four, Lucas Oil Stadium

May 29—Indianapolis 500, Indianapolis Motor Speedway

July 24—Allstate 400 at the Brickyard, Indianapolis Motor Speedway

2012

February 5—Super Bowl XLVI, Lucas Oil Stadium

March 1-4—NCAA Big Ten Women's Tournament, Conseco Fieldhouse

March 8-11—NCAA Big Ten Men's Tournament, Conseco Fieldhouse

May 28—Indianapolis 500, Indianapolis Motor Speedway

July 31—Allstate 400 at the Brickyard, Indianapolis Motor Speedway

September—BMW Championships, Crooked Stick Golf Club (dates to be announced)

Ground was broken on July 22, 1997, to create the landmark facility that has risen 14 stories into the Indianapolis skyline. Modeled after Indiana's old high school and college field houses, the building is an experience in itself. Featuring an eye-catching half-barrel type roof with a red-brick and steel interior, the Fieldhouse has huge skylights at the bottom of the building that bathe the arena bowl in natural light during the day and offer an awesome view of the city skyline at night.

Other features include two huge glass curtain walls facing east and west, a grand staircase, seating bowl, large memorabilia cases on each side of the entrance to the seating bowl, roll-out bleachers at the south end, 20- to 22-inch seats, and retro light fixtures. The box office has old-fashioned teller cages with vintage billboards above them.

i The world's largest crane was brought in to install tresses on top of Conseco Fieldhouse. The crane was so large it was disassembled before being brought into the structure and reassembled on the ground level once inside.

The Pacers were born in 1967 when six investors bought a franchise in the proposed American Basketball Association. The nickname "Pacers" was picked, it is said, because it reflects the state's history with harness racing pacers and the pace car used for running the Indy 500. For their first seven years, the Pacers played in the Indiana State Fairground Coliseum, now called the Pepsi Coliseum. In 1974 they moved to the great new Market Square Arena in downtown Indianapolis, where they stayed for 25 years. The

Pacers were the most successful team in ABA history, winning three ABA Championships in four years. In all, they appeared in the ABA Finals five times in the league's nine-year history. The Pacers were one of four ABA teams that joined the NBA in the ABA-NBA merger in 1976. Pacers team members have included Roger Brown, Mel Daniels, Bobby "Slick" Leonard, George McGinnis, Jermaine O'Neal, Rik Smits, Reggie Miller, and Larry Bird (now team president). Pacers tickets range from $15 to $500.

i Boomer and Bowser are the official mascots for the Pacers, while Freddy Fever leads the cheers as the official mascot for the Fever. Rowdy is mascot for the Indians.

INDIANA FEVER
Conseco Fieldhouse
125 S. Pennsylvania St.
(317) 917-2500
www.consecofieldhouse.com
The Fever, Indiana's WNBA team, brings the thrills of women's professional basketball from June through Aug. Since their inaugural season in 2000, the Indiana Fever has had a fast start as a WNBA franchise. See the above listing for more information about Conseco Fieldhouse. Fever tickets range from $14 to $79.

i Have you always dreamed of proposing to your girlfriend or boyfriend at a Pacers or Fever game? Now you can make a proposal of a lifetime in front of more than 18,000 guests at Conseco Fieldhouse. A $200 tax-deductible donation to Pacers Foundation, Inc. will get your personal message in lights on the center scoreboard at Conseco Fieldhouse during Pacers or Fever home games. A $225 tax-deductible donation to Pacers Foundation includes your message and a color photo of your proposal as it appears on the scoreboard.

FOOTBALL

INDIANAPOLIS COLTS
Lucas Oil Stadium
7001 W. 56th St.
(317) 297-7000
www.lucasoilstadium.com
The new, state-of-the-art, 63,000-seat stadium is the permanent home of the Indianapolis Colts, as well as a venue for future NCAA Division I Men's and Women's Final Fours. Lucas Oil Stadium will also play host to the 2012 Super Bowl.

With a grand opening on August 14, 2008, the $719 million stadium has an infill playing surface, seven locker rooms, exhibit space, meeting rooms, dual two-level club lounges, 137 suites, retractable sideline seating, spacious concourses, and much more. Football games can be played indoors or outdoors using the retractable roof and operable north window. Concerts can be played indoors or outdoors in full-stadium or reduced-house configurations. The retro look to the new stadium is a result of Indianapolis's affinity for the historic field-house appearance of sports venues from decades ago. Conseco Fieldhouse, Hinkle Fieldhouse, and the Pepsi Coliseum are other examples of large sports venues, both old and new, around the city with the same type of design.

After nearly 40 years in Baltimore, the Colts moved to Indianapolis in 1984. With coaches such as Don Shula and players like Johnny Unitas, the Colts had won two World Championships and the 1971 Super Bowl for Baltimore. However, owner Robert Irsay wanted Baltimore to upgrade the team's stadium. Negotiations reached such an acrimonious point that Irsay began shopping his team around to other cities. Indianapolis was one of those. In late March 1984 a deal was struck and Mayflower moving trucks (chosen because Indy was Mayflower's headquarters) arrived in the dead of night and moved the Colts gear to Indianapolis. That secretive move is often referred to as "the midnight ride of the Colts."

The Indianapolis Colts hosted their first AFC Conference Championship Game in the RCA Dome on January 21, 2007. Before a sellout crowd, the Colts staged the biggest conference championship comeback in history to defeat the New England Patriots, 38-34, and earn their first trip to the Super Bowl since moving to Indianapolis in 1984.

In 2007 the team won its first Super Bowl since moving to Indianapolis, defeating the Chicago Bears 29-17. Quarterback Peyton Manning and former coach Tony Dungy are heroes in Indianapolis, not only for their sports expertise but also for their excellent sportsmanship and efforts to help the community and young people in particular.

Colts tickets start at $44.

HOCKEY

INDIANA ICE
Indiana State Fairgrounds Pepsi Coliseum
1202 E. 38th St.
(317) 927-7622
www.indianaice.com

Built in 1939, the Indiana State Fairgrounds Pepsi Coliseum has a permanent seating capacity of 7,659 and is used for concerts, ice-skating, rodeos, trade shows, and sporting events. It is home to the Indiana Ice, members of the United States Hockey League.

A historical landmark, the Pepsi Coliseum was the first home of the Indiana Pacers and the centerpiece of the Indiana State Fairgrounds. Built of brick and Indiana limestone, the structure was also home to the Indianapolis Capitals of the American Hockey League for 12 seasons when it opened, including two league championship seasons in 1942 and 1950.

Hockey great Wayne Gretzy began his professional career in 1978 with the Indianapolis Racers. The then 16-year-old Gretzy played his first eight games with the Racers, scoring three goals and three assists.

Banners draping the walls proudly salute the many uses of this structure. The arena hosted a concert by the Beatles in 1964, the only appearance by the Fab Four in Indiana. Another banner commemorates a speech by young Democratic presidential candidate John F. Kennedy in front of a capacity crowd in 1960. In 2003 George W. Bush was the first sitting U.S. president to speak at the Coliseum.

Renovations and improvements have been made to the Coliseum over the years, including a video screen on the east wall and new seats throughout the arena. But four rows of original wooden seats remain intact in each corner of the Coliseum. Fans still use those old seats.

The Indiana Ice is a Tier 1 ice hockey team formed in 2004 when it was purchased from the former Danville, Illinois, team, the Danville Wings. The Ice play in the Eastern Division of the United States Hockey League. Ice players who have gone on to the NHL include Joel Rechlicz and John Carlson. Ice tickets start at $9.

As a renowned hotbed for sports, Indianapolis is also headquarters for several national governing bodies. Among those are the Black Coaches Association, National Collegiate Athletic Association (NCAA), National Federation of State High School Associations, USA Gymnastics, USA Track & Field, U.S. Diving, and U.S. Synchronized Swimming.

OTHER SPORTS FACILITIES

EAGLE CREEK PARK
7840 W. 56th St.
(317) 327-7110
www.eaglecreekpark.org

Eagle Creek is one of the country's largest municipally owned parks. It encompasses more than 1,300 acres of water and 3,900 acres of land. Its regatta course is one of only two in the U.S. sanctioned for international competition by the International Federation of Rowing Associations and has been the site of past U.S. Rowing National Championships. In 1994 the course hosted the

(Q) Close-up

Sports-related Organizations Headquartered in Indianapolis

American College of Sports Medicine

Central Indiana Tennis Association

Coca-Cola Circle City Classic

Great Lakes Valley Conference

Indiana High School Athletic Association

Indiana Horse Council

Indiana Golf Association

Indiana PGA

Indiana Sports Corporation

Indiana Swimming Inc.

Indiana University Sports Medicine Drug Identification Lab

Indiana Youth Soccer Association

International Institute of Sport, Science and Medicine

Horizon League

National Association of Governors' Councils on Physical Fitness and Sports

National Institute for Fitness and Sport

National Youth Sports Corporation

World Rowing Championships, the first time the event was held in the United States. The Park also features an archery range designed according to world-class specifications and two competition fields. Eagle Creek has a 36-hole golf complex that has been rated one of the top 50 public courses in the country by *Golf Digest*.

HINKLE FIELDHOUSE
Butler University
4600 Sunset Ave.
(317) 283-9375
When it opened in 1928 on the Butler University campus, Hinkle Fieldhouse was the largest basketball arena in the United States and remained so for 20 years. Originally called Butler Fieldhouse, it was renamed in 1966 to honor Paul D. "Tony"

Hinkle (1899–1992), basketball coach at Butler for 41 seasons ending in 1970.

Now it is listed in the National Register of Historic Places and was the inspiration for the design of Conseco Fieldhouse, home of the Indiana Pacers. The 10,800-seat Fieldhouse is the home court for Butler University's basketball teams. It was also the site of the first U.S.S.R.-U.S. National Team basketball game and volleyball events for the Pan Am Games. Scenes from the blockbuster movie *Hoosiers* were filmed in the Fieldhouse.

INDIANA UNIVERSITY MICHAEL A. CARROLL
TRACK & SOCCER STADIUM
1001 W. New York St.
(317) 274-5555
www.iupui.edu

Built in 1982 at a cost of $7 million, the Indiana University Michael A. Carroll Track & Soccer Stadium features a nine-lane, 400-meter rubber track that is considered one of the world's fastest. Resurfaced with a new track in 1997, the stadium contains 12,100 permanent spectator seats and is adjacent to several athletic fields for softball, soccer, and volleyball. The USA Outdoor Track & Field Championships were held at the track in 1997, 2006, and 2007.

Both the Indiana University-Purdue University Indianapolis men's and women's soccer teams train at the stadium, located on the IUPUI campus. The stadium is used as a training ground by members of all 14 IUPUI sports, while the soccer team will occasionally host a home match on the grass field as well. During summer, the facility is used for IUPUI Sport Complex Summer Camps, as well as benefit walks and runs.

INDIANA UNIVERSITY NATATORIUM
901 W. New York St.
(317) 274-3518
www.iupui.edu
Built in 1982, the Indiana University Natatorium is one of the prime swimming and diving venues in the world. This facility boasts a swimming pool with adjustable lengths and an 18-foot-deep diving pool featuring five platforms and three springboards. Speed is built into the pool; it is exactly the right depth to reduce reverberation from the bottom.

Events held here include U.S. Olympic swimming, diving and synchronized swimming trials, and NCAA Championships. The Natatorium is also home to the annual IHSAA boy's and girl's swimming championships, along with housing various swimming clubs from across the Midwest. The IU men's and women's swimming and diving teams have called the Natatorium home since their inception in 1998.

Greg Louganis, Michael Phelps, and Jenny Thompson are among those who have competed at this facility, known as one of the world's fastest pools. The seating capacity of the Natatorium is 4,700, making it the largest indoor pool

in the United States. There is also room for additional seating of 1,500 on deck.

The depth of the pool is 9 feet at the ends and 10 feet at the center. Water temperature is kept at 70 degrees. The main pool contains six underwater windows for TV cameras and coaching. It takes one million gallons of water to fill the main pool. To date, there have been 90 American records and 12 world records set in the pool.

INDIANA/WORLD SKATING ACADEMY
Pam American Plaza
(317) 237-5565
www.iwsa.org
Part of Pan American Plaza, the center features two indoor skating rinks. The Olympic Rink, one of the few 100-by-200-foot Olympic-size rinks in the United States, is used for ice-sport training, classes, and public skating. The American Rink is an 85-by-200-foot rink that seats 1,000 spectators. The Research Center houses the Human Performance Lab, where skaters' strengths and weaknesses are tested in regard to their physical conditioning.

INDIANAPOLIS TENNIS CENTER
150 University Blvd.
(317) 278-2100
www.iupui.edu
The Indianapolis Tennis Center features an 8,000-seat stadium court, a 2,000-seat grandstand court, six indoor courts, 14 outdoor hard courts, and four outdoor clay courts. The Tennis Center is the permanent site of the Indianapolis Tennis Championships, an event of the U.S. Open series that has attracted top players such as Lleyton Hewitt, Andy Roddick, James Blake, and Robbie Ginepri.

i Indianapolis composers Albert and Harry Von Tilzer wrote "Take Me Out to the Ball Game."

LITTLE LEAGUE BASEBALL CENTRAL REGION HEADQUARTERS
9802 E. Little League Dr.
(317) 897-6127
www.littleleague.org
The headquarters is responsible for chartering

and serving all 1,000 leagues for the 13 Midwest states that make up the central region of Little League Baseball. The facility hosts annual summer camps for approximately 800 players and year-round leadership training for members. The complex includes six playing fields, a dormitory, swimming pool, tennis and basketball courts, a cafeteria, and administrative building.

MAJOR TAYLOR VELODROME AND LAKE SULLIVAN BMX TRACK
3469 Cold Spring Rd.
(317) 327-8356
www.indy.gov
This world-class bicycle-racing track is named after one of the sport's 19th-century greats.

Born and raised in Indy, Marshall "Major" Taylor was once known as the fastest man on earth. In 1899, when bicycling was a major sport, he became the first black athlete to win the coveted title of world champion bicycle racer—and one of the first black athletes to hold a world champion title in any sport. In 1982, when bicycle racing began enjoying a resurgence in popularity, Indianapolis honored the memory of its native son by building one of the best racing tracks in the country and naming it the Major Taylor Velodrome. The Velodrome today hosts many world-class cycling events.

The 333¹/₃-meter track is smooth concrete with 28-degree banking in the turns. The 33-foot concrete apron also offers a great place for in-line skating. Although the track is used by many elite bicycle racers, it is suitable for ages 10 and up. Clinics, organized group instruction, and individual open riding times are available.

The track, one of only 18 velodromes in the country, hosts many national and international biking competitions as well as remote-control car races and concerts. Next to the track is the Lake Sullivan BMX Track, a bicycle motocross track certified by the American Bicycle Association and sanctioned by the National Bicycle League (NBL). The track offers open riding, weather permitting.

The Velodrome accommodates up to 5,000 spectators and has hosted the Grand Prix of Cycling and the EDS Senior Track Cycling Championships.

In 1996 the Velodrome and BMX track were privatized and now are operated by the Indiana Bicycle Coalition, a nonprofit bicycling advocacy group.

NATIONAL INSTITUTE FOR FITNESS AND SPORT (NIFS)
250 University Blvd.
(317) 274-3432
www.nifs.org
NIFS is a state-of-the-art fitness and research center dedicated to health and physical fitness research, education, and training. Open to athletes, as well as the public, the institute's fitness center offers complete fitness appraisals and has a 200-meter indoor track, regulation-size basketball floor, rubberized workout floor, weight training, and cardiovascular exercise equipment and fitness classes.

WILLIAM KUNTZ SOCCER CENTER
1502 W. 16th St.
(317) 327-7194
Built for the Pan American Games, this facility includes a competition field with 4,500 permanent spectator seats and a practice field that seats 2,000.

Looking for a reason to cheer?

These are the professional sports teams in Indianapolis and where they play:

NFL—**Indianapolis Colts** (Lucas Oil Stadium)

NBA—**Indiana Pacers** (Conseco Fieldhouse)

WNBA—**Indiana Fever** (Conseco Fieldhouse)

Triple-A Minor League Baseball— **Indianapolis Indians** (Victory Field)

United States Hockey League— **Indiana Ice** (Pepsi Coliseum)

MOTORSPORTS

The thunder of revving engines mingles with the roar of more than a quarter million people in the grandstands around Indianapolis Motor Speedway. When the checkered flag falls, 33 powerful open-wheel cars blast off in an awesome show of high-octane power known as the Indy 500. An American icon, the most famous auto race in the world is now over a century old. It has helped turn the Hoosier city of Indianapolis into the racing capital of the world.

Add in the presence of MotoGP, the National Hot Rod Association's national drag-racing championships and a full menu of stock, sprint, and midget car racing, and Indy is unchallenged in its passion and support for life in the fast lane. Motorsports in Central Indiana are a significant local industry, paying more than $425 million in annual wages and employing nearly 9,000 workers. Between Memorial Day and Labor Day, no place hosts more heart-pounding auto racing than Indianapolis.

And it all started with a crazy idea.

In the early part of the 20th century, Indiana was the second largest manufacturer of automobiles in America. Hoosier cars tended to be more expensive and better quality than those made in Michigan, but all vehicles then could have used a higher testing standard. In 1905, Indianapolis auto parts manufacturer Carl Fisher was helping racing friends in France when he observed that Europeans had an edge over the American automobile industry. What his country needed, Fisher decided, was a good way of testing cars before putting them on the road.

i The Indianapolis 500 consists of 200 laps around the track. It is called the 500 because it covers 500 miles.

At the time, American racing was just getting a foothold on horse tracks and even on public roads. But a good automobile racetrack would go a long way, Fisher reasoned. He pitched the idea to three friends and fellow businessmen—James Allison, Arthur Newby, and Frank Wheeler.

Together the four men bought a 328-acre plot of land northwest of downtown Indianapolis for $72,000. But the first race at the new speed-

way wasn't vehicles. It was balloons. Through the track wasn't completed, on the evening of June 5, 1909, nine gas-filled balloons lifted off at the newly christened Indianapolis Motor Speedway, racing for bragging rights and silver trophies. The winner of the Speedway's first competitive event, University City, landed 382 miles away in Alabama after spending more than a day aloft.

The Speedway's track, surfaced with a combination of crushed stone and asphalt, opened for its first auto race on Aug. 19, 1909. Paying $1 for one of the grandstand seats or 50 cents for the first- and second-turn bleachers, between 15,000 and 20,000 spectators came for the big event. Impatient drivers didn't wait for the official start, and flagman Fred Wagner had to stop the field three times and finally begin it from a standing start.

The race was a treacherous one. The track's surface broke up from the heat and the traffic, resulting in the deaths of two drivers, two mechanics, and two spectators. Louis Schwitzer won the first race of the day in his Stoddard-Dayton. But the disaster pointed out the necessity of repaving the track. This time they used street-paving bricks—3,200,000 of them, in fact.

The job took 63 days. By the time the project was finished, the track had already been nicknamed "the Brickyard."

The new brick surface did the job, and the first official race on the new track took place on Dec. 17, 1909. However, fans didn't continue to pack the stands. To draw the public, Fisher and his partners decided they needed something bigger, something unheard of—a really spectacular one-day annual event instead of a series of minor races. That's how the Indy 500 was born.

The inaugural Indianapolis 500-Mile Race was announced for Memorial Day 1911. Making it 500 miles was a big deal, meaning the race would last almost a workday between mid-morning and late afternoon. Fisher himself drove the pace car, leading the race-car pack for a lap around the track before exiting as the checkered flag dropped and the race officially began.

i Louis Meyer was the first driver to drink milk after winning the Indianapolis 500 in 1936. Meyer's mother had always encouraged him to drink milk, so he reached for it on a hot day.

Spectators were mesmerized from the start. The man who would eventually become the race winner, Ray Harroun, didn't have a ride-along mechanic—the only car in the field that didn't. Mechanics gave a much-needed second set of eyes to warn of impending danger. So Harroun mounted a mirror above the cowling of his single-seat Marmon Wasp, built less than 5 miles from the track. Some historians say that was the first use of a rearview mirror. Using the mirror to watch for traffic, Harroun successfully avoided accidents for 200 laps and crossed the finish line with a time of six hours, 42 minutes, and eight seconds. He covered 500 miles with an average speed of 74.59 mph.

But there are those—including pioneer race-car driver Ralph Mulford—who claim another man actually won that first race. On the 13th lap, a multicar accident on the main straightway in front of the scoring stand sent the scorers (many of them Fisher's friends and untrained) scurrying.

For several laps, no one was scoring the race. That's when Mulford claimed he wasn't credited with a lap he completed—a lap that would have made him the winner. Mulford went to his grave contending he had been the first 500 winner.

Along with the scoring controversy, that first race brought death. On lap 13, Arthur Greiner crashed his Amplex, killing his riding mechanic, Sam Dickson.

Since that inaugural race, the Speedway has seen many changes. In 1927 the original partners sold the Speedway to World War I flying ace Eddie Rickenbacker and some Michigan investors. Rickenbacker had been a former Indy 500 driver. The race grew in stature but was suspended because of World War II. By 1945 the track was in dire shape and seemed headed for destruction. That's when Terre Haute businessman Anton Hulman Jr. bought it for $75,000—a fortuitous purchase for the Hulman family and the famed Indy 500.

President of Hulman & Co., Anton Hulman Jr. had made his fortune marketing the company's Clabber Girl into the nation's top-selling baking powder. And Hulman was up to the challenge of getting the dilapidated track ready for a race in May 1946. Pumping millions of dollars into the Indianapolis Motor Speedway, Hulman began a giant improvement project. He built an eight-story control tower, added thousands of new infield seats, built a tunnel under the backstretch, and added a safer pit area walled off from the main stretch.

In 1957 the 500 Festival began to organize community activities to celebrate "the Greatest Spectacle in Racing." The 500 Festival Parade became a major event, drawing thousands of people to downtown Indianapolis. Now, the 500 Festival is organized each May for a full month of celebrations honoring the Indy 500. Highlights include the country's largest half-marathon, the downtown parade, memorial celebrations for the nation's service men and women, Kid's Day festivities, and Community Day at the Indianapolis Motor Speedway.

Gentlemen (and ladies) start their engines at the Indianapolis Motor Speedway long before race day. Throughout May, hordes of racing fans knock off work and head to the track for qualifications, when drivers vie for the 33 coveted positions of the Indianapolis 500. Crowds are thickest on Pole Day, the first round of qualifications; Bump Day, the final chance for racers to make the starting grid; and Carb Day, the last practice before race day, followed by a free rock concert.

The track itself has changed over the years. Although the bricks were an important part of its identity, they weren't a good racing surface. They tended to shift when the ground froze and thawed, and any moisture made them slick. Hulman resurfaced the track and replaced the grandstands and other facilities. By 1961 all that was left of the old brick track was a 3-foot section at the start-finish line. It is still there today. The rest has been covered with asphalt.

Hulman continued to oversee the 500 until his death on Oct. 27, 1977. Hulman's only child, Mari Hulman, married race driver Elmer George in 1957. Their second child and only son, Anton "Tony" Hulman George, would become IMS president in 1989 and remain in that position until he resigned June 30, 2009. Today, the Hulman family still owns the track and operates it as a privately run enterprise.

Under Tony George, the track began to diversify. In 1994 the Speedway hosted its first stock-car race, the Brickyard 400, which today ranks among NASCAR's most prestigious events. George also built a road course in the oval's infield to host the Formula 1 World Championship for Grand Prix–style racing from 2000 to 2007. F1 was replaced by the Red Bull Indianapolis GP, a road race for Grand Prix–level motorcycles.

Although Indianapolis has grown into a destination for big-time pro sports, the Indianapolis Motor Speedway is still what put Indy on the fast track. Visit in May or for any other race and see what all the shouting is all about. A century of

i Troy Ruttman was the youngest winner of the Indy 500—22 years, 80 days when he won in 1952. Al Unser was the oldest—47 years, 360 days when he won in 1987.

i Planning on attending the Indy 500? Don't forget to take plenty of sunscreen, a hat, seat cushion, binoculars, and earplugs.

speed has made Indy the racing place to be. If you want to try your hand at putting the pedal to the metal, marvel at some of the early race cars, or kiss the bricks yourself (as Indy 500 winners do), here are some suggestions. Remember to check times and prices before you start your engine.

THE SPEEDWAY

INDIANAPOLIS MOTOR SPEEDWAY
4790 W. 16th St.
(317) 484-6784
www.indianapolismotorspeedway.com
To test and showcase automobiles at the turn of the 20th century, entrepreneur Carl Graham Fisher and three other investors conceived the Indianapolis Motor Speedway and arranged for its construction. Completed in 1909 and initially paved with bricks—hence, its nickname "the Brickyard"—the 2½-mile oval began to host automobile and motorcycle races.

Under the post–World War II ownership of Anton "Tony" Hulman, his grandson, Tony George, and now Hulman's family, the Indianapolis Motor Speedway has grown into the largest spectator sporting facility in the world, with more than 250,000 permanent seats. The Speedway plays host to the Indianapolis 500 and the Allstate 400 at the Brickyard, the two largest single-day sporting events in the world.

Here are some major events and attractions at the Speedway:

The Indianapolis 500

On May 30, 1911, the Indianapolis Motor Speedway hosted the first Indianapolis 500-Mile Race. The Indianapolis 500, a part of the Indy Racing League, is widely known as "the Greatest Spectacle in Racing." The 500-mile race in 2010 will run on Sunday, May 30. In 2011, the race is set for Sunday, May 29. Tickets range from $20 for general admission to the infield (bring your own chair) to $150 for the best reserved seating. For tickets and a calendar of events, contact the Indy 500 at www.Indy500.com or call 800-822-4639.

 The first televised sporting event in Indiana was the 1949 Indy 500.

The Allstate 400 at the Brickyard

The first Allstate 400 at the Brickyard (formerly the Brickyard 400) took place in Indianapolis in 1994 and is now one of most anticipated events in the NASCAR Sprint Cup series. The 2010 race is scheduled for Sunday, July 25.

Red Bull Indianapolis GP

Motorcycle racing returned to the Indianapolis Motor Speedway for the first time in nearly a century with the Red Bull Indianapolis GP on Sept 14, 2008. The event featured MotoGP, the world's premier motorcycle road-racing series. The first vehicles to race at the Indianapolis Motor Speedway were motorcycles in 1909. The inaugural Red Bull Indianapolis GP race took place on the new 16-turn, 2.601-mile (4.186-kilometer) motorcycle road course at the Speedway. The 2010 race will take place on Sunday, Aug 29.

Brickyard Crossing

Designed by the legendary Pete Dye, Brickyard Crossing is one of the top public golf courses in America. It also provides the unique experience of playing four holes inside the famed oval circle of the Indianapolis Motor Speedway. (See the Golf chapter for more information.)

The Speedway does not give passes to leave and come back, so bring what you need before entering the gate.

Indianapolis Motor Speedway Hall of Fame Museum

A National Historic Landmark, the Hall of Fame Museum attracts visitors from around the world. It houses one of the most diversified collections of antique and classic passenger automobiles and racing cars in the world. Approximately 75 cars are always on display, representing a widely diversified collection of early-day passenger cars, European sports cars, motorcycles, and other special interest vehicles, plus more than one-third of all the Indianapolis 500 winners, including the 1911-winning Marmon "Wasp."

Also on display are trophies, photographs, helmets, uniforms, goggles, and other artifacts. A historic video is shown every 20 minutes in a 48-seat theater at no additional cost, while bus rides around the track are offered for an additional fee ($3 for adults, $1 for children ages 6 to 15) when the track is not in use. The museum is open 9 a.m. to 5 p.m. daily, closed Christmas Day. Extended hours are offered during the month of May. Admission is $3 for adults, $1 for children ages 6 to 15. (See the Attractions chapter for more details.)

Gasoline Alley at the Indianapolis Motor Speedway is the road the race cars and drivers take between the garages and the race track during the Indy 500. Hang out there for a chance to see and photograph famous people and drivers.

Grounds Tour: Behind-the-Scenes at IMS

A unique behind-the-scenes "grounds tour" of the Indianapolis Motor Speedway gives unprecedented access to the Speedway's most important landmarks, including the Gasoline Alley Suites, the four-story Media Center, the Bombardier Pagoda's timing and scoring suite, the victory platform, the Gasoline Alley garage area, and the start/finish line, where fans can stand on the famous "Yard of Bricks." If they are so inclined, fans also can kiss the bricks as Indy 500 winners do. The 90-minute guided tour of the 2.5-mile oval offers an in-depth view of the Speedway's evolution over the last century. Grounds Tours get underway in March and continue on select days through Thanksgiving weekend. Tours depart from the Hall of Fame Museum four times a day—9:30 and 11:15 a.m., and 1:15 and 3 p.m. The tour costs $25 for adults and $10 for children ages 6 to 15. Tickets also include admission to the museum.

INDY RACING EXPERIENCE
(888) 357-5002
www.indyracingexperience.com
During this thrilling experience, an Indy Racing League driver pilots an IndyCar that's been specially built with a second seat. Participants are strapped into the "backseat" and taken for a fast-paced spin around the Indianapolis Motor Speedway's 2½-mile oval. Lap speeds approach an average of 180 mph. There is also a single-seat experience enabling you to be the driver. The Indy Racing Experience also offers the Ultimate Experience—a 3-lap drive followed by a 2-lap ride. The regular ride or drive is $499. The combo is $599. Each driver must be 18 years or older, under 6 feet, 5 inches in height, and under 250 pounds. Check for dates when the experience is offered.

RICHARD PETTY DRIVING EXPERIENCE
(800) 237-3889
www.1800bepetty.com
The Richard Petty Driving Experience takes you one step closer to experiencing firsthand the thrill and excitement of stock-car racing. The program offers several choices. A "ride-along" at $109 lets you ride shotgun in a two-seat NASCAR-style stock car driven by a professional instructor for a 3-lap qualifying run at speeds up to 165 mph. Driving experiences where you get to be in the driver's seat run from the Rookie Experience (8 laps over one session for $399) to the Brickyard Experience (24 laps over three sessions for $2,199).

OTHER ATTRACTIONS

FASTIMES INDOOR KARTING
3455 Harper Rd.
(317) 566-0066
www.ftik.com
Race European-style karts at speeds in excess of 40 mph at the Midwest's only indoor, two-level track. Both the young and the young at heart will enjoy this heart-stopping racing excitement. Open weekdays from 11 a.m. to 10 p.m. and weekends from 11 a.m. to 11 p.m. The cost is $20 for an eight-minute race around the track, plus a $2 one-time charge for a head sock to wear under the helmet.

Keep the sock and use it next time. A race suit and helmet are provided.

INDIANA STATE FAIRGROUNDS
1202 E. 38th St.
(317) 927-7500
Used once a year for auto racing, the Indiana State Fairgrounds is part of an annual May tradition with A. J. Foyt's Hoosier Hundred. Known as the "Track of Champions," the dirt oval has seen famous drivers such as Foyt, Al Unser, and Tony Stewart compete in the 100-mile event.

i On the final day of qualifying on May 22, 1977, Janet Guthrie became the first female to qualify for the Indy 500. Her ninth-place finish in 1978, with a team she formed and managed herself, was the best by a woman until 2005 when Danica Patrick became the highest-finishing woman by coming in fourth, earning Chase Rookie of the Year honors. Patrick is also the first woman to lead a lap in the prestigious race.

INDIANAPOLIS SPEEDROME
802 S. Kitley Ave.
(317) 353-8206
www.speedrome.com
Edge-of-your-seat action abounds with United States Auto Club modified competition and hair-raising World Figure 8 challenges. Don't miss the demolition derbies or midget and pro-stock action at this east-side facility that has promoted motorsports since 1941. Some of auto racing's greatest drivers have raced at the Speedrome, including A. J. Foyt, Darrell Waltrip, Michael Waltrip, John Andretti, Johnny Rutherford, Lloyd Ruby, Gary Bettenhausen, Mel Kenyon, Bobby Allison, and Tony Stewart.

The Speedrome was founded in 1941 by the Sexton family and remained under their ownership until 1974. When the new Indianapolis Speedrome opened on Sept. 9, 1941, it featured the open-cockpit, single-geared "doodlebugs."

The government stopped all auto racing during World War II to conserve fuel and rubber. When the war ended, the nation's race fans were ready and a new form of racing captured their attention—stock cars. The fifth of a mile oval track featured mainly midget cars until 1951, when exciting Figure 8 racing was introduced. With hairpin turns and action galore, the Figure 8s race diagonally through the infield, trying to avoid each other at the intersection. Each year a three-hour World Figure-8 Endurance Race is held that draws cars and fans from across the country.

In 1997 the track was bought by Jake Cohen, a Speedrome Hall of Fame member, and his sons Bill and Joel. The one-fifth-mile asphalt, oval, and figure 8 track now hosts Late Model, Figure 8, stock car, midget, Legend, I-Car Jasper Modified, and Bomber races from Mar through mid-Nov. Admission starts at $10 for adults, $5 for ages 6 to 11.

O'REILLY RACEWAY PARK
10267 E. US 136
(317) 291-4090
www.oreillyracewaypark.com
Recently named one of the top 12 racing venues in the world by *Racer* magazine, the .683-mile oval features grandstand seating, 12 VIP suites, race control, a broadcast booth, and pressroom. The oval plays host to a jam-packed season spanning Mar through Nov and notable series such as the ASA ACDelco Series and NASCAR's Nationwide and Craftsman Truck Series. The Park is home to a Labor Day weekend tradition—the NHRA's Mac Tools U.S. Nationals, which features roaring top-fuel dragsters, funny cars, and pro-stock cars. More than 1,100 drag-racing entries and 100,000 fans attend the richest drag racing event in the world.

O'Reilly started in 1958 when four business-men, Tom Binford, Frank Dickie, Roger Ward, and Howard Feiger, invested $5,000 each for development of a raceway park. The group bought a 267-acre farm about 7 miles from Indianapolis Motor Speedway and constructed a multipurpose racing facility. The original intent was to design a 15-turn, 2.5–mile road course. They also decided to add a quarter-mile drag strip in the long straightway of the 2.5-mile-long road course design.

The drag strip was the first of the three courses to be completed. The raceway's first event was held in the fall of 1960. That same year, a handshake agreement between Binford and NHRA founder Wally Parks brought the historic event to O'Reilly. Signed under a tree in Detroit Dragway's pits, the three-year pact led to O'Reilly eventually becoming the home of the NHRA's biggest annual event. The NHRA bought the whole facility in 1979 and set about making improvements. In 2006 the track announced its first track entitlement with O'Reilly Auto Parks. Long known as Indianapolis Raceway Park, the track is now known as O'Reilly Raceway Park at Indianapolis.

i The fewest cars to finish the Indy 500 was seven in 1966. On the first turn of the first lap, a 16-car tangle eliminated 11 cars, including A. J. Foyt. Miraculously, the only injuries were to Foyt, who suffered a cut finger and bruised knee when he climbed out of his car and scaled a high wire fence to reach the stands. Then, with 25 miles to go, Jackie Stewart appeared to have the race in hand. But his car lost oil pressure and he was sidelined. Briton Graham Hill was the surprise winner. Some even said he never passed a car all day long; he just stayed clear of wrecks and kept his car running.

WHITELAND RACEWAY PARK
10267 E. US 136
(317) 535-7291
www.whitelandraceway.us
Built in 1958, this outdoor track is the oldest karting track in the country. Many professional drivers got their start at Whiteland Raceway Park, including Tony Stewart and John Andretti. Visitors can rent a kart by a single ride or by the hour and may even see an IndyCar veteran taking a few laps.

When racing at Whiteland, the track will be something new nearly every week, with two different layouts running clockwise and counterclockwise. Kart rides cost $12 for six minutes. Helmets are provided at no extra cost. Closed toe shoes, long pants, and sleeved shirts are required. Riders must be at least 16 years old to participate (with parental consent).

GOLF

Few states take their basketball more seriously than Indiana. But Hoosiers also have an affinity for another ball—the small round one that golfers like to slug around a course. Not surprisingly, Indiana boasts some of the most scenic, highest-quality, easily accessible, and reasonably priced golf courses in the Midwest. After all, look at who calls Indy his home. Considered to be one of the most influential course architects in the world, Pete Dye and his wife, former amateur champion Alice Dye, live in Indianapolis.

Now in his 80s, Pete is still designing courses and playing them. One of his most famous local works is the private course in nearby Carmel. Built in 1964, the course transformed a flat cornfield into a Scottish-style links. Legend says that the new course got its name when Pete and one of the club directors were walking the uncompleted back nine. Pete picked up a gnarled stick and swung at some stones. The name stuck. Crooked Stick has played host to many championships, including the 2009 U.S. Men's Senior Open.

The crown in the Indy golf scene is likely the Pete Dye course that millions of viewers have seen during the Indy 500 race. Often called the nation's most unique links, Brickyard Crossing has golfers playing inside and outside the famed Indianapolis Motor Speedway racing oval. Pete integrated concrete pieces from the speedway's outer retaining wall into the design of the golf course. Holes 7, 8, 9, and 10 of the course are located within the race track's infield. The remaining holes border the east side of the track. While the "inside holes" are certainly the most well known and photographed—especially on race days—the "outside holes" have a prevailing southwest wind, making for challenging play.

For some of the most heavenly golf, drive about 100 miles south of Indianapolis to the old resort town of French Lick. There you can find three great golf courses with designer names— Pete Dye, Tom Bendelow, and Donald Ross—all within 5 miles of each other. (For more about French Lick, be sure to see the Day Trips and Weekend Getaways chapter). The icing on the cake is the new Pete Dye Course at French Lick. Opened in 2009, the course is already receiving raves and will host the PGA of America 2010 Professional National Championship. Visually stunning, the dramatic hilltop course is etched into one of the highest elevations in Indiana. On a clear day, from the 900-foot elevation, you can see 30 to 40 miles.

This chapter includes a selection of area courses that are open to the general public. Please note that prices were in effect at publication time and are subject to change. If you're a golfer who prefers the old-fashioned way of golfing—walking rather than riding a cart—Indy offers some wonderful courses where you can stretch your legs. Most courses also give a nice discount for senior citizens and feature specials that can save you money. So line up a tee time (very handy to do online), lace up your shoes (many courses no longer allow steel spikes because they tear up the greens, so check ahead of time), slather on some sunscreen, and plop on a shady hat. Fore!

GOLF COURSES IN AND AROUND INDY

Indianapolis

BRICKYARD CROSSING
4400 W. 16th St.
(317) 492-6572
www.brickyardcrossing.com

If you're an auto race fan as well as a golf lover, here's your chance to enjoy a bit of both. Called the nation's most unique links, Brickyard Crossing has golfers playing inside and outside the famed Indianapolis Motor Speedway's racing oval. The 18-hole championship course was designed by Pete Dye and provides one of the most unusual golfing opportunities you'll ever experience. Holes 7, 8, 9, and 10 of the course are located within the racetrack's infield. The remaining holes border the east side of the track. An enticing offer is the stay-and-play package. Guests get a round of golf and one night's stay for the rate of $99 per person, based on double occupancy. That practically gives you a hotel room for 10 bucks. Greens fees are about $90, which includes a cart (usually $45). There is also a great Driving Force program that offers golfers the chance to drive a real race car, enjoy private golf lessons, and play a round. The facility includes a pro shop, restaurant, instruction facilities, banquet facilities, and driving range. The course is open mid-Mar through Nov.

> **i** When you play golf in Indianapolis, you will be teeing off at about 711 feet above sea level.

COFFIN GOLF CLUB
2401 Cold Spring Rd.
(317) 327-7845
www.coffingolf.com

Designed by Pete Dye understudy Tim Liddy, the Coffin Golf Club is a beauty of a city course with mature trees and a winding river. Because Coffin is a public course, the fees are reasonable—$23 for Mon through Thurs, $25 for Fri, Sat, Sun, and holidays, with a cart rental of $17. The Coffin fea-tures 6,789 yards of golf from the longest tees for a par of 72. Despite the economical price, the Coffin staff pays attention to service and detail. Some say it's comparable to exclusive private clubs. Fairways are closed in on all sides by trees, water, and rough. If you tend to get claustrophobic, this Coffin might be a bit scary.

> **i** It's not unusual to see deer, squirrels, and other wildlife at Eagle Creek Golf Course in Indianapolis.

EAGLE CREEK
8802 West 56th St.
(317) 297-3366
www.eaglecreekgolfclub.com

Enjoy 36 holes of Pete Dye championship golf at Eagle Creek Golf Club, which served as host to the prestigious USGA Public Links Championship in 1982 and is consistently ranked as one of Indiana's top public courses in different publications. With its natural parkland setting, Eagle Creek lets golfers enjoy numerous nature areas, wetlands, animal habitats, and rolling terrain. Eagle Creek features the Sycamore Course and the Pines Course. On the Sycamore, take special note of the 6th hole and don't hit the ball left. That will court danger with a front green-side bunker and thick woods. Instead, bail out right and take a par on this challenging par 3 hole. On the Pines Course, watch out for hole No. 8 and its abundant bunkers. Hitting the green is the secret to making par on this par 3 hole. Greens fees are $35 with cart Mon through Fri, $44 on weekends. For a good deal, choose a stay-and-play package that includes one night's stay at a local motel, along with 18 holes of golf and a cart for $69 per person (based on double occupancy) Mon through Fri, and $79 per person (based on double occupancy) on the weekend.

THE FORT GOLF RESORT
6002 N. Post Rd.
(317) 543-9597
www.thefortgolfcourse.com

Famed golf course architect Pete Dye took this 238-acre natural setting and created an 18-hole championship layout that is both beautiful and challenging. The facility includes a driving range, restaurant, and banquet rooms. It is open mid-Mar through Nov.

The 7,148-yard, par 72 design features tree-lined fairways, rolling hills, and the Dye trademark undulating greens. No metal spikes are allowed. The Fort Golf Resort is a soft-spike-only course. Players also must wear golf attire, meaning shirts must have collars. Tank tops, T-shirts, cutoffs, and athletic shorts are not permitted. After all, this was once a military garrison. From 1903 to 1995 it was formerly Fort Benjamin Harrison. As such, the military get a greens-fee break. Regular fees are $66 with $13 for a cart. The military greens fee is $49.50. For a treat, stay in the Benjamin Harrison House, which originally served as VIP lodging for high-ranking military guests. Now its VIP suites, two-room suites, and single guest rooms offer fine accommodations at quite reasonable prices. The VIP King, for example, goes for $159 a night and offers an 8-foot-by-12-foot walk-in closet, kitchenette, and sitting room with sleeper sofa. Or three nicely decorated, fully furnished officers' homes are available, each with three bedrooms, two sofa beds, and two and half baths. Rates for the homes are $229 a night.

i Wonder where the Fort Golf Resort got its name? It actually was an Indianapolis fort. It is part of a 1,700-acre historical nature preserve that was Fort Benjamin Harrison from 1903 to 1995. The resort also offers some of the most interesting golf lodging in the state—Benjamin Harrison House, where visiting military officers used to stay.

SUNRISE GOLF CLUB
9876 Westfield Blvd.
(317) 574-0427
Opened in 1995 and designed by Pat Gavigan, Sunrise Golf Club is a fairly challenging 9-hole course. Four holes are wide open, built in a field with most of the 20 bunkers. Five holes lead through a wooded area and have narrow fairways. The course features 3,279 yards of golf from

the longest tees, with a par of 35. The signature 8th hole requires two uphill shots. Sand on the left and two bunkers in the middle of the fairway make this the most difficult hole on the course. Open Mar 15 through Nov 15, Sunrise costs about $20 for a round of golf. The facility includes a driving range with mats and grass, covered tees, a clubhouse, and pro shop.

i Pete Dye's real first name is Paul. The legendary golf course designer was born December 29, 1925, in Urbana, Ohio, and lives in Indianapolis.

Camby

HEARTLAND CROSSING
6701 S. Heartland Blvd.
(317) 630-1785
www.heartlandcrossinggolf.com
This course, designed by professional golfer Nick Price and golf course architect Steve Smyers, is played over rolling terrain. It is known for its large bunkers that frame the greens and define the fairways. Throughout the course, the dramatically shaped bunkers create angles difficult for even the best golfers to negotiate. The fairways are almost entirely unencumbered by houses. Liberal use of fescue, prairie grasses, and wildflowers create a pleasant scene. Bent-grass tees, fairways, and greens complement the Kentucky bluegrass rough. Greens fees are $45 with cart.

i Most golf courses allow you to book your tee times online. Scorecards often can be downloaded from golf course Web sites as well.

Carmel

BROOKSHIRE GOLF CLUB
12120 Brookshire Parkway
(317) 846-7431
www.brookshiregolf.com
Open year-round and offering 18 holes, Brookshire Golf Club was voted the area's most photogenic course by readers of a local magazine. Brookshire offers challenging play on blue/rye

fairways and bent-grass greens. The excellent practice facilities include a driving range, putting greens, pitching greens, and practice bunkers. Regardless of age, no more than two people are allowed in a golf cart. Golfers must have their own sets of clubs. Greens fees are $35, including a cart.

PLUM CREEK GOLF CLUB
12401 Lynnwood Blvd.
(317) 573-9900
www.plumcreekcc.com
Designed by nationally acclaimed golf architect Pete Dye, Plum Creek is one of the premier semiprivate clubs in the state. Site of the 2004 IWGA Mid-Amateur Championship and 2003 Indiana State Open, Plum Creek's par 72 layout is equipped with multiple water features, strategically placed sand bunkers, and large undulating greens. The facility includes a snack bar/lounge, banquet rooms, pro shop, driving range, short game area, and instructional programs offered by PGA Golf Professionals. Plum Creek Country Club also features a swimming pool and tennis court. Greens fees are $59 with cart Mon through Thurs, $69 on weekends.

PRAIRIE VIEW GOLF CLUB
7000 Longest Dr.
(317) 816-3100
www.prairieviewgc.com
Prairie View has won accolades for "Best Course," "Best Par 3," "Most Beautiful" and other categories. As Indiana's only course designed by the renowned Robert Trent Jones Jr. company, Prairie View opened to much acclaim in 1997. *GOLF Magazine* said, "Prairie View could exist comfortably in golf meccas such as Pinehurst and Hilton Head." *Golf Digest* listed Prairie View in the top 10 best new upscale public courses in the U.S. Located on 206 acres along the White River, Prairie View blends 18 holes of traditional golf, a full-service clubhouse, pro shop, locker room, and driving range. Water features are a delight, with a clear running stream that meanders through four holes, natural wetlands, and five lakes. Ninety white-sand bunkers are strategi-

cally placed throughout the course. Pulling onto Longest Drive, golfers enjoy a winding road leading to Prairie View and its 1830s-era architecture clubhouse. A white picket fence, prairie grass, and wildflowers make the 15,000-square-foot facility a beauty to behold.

Cicero

BEAR SLIDE GOLF CLUB
6770 E. 231st St.
(317) 984-3837
www.bearslide.com
One of the most difficult courses in the state, Bear Slide has been ranked by *Golf Digest* as one of America's top 75 affordable golf courses and the eighth best of the almost 500 courses in the state. *GOLF Magazine* lists it on the top-tier "must-play" list. The front nine has a Scottish-links design with large mounding and rough areas, while the back nine offers a traditional rolling, wooded layout with doglegs and elevation changes. Three large lakes on the property come into play on several holes, and the greens are of all sizes and slope. The facility includes a pro shop, banquet facility, snack bar, and driving range. Greens fees are $45 with cart on Mon through Thurs and $55 on weekends and holidays.

Fishers

GRAY EAGLE GOLF CLUB AND ACADEMY
12500 Brooks School Rd.
(317) 845-2900
www.grayeaglegolf.com
Gray Eagle features an 18-hole course catering to golfers of all skill levels. The course highlights include bent-grass tees, greens, and fairways. Water comes into play on several holes requiring accurate iron shots to score well. The facility also features the Gray Eagle Golf Academy for year-round play on state-of-the-art golf simulators. Greens fees are $35 with cart. Gray Eagle is a soft spike-only facility. No metal spikes are allowed. Appropriate golf attire is required. No tank tops, cut-off shorts, or turf shoes allowed. A shirt and shoes must be worn at all times.

IRONWOOD GOLF CLUB
10955 Fall Rd.
(317) 842-0551
www.ironwoodgc.com
Open year-round, Ironwood Golf Club offers three nines—Lakes, Valley, and Ridge—that are scenic, challenging, and playable. Created by R. N. Thompson, Ironwood has greens fees of $35 with carts on weekdays, $48 on weekends and holidays. Golf carts are mandatory on Fri, Sat, Sun, and holidays until noon. The facility also offers a driving range, snack bar, pro shop, pool, tennis courts, and recently renovated clubhouse.

RIVER GLEN COUNTRY CLUB
12010 Clubhouse Dr.
(317) 849-8274
www.riverglencc.com
Open mid-Mar through Nov, this 18-hole course features rolling hills and lots of water challenges, with many traps and difficult par 4s. Designed in 1990 by Gary Kern, River Glen appears much older because of its towering trees and mature landscape. The course runs alongside White River and is lined with woods where abundant wildlife can be glimpsed. River Glen County Club includes a driving range, snack bar, swimming pool, and tennis court. Greens fees are $32 Mon through Thurs and $42 Fri, Sat, and Sun, with $10 cart rental. Cart rental is required until 2 p.m. on weekends and holidays and from 10 a.m. to 4 p.m. on Fri.

Lebanon

THE TROPHY CLUB
3887 North US Hwy. 52
(888) 730-7272
www.thetrophyclubgolf.com
Designed by Tim Liddy and built in 1998, the Trophy Club was formed on 247 acres of natural beauty with Prairie Creek meandering through the rolling terrain. The course features a links-style layout, with large greens built to USGA specifications, four sets of tees, and 60-yard-wide, bent-grass fairways. Taller-growing bluegrass and fescue frame and define each hole. A favorite hole is lucky 13, a 481-yard par 4 with a narrow entry to the green.

Skirting the right side and rear of the 13th green is a creek. The Trophy Club, which was named the top public golf course in Indiana by *Golf Digest* in 2007–2008, is open Mar through Dec. Greens fees are $45 Mon through Thurs, cart included, and $47 on Fri, Sat, and Sun. The facility includes a clubhouse, full service pro shop, the Hogan Bar and Grill, practice facilities, and a 100-seat pavilion room.

Noblesville

FOREST PARK GOLF COURSE
701 Cicero Rd.
(317) 773-2881
www.forestparkgolf.com
Hamilton County's oldest golf course, this nine-hole jewel reminds golfers of how golf used to be in design and price. Designed by Bill Diddle, Forest Park was the result of dedicated golfers who wanted a quality, inexpensive course to play. The course opened on June 16, 1927. With 3,004 yards and a par of 35, the course has sand traps on all nine holes. Greens fees are a bargain at $11 Mon through Fri and $14 on weekends and holidays. Carts at $6.50 are not mandatory and are free on Mon with greens fees. Open Mar 15 through Nov, Forest Park features undulating greens and wide furrows. Walking is allowed but metal spikes are not permitted. Rental clubs are available for $5. Alcohol is allowed but must be purchased on the course.

> **i** It was the era of Bobby Jones, Walter Hagan, and Tommy Armour. Folks in Noblesville were inspired to build their own golf course. Being good Hoosiers, they rolled up their sleeves and got to it. Ten men working in seven tractor teams got it done with advice from designer Bill Diddle and plenty of volunteer labor and donations. About a year after ground was broken, Forest Park Golf Course was turned over free of debt to the city. At a cost of about $4,000, Forest Park opened for play June 16, 1927. A season pass sold for $7.50 and greens fees were 50 cents. Still a popular course, Forest Park is the county's first and oldest golf course.

FOX PRAIRIE GOLF COURSE
8465 E. 196th St.
(317) 776-6357
www.foxprairie.com

Open mid-March through Nov, Fox Prairie Golf Course was given a three-star rating by *Golf Digest*. The 18-hole course features mature trees on each hole, totally renovated sand bunkers, four sets of tees, very large greens, and a new clubhouse. Opened in 1970, Fox Prairie was designed by William Newcomb on a former dairy farm. In 2002 nine holes were added based on Steve Frazier's design. Today Fox Prairie features three nine-hole courses playable in three 18-hole combinations, at the most affordable rates in Hamilton County. Many of the fairways are tight with wooded areas on either side. Five ponds and plenty of native grass add to the course's beauty and challenge. The signature hole on the East Course, No. 6, is an interesting par 4 from 223 to 313 yards with three tee boxes and two crisscrossing landing pads. Greens are always in good shape even after heavy rains. Greens fees are $26 Mon through Fri, $32 on weekends and holidays. Carts at $15 are not mandatory but even strong walkers might feel winded by game's end.

PEBBLE BROOK GOLF CLUB
3110 Westfield Rd.
(317) 896-5596
www.pebblebrookgolfclub.com

Open mid-Mar through Nov, Pebble Brook's two 18-hole championship courses are well manicured with mature trees and water hazards. The facility includes a restaurant and lounge with large-screen TV. Opened in June of 1974, the South Course is the original one. The South Course is also the traditional one with tree-lined fairways and an occasional bunker. Many of the bent-grass greens are flat with older traditional layouts. The first and 10th tees are close to the clubhouse for easy access to the snack bar and grillroom. Built in 1990 by architect Ron Kern, the North Course features a modern Scottish links–style design with native grasses and scenic lakes. Lush bent grass gives a Scottish rolling effect. The ninth green and 10th tee is one of the

farthest points from the clubhouse, so golfers are invited to grab a complimentary beverage cooler in the snack bar to take some drinks on the journey. Both courses offer multiple sets of tee markers to fit every golfer's skill level. Built in 1998, the shaker-roofed clubhouse features men's and women's locker rooms, a grill, snack bar, meeting rooms, and golf shop. The clubhouse offers indoor and outdoor dining with a nice view of the golf courses. Greens fees are $39 with a golf cart on Mon through Fri, $49 on Sat, Sun, and holidays. You can save about $10 on a golf cart charge by walking.

PURGATORY GOLF CLUB
12160 E. 216th St.
(317) 776-4653
www.purgatorygolf.com

Despite its name, Purgatory is a heavenly course with a wicked sense of humor. Holes have names like Everlasting Torment and Sweet Misery. The 16th hole, Blinding Cloud of Smoke, is completely lined with bunkers, so that when you get to the green and look back towards the trees, the bunkers disappear—just like smoke. Creative bit of thinking there.

Designed by Ron Kern and opened in 2000, Purgatory was the longest non-mountain course in the world at 7,754 yards. That didn't last long with the quick rush to lengthen courses. Still, Purgatory was named one of the top 50 public courses in the Readers' Choice Award for 2009 by *Golf World* magazine. One of the club's defining features is the bunkering. There are over 125 bunkers on the course. These bunkers define the holes visually and outline many of the fairways. With a minimum of six tees on each hole, the course tempts golfers of all skill levels. Bent grass is used on the greens, tees, and fairways, but the rough is covered in tall-grass fescues, which change color based on the water content of the soil. As a result, in autumn the tall grass becomes a beautiful golden brown. Greens fees are $60 with a cart Mon through Thurs, $75 Fri, Sat, Sun, and holidays. Deduct $10 if you'd rather walk. Now for the most-asked question—why was it named Purgatory? The story goes that the name was picked because in religious mythology, Purgatory is where souls pay for their earthly errors to gain entry into heaven. It's said that the name is fitting for the course because it conjures up images of overcoming obstacles to reach happiness. Golfers might agree.

> **i** Purgatory Golf Club in Noblesville has three on-course bathrooms. That means you never get more than four holes without passing a bathroom. The bathrooms have separate men's and women's facilities, along with hot running water, mirrors, and seat covers.

STONY CREEK GOLF CLUB
11800 E. 166th St.
(317) 773-1820
www.stonycreekgolfclub.com
Designed by Sam Taylor and opened in 1990, Stony Creek Golf Club offers bent-grass tees, fairways, and greens with rolling hills, and mature trees. Wide, undulating fairways lead to large greens. Water hazards from ponds and three streams comes into play on nine holes, with sand traps in play on six holes. Well-manicured fairways highlight the course, with two holes featuring sharp dogleg fairways. Six of the large greens are well bunkered. The greens are often tucked away within the trees, surrounded by powdery sand. An additional par 3, nine-hole course designed by Sam Taylor opened in 2001. From the longest tees, the nine-hole course offers 1,022 yards of golf, with a par of 27. The nine-hole course is great for working on a short game or squeezing in a quick round of golf. The course's holes offer two tee boxes from which to choose. Greens fees are $22, plus $8 for a cart, on Mon through Fri, $31 with $14 more for a cart on weekends and holidays. Walking is allowed. Plan to play the 18 holes in four hours. Rangers and clocks will monitor your speed of play to be sure you do. The facility includes a driving range and a full-service snack bar. The large 330-yard driving range gets a lot of use and can comfortably hold 30 golfers. It includes a chipping area with greenside practice bunkers, as well as two practice greens. A bucket of 30 balls is $3.

Westfield

WOOD WIND GOLF CLUB
2302 W. 161st St.
(317) 669-8550
www.woodwindgolf.com
Designed by Ronald Kern and Gary Kern, Wood Wind Golf Club opened in 1990. In 2007 the facility was bought by the Estridge Companies and given a major renovation. Among the upgrades are 64 new Club Car golf carts, a renovated clubhouse with nice dining area and pro shop, a redone pavilion that seats up to 175 people, a new entrance and exit design for the club, extensive landscaping, a new parking lot west of the clubhouse, and a new 5,000-square-foot putting green adjacent to the south side of the clubhouse. The course itself is in great shape, immaculate and challenging to play. With bent grass from tee to green, the course features 6,519 yards of golf from the longest tees, with a par of 71. The course has rolling hills, a winding creek, ponds, trees, cement cart paths, and over 90 sand bunkers. The championship course offers year-round golf and was given a three-and-a-half star rating by *Golf Digest*. Greens fees are $45 with cart on weekdays, $56 with cart on weekends and holidays. Carts are $15 on weekdays, $17 on weekends. Wood Wind is popular for not making golfers feel rushed, yet making sure that no group is crowded by another.

ANNUAL EVENTS

Hoosiers love to celebrate. And we find plenty of reasons to do so. From the first crocus of spring to the sweet strawberries of summer, from the reddish leaves of autumn to the swirling snow of winter, we host festivals and fairs and gatherings of all sorts. Just about any weekend of the year, you can find at least one event taking place in and around Indianapolis. From art to antiques, caroling to chocolates, gardening to gems, horsepower to hayrides, there's something for everyone.

It's not surprising that many events are organized around our Hoosier passion for sports. The month of May is one long party with the famous Indy 500 as the guest of honor. More details about sports and sporting events can be found in the chapters on Spectator Sports and Motorsports. We are also mighty proud of our heritage, and we host events in our neighborhoods and at churches to celebrate it. For a true taste of French or German cooking or any international cuisine, get the real thing at one of these street fairs. In this chapter, we'll share a smattering of great ways to have fun in Indy. Many more events are offered, of course, and it's a wonderful way to meet folks and find out what Indianapolis is all about. After all, we're known for our Hoosier Hospitality and those aren't just words. We mean it.

JANUARY

HEARTHSIDE SUPPERS
Conner Prairie
13400 Allisonville Rd., Fishers
(800) 966-1836
www.connerprairie.org
By lantern light, follow a costumed interpreter down a wooded path to the historic 1823 William Conner home. In the Conner kitchen, warm yourself by the fireplace before you help prepare the evening's meal. Everything centers on the hearth for this 19th-century food preparation. Hearthside Suppers began in 1984 and are a popular winter activity at the living-history village north of the city. Learn to eat with a knife (forks weren't in use yet), sip on hot cider, and enjoy a delicious multicourse meal that you helped fix with low-tech cooking methods. With foods that would have been available during the Indiana winter months, the meal might consist of chicken pie, barley soup, cabbage salad, sliced cheese, hearth bread, apple butter, brandied peaches, and orange fool (a spongy cake). After dinner,

play old-fashioned parlor games and tour the restored home. Guests leave with a full stomach and a copy of receipts (recipes) for the evening's meal. The cost is $55 per person. Reserve early for these popular dinners, which continue through March.

> **i** Try this warm drink to take off the wintry chill: spiced cider as served at Conner Prairie's Hearthside Suppers. To one gallon of cider, add a bag of spices and heat over a trivet until hot. For the spice bag, add 6 cloves, 1 broken cinnamon stick, and 3 whole allspices. When hot, remove the spice bag and serve.

INDIANAPOLIS HOME SHOW
Indiana State Fairgrounds
1202 E. 38th St.
(800) 395-1350
www.indianapolishomeshow.com
When snow covers the ground, the Indianapolis Home Show gives a preview of spring with gardening projects, blooming plants, flowering

trees, and decorating tips. Almost 90 years old, the show is the nation's oldest and the Midwest's largest home-focused extravaganza. The show features thousands of products, decorations, construction, and remodeling ideas for visitors to gather and compare. It's also a great place to showcase new products. The fee is $15 for adults, $5 for children 6 to 12.

> **i** The Indianapolis Home Show showcases an amazing feat—a fully constructed, decorated, and landscaped home built inside Expo Hall in less than 30 days.

DEVOUR DOWNTOWN
Various Restaurants
www.devourdowntown.org
Chase away the winter blues and enjoy some tasty cuisine at the annual Devour Downtown. This is a good time to get out and try Indy's most talked about restaurants. About 35 participating restaurants stretch from the Wholesale District to Mass Ave and Fountain Square. Special three-course $30 menus are a real bargain. Started in 2005, the event has proven so successful that it has been extended to two weeks and happens twice a year, in the winter and again in the summer. It's a perfect excuse to escape the winter doldrums and try some top cuisine.

FEBRUARY

INDIANA BOAT, SPORT AND TRAVEL SHOW
Indiana State Fairgrounds
1202 E. 38th St.
www.indianaboatsportandtravelshow.com
(877) 892-1723
For over half a century, the city's oldest sports show has drawn outdoor and travel enthusiasts to dream, purchase, and check out the latest in hunting, fishing, camping, and boating equipment. With over 600 exhibitors, it's a great place to spend a winter day planning for summer. From canoes to cruisers, RVs to tents, this show has it all. Travel and tourism booths from throughout the U.S. and Canada are ready to show you what's great about their attractions and help you plan a

visit. The fee is $10 for adults, $7 for children 6 to 12, and free for children 5 and under.

MARCH

ST. PATRICK'S DAY PARADE
Downtown
(317) 884-3836
www.indystpats.com
Plop on a green hat, a green shirt, or even an "I'm Irish" button and head downtown for this festive event. You have to get up early on March 17th to catch the colorful kickoff—turning the White River Canal green. Free breakfast and coffee is usually served as long as it lasts. Shortly after 6:30 a.m., city officials pour dye into the canal, which produces a brilliant green fountain for the rest of the day. A pipe-and-drum band and Celtic dancers are usually on hand to help wake you up. Sponsored by the Indy Sports Foundation, the day's celebration includes a parade and Shamrock Indy Fun Run and Walk. The parade features more than 100 units, including floats, motorcycles, horses, bands, and dancers. The Gordon Pipers are a popular strut with their bagpipes and swinging kilts.

> **i** The Indianapolis Convention & Visitors Association maintains a great listing of area events at www.visitindy.com.

APRIL

EARTH DAY INDIANA FESTIVAL
American Legion Mall
Meridian and North Streets
(317) 767-3672
www.earthdayindiana.org
On the last Saturday of every April, thousands of Hoosiers head to downtown Indianapolis to attend one of the nation's largest Earth Day festivals. The free outdoor festival combines 130 environmental and conservation exhibits with live music from some of Indiana's best new bands, special activities for kids, and good food. Learn how to make a compost pile for your home or find out how to create a rain barrel to water your

garden. Get information on backyard habitats, downsizing your carbon footprint, green advocacy, the latest energy savers, and locally grown food. Maybe take home a free tree to plant or help your child check for the correct pressure in bicycle tires. Above all—Live Green and Prosper.

MAY

500 FESTIVAL KICK-OFF
Monument Circle
(317) 482-6700
www.500festival.com
Start the exciting month of May by spending lunchtime with the Indianapolis 500 pace cars and princesses at the first part of the monthlong 500 Festival. Live music, free giveaways, and free lunch for the first 500 people always draw a big crowd.

ONEAMERICA 500 FESTIVAL MINI-MARATHON
Military Park, New York and West Streets
(317) 492-6700
www.500festival.com
Some 35,000 runners take to downtown streets for the nation's largest half-marathon, part of the monthlong Indianapolis 500 festivities. With 120 entertainment groups and spirit squads lining the 13.1-mile course, the Mini-Marathon has arguably the most entertainment of any road race in the world. Fans say it might be one of the largest four-hour music festivals anywhere. The Mini is a fun, family-oriented community event with participants ranging in age from 10 to 80 plus. In the past, participants have represented all 50 states and seven countries. Register early for the run. The post-race party is free and open to the public. Spectators can watch the action at the finish line and perhaps witness a marriage proposal or two.

ZOOPOLIS 500
Indianapolis Zoo
1200 W. Washington St.
(317) 630-2001
www.indyzoo.com
In a salute to the Indy 500, two tortoises head—slowly—to the checkered flag. The annual race

also marks the move of the Aldabra tortoises (Lyn and A.J.) from their winter holding area to their summer home. The event includes a number of prerace activities before the two racers lumber to the finish line, lured by the reward of fresh broccoli and fruit. The tortoises are the zoo's oldest residents, and most race fans know where they got their names. Named for Indy 500 legend A. J. Foyt, A.J. weighs about 485 pounds and joined the zoo in 1963. He's likely more than 60 years old. Named for race favorite Lyn St. James, Lyn tips the scales at almost 150 pounds and could be as much as 100 years old. Native to the Aldabra Island between the coast of Kenya and the northern tip of Madagascar, these giant tortoises have a life expectancy of more than a century. The race is free with zoo admission.

BROAD RIPPLE ART FAIR
Indianapolis Art Center
820 E. 67th St.
(317) 255-2464
www.indplsartcenter.org
Munch on a grilled turkey leg, watch bricks being made, dance to some cool jazz, throw (create) your own ceramic pot, and see the marvelous work of more than 225 artists from the United States and Canada. Established in 1971, the Broad Ripple Art Fair is a favorite for browsers and buyers. The event also features booths from local cultural organizations, a children's creative area, gourmet food courts, a beer and wine garden, and live entertainment on four stages and in the Frank M. Basile Auditorium. Admission at the gate is $15 for adults and $2 for children 3 to 12; children under 3 are free. Proceeds from the two-day event fund Art Center programs.

INDY 500 MILE RACE AND PARADE
Indianapolis
(317) 492-6747
www.indianapolismotorspeedway.com
The legendary Indianapolis 500-Mile Race is held annually over the Memorial Day weekend at the Indianapolis Motor Speedway. The event lends its name to the "IndyCar" class of formula, or open-wheel, race cars that have competed in it. Billed

as "the Greatest Spectacle in Racing," it is one of the oldest and richest motorsports events in existence. Expect to see celebrities enjoying themselves at the Brickyard. Arrive early, bring plenty of sunscreen, and drink loads of water. (See the Motorsports chapter for more information).

JUNE

STRAWBERRY FESTIVAL
Monument Circle
(317) 636-4577
More than 12,000 pounds of strawberries, 18,000 sweet biscuits, mounds of whipped topping, and mountains of ice cream are savored during the delicious Strawberry Festival. Starting at 9 a.m., volunteers dish out bowls of the sweet treat until they run out. The works with everything goes for $6 a bowl, or pick what you want for $2 a al carte. Proceeds benefit charities.

ITALIAN STREET FESTIVAL
Holy Rosary Catholic Church
520 Stevens St.
(317) 767-7685
www.italianheritage.org
Authentic Italian food is a top draw at the Italian Street Festival. And these folks sure know how to cook. Toasted ravioli, antipasti, Italian sausage, sweets galore, and plenty of wine are sold at more than 30 food stands in a festive setting with strands of twinkling lights. Italian music and an Old World–style procession with a statue of the Blessed Virgin add to the Italian feel at the free festival. People often follow the procession into the church for the second of two Masses on Saturday night.

INDIAN MARKET AND FESTIVAL
Eiteljorg Museum
500 W. Washington St.
(800) 622-2024
www.eiteljorg.org
Make a mask, toss a corncob dart, hear a story-teller, watch a Native American dancer, and enjoy Indian tacos. The Indian Market and Festival draws nearly 130 Native American artists from across the country to share their art. Dancers and singers add to the festive atmosphere. This is a great place to buy beautiful jewelry and original artwork. Tickets are $10 at the gate; children 17 and under are admitted for free.

INDIANAPOLIS AIR SHOW
Mt. Comfort Airport
3867 Aviation Way, Greenfield
(317) 335-7252
www.indyairshow.com
Precision flybys, the U.S. Navy's Blue Angels, historic fighter planes, bombers, and aerobatics delight visitors to the Indianapolis Air Show. The show has in the past also featured hot-air balloon rides, antique car shows, military history exhibits, giant-scale radio-controlled aircraft, and competitions. Admission at the gate is $20 for adults, $10 for children 6 to 12. Smoking is not permitted on the grounds of the airport. Smoking in cars parked in the general parking area, prior to entering the event, is allowed.

BREW-HA-HA
Mass Ave Arts District
700 N. Park Ave.
(317) 635-2381
Beer, beer, and more beer. What's not to like? Cold beer, hot music, and a great time keep people coming to this beer-tasting festival and block party in Indy's Mass Ave Arts District in front of the Phoenix Theatre. Sample the best in craft beer from around the region and the nation. Tickets are $25 and include beer sampling. Designated drivers tickets (no alcohol allowed) are $10. Cheers!

VINTAGE INDIANA WINE AND FOOD FESTIVAL
Military Park
601 W. New York St.
(800) 832-9463
www.vintageindiana.com
Celebrate the fruit of the vine. More than 100 award-winning wines from Hoosier wineries are available for sampling, along with food from culinary experts. Browse artists' booths and enjoy live music. Tickets are $15 at the gate for adults, which includes a souvenir wine glass to the first

10,000 people. An ID is required and every guest is carded at the gate. Tickets for designated drivers cost $10 at the gate and include unlimited soft drinks. Designated drivers may not sample wine but can purchase bottles to take home. Designated drivers include any adult over the age of 21 who does not wish to consume alcohol. Admission costs $5 for children 6 to 20 and is free for children 5 and under.

TALBOT STREET ART FAIR
Talbot Street between 16th and 20th Streets
(317) 745-6479
www.talbotstreet.org
Held for over half a century, the Talbot Street Art Fair is a top-ranked, juried exhibition featuring more than 250 artists and crafts from around the country. One of the city's oldest festivals, the Talbot Street Art Fair was started in 1955 by Herron School of Art students as a venue to sell their work at the end of the semester. One of the last free art fairs around, the festival is a great place to shop for excellent artwork.

LET'S MEET PBS KIDS IN THE PARK
St. Clair Street to North Street, between Meridian and Pennsylvania Streets
(317) 715-2005
www.wfyi.org
Come to the park and meet Clifford the Big Red Dog, Cookie Monster, Curious George, Miss Rosa, Snook, and many more PBS kids' show characters. Multiple stages feature nonstop entertainment, plus education and carnival-style activities. Hosted by some of Central Indiana's leading arts and service organizations, activities have included crafts, games, exhibits, train rides, face painting, balloon artists, craft dough, bubble-making stations, and children's book giveaways. The family fun is free.

JULY

GLORIOUS FOURTH AT CONNER PRAIRIE
Conner Prairie
13400 Allisonville Rd., Fishers
(800) 966-1836
www.connerprairie.org

Celebrate the nation's birthday with an old-fashioned party. Help decorate Prairietown, march with the militia, play old-time baseball, eat watermelon, and see who can spit the seeds the farthest. Enjoy games like croquet and sack races. Honor Independence Day with a flag presentation, Declaration of Independence reading, patriotic songs, and recognition of war veterans. Regular admission to Conner Prairie is $12 for adults and $8 for children 2 to 12.

> **i** In 1957, Muhammad Ali, as the young Cassius Clay, boxed as an amateur at the Indiana State Fair.

INDEPENDENCE DAY FIREWORKS
The best seats for downtown's annual Fourth of July fireworks are at Indiana War Memorial Plaza, Central Canal, and Victory Field baseball stadium after the Indianapolis Indians game.

INDIANAPOLIS INTERNATIONAL FILM FESTIVAL
Indianapolis Museum of Art
4000 Michigan Rd.
(317) 567-1368
www.indyfilmfest.org
Movie lovers are in heaven at the Indianapolis International Film Festival. Started in 2004, the Film Festival now screens more than 100 films at one lovely venue, the Indianapolis Museum of Art. The 11-day, star-studded celebration of movies represents more than 50 nations from around the world. The festival aims to promote innovative and independent films that might not otherwise receive wide distribution. Settle into a comfy theater seat and watch future Oscar winners. Individual tickets are $10 per show but may be purchased in bundles of 10 for a discount. Check the Web site for a listing of movies to be shown.

INDIANA BLACK EXPO SUMMER CELEBRATION
Various locations
(317) 925-2702
www.indianablackexpo.com
Stars galore light up the annual Indiana Black Expo

Summer Celebration. First held in 1971, the event highlights the cultural, artistic, historical, and economic accomplishments of African-Americans. Stretching over 11 days, Black Expo includes business workshops, health and wellness programs, employment opportunities, spiritual enrichment, exhibits, youth activities, and entertainment. But the party is always at the downtown concerts. Celebrities for 2009 included Eric Benet, Jamie Foxx, Magic Johnson, the Sugar Hill Gang, and Ginuwine. Admission is charged for events at various locations.

i Indiana Black Expo Summer Celebration is the largest African-American event in the nation, with over 300,000 people in attendance. Indiana Black Expo started in 1971.

BRICKYARD 400
Indianapolis Motor Speedway
4790 W. 16th St.
(317) 492-6700
www.brickyard400.com
Watch the best NASCAR drivers start their engines for the Brickyard 400 at the famed oval of the Indianapolis Motor Speedway. First held in 1994, drivers compete in 400 miles in 160 laps. Some of NASCAR's top drivers have won the Brickyard 400 (formerly known as the Allstate 400 at the Brickyard), including Dale Earnhardt, Bill Elliott, Jeff Gordon, Dale Jarrett, Bobby Labonte, and Tony Stewart. Ticket prices vary, usually from about $75 up to $1,000.

i In 1852, the first Indiana State Fair was held in what is now Military Park in downtown Indianapolis, making Indiana the sixth state to begin holding a state agricultural fair. Now held at the Indiana State Fairgrounds on East 38th Street since 1892, the State Fair is a huge extravaganza that stretches more than two weeks.

AUGUST
INDIANA STATE FAIR
Indiana State Fairgrounds
1202 E. 38th St.
(317) 927-7500
Watch pigs race for the finish line (and Oreos), see a baton-twirling contest, cheer on a tractor pull, and pick the winner in the giant pumpkin competition. The Indiana State Fair has myriad contests, plus entertainment and food galore. Favorite fair food has included chocolate-covered bacon, deep-fried green beans, cone pizza, pork chops, roasted corn on the cob, lamb kabobs, elephant ears, and lemon shake-ups. Amusement rides and games line the midway. At the heart of the fair are the dedicated members of 4-H who spend hours washing, brushing, and fluffing their animals for the competitions. Started in 1852, the Indiana State Fair grew from 12 days to 17 in 2009 to accommodate all the festivities. Legendary performers who have graced Indiana State Fair stages include Johnny Cash, Dolly Parton, Randy Travis, Garth Brooks, Bruce Springsteen, the Jackson 5, the Beatles, Reba McEntire, Def Leppard, Rascal Flatts, New Kids on the Block, and Kanye West. General admission is $8 for adults, free for children 5 and under.

i In 1956, Elvis Presley did one of his first television interviews at the Indiana State Fair shortly after recording "Heartbreak Hotel."

GEN CON INDY
Indiana Convention Center
100 S. Capitol Ave.
(800) 529-3976
www.gencon.com
Stare at jaw-dropping costumes. Or better yet, wear one of your own. Gen Con Indy is the longest-running show in the gaming industry, with consumer fantasy, electric, sci-fi, and adventure games. Check out the newest games and get a sneak peek at the latest editions. Gen Con hosts all types of games and events—board games, card games, celebrity appearances, electric gaming, anime, film festivals, miniature games, live-action and stan-

dard role-playing games, trading card games, and more. It includes an art show, exhibit hall, costume contest, game auction, seminars, workshops, and events for the whole family. Gen Con even offers such traditional crafting activities as knitting, scrap booking, and beadwork. Or you can take part in Irish dancing, belly dancing, and self-defense. A one-day badge is $48 at the door. Children 8 and under are free with an accompanying adult.

i The tradition of Oktoberfest dates back to the early 1800s when Crown Prince Ludwig married Princess Theresa Charlotte Luise of Saxe-Hildburghausen and the city of Munich celebrated for days in grand style. Indianapolis's Oktoberfest is the largest such celebration in the state, attracting 15,000 people annually.

OKTOBERFEST
Indiana State Fairgrounds
1202 E. 38th St.
(317) 888-6940
www.indianapolisgak.com
Sure, we know it's not October. But there's no reason not to start the celebration a bit early. Stretching over two weekends in late Aug and early Sept, Oktoberfest is produced by the German-American Klub of Indianapolis. Oktoberfest features authentic, traditional German cuisine like *frikadellen* (German hamburgers), bratwurst, knockwurst, sauerkraut, and German-style potato salad. In addition, a wide variety of German and domestic beers are available in the popular German Bier and Wein Garten. Visitors can also enjoy live music, dancing, carnival rides, and games like bingo and Monte Carlo. Admission at the gate is $6 for adults, free for children 10 and under.

i Visitors to Oktoberfest can take a sentimental journey on the Oktoberfest Train from the Fishers Train Station to the State Fairgrounds. Indiana Transportation Museum officials will operate the train all five days of the event. Round-trip tickets are $14 for adults, $9 for children 3 to 12, and free for children 2 and younger.

SEPTEMBER

INDIANAPOLIS GREEK FESTIVAL
Holy Trinity Greek Orthodox Church
3500 W. 106th St., Carmel
(317) 733-3033
www.indygreekfest.org
Souvlaki, dolmades, spanakopita. *Opa!* And that doesn't include the desserts. Greek food and culture are spotlighted at this festival. Now almost 40 years old, the Greek Festival also has plenty of music and dancing. Watching the youngsters in their Greek outfits hold hands and dance like in the Old Country is charming. Save room for tempting desserts such as *diples*—delicately rolled pastry, lightly fried and topped with honey and cinnamon; *galaktoboureko*—phyllo dough filled with custard and topped with syrup; and *koulourakia*—butter cookies sprinkled with sesame seeds. You don't have to know how to pronounce them or spell them; just point, pay, and eat. Admission is $5 at the gate; kids under 12 get in free.

i For the Indianapolis Greek Festival in September, save money with this bargain—buy an advance ticket book for $15. It has $15 in food coupons, so the regular admission of $5 is free.

PENROD ART FAIR
Indianapolis Museum of Art
4000 Michigan Rd.
(317) 923-1331
www.penrod.org
One of the biggest one-day art fairs in the nation, the Penrod Art Fair has a beautiful setting, art galore, and plenty of food and entertainment. Held in the gardens of the Indianapolis Art Museum, the almost 5-year-old juried show features more than 300 local and national artists showing and selling their work. Pieces range from woodworking and watercolors to pottery and paper cutting, with excellent jewelry, etchings, photography, sculpture, fabrics, and even birdhouses. Six stages of entertainment ensure something for everyone. Tickets are $15.

ℹ Site of the annual French Market, St. Joan of Arc Church in Indianapolis was built in 1929. The church was one of the very first churches in the world named for the "Maid of Orleans."

FRENCH MARKET
St. Joan of Arc Church
4217 N. Central Ave.
(317) 849-4709
www.sjoa.org

Beef bourguignon, ratatouille, onion soup, pate, Provençal chicken, white cheese pizza, crawfish étouffée, tarte flambé, beignets, éclairs, madeleines, and plenty of strong cappuccino. Yum! You don't have to go to France to savor such tasty cuisine. It's all at the French Market, one of Indy's major neighborhood festivals, with live entertainment, artisan booths, children's games, and plenty of French and American cuisine. The annual event raises funds for the maintenance of St. Joan of Arc Church and School. Free admission.

INDY JAZZ FEST
Various venues
(317) 966-7854

For more than a decade, the Indy Jazz Fest has been heating up Sept. Big names always make their way to the Indy Jazz Fest, where music lovers might hear a Grammy winner one day and discover a new bossa nova artist the next. Look for shows at venues around the city before the weekend's headlining acts take to the White River State Park's amphitheatre.

IRISH FEST
Military Park
100 N. West St.
(317) 713-7117
www.indyirishfest.com

Cast your vote for the hairiest legs and the bonniest legs in the kilt contest. Watch authentic sheep herding with border collies. At the annual three-day Irish Fest, the schedule is jam-packed with fun and food. Bagpipes and kilts are everywhere. The Sunday festival kicks off with a Celtic Mass at the Claddagh Stage, followed by an authentic Irish breakfast for a small fee. Sunday is also a good time to get free admission. Just bring a minimum of three nonperishable food items to benefit St. Vincent de Paul food bank before 11:30 a.m. and get in the festival free. Otherwise, tickets are $13 at the gate for adults and $10 for students 14 to 18, and free for children 13 and under. Hotels often offer great packages for the Fest. In 2009 the Omni Severin Hotel featured a rate of $99 per night, which included two festival tickets and transportation to the festival. Stay downtown and party to your heart's content, then sleep in a nearby hotel bed.

ℹ At the Irish Fest in September, contestants try to impress judges with their wit and charm as they vie for the best Irish toast—that's the salute said before a stout drink, not the burned bread kind. A sample toast: "Here's to the beer we love to drink, And the food we love to eat / Here's to our wives and sweethearts, May they never meet. / Here's champagne for our real friends, And real pain for our sham friends / And when this journey finally ends, May all of us find peace. *Sláinte!*"

RIB AMERICA FESTIVAL
Military Park
601 W. New York St.
(317) 566-2118
www.ribamerica.com

Barbecue and bands combine for a rocking good time. Buy a strip of tickets (seven for $10) and munch your way around the festival. Food, beverage, and game vendors accept only tickets, no cash, so look for the ticket tents. Favorites are countless slabs of ribs, pulled-pork sandwiches, roasted corn on the cob, spiral spuds, funnel cakes, deep-fried Oreos, bratwurst, barbecued chicken, and waffle cones. Alcoholic and nonalcoholic drinks are for sale. Musicians like Morris Day and the Time have played, as have "tribute bands" for such diverse groups as the Beatles, Eagles, and Guns N' Roses. Admission is free before 5 p.m. on Fri and before 1 p.m. on Sat, Sun, and Mon. Otherwise, admission is $5 for adults;

children under 12 are admitted free. The Rib America Festival is held rain or shine.

FIESTA INDIANAPOLIS
American Legion Mall
Pennsylvania Street between St. Clair and
North Streets
(317) 890-3292
Taking place during National Hispanic Heritage Month, Fiesta is the premier Latino cultural celebration in Indiana. Since 1980, Fiesta has celebrated, educated, and shared the Latino culture through art, music, dance, food, and cultural activities. It's a huge outdoor party where the Americas come together.

OCTOBER

CIRCLE CITY CLASSIC
Lucas Oil Stadium
500 S. Capitol St.
(317) 237-5222
www.circlecityclassic.com
Superstars, gridiron heroes, and other legends are featured at the annual weekend celebrating African-American cultural excellence and educational achievement. Highlights include a football showdown between two historically black colleges and a parade extravaganza with marching bands, drill teams, and special entries performing on Pennsylvania, Ohio, and Meridian Streets. Arrive early to get a good viewing spot. This is an Indy favorite. The parade is free; game tickets start at $10. Born in 1984, the Circle City Classic uses proceeds to help fund scholarships and support youth initiatives. The first football game pitted the Mississippi State Delta Devils against the Grambling State Tigers. It's all in good fun, but fans do care which team wins. With fans thundering their support, Mississippi beat Grambling in 1984 with a score of 48-36.

HAUNTED HOUSE
Children's Museum
3000 N. Meridian St.
(317) 334-3322
www.childrensmuseum.org

It's a spooky good time at this event filled with friendliness, fright, and fun. Since 1964, the Children's Museum has been sponsoring a Haunted House. Each year the name, theme, costumes, and decorations change. But if you look closely, some of the same props and scenes are reworked to fit the new motif. Themes over the years have included Haunted Safari, Haunted Shipwreck, Haunted Castle, Ghost Grand Hotel, and Monster Manor. In 2009 the theme was the Quest for the Lost Mummy, a fitting salute to celebrate the Children Museum's exhibit of King Tut's treasures. Much less gruesome than many local haunted houses, the Children's Museum even offers lights-on tours for the littlest kids to show them there is nothing to be afraid of in the dark. Museum admission is not required, but a separate admission fee is charged.

NOVEMBER

CHRISTMAS GIFT AND HOBBY SHOW
Indiana State Fairgrounds
1202 E. 38th St.
(800) 215-1700
www.christmasgiftandhobbyshow.com
For more than 60 years, shoppers have flocked to the Christmas Gift and Hobby Show with shopping lists in hand. Nearly five acres of wild, wacky, and wonderful holiday gifts are featured, all under one roof and thousands under $20. Entertainment and celebrities also add to the merriment. More than 350 exhibitors display an incredible array of gifts—running a gamut of home decor, sports memorabilia, books, jewelry, dolls, apparel, designer-inspired accessories, collectibles, and much more. The largest of its kind in the Midwest, the show boasts that it has something for everyone, including an array of holiday foods and locally produced wine. Of course, the merry man in red makes an appearance. The fee is $10 for adults; children 12 and under are admitted free.

CIRCLE OF LIGHTS
Monument Circle
www.qc-indy.com

For almost 50 years, thousands of Hoosiers have braved the cold on the Friday night after Thanksgiving to enjoy a beloved holiday tradition—the lighting of almost 5,000 colored lights strung from the 284-foot-tall Soldiers and Sailors Monument. Another 60,000 twinkling lights in trees add shimmer to the scene. Each year a local child is picked from a coloring contest to help "flip the switch." Live entertainment adds to the festivities. Arrive early to get a good spot for all the celebration. The tree lighting takes place shortly after 7:30 p.m., but entertainment with top-notch performers starts at 6 p.m. Circle of Lights is presented free by the Contractors of Quality Connection and Electrical Workers of IBEW 481.

CONSERVATORY CROSSING

Garfield Park Conservatory and Sunken Garden
2450 S. Shelby St.
(317) 327-7183
www.garfieldgardensconservatory.org
Enjoy the Conservatory decked out in its holiday best with a brilliant display of poinsettias and model trains. A train village and thousands of twinkling lights create a fairyland. Garfield Park Conservatory houses 10,000 square feet of plants from the world's tropics. Even if it's snowing outside, the conservatory is always in full bloom. Admission is $2 for adults, $1 for children, or $5 for a family.

DECEMBER

CONNER PRAIRIE BY CANDLELIGHT

Conner Prairie
1300 Allisonville Rd., Fishers
(800) 966-1836
www.connerprairie.org

Snuggle in a warm coat and hat while you journey back to Christmas Eve 1836, when Prairietown residents are preparing for the holidays. Each has a story to tell. Mr. McClure, the town carpenter, is putting the finishing touches on handcrafted gifts. The Ullman's describe their Hanukah celebration. Meet the German Pennsylvania version of Santa Claus. Back then, Christmas wasn't quite the big celebration it is today. Savor the simplicity as you stroll along lantern-lit paths and meet costumed interpreters. Stay for a cozy dinner inside. Reservations are required for the buffet-style meal with such favorites as glazed ham with golden raisin sauce, chicken cordon bleu, green beans almondine, macaroni and cheese, and sweet potatoes with cinnamon, followed by warm cherry crisp and holiday cookies. Admission is $12 for adults, $10 for children 2 to 12. Dinner is $15.95 for adults and $7.95 for children 12 and under.

INDIANAPOLIS AUTO SHOW

Indiana Convention Center
100 S. Capitol Ave.
www.indyautoshow
Held the weekend after Christmas, the Auto Show gives car lovers a head start on next year's Christmas wish list. Presented by the Indianapolis Auto Dealers Association, the show features about 400 vehicles from almost 40 manufacturers. Concept cars, the latest technology, daily giveaways (culminating in a drawing for a new vehicle), and celebrities add to reasons to attend. If nothing else, it's a good place to dream, stretch your legs, and walk off some of the holiday goodies. Admission is $7 for adults; children under 12 enter free with an adult. All active-duty military, police officers, and firefighters are admitted free with identification.

DAY TRIPS AND WEEKEND GETAWAYS

The challenge with this chapter—as with so many other chapters—is not enough space for all the goodies I would like to share. When I sat down with a map to choose which day trips and weekend getaways to spotlight, the map was soon filled with more red dots for possible places than there was room in this book to put them all.

Since Indianapolis is situated in the middle of the state, it offers easy access in any direction to a myriad of fascinating destinations. Many of the suggested sites are close enough so that you can make it back to Indianapolis for the evening and still feel as though you had a wonderful getaway. Using Indy as your base, you can howl with the wolves in Battle Ground, understand how the Amish live in Nappanee and Shipshewana, learn about the Underground Railroad stations run by Quakers in Fountain City, read World War II correspondent Ernie Pyle's writings at his Dana birthplace, see where rebel actor James Dean is buried in Fairmount, marvel at the penny ceiling in Marengo Cave, inspect a fossil bed in Clarksville, walk the same halls automotive giants once did in Auburn, watch windmills in Kendallville, be entertained by Garfield the cat in Muncie, celebrate July 4th at the famed Madison Regatta on the Ohio River, and so much more. See what I mean about a wealth of activities? These tantalizing attractions aren't even among the ones I have listed. (But if their mention has sparked your interest, you can contact Indiana Tourism at www.VisitIndiana.com for more information.) If you're not familiar with the Hoosier state, you might be surprised at how varied the terrain and towns are. After traveling around Indiana for decades, I have discovered so many attractions I never expected to find and hope to return to explore once again.

The list below is only a start. If your favorite is not included, maybe it will be in the next edition. So get out there and see what you discover. Adventure awaits.

BLOOMINGTON

Home of Indiana University, Bloomington is a lively city and the setting for the 1979 movie *Breaking Away*. The film spotlighted IU's Little 500 bike race held each April. With its local limestone architecture and shady trees, the university is a beautiful campus for a stroll. Founded in 1824 as the first college west of the Allegany Mountains, IU offers top-notch attractions like the Mathers Museum of World Cultures, IU Art Museum, Kinsey Institute Gallery, and IU Opera Theater, said to be acoustically perfect. If you're lucky, you might catch a performance of native son and acclaimed violinist Joshua Bell.

Founded in the late 1970s, the Tibetan Mongolian Buddhist Culture Center is the only one in the nation. How did such a gem come to be in Bloomington? The Dalai Lama's brother lived here for many years until his recent death. Thubten J. Norbu, the Dalai Lama's oldest brother in a family of 16 children—seven of whom survived infancy—came to Bloomington as an IU professor. Open to the public, the center features traditional Buddhist temples, colorful scrolls, and a permanent sand mandala, among other gems. The Dalai Lama has visited Bloomington many times; the next scheduled visit is May of 2010.

With over 12,500 acres of water, Lake Monroe is the state's largest man-made lake and a major recreational playground. Opened to the public in 1965 and located 10 miles southeast of Bloomington, the lake has a privately owned marina—Fourwinds Resort and Marina—as well as public marinas, boat rentals, hiking trails, picnic areas, a swimming beach, and campground. Rent a pontoon and watch a marvelous sunset over Lake Monroe.

ℹ️ Encompassing more than 475,000 square feet, the Indiana Memorial Union at Indiana University in Bloomington is one of the largest student union buildings in the world. Inside are a 186-room hotel, seven-story student activities tower, restaurants, theater, bowling alley, convenience store, bookstore, travel agency, bank, and meeting rooms.

Stop by the Monroe County History Center in the historic Carnegie Library building downtown and pick up a self-guided walking tour about Hoagy Carmichael. The museum itself has some neat exhibits and a special one on Hoagy to get you started. Born Nov. 22, 1899, in Bloomington, Hoagland Howard Carmichael went on to become a famed jazz pianist, songwriter, singer, actor, and bandleader. Among his most loved tunes are "Stardust" and "Georgia on My Mind." Hoagy died in 1982 and is buried in Rose Hill Cemetery in Bloomington.

If you're in the mood for music, Bloomington clubs offer a variety of late-night entertainment—Second Story, Bluebird, and Café Django are just a few that feature everything from folk to funk. It's not uncommon to see resident rocker John Mellencamp around town or the man called "the best rock and roll drummer in the world," Kenny Aronoff, hitting the golf links. Both live here.

Now that you've worked up an appetite, check out the almost 100 restaurants in the downtown area. The variety is surprising and mouth-watering. For a town its size (population 70,000), Bloomington has a smorgasbord of ethnic and specialty restaurants and bars. Choices include Greek, Cajun, French, Irish, Yugoslavian, American, Chinese, and Tibetan. Just park your car on the courthouse square, start walking, and you are bound to find a restaurant that appeals to you.

Located just north of Bloomington, Oliver Winery is the oldest and largest winery in Indiana. Founded in 1972, the winery got its start in the basement of the Oliver family home, where IU law professor William Oliver made wine from grapes stomped by his own and neighborhood children. The tasting room is surrounded by beautifully landscaped gardens and limestone sculptures. An on-site picnic ground features a shimmering pond, sunny meadow, and wooded hillside. Buy a bottle of Oliver wine, get some of the bread and gourmet cheese that Oliver offers, and enjoy an outdoor feast.

For more information contact the Bloomington Convention & Visitors Bureau at (800) 800-0037 or www.visitbloomington.com.

Bloomington is less than an hour south of Indianapolis via SR 37.

ℹ️ The Little 500 at Indiana University in Bloomington is the nation's largest collegiate bicycling event. Started in 1951, the relay race features four-member student teams pedaling around a quarter-mile cinder track.

BROWN COUNTY, INDIANA

When Chicago painter Adolph Shulz visited Brown County in the early 1900s, he wrote that "a sense of peace and loveliness never before experienced came over me." Shulz and his wife Ada quickly made the unique hill country their home, along with other celebrated artists such as T. C. Steele.

Today, that "Peaceful Valley" is filled with artisans seeking the same inspiration, tranquillity, natural beauty, and genuine hospitality that their predecessors found. The century-old Art Colony of the Midwest boasts award-winning artists in a wealth of mediums. An unofficial estimate notes that at least 100 artists live in Brown County.

Long known for its tradition of handicrafts, Brown County is home to artisans who seem able to create something beautiful from almost anything. That's part of the hill heritage of "using up, making do, or doing without." Unique crafts can be found at many shops, studios, and festivals throughout the area.

Name it—paintings, ceramics, holography, photography, braided rugs, candles, blown glass, hammered copper pots, wrought iron, quilts, furniture, dolls, dollhouses, toys, birdhouses, stained glass, corn fiber brooms, rag rugs, leatherwork, mountain dulcimers, jewelry, carving, pottery, weaving—somebody here makes it.

Contact the Brown County Convention & Visitors Bureau at (812) 988-7303 or www.brown county.com

Brown County is about an hour south of Indianapolis. Some great places you might want to visit in Brown County are listed below.

Nashville

The 4-square-mile county seat of Nashville, with a population of under 1,000, might boast a higher percentage of artisans than any other town in America. The town features more than 300 specialty shops, art and crafts studios, and galleries brimming with unique wares. Spectacular in every season, Brown County offers a return to a quieter time and a chance to see what gifted artists can create in a spectacular setting.

From bustling restaurants to cozy bistros, Nashville offers a wide selection of dining spots. Located in the center of Nashville at 105 S. Van Buren St. (800-370-4703), the Artists Colony Inn Bed and Breakfast is great for an overnight stay and meal. Smoked grilled pork chops served with sliced apples in brown sugar sauce are a favorite, as is Adolph's Country Style Meatloaf Dinner with real mashed potatoes, gravy, and vegetable of the day. The inn is noted for its Sun Fries, thinly sliced sweet potatoes served with the inn's special brown sugar sauce.

As the oldest commercial building in Nashville, the Hobnob (812-988-4114), at the corner of Main and Van Buren Streets, has served as a meeting place for tourists and locals alike for decades. Much has changed since the building was erected in 1868, but the Hobnob's menu continues to please. The Hill County Breakfast is a filling way to start the day—two eggs cooked to

order, a side of sausage, bacon, or ham, and a side of biscuits, gravy, and toast. All breads, pastries, and Danish are baked at the Hobnob daily.

The Nashville House on the corner of Main and Van Buren streets has a devoted following for its fried chicken, ham cured in a small packing house nearby, slow-roasted turkey, and homemade fried biscuits and apple butter made in its own kitchen.

Brown County State Park

One of the most visited state parks in the nation, Brown County State Park offers 15,000 acres of natural wonders and the lovely Abe Martin Lodge. Located in the hills of Brown County off Highway 46, Indiana's largest state park includes nearly 20 miles of roads with numerous scenic vistas, campgrounds, hiking trails, mountain bike trails, horse-riding facilities, and a nature center. Also available are tennis courts, picnic shelters, playground equipment, and a swimming pool.

Contact Brown County State Park at (812) 988-6406 or www.browncountystatepark.com.

Bean Blossom

The "high lonesome" sound created by Bill Monroe still floats over the hills he loved in Brown County. Performing in the area in 1951, the Grand Ole Opry star saw the 55-acre site and bought it a month later for his home away from home. Located up the hill from Nashville, the Bill Monroe Musical Park and Campground in Bean Blossom celebrates the legendary bluegrass musician with the annual Bill Monroe Memorial Bean Blossom Bluegrass Festival held for eight days in June. Attracting the best in bluegrass musicians, the festival originated in 1967 when Bill Monroe put on a two-day event. Bill Monroe died in 1996. He was buried a day before he would have turned 85 years old.

The park is also home to the Bill Monroe Bluegrass Hall of Fame & Country Star Museum. A walkway of stars paves the entry to the museum, with Hollywood-style bronze stars for bluegrass greats, family, and friends. The museum tells the story of how Bill Monroe found his musical way to Bean Blossom. On display is Monroe's personal collection of memorabilia of his life, as well as instruments, clothing, pictures, and more donated by legendary stars like Jimmy Martin, Jim & Jesse, Porter Wagoner, Flatt & Scruggs, Loretta Lynn, Dolly Parton, Johnny Cash, and George Jones.

In the courtyard of the museum is Uncle Pen's Cabin, a replica of the cabin once owned by Pendleton Vandiver, Bill Monroe's uncle. After Monroe's parents died, he went to live with his Uncle Pen as a teenager. Monroe memorialized his Uncle Pen in a song.

Contact the Bill Monroe Musical Park and Campground at (812) 988-6422 or www.bean blossom.com.

Story

The hills and hollers of Brown County are dotted with small towns. But the little spot known as Story may be the tiniest around. Barely a dot on Indiana maps, Story has a population of three. Plus a ghost.

To get to Story, you follow a winding country road and turn back the hands of time. The heart of the community is the old Story Inn, standing solidly like a monument to another era. Story was named after the community's resident physician, George Story, during the post–Civil War years. Story and his kin were timber harvesters from southern Ohio who were attracted to the Hoosier area by the vast expanses of virgin hardwoods. A post office called Story was established May 25, 1882. Characterized as a boomtown in the late 1800s, Story was the largest settlement in the area at the turn of the 20th century.

Today, the town consists of less than a dozen buildings. The entire village is owned by Rick Hofstetter and his wife Angela. They live in Story along with their bar manager. The Story Inn is now a noted place for gourmet meals and wine tastings. Several buildings have been turned into guest cottages, many with kitchenettes and hot tubs. Four rooms also are available for guests over the restaurants. Creaky wooden stairs lead to comfortable guestrooms and, as Indiana's oldest bed and breakfast, the rooms remain true to their 19th-century charm. Don't look for televisions, radios, phones, or clocks.

What many guests do hope to see is the legendary Blue Lady. The first room to the left at the top of the stairs is reported to be haunted by a woman wearing a long blue dress. Guest books dating back to the 1970s record weird happenings in the middle of the night. In the bedroom, the lady in blue has been seen standing by the bed, reflected in the window or the mirror. Guests have talked about the smell of perfume or finding their belongings moving about the room. A blue lamp next to the bed is said to summon the Blue Lady. Light it, legend says, and the she will come and visit you.

Contact the Story Inn at (812) 988-2273 or www.storyinn.com.

Story is 14 miles southeast of Nashville.

> **i** Columbus, Indiana, is ranked sixth in the nation for architectural innovation and design by the American Institute of Architects, on a list that includes the much larger cities of Chicago, New York, Boston, San Francisco, and Washington, D.C.

COLUMBUS, INDIANA

Walk out a church designed by Eliel Saarinen, cross the street, pass a Henry Moore sculpture, and enter a library designed by I. M. Pei. Where can you do that?

Where else in the country are such architectural treasures gathered in such a relatively small place? Like the famed explorer for which the city is named, Columbus has dared to go to great heights in its architectural quest.

No small town—and few big cities—in America can match Columbus for its modern architecture, which has earned praise across the nation. With more than 60 buildings designed by some of the world's greatest architects, residents love to show visitors around their hometown. Local lore says that the county jail in downtown Columbus looks so good that a visitor once tried to check in.

A few years ago when a bridge was built at the downtown entrance on Second Street, the city's leaders demanded a signature structure. That cable-stayed bridge, with four tall red pylons, is lighted at night and frames the 1874 country courthouse and its tower. Many people don't realize that you can walk out onto that bridge on a very safe platform and look down into the river.

The city's love affair with architecture began in the early 1940s when its First Christian Church needed a new building for a growing congregation. In a daring move, the church selected modern architect Eliel Saarinen. The church, with its 166-foot bell tower instead of a steeple, broke with tradition and was one of the first modern religious buildings in the nation with simple clean lines and no stained glass.

i Chuck Taylor, for whom the Converse All Star shoe is named, was a basketball player, salesman, and shoe endorser from Columbus. He played on the Columbus High School Bulldogs team from 1914 to 1918. Until the mid-1970s, the beloved shoe design, nicknamed "Chuck's," captured 50 percent of the athletic shoe market.

As Columbus grew in the years following World War II, new schools became necessary for the baby boom. In 1957, Cummins Engine Co., under the guidance of CEO J. Irwin Miller, made an offer to pay the architectural fees for the design of new school buildings. Later, the offer was extended for all public buildings. Since then, the Cummins Foundation has spent more than $20 million on more than 50 community projects.

Among the many treasures is the Bartholomew County Veteran's Memorial, erected in 1997. Designed by Thompson and Rose Architects and awarded the Boston Society of Architects Unbuilt Architecture Design Award, the memorial is located on the County Courthouse lawn and has 25 limestone pillars, each 40 feet high. To fully appreciate the solemnity and impact of the memorial, walk inside the pillars. Engraved on the columns inside are letters from Bartholomew County people who died in 20th-century wars. The words are often simple expressions from service men and women to loved ones back home. When you read about someone who says how much he misses his mom and her cooking, it makes you realize that these letter writers never made it back home.

One of the best ways to learn the Columbus story is to take a guided tour aboard the visitor center bus. During the two-hour tour led by tour guides, visitors travel throughout the community, looking at historic and modern building exteriors, landscaping, parks, and public art. Guests on the tour also get an inside look at two buildings. Tours start at the Columbus Area Visitors Center at 10 a.m. each weekday, 10 a.m. and 2 p.m. on Sat, and 1 p.m. on Sun, from Mar through Nov. In Jan, Feb, and Mar, tours are offered on Sat only. The fee is $12 for adults, $7 for children, and free for children 4 and under. Self-guided tour maps also are sold in the visitor center gift shop.

Contact the Columbus Area Visitors Center at (800) 468-6564 or www.columbus.in.us.

Columbus is about a 45-mile drive down I-65 south from Indianapolis.

i Race-car driver and 2007 Brickyard 400 winner Tony Stewart is a local boy made good. See a mural of Tony at the downtown Dairy Queen, where the owner was an early fan and sponsor.

FRENCH LICK AND WEST BADEN

These two towns are often mentioned in the same breath because they are so close together and share so much—including two "sister" hotels. The West Baden Springs Hotel and French Lick Hotel both recently underwent more than $400 million in preservation and renovation work by Gayle and Bill Cook and their son Carl of Bloomington.

i In 1917, Chef Louis Perrin at the French Lick Springs Resort ran out of orange juice and served tomato juice instead, reported to be the first known serving of its type.

The French Lick/West Baden area offers 8,800-acre Patoka Lake, Big Splash Adventure Waterpark & Resort, Paoli Peaks Ski Resort, French Lick Scenic Railway, French Lick Winery, and much more.

Contact the Orange County Convention & Visitors Bureau at (866) 960-7792 or www.visit frenchlickwestbaden.com.

French Lick and West Baden are about 100 miles south of Indianapolis.

French Lick Springs Hotel

French Lick has long been a mecca for people seeking to improve their health. More than 200 years ago, French traders were drawn to the area of French Lick because their livestock, attracted by the rich springs, flocked here to lick the mineral rich waters and rocks. That's why the valley was called "The Lick."

Seeing the potential for the area, Dr. William Bowles bought some land around the mineral springs and opened a swanky spa resort in 1845. The hotel became an immediate success as people flocked from hundreds of miles to experience the touted healing powers of the mineral waters. Dubbed Pluto Water because it came from the depths of the Earth, the water was said to have 22 different minerals in it and would cure what ailed you. Now this classic hotel has been restored to its famed charm and grandeur. From the distinct mosaic and marble flooring to the state-of-the-art spa and 24-hour French Lick Casino, the hotel has amenities galore. Indoor and outdoor pools, hot tub, casual and fine dining options, shops, riding stables, bowling alley, golf course, and much more can be enjoyed.

Contact French Lick Springs Hotel at (888) 936-9360 or www.frenchlick.com

West Baden Hotel

The story of the West Baden Hotel began long ago, when the West Baden/French Lick valley was a busy resort area. Dr. John Lane acquired property a mile away from the French Lick Spring Hotel in 1855 and named his hotel West Baden Springs after the famous springs in Wiesbaden, Germany. Indiana banker Lee Sinclair took over the property and in 1902 constructed a sophisticated resort. With its one-of-a-kind domed atrium spanning 200 feet, the National Historic Landmark has been called the "Eighth Wonder of the World." Rooms rise in six tiers around the dome, and balcony rooms provide a panoramic view of the atrium.

Not to be outdone by his rival up the road, Sinclair promoted his Sprudel water, which means "spring" in German. The hotel became the social playground of the wealthy elite, sports heroes, politicians, even gangsters like Al Capone and John Dillinger. But the Great Depression of 1929 ended those glory days. Many of the guests were ruined financially, and the hotel never recovered from the shock. Over the years, this crown jewel of the valley fell on hard times and sat deserted. In 1991 a portion of the hotel collapsed.

That's when the medical-device entrepreneur Bill Cook of Bloomington stepped in to fund an amazing restoration and renovation project. In 2007 West Baden Springs Resort was officially opened. Three-fourths of a century after the last guest checked out, visitors again checked in. And that's what they have been doing ever since.

Contact West Baden Springs Hotel at (888) 936-9360 or www.frenchlick.com.

i Deep below the earth in southern Indiana is a sea of limestone that is one of the richest deposits of top-quality limestone found anywhere on earth. New York City's Empire State Building and Rockefeller Center, as well as the Pentagon, the U.S. Treasury, a dozen other government buildings in Washington, D.C., and 14 state capitols around the nation are built from this sturdy, beautiful Indiana limestone.

NEW HARMONY

It might seem a strange place to create Utopia. But two different leaders chose this southwestern Indiana spot for what they thought would be the ideal life. Although neither community lasted, each left an indelible mark on New Harmony and on the world.

New Harmony was a community that began almost 200 years ahead of its time. Two communal societies were located here, back to back. Of course, George Rapp probably didn't realize what an important step he was taking when he bought 20,000 acres of land along the Wabash River in 1814. "Father" Rapp led a group of 800 Harmonists to the United States from Germany to escape religious persecution. They came to Indiana from Pennsylvania.

Within a year, the Harmonists had created a planned community in the wilderness of the Indiana territory. From 1814 to 1824, the Harmonists perfected a cosmopolitan and industrious community while awaiting the millennium. The Harmonists also believed in celibacy, which is why the society died out near the end of the 1800s.

By 1824, more than 180 structures stood in New Harmony. The land had been planted with large vineyards and orchards. A portable greenhouse was constructed for raising oranges and lemons. Over 20 products were being marketed as far away as Pittsburgh and New Orleans. But in 1825 the Harmonists decided to return to Pennsylvania. Difficulties in shipping goods, problems with malaria, and a hope to rekindle the spirit of Rapp's followers may have contributed to the decision.

So Rapp sold the entire town to a wealthy Welsh-born social reformer named Robert Owen. Owen hoped to create a model community where educational and social equality would prosper. Owen and his partner, geologist William Maclure, paid $150,000 for the town. Sadly, harmony did not reign in the utopia. Owen's dream failed and was dissolved in 1827. Owen returned to Scotland but his daughter and four of his sons remained in New Harmony, along with Maclure and other "Owenites."

Today, visitors can enjoy the Roofless Church, an interdenominational spiritual retreat. The New Harmony Inn is a peaceful place to stay; dine in its Red Geranium Restaurant, well known for its hearty fare and lemon pie. Be forewarned, however, that the pie is definitely lemony and tart.

The town also has plenty of shops brimming with antiques, books, and handmade gifts. Galleries and garden shops continue the 19th-century tradition. Take time to walk the Cathedral Labyrinth, patterned after one dating back to the 12th century, the Cathedral of Notre Dame's labyrinth in Chartres, France.

Christians have used it in symbolic pilgrimages, and variations of the rite are documented throughout history. For instance, European coastal fishermen would walk a labyrinth ceremoniously before heading out to sea. During the Harmonist era here, the garden maze, with a small temple at the center, was considered a place to relax after a long workday. Unlike a maze, a labyrinth has no dead ends or wrong turns. It is not a puzzle. It is meant to calm the spirit—a fitting symbol for New Harmony.

Contact Historic New Harmony at (800) 231-2168 or www.usi.edu.

New Harmony is about three and a half hours west of Indianapolis.

INDIANA DUNES

Singing sands caress the air. Waves crash on sandy shores. Dunes tower almost 200 feet into the horizon. More than 350 species of birds and over 1,100 flowering plant species and ferns call this marvel home. And all of this sand and water wonder is located in Indiana.

That's right, some of the largest sand dunes this side of the Sahara are in the Hoosier state. Authorized by Congress in 1966, Indiana Dunes National Lakeshore offers a wealth of diverse natural beauty located within an urban setting. Once in danger of being turned into an industrial complex, the gift from Mother Nature was preserved as a national park through the efforts of environmentalists, officials, and local folks who knew they had something too good to lose. Stretching along

Lake Michigan's southern shoreline, the dunes provide an ecosystem unlike any other. With 18 miles of shoreline, the park encompasses 14,000 acres of forest, marsh, dune, and beach.

Among the most popular dunes is Mount Baldy. An impressive 125 feet tall, Mount Baldy is the largest "living" dune that marram grass and cottonwood trees cannot hold in place. Getting its name because of the lack of vegetation on its "top," Mount Baldy actually moves south at a rate of 4 to 5 feet each year, burying all woodlands in its path. On a clear day, you can see the Chicago skyline from atop Mount Baldy.

Contact Indiana Dunes National State Park at (219) 926-7561 or www.nps.gov/indu.

Indiana Dunes is about 175 miles north of Indianapolis.

SANTA CLAUS

Yes, there is a Santa Claus. And the small southern Indiana town (population 2,164) with that name celebrates Christmas all year long.

Christmas is always in the air. Santa's Lodge has year-round lighted Christmas trees in the lobby and a huge permanently frozen snowman on the front lawn. St. Nick's Restaurant, Lake Rudolph Campground & RV Resort, Frosty's Pizza, Holiday Foods, Ho Ho Ho Holdings, and more carry on that Yule heritage.

The town's fire trucks are named after reindeer Rudolph, Dasher, and Blitzen. Streets boast signs like Silver Bell Terrace, Kringle Plaza, Prancer Drive, Christmas Boulevard, and Evergreen Plaza. Then there's Holiday World & Splashin' Safari, formerly Santa Claus Land, opened in 1946 as the world's first theme amusement park, where Santa is a major attraction even on hot summer days.

At the Santa Claus Post Office, more than 500,000 pieces of mail arrive each year for the special holiday postmark designed by a local student. Letters from children also find their way to the Hoosier post office. Some of them are just addressed to Santa Claus at the North Pole, but they make it here. Those special letters—about 10,000 of them—from children are answered by a group of volunteers known as Santa's Elves.

Founded in 1850 by German settlers, the town originally was named Santa Fe. But the state already had a Santa Fe and the government said a new name was necessary. As legend recalls, townspeople gathered at the church on Christmas Eve to discuss a new name and were deep in debate. Suddenly the wind blew the church doors open, snow was falling outside, and the sound of sleigh bells chimed in the distance. The children started chanting "Santa Claus, Santa Claus," the story goes. And the townspeople decided that would be a good name for their town.

If you're visiting in the summer, Holiday World & Splashin' Safari is great for people of all ages. Consistently voted No. 1 for cleanliness and friendliness, Holiday World offers enough thrilling rides, live shows, tasty food, and unexpected museums to keep anyone amused. Holiday World also offers free unlimited soft drinks, free sunscreen, and free parking—a wonderful perk for budget-minded families.

A free museum in Santa Claus tells the history of the town and of Holiday World. At Santa's Candy Castle, kids can log on to an exclusive North Pole Network, an interactive computer lab connected to the North Pole where you can chat with an elf, tell Santa what you want for Christmas, and find out if you're on Santa's Good List. Kids that make the list get an official Good List Certificate to take home.

While you're that close, drive down the road to where Abraham Lincoln lived from age 7 to 21. You can see the Lincoln Boyhood National Memorial where the Lincoln cabin was located, and costumed interpreters carry out the tasks of the day. Visit the simple grave where his mother is buried. Nancy Hanks Lincoln died when "milk sickness" struck the Little Pigeon Creek settlement. The illness developed when a person ate the butter or drank the milk of a cow that had eaten snakeroot plant. The sickness was nearly always fatal.

Dying in childbirth at age 20, Abe's sister Sarah Lincoln Grigsby is buried with her baby in the churchyard behind the Little Pigeon Creek

Baptist Church in Lincoln State Park. The park is also the site of an excellent amphitheater, which premiered a new Lincoln play in 2009.

The newest Abraham Lincoln attraction is the Bicentennial Plaza inside Lincoln State Park. The impressive monument was unveiled in 2009, featuring 94 Indiana limestone pieces with a circular plaza 58 feet in diameter. A pathway leads to eight pillars tracing Abe's development as he grew in these woods and his height at different ages from 7 to 21. Behind the wall, a large bronze bust portrays Lincoln at the end of is life.

Driving the short distance from Santa Claus to Lincoln City, you'll pass Buffalo Run Farm, Grill & Gifts. With two cabins and a tepee behind it, Buffalo Run sits on property where Lincoln's cousin, Dennis Hanks, once lived. Buffalo Run is a neat place to lunch with a fresh-cooked buffalo burger.

Contact the Spencer County Visitors Bureau at (888) 444-9252 or www.legendaryplaces.org.

Santa Claus is about three hours south of Indianapolis.

i The first automobile produced by South Bend–based Studebaker Brothers Manufacturing Co. in 1902 was powered by electricity and had a top speed of 13 mph.

SOUTH BEND

Willy Wonka would love this place. The South Bend Chocolate Museum honors the delicious cocoa bean with one of the world's largest displays of chocolate-related items. The attraction features such gems as a 1,300-year-old Mayan chocolate pot and a chance to make your own chocolate spoon. Tours end with sweet samplings of famed South Bend Chocolates from the company that produces 4,000 pounds of chocolate daily.

What's an Indiana city without sports and cars? South Bend is famed for both. Hometown of the gold-domed University of Notre Dame and its Fighting Irish, South Bend boasts America's winningest college football team. Looming over

Notre Dame Stadium is the 132-foot-tall mural of "Touchdown Jesus," so nicknamed because the resurrected Christ has his arms raised like a referee signaling a touchdown. The College Football Hall of Fame shares stories of the legends, the action, and such oddities as the Flying Wedge belt equipped with handles so players could hold on securely to teammates for the deadly football barrier.

i Born in South Bend, Dale Messick was one of the first female comic strip artists and creator of glamorous, redheaded Brenda Starr, a 1940s reporter who searches the globe for interesting news. In the 1950s, the strip appeared in more than 250 newspapers. Messick died in 2005 at age 98.

The Studebaker National Museum spotlights a story stretching back to 1852, when two brothers, Henry and Clem Studebaker—with only $68 in cash—started a blacksmith shop in South Bend. Once the largest producer of horse-drawn vehicles in the world, Studebaker joined the "horseless contraption" revolution with its first automobile in 1902. The company closed in 1966. Showcasing an awesome automobile collection, the museum salutes the only company to span the time from settlers' wagons to high-performance automobiles.

Contact the South Bend/Mishawaka Convention and Visitors Bureau at 800-519-0577 or www.exploresouthbend.org.

South Bend is about 140 miles north of Indianapolis.

VINCENNES

Selling newspapers on a corner, the redheaded kid was asked by an out-of-towner what there was to do in the tiny Indiana burg of Vincennes. Gesturing across the street to a theater, the nine-year-old answered that a famous comedian was going to appear that night. When the stranger asked if the boy would be in the audience, the youngster said that he didn't have the money and had to finish selling his papers.

Upon hearing that, the stranger bought the remainder of the papers—paying $1 for three newspapers that sold for three cents each at the time. He also said a seat would be waiting in the theater for the boy. When the show began and the performer walked out from behind the curtain, the boy was shocked. The star of the show was old-time entertainer Ed Wynn—the stranger who had bought the boy's newspapers.

During intermission, the performer invited the boy backstage and held him up to peer through the curtains. That was Red Skelton's first look at an audience. When he grew up, Red had one of the most popular television shows of the day. He also starred in more than 30 movies, wrote 5,000 musical pieces and several children's books, and created paintings. Some of his clown portraits sold for more than $80,000 each. Red died in 1997, but his memory is honored in his birthplace with a wonderful $16.8 million theater dedicated in his honor in 2006—the Red Skelton Performing Arts Center at Vincennes University.

Founded in 1732, the oldest city in Indiana offers a wealth of history. You can visit the William Henry Harrison mansion known as Grouseland, built in 1803 by the nation's ninth president. Hear the tale of how, if not for bad aim, the nation might have lost its ninth and 23rd presidents all in one fatal shot. A bullet hole in the shutter at the mansion recalls that lucky incident. Harrison was walking the floor with his infant son, John Scott Harrison, when someone took a shot at him. They missed. The son he was carrying went on to have a son who would become our 23rd president. Of course, William Henry Harrison himself went on to become president as well.

i The nickname of the sports teams for Vincennes Lincoln High School is the "Alices." The school picked that name in honor of local author Maurice Thompson, who wrote the 1900 book *Alice of Old Vincennes,* set during the American Revolution.

Stop by the George Rogers Clark National Historical Park to learn more about the Revolutionary War hero. Built in 1931, the memorial is an eye-catching round building with seven murals depicting Clark's military campaigns. Inside, a larger-than-life bronze statue of Clark stands atop a marble pedestal. During the summer, living-history programs often take place here to re-create camp life with military drills and firearms demonstrations.

Next is St. Francis Xavier Cathedral, Indiana's oldest parish church. Dating from 1749, the cathedral recently completed a massive renovation and is a real beauty to behold. Beside the cathedral, dark cedars shelter the Old French Cemetery, where priests, parishioners, Indians, soldiers, and African slaves lie buried, many in unmarked graves. The first interment was in 1741, the last in 1846, Behind the cathedral in a modern redbrick building is a treasure house—the Brute Library. The oldest library in Indiana, it contains more than 11,000 rare books, including the Bible that St. Elizabeth Seton was holding when she died.

For some more history, visit the Vincennes State Historic Site, which consists of the Log Cabin Visitor Center, Indiana Territory Capitol, Elihu Stout Print Shop, Maurice Thompson Birthplace, Old State Band, and Fort Knox II. Vincennes is also home to Vincennes University, Indiana's first college. Founded in 1801, it is the only college in the nation founded by an individual who would later become president of the United States, William Henry Harrison.

RELOCATION

Indianapolis is a city of neighborhoods with a huge variety of housing options. Hoosiers live in historic homes, modern houses, high-rise condos, downtown lofts, apartments, farmhouses, mansions, cottages, and town houses in neighborhoods that are as diverse as the people who live in them.

Newcomers arrive daily, lured by Indy's low cost of living, affordable housing, opportunities for higher education, excellent health care facilities, and overall quality of life. Indianapolis is one of the most affordable cities of its size. Its cost of living consistently ranks below the national average. Housing in Indianapolis is among the most affordable in the county, with the average sale price of a home at $136,800. The average apartment rent per month is $643.

If you are relocating in Indianapolis, have recently moved here, or are in the market for a new home in the area, this chapter is for you. The following pages are filled with information about Indy neighborhoods and a list of resources that will come in handy. It's not possible to profile all the neighborhoods around the city, but these will give you an idea of the wonderful areas to consider. Indianapolis is a great place to visit and an even better place to call home.

DOWNTOWN INDIANAPOLIS

A thriving success story and model for revitalization, downtown Indianapolis is a dynamic and growing residential market. Downtown attracts young professionals, empty nesters, students, and more and more families. It's easy to see why. Living downtown means easy access to the area's more than 210 shops, 300 restaurants and bars, 18 museums and historic sites, 24 memorials and parks, eight major sports venues, countless performing arts, theaters, entertainment, and recreation options, numerous art galleries, and many other interesting attractions. Living downtown also means skipping the daily commute and suburban traffic jams and having time after work for family, friends, and fun. It means saving fuel and wear and tear on an automobile by not having to drive daily to and from work.

No wonder downtown Indianapolis has become the hot spot to live. Downtown living offers a mix of historic neighborhoods, luxury condos, lofts, and apartments. Currently, almost 20,000 people live downtown. The goal is to double that population to 40,000 by the year 2020.

Even during a tough economy, downtown Indianapolis has seen strong demand and occupancy levels, driving the surge in residential development. This has led to more than 2,223 new residential units currently in the works, totaling more than $375 million. These houses, condos, and apartments are scheduled to begin or be completed by 2013. Several options, from custom condos to row houses, are available for those looking to own a home or condo downtown. There are 21 projects totaling 547 new homes being developed. Prices start at about $125,000. In 2008, 211 residential units totaling $61.5 million were completed. Since 2000, 2,721 residential units totaling more than $387 million have been built.

Downtown Indianapolis offers several rental options. Nine projects being developed include 1,676 apartments. Rental rates begin at about $600. Downtown devotees can also choose to live in a variety of recently constructed residential projects ranging from apartments overlooking the downtown canal to renovated lofts in the heart of the central business district. More than 50 residential developments with 2,500 units were completed from 2000 to 2008. For more information about downtown living, visit www.indydt.com or call (317) 237-2222.

NEIGHBORHOODS

BROAD RIPPLE VILLAGE
www.discoverbroadripplevillage.com
About 20 minutes from downtown, this north-side neighborhood features eclectic shops and vintage boutiques, a variety of restaurants—many with al fresco dining—artists and art galleries, and bars and pubs with live entertainment. Parks in Broad Ripple Village are connected by the nationally recognized Monon Trail.

Broad Ripple is bordered on the north and west by the White River, on the south by Kessler Boulevard, and on the east by Keystone. While known for its thriving nightlife and music scene, Broad Ripple is also a popular residential neighborhood with its unique architecture, neat bungalows, and well-tended lawns.

i Neighborhood home tours offer great ways to get an inside peek into these popular areas. Check out neighborhood association Web sites to see when one may be offered.

BUTLER TARKINGTON
www.butlertarkington.org
This lovely neighborhood draws its name from Butler University, which relocated to the district in 1928, and Booth Tarkington, a well-known Hoosier author who once lived in the area. The Butler-Tarkington area is bordered by 38th and Meridian Streets and the old Central Canal.

The electric street trolleys spurred the development of the area because they allowed city residents to be able to commute to homes farther from the city's core. Soon streets were lined with gracious mansions. Today, the popular area has a small but vibrant shopping district, beautifully restored homes, and a number of parks and recreational facilities. Affordable fixer-upper homes are still available.

CASTLETON
Once a railroad stop, Castleton is now a bustling commercial area with the largest mall in the state, Castleton Square Mall. The area also has office parks, restaurants, hotels and motels, and shops galore. Located in the northeast corner of Indy at the southern terminus of I-69, Castleton is home to about 40,000 residents. The residential neighborhood contains a mix of two-story and ranch-style houses, which are much in demand because of the area's easy access to commercial amenities and Indy's interstate road system.

CHATHAM ARCH
Located northeast of downtown, Chatham Arch was one of the first neighborhoods that sprang up outside of the city's original Mile Square. Filled with character, Chatham Arch offers small restored cottages, tree-shaded streets, unusual street patterns, architectural variety, and jogging trails. Most architecture is Queen Anne inspired with gabled cottages and embellished porches.

The district includes a Tudor Revival firehouse on 11th Street that a recent owner converted into a residence. Among several buildings linked to the African-American heritage of Indianapolis is Allen Methodist Episcopal Church. Located at 629 E. 11th St., the church and an adjoining sanctuary are part of an African-American community that once flourished in the area. Bordered by I-65, Chatham Arch offers easy access to the city's freeway system.

CLERMONT
Home to the Indianapolis Motor Speedway, Clermont was once a neighborhood of railroad workers. Economic development has grown in the area with a mix of restaurants, shops, and houses.

COTTAGE HOME
www.cottagehome.info
East of Chatham Arch, Cottage Home gets its name from the style of house built here between 1870 and 1900. Early residents built modest frame cottages in a variety of styles, including shotgun and Queen Anne. Many of the cottages

feature turned posts and spindles, gingerbread trim porches, brackets, and fish-scale shingles. Considered the gem of the neighborhood, one architectural exception is the brick residence at 711 Dorman St. Built for Frederick Ruskaup in 1892, this brick mansion was designed by city architects Vonnegut & Bohn. After significant decline, Cottage Home experienced a restoration boom in the mid 1980s and boasts one of the city's most active neighborhood associations.

FALL CREEK PLACE
www.fallcreekplace.com
Once known as "Dodge City" because of its high crime rate, Fall Creek Place has turned itself around. With the help of a $4 million federal grant in 2001, Fall Creek Place cleaned up its act and the surrounding area. Vacant lots, abandoned houses, and dilapidated homes were acquired; new streets, sidewalks, lighting, utilities, and trees were installed; and special financing packages were assembled for home buyers. Today, more than 400 new families join many longtime residents in a once-again thriving neighborhood. Tree-lined streets share space with Victorian homes and new homes. A neighborhood association sponsors annual events such as neighborhood cleanups, group dinners, garage sales, and more. Fall Creek Place is bounded by Meridian Street on the west, Fall Creek Parkway on the north, College Avenue on the east and 22nd Street on the south.

> **i** The National Association of Home Builders and Wells Fargo ranked Indianapolis the most affordable major housing market in the U.S. for the fourth quarter of 2008.

FLETCHER PLACE
www.fletcherplace.org
Named for Calvin Fletcher, whose farm originally encompassed most of the land in the area, Fletcher Place was originally platted in 1857. The neighborhood is a designated historic district with many notable structures, including the Andrew Wallace House, likely designed by noted architect Francis Costigan. Early settlers to the area came from both the South and the East, with Fletcher himself from New England. As it was from the beginning, Fletcher place is a working-class community made up of a variety of ethnic groups. The borders of Fletcher Place are Louisiana Street on the north, I-65 to the south, East Street to the west, and I-70/I-65 to the east.

FOUNTAIN SQUARE
www.discoverfountainsquare.com
South of Fletcher Place, Fountain Square is the oldest area of the city inside the central business district to function continually as a recognized commercial area. In 1835, Calvin Fletcher and Nicholas McCarty purchased a 264-acre farm to plat what became the Fountain Square neighborhood. Much of the development was fueled by a large number of German immigrants settling in the area. German and German-American merchants helped establish much of the character of Fountain Square. Fountain Square also played an important part in the city's theater heritage. From 1910 to 1950, Fountain Square had more operating theaters than anywhere else in Indianapolis. Urban renewal has been an ongoing process, with more than $1 million to be invested in the next few years to restore the signature fountain, create a new public plaza, make improvements to streets, and upgrade the lighting, curbs, and sidewalks.

HERRON-MORTON PLACE
www.herron-morton.org
Herron-Morton gets its name from two sources. In 1861 the area was a Civil War induction center named Camp Morton, in honor of Governor Oliver Perry Morton. In the 1890s, three businessmen purchased the area and renamed it Morton Place. Later the neighborhood became home to the John Herron Art Institute building, establishing the area's artistic reputation. Famed Hoosier artist T. C. Steele once resided in the Herron-Morton Place neighborhood.

Once the home of city movers and shakers, Herron-Morton Place lost many of its buildings to fire, neglect, and demolition. Today, New Jersey

Street still has its original esplanades and is a good example of what the northern half of the neighborhood used to be.

Renovation continues on Herron-Morton's grand Victorians, Italianates, and Queen Annes. The neighborhood is bounded by 16th Street on the north, 22nd Street on the south, Pennsylvania Street on the west, and Central Avenue on the east.

HOMECROFT

Located about 5 miles south of downtown, Homecroft was a development of the Frank Gates Real Estate Company in the 1920s. A typical suburb for middle-class families, Homecroft was a way for many to realize the American dream of buying their own homes. Most homes are modern-period styles popular at the time—brick- or stone-veneered houses with Tudor Revival or Colonial Revival elements. Today, Homecroft still retains its suburban feel and community togetherness. Well-kept single homes are shaded by mature maple trees. Banta Road, Tulip Drive, Orinoco Avenue, and the Penn railroad tracks form its borders.

i The Abraham Lincoln funeral train procession, which traveled from Washington, D.C., to Illinois, passed through what is now the neighborhood of Irvington.

IRVINGTON
www.irvingtonbuzz.com

Founded in 1870, Irvington was named after Washington Irving, author of *The Legend of Sleepy Hollow* and *Rip Van Winkle*. Irvington was one of the earliest planned suburbs of Indianapolis. The community was laid out with curving streets that followed the natural topography and the designed open spaces. The site of Butler University from 1875 to 1928, Irvington acquired a reputation for the arts during the early 1900s and is often referred to as the cultural gateway to Indy's east side. Artists still seek housing in this community with its bohemian charm. Irvington is also the city's newest locally protected historic area and the largest National Register Historic District in Marion County.

The area contains excellent examples of every major American architectural style from 1870 to 1950, including Italianate, French Second Empire, Victorian Gothic, Queen Anne, Colonial Revival, and Tudor Revival. Irvington is best known for its lovely collection of Arts and Crafts architecture, including the only known example of a Gustav Stickley designed house in Indiana. At the center of Irvington is a small circular park surrounded by a roundabout where streets intersect. The park features a fountain, a bust of Washington Irving, and personalized brick paths. Irvington is bordered by 10th Street, Brookville Road, and Edmondson and Kitley Avenues.

i For almost seven decades, the fine residents of Irving have been scaring the living daylights out of some folks. The Historic Irvington Halloween Festival features a street fair with food and arts and crafts vendors, plus a costume parade and live music. But it's the Haunted Irvington Tour led by paranormal specialists that can give you shivers. The walking tour highlights different Irvington homes, along with chilling accounts of reported ghost sightings and stories.

LITTLE FLOWER
www.littleflowerneighborhood.com

Developed in the 1920s, the Little Flower neighborhood on the city's east side got its name from the Little Flower Catholic Church, still an anchor in the area. One of the top private schools in the state, Father Scecina Memorial High School was added to the community in 1953. The majority of the homes are in the Arts and Crafts, California Bungalow, and Tudor Revival styles. Shady mature trees are a bonus, as are large front porches on many of the homes. Little Flower is bounded by 16th Street, 10th Street, Emerson Avenue, and Sherman Drive. Little Flower has an energetic neighborhood association.

i In the historic Irvington neighborhood, 78.1 percent of the homes were built before 1960.

LOCKERBIE SQUARE

www.lockerbiesquare.org

Indianapolis's oldest surviving neighborhood, Lockerbie Square was made famous in the late 19th and early 20th centuries as the home of Hoosier poet James Whitcomb Riley. It was the city's first historic district placed in the National Register of Historic Places. The neighborhood takes its name from George Murray Lockerbie, a man from Glasgow, Scotland. The name means "Loki's Village" in Old Norse. The completely restored neighborhood features a wealth of architectural styles.

Located less than half a mile from the very center of Indianapolis, Lockerbie Square seems a world away. Rich in history and charm, the neighborhood has tree-lined cobblestone streets, small homes, wrought iron fences, tiny flower gardens, a few mansions, and a population of about 400. Lockerbie Square is considered one of the best examples of Victorian renovation in the country. It is bounded by Michigan, New York, Davidson, and East Streets.

MERIDIAN-KESSLER

www.mkna.org

A large and diverse neighborhood, Meridian-Kessler features older Meridian Street mansions and much more modest homes owned by do-it-yourself restorers. Located about 4 miles north of downtown, Meridian-Kessler is bounded on the north by Kessler Boulevard, on the east by the Monon Trail greenway corridor, on the south by 38th Street, and the west by Meridian Street. Meridian Street forms a shared boundary with the adjacent Butler-Tarkington neighborhood.

In 1905, famed landscape architect George Kessler redesigned Maple Road into an excellent urban parkway. The neighborhood population boomed in the early 1920s and grand homes were built along Meridian Street, Pennsylvania Street, and Washington Boulevard. The Meridian-Kessler Neighborhood Association was formed in 1965 and continues to actively work to unify the community and protect the neighborhood's charming character.

NORA

Located on the north side of Indianapolis, Nora is bounded by Meridian Street on the west, Castleton on the east, Ravenswood on the south, and 96th Street on the north. Home to North Central High School, Nora got its name back in the 1870s when Swedish immigrant Peter Lawson was appointed postmaster there. Lawson named the community after his home parish in Sweden. He also opened a grocery store with the post office and that is where the young community began to grow. The residential area of Nora features ranch homes and traditional-style brick homes.

OLD NORTHSIDE

www.oldnorthside.org

Located about a mile north of downtown, Old Northside was the fashionable home of many prominent leaders in the late 1800s. Around 1914, the neighborhood had reached its peak as a leading residential area. It then began a slow decline during which a significant number of original homes were demolished. In 1978 the area was placed in the National Register of Historic Places. Since then, old structures have been renovated and appropriate fill-in housing has been built to make Old Northside a premier neighborhood once again.

Formed in 1976, the Old Northside Neighborhood Association has kept a steady focus on preserving the neighborhood. Bounded by I-65 and Pennsylvania, Bellefontaine, and 16th Streets, the area boasts a wide array of homes from Italianate and Queen Anne mansions to small Carpenter cottages.

> **i** In 2009, Indianapolis ranked first on CNN/*Money's* list of the top 10 cities for recent graduates.

RANSOM PLACE

The most intact 19th-century neighborhood associated with African Americans in Indianapolis, Ransom Place was named after Freeman Ransom (1882–1947), an attorney and general manager of Walker Manufacturing Company, a cosmetics firm founded by Madam C. J. Walker. The neighborhood is a surviving fragment of a much larger black neighborhood that surrounded Indiana Avenue, which was home to many African-American business and civic leaders.

Houses are primarily wood-frame, one-story dwellings. The Ransom Place Historic District was added to the National Register of Historic Places in 1992 for its significance in the history of the city's African-American community. The 6-block district is bounded by 10th Street on the north, Paca Street on the west, St. Clair Street on the south, and Dr. Martin Luther King Jr. Street on the east.

ST. JOSEPH
www.stjoeneighborhood.org
Located just north of downtown, St. Joseph is a historic district with homes and buildings dating back to the late 1800s. The neighborhood provides a significant example of rowhouse buildings as well as architectural styles including Queen Anne, Tudor Revival, Italianate, Carpenter-Builder, and others. The area is bounded by I-65, Fort Wayne Avenue, Central Avenue, and Pennsylvania Street.

UNIVERSITY HEIGHTS
www.uheights.us
Located around the University of Indianapolis, this neighborhood offers an affordable alternative to Indy's more expensive neighborhoods. Bungalows are similar in style but more reasonably priced than in other areas. University Heights is bounded on the north by Hanna Avenue, the south by Lawrence Avenues, east by Keystone Avenue, and west by Madison Avenue. University Heights has a neighborhood association.

WILLIAMS CREEK
With large lawns and wooded areas, Williams Creek is an affluent residential area about 8 miles north of downtown. It is part of Indianapolis but retains a functioning town government. Featuring beautiful rolling terrain combined with Victorian and Tudor architecture, Williams Creek is one of the most desirable neighborhoods. Some homes have been in the same family for generations.

i Williams Creek is the neighborhood where the parents of American writer Kurt Vonnegut lived when he wrote a letter home from Europe after surviving the bombing of Dresden as a POW in 1945. Vonnegut and other American prisoners of war were in an underground slaughterhouse meat locker used by the Germans as a war camp. The Germans called the building *Schlachthof Funf* ("Slaughterhouse Five"). Vonnegut said the aftermath of the attack was "utter destruction" and "carnage unfathomable." This experience was the inspiration for his famous novel *Slaughterhouse Five* and is a central theme in at least six of his other books.

WOODRUFF PLACE
www.woodruffplace.com
Laid out by James Woodruff in 1872, Woodruff Place was envisioned as a quiet neighborhood in a parklike setting. Wide grassy esplanades were adorned with statuary and urns throughout the neighborhood. After years of decline, Woodruff Place was named to the National Register in 1972 and the area has enjoyed restoration and preservation. Today, Woodruff Place attracts a wide variety of people seeking a lovely neighborhood just minutes from downtown. The Woodruff Place Civil League has a large membership that organizes annual fund-raising events such as a flea market, Victorian home tour, July 4th parade, children's Halloween party, and other activities.

i Woodruff Place is said to be the inspiration for the setting of Booth Tarkington's 1918 novel, *The Magnificent Ambersons,* which won the Pulitzer Prize. Tarkington once lived in Woodruff Place.

Woodruff Place boasts a variety of architectural styles, including some mansions dating from 1875 to 1917. The oldest surviving residence in Woodruff Place is the J. Francis Burt House, constructed in 1875 as an early example of Eastlake or Late Stick style. While Victorian styles predominate, there are also many spectacular examples of Queen Anne–style homes throughout the neighborhood. In 2001 Woodruff Place was awarded $500,000 from the state to help restore the East Drive esplanades and fountains. Woodruff Place is bounded by 10th, Michigan, and Tecumseh Streets and by West Drive.

DRIVER'S LICENSE

INDIANA BUREAU OF MOTOR VEHICLES
5155 S. Meridian St.
(317) 786-9342
www.in.gov/bmv
You must obtain a driver's license and have your vehicle registered and titled in Indiana within 60 days of establishing Indiana residency. To obtain a first-time Indiana license, you must successfully pass both a written and vision test, forfeit the license from the previous state where you lived, and present one primary identification document, one secondary document, one proof of Indiana residency document, and one proof of social security number; or two primary documents, one proof of residency, and one proof of social security number.

Licenses from foreign countries are not accepted as identification; only original documents or those certified by the issuing agency are accepted. Indianapolis has branches of the Indiana Bureau of Motor Vehicles throughout the city.

It is illegal to drive without liability insurance in the State of Indiana. This is a Class A infraction that subjects the violator to a 90-day license suspension on the first offense and a one-year suspension for repeat violations within a three-year period.

If your license is suspended for driving without insurance, the fines for reinstatement range from $150 to $500 and depend on the number of past offenses, if any.

The first time you are convicted of drunk driving in Indiana, you will pay court costs and fees of $300 or more. You also can be fined up to $5,000. You will also face jail time, not exceeding one year. Your driver's license will be suspended for a minimum of 30 days, followed by a probationary period in which you will be allowed to drive only to work and back. It is also possible that you will be placed on probation and ordered to enroll in a substance-abuse course at your own expense. If the court rules, you may need to install an ignition interlock on your car, attend a victim-impact panel, and submit to chemical testing for drug and alcohol abuse.

MEDICAL AND DENTAL REFERRAL SERVICES

INDIANAPOLIS DISTRICT DENTAL SOCIETY
(317) 471-8131
www.indydentalsociety.org

INDIANAPOLIS MEDICAL SOCIETY
(317) 639-3406
www.imsonline.org

INDIANA OSTEOPATHIC ASSOCIATION
(317) 926-3009
www.inosteo.org

INDIANA UNIVERSITY MEDICAL PHYSICIAN REFERRAL
(for all Clarian hospitals)
(800) 265-3220
www.medicine.iu.edu

PET LICENSES

HUMANE SOCIETY OF INDIANAPOLIS
7929 N. Michigan Rd.
(317) 872-5650
www.indyhumane.org
In Marion County, dogs and cats must be given shots on an annual basis. Marion county code requires that dogs and cats wear a permanent means of identification at all times, either a collar with owner's name, address, and phone number or an implanted microchip with a registered identification number. Both the Humane Society and Indianapolis Animal Care & Control can provide this service. Cats and dogs must be kept under control—leashed if off their property;

otherwise restrained by fence or wall. Pet owners will be fined for violations. The Mayor's Action Center handles animal control requests (317) 327-1397.

SCHOOL REGISTRATION

Indiana's compulsory school-attendance law requires all children to attend a school taught in English from the start of the school year in which a child turns seven or at the age of seven if home-schooled or attending a private or nonaccredited school. Kindergarten is not required, but a child must be 5 years old on or before Aug. 1 to enroll in a public kindergarten.

Parents must provide the child's birth certificate, immunization records, and transcripts. Check with individual schools for additional proof of residency requirements, exemptions, and intra-district transfer options. Parents interested in home schooling can obtain more information by contacting the Indiana Association for Home Educators, 320 E. Main St., Greenfield; (317) 467-6244; www.inhomeeducators.org.

UTILITIES

AT&T
(800) 742-8771
www.att.com

BRIGHT HOUSE NETWORKS
(317) 972-9700
www.mybrighthouse.com

CENTRAL INDIANA POWER
(317) 477-2200
www.cipower.com

CITIZENS GAS
(317) 924-3311
www.citizensgas.com

COMCAST
(888) 266-2278
www.comcast.com

DUKE ENERGY
(800) 521-2232
www.duke-energy.com

EMBARQ
(888) 723-8010
www.embarq.com

INDIANA-AMERICAN WATER CO.
(800) 492-8373
www.amwater.com

INDIANAPOLIS DEPARTMENT OF PUBLIC WORKS
(317) 327-4000
www.indygov.com

INDIANAPOLIS POWER & LIGHT
(317) 261-8222
www.iplpower.com

INDIANAPOLIS WATER
(317) 631-1431
www.indianapoliswater.com

LONGVIEW COMMUNICATIONS
(866) 611-6565
www.longviewcomm.com

SOUTH CENTRAL INDIANA REMC
(765) 342-3344
www.sciremc.com

SPRINT
(800) 877-4646
www.sprint.com

VECTREN ENERGY
(800) 777-2060
www.vectren.com

VERIZON WIRELESS
(800) 922-0204
www.verizon.com

VOTER REGISTRATION

To register, you must be a citizen of the United States, be 18 years old, have lived in your precinct for at least 30 days (except certain military voters), and not be currently imprisoned after being convicted of a crime. You can obtain an application online at www.in.gov/sos/elections. A list of voter registration offices is available at the Web site. You can also mail your application to the registration office at the Indiana Election Division, 302 W. Washington St., E-204. For more information call (317) 232-3939.

i Looking for a reputable real estate company and agent? Contact the Metropolitan Indianapolis Board of Realtors, 1912 N. Meridian St.; (317) 956-1912; www.mibor.com. The board was first incorporated in 1924 and has 6,500 members who work out of 1,687 offices, 27 of which are multi-office companies.

REAL ESTATE AGENCIES

Indianapolis has plenty of Realtors to bring housing seekers and sellers together. Below is a sample of some in the Indianapolis area.

ADVANCED REALTY
1188 N. Raceway Rd.
(317) 298-0961
www.advancedrealtyllc.com

CENTURY 21 SCHEETZ ON THE AVENUE
643 Massachusetts Ave.
(317) 814-5500
www.c21scheetz.com

CLASSIC REALTY
6307 S. Meridian St.
(317) 786-7861
www.classicrealtyindy.com

DALE HAMMOND CARPENTER REALTORS
790 City Center Dr., Carmel
(877) 302-2728
www.indyhouses.com

THE EVELO TEAM
Keller Williams Realty
11800 Exit 5 Parkway, Suite 102, Fishers
(317) 863-4663
www.homes4friends.com

F.C. TUCKER
342 Massachusetts Ave.
(317) 686-0612
www.talktotucker.com

FLOCK REAL ESTATE GROUP
442 Massachusetts Ave.
(888) 500-1085
www.flockrealty.com

LANDRIGAN & COMPANY
55 Monument Circle
(317) 687-8888
www.landrigan.com

RE/MAX SELECT REALTORS STEVE WADE
4455 Southport Crossings Dr.
(317) 888-9233
www.remax.com

SUMMIT REALTY GROUP
111 Monument Circle, No. 4750
(317) 713-2100
www.summitrealtygroup.com

i According to the *Wall Street Journal*, Indianapolis ranked No. 1 in the nation on the Value for Money Index in 2008.

RESOURCES

CENTRAL INDIANA BETTER BUSINESS BUREAU
22 E. Washington St., Suite 200
(317) 488-2222
www.indybbb.org

GREATER INDIANAPOLIS CHAMBER OF COMMERCE
111 Monument Circle, Suite 1950
(371) 464-2222
www.indychamber.com

HUMANE SOCIETY OF INDIANAPOLIS
7929 N. Michigan Rd.
(317) 872-5650
www.indyhumane.org

INDIANA DEMOCRATIC PARTY
One N. Capitol, Suite 200
(800) 223-3387
www.indems.org

INDIANA STATE REPUBLICAN PARTY
47 S. Meridian St.
(317) 635-7561
www.indgop.org

INDIANAPOLIS BLACK CHAMBER OF COMMERCE
3921 N. Meridian St., Suite 230
(317) 924-9840
www.indianapolisbcc.org

INDIANAPOLIS CITY COUNTY BUILDING
200 E. Washington St.
(317) 327-3601
www.indy.gov

INDIANAPOLIS CONVENTION & VISITORS ASSOCIATION
30 S. Meridian St., Suite 410
(800) 323-INDY
www.indy.org

INDIANAPOLIS DOWNTOWN, INC.
Chase Tower
111 Monument Circle, Suite 1900
(317) 237-2222
www.indydt.com

INDIANAPOLIS FIRE DEPARTMENT
555 N. New Jersey St.
Nonemergency: (317) 327-6041
Emergency: 911
The Indianapolis Fire Department is composed of seven battalions encompassing 38 stations. Each station is as individual as the neighborhood it serves.

INDIANAPOLIS-MARION COUNTY PUBLIC LIBRARY
Central Library
40 E. St. Clair St.
(317) 269-1700
www.imcpl.org
The Indianapolis–Marion County Public Library is made up of the Central Library, 22 branches, and the Library Services Center.

INDIANAPOLIS METROPOLITAN POLICE DEPARTMENT
50 N. Alabama St.
Nonemergency: (317) 327-3811
Emergency: 911
www.indy.gov

INDIANAPOLIS POST OFFICE
456 N. Meridian St.
(317) 464-6825
Numerous other locations around the city

MARION COUNTY COURTHOUSE
200 E. Washington St.
(317) 327-4740
www.indy.gov

MARION COUNTY DEMOCRATIC PARTY
603 E. Washington St., Suite 100
(317) 637-3366
www.marioncountydemocrats.org

MARION COUNTY REPUBLICAN CENTRAL COMMITTEE HEADQUARTERS
47 S. Pennsylvania Ave.
(317) 635-8881
www.indyrepublicans.com

HEALTH CARE AND WELLNESS

If you're going to get sick, Indianapolis is a good place to do it. Everyone knows that Indianapolis is the heart of motor sports, but the city is also a leading center for the health care industry. Metro Indianapolis has an abundance of quality hospitals, including teaching hospitals and those with state-of-the-art and specialized facilities. There are 404 physicians per 100,000 residents in Indianapolis, compared to the U.S. average of 170.

On the business side of the ledger, health care plays an important role in Indianapolis. Pharmaceutical giant Eli Lilly and Company has its world headquarters in Indy. The company was founded in Indianapolis in May 1876 by Colonel Eli Lilly, a 38-year-old pharmaceutical chemist and Civil War veteran. He saw firsthand the bloody casualties of war and was frustrated by the poorly prepared and often ineffective medicines of his day. His goal was to found a company that manufactured pharmaceutical products of the highest possible quality, based on the best science of the day, and to develop medicine that would be dispensed by physicians rather than by quick-talking sideshow hucksters.

Lilly's business flourished but he still wasn't satisfied with traditional methods of testing the quality of his products. Instead, Lilly hired a young chemist in 1886 and established his own basis and techniques for quality evaluation. Eventually, the company expanded to include the discovery and development of new and better pharmaceutics. Over the years, Lilly's son and his two grandsons each served as president of the company.

Today, Eli Lilly and Company is a major employer and contributor to the welfare of Indianapolis. From the original shop where Lilly, his 14-year-old son, Josiah, and another employee were the only workers, Eli Lilly and Company has grown to have almost 39,140 employees worldwide. Lilly is consistently ranked as one of the most charitable companies in the world, and the Lilly Foundation, which is made possible by donations from Eli Lilly and Company, is an important source of this charitable work. In its last annual report, the Foundation donated more than $29 million to charities.

METROPOLITAN HOSPITALS

COMMUNITY HEALTH NETWORK
1500 N. Ritter Ave.
(800) 777-7775
www.ecommunity.com

More than 50 years ago, residents on the east side of Indianapolis decided they didn't want to drive all the way downtown for health care. They wanted something closer to home. Volunteers started going door to door to raise funds for the new facility. Before long, businesses and private citizens pitched in for what was called "the swiftest, most effective fund-raising campaign of our time."

i Community Health Network was named among the 100 "most wired" hospitals in the United States for 2009 by Hospital & Health Networks. Community has been implementing cutting-edge technology to connect electronic medical records and other clinical data across network facilities

A farmer donated 28 acres on 16th Street and Ritter Avenue for the new facility, and ground was broken in 1954. Then Vice President Richard Nixon was on hand for the kickoff ceremony. When it opened, the new $5 million, 300-bed hospital featured the novelty of air-conditioning and piped-in oxygen. Residents could proudly say it was their hospital. They helped build it. The name "Community Hospital" was chosen to reflect the massive involvement of the eastside community to help secure a hospital.

Over the years, Community has grown into an integrated health network known as Community Health Network. Community now has five hospitals and more than 70 sites to serve people of central Indiana. The four local hospitals—a fifth is in nearby Anderson—and their services are:

COMMUNITY HOSPITAL EAST
1500 N. Ritter Ave.
(317) 355-1411
www.ecommunity.com
Community Hospital East began in 1956 to answer a need for accessible, high-quality health care. The hospital started with 300 beds and 111 employees. Ten years later, the psychiatric inpatient units and the coronary care unit opened at Community Hospital East. A cardiac catheterization lab, ambulatory care, and the Family Practice Residency Program soon joined those services. Also added were 250 new beds, Hook Rehabilitation Center, Gallahue Mental Health Center, the Pain Center, and Community Regional Cancer Care.

In 1988 the Same-Day Surgery Center opened at Community Hospital East, followed by a new main lobby, entrance, and professional building three years later. Indiana Surgery Center East was opened in 1999, the Center for Interventional Radiology in 2004, and the $7 million Radiation Oncology Treatment Center in 2007. The facility contains a 24-hour emergency room with state-of-the art equipment.

COMMUNITY HOSPITAL NORTH
7150 Clearvista Dr.
(317) 621-6262
www.ecommunity.com
Opened in 1985, Community Hospital North started with a 100-bed, acute-care inpatient capacity, emergency department, inpatient and outpatient surgery, and support services.

Since then, the hospital has more than doubled in size, with 282 private patient guest suites, the largest collection of private labor and delivery suites (60 beds) in the country, a neonatal intensive care unit with private rooms, and 48 private inpatient surgical-care suites on the second floor. A new five-story professional office building is connected to the hospital and a new six-story parking tower.

i In 1964, Community Hospital of Indianapolis needed more space and opened "The Towers." The building's radical design—with two circular towers allowing central stations to observe patients at all times—was dubbed the "Hospital of the Space Age" and was one of the first of its kind in the nation.

COMMUNITY HOSPITAL SOUTH
1402 E. County Line Rd.
(317) 887-7000
www.ecommunity.com
An acute-care hospital, Community Hospital South offers a vast array of surgical capabilities, maternity care, emergency room services, and cardiovascular care. A $130 million expansion currently underway is scheduled to be completed in June 2010.

The expansion includes six state-of-the-art operating suites to accommodate all types of surgery and the latest technologies. The project will add 194,000 square feet to the existing structure and will feature a five-story patient tower with all-private patient rooms, creating a healing environment focused on patient safety and quality interactions between caregivers, patients, and families. Existing units are being renovated to complement the new structure, increasing inpatient capacity from 100 private and semiprivate beds to 150 all-private rooms.

INDIANA HEART HOSPITAL
8075 Shadeland Ave.
(317) 621-8000
www.hearthospital.com
Opened in February 2003, Indiana Heart Hospital concentrates on heart care. Designed by cardiac

doctors and nurses, the facility offers innovative services such as the only 24-hour emergency room for heart care in Indiana, a cardiologist always on-site for emergencies, and advanced digital technology to ensure faster and more effective care.

The hospital offers complete integrated cardiovascular care, including heart surgery, bypass surgery, angioplasty, outpatient cardiac rehabilitation, and more. Heart physicians and specialists include cardiologists, vascular surgeons, cardiothoracic surgeons, and nurses. In addition to being a fully accredited chest-pain center, The Indiana Heart Hospital carries accreditations in cardiovascular diagnostic testing, such as nuclear cardiology, positron emission tomography (PET), and echocardiography, and is the recipient of numerous awards for clinical excellence in heart attack and congestive heart failure care.

INDIANA ORTHOPAEDIC HOSPITAL
8450 Northwest Blvd.
(800) 223-3381
www.orthindy.com
In 1962, Dr. Donald Blackwell and Dr. F. Robert Brueckmann founded a partnership that became the foundation for what is known today as OrthoIndy. Ranking among the largest private full-service orthopedic groups, OrthoIndy is the largest orthopedic group in Indiana and the Midwest. Currently, the group consists of more than 60 physicians who specialize in primary care, physical medicine, and rehabilitation, in addition to anesthesiology. Serving patients from 11 convenient locations, OrthoIndy's specialties include bone-tumor and soft-tissue oncology, cartilage restoration, the foot and ankle, general orthopedics, the hand and upper extremity, the hip, the knee, nonoperative spinal care, pediatric orthopedics, physiatry and pain management, the shoulder, sports medicine, total joint replacement, and trauma.

INDIANA UNIVERSITY HOSPITAL
550 N. University Blvd.
(317) 274-5000
www.clarian.org

What is today known as Indiana University Hospital, a Clarian Health Partner, began over a century ago as Long Hospital. Considered very modern for the time, Long Hospital featured 106 beds, 18 private rooms, two operating rooms, and X-ray equipment. In 1963 plans for a successor to Long Hospital were announced, and in 1970 Indiana University Hospital opened.

Today, Indiana University Hospital has hundreds of beds, treats more than 50,000 patients each year and features the most modern technology. Working side by side with the Indiana University School of Medicine—the state's only medical school—the hospital provides an environment for advanced medical care. As a major teaching hospital and a recognized leader in technology, Indiana University Hospital offers patients access to treatment, therapies, and procedures found only in the most advanced academic medical centers.

i Possibly the most widely known success story at Indiana University Hospital involves seven-time Tour de France champion Lance Armstrong. When diagnosed with testicular cancer, Armstrong selected the team at the IU Simon Cancer Center for his care. (IU Simon Cancer Center is a partnership between Clarian Health and Indiana University School of Medicine.) Armstrong's recovery from cancer and domination of the Tour de France have served as an inspiration to thousands of people facing cancer in their own lives.

METHODIST HOSPITAL OF INDIANA
I-65 at 21st St.
(317) 962-2000
www.clarian.org
Dedicated in 1908, Methodist Hospital was recognized in 2007 as the top-ranked hospital in the country for quality and safety by University Health Consortium. Methodist is nationally ranked for transplant care, orthopedic services, and urology care and has an award-winning cardiac critical-care unit. Methodist is well known for its excellent Level One Trauma Center, one of only two in the

state. In addition, Methodist is a nationally ranked organ transplant center based on total transplant volume (bone marrow, heart, intestine, kidney, liver, lung, and pancreas)—one of only a few centers nationally to have each of these programs certified by Medicare.

Methodist has the largest neuroscience critical-care unit in the country and one of the largest critical-care departments in the country. The hospital has specialists on-site 24 hours a day. Methodist offers a nationally ranked urology program and is home to the International Kidney Stone Institute.

i In 1982, Methodist Hospital of Indiana performed the world's first successful heart transplant at a private hospital. In 2006, it was the first in the nation to perform a simultaneous lung and pancreas transplant.

PEYTON MANNING CHILDREN'S HOSPITAL AT ST. VINCENT
2001 W. 86th St.
(317) 338-2345
www.stvincent.org
Opened in 2003, Peyton Manning's Children's Hospital at St. Vincent offers a full range of pediatric services and state-of-the-art facilities to patients from newborns to teens. The facility was thoughtfully designed for children in a whimsical space that is kid-size and child-friendly. The hospital has grown to 46 private inpatient beds, 15 beds in the Pediatric Intensive Care unit, 85 beds in the Newborn Intensive Care unit, and 18 beds in the Hilbert Pediatric Emergency Department, the first pediatric emergency room in the state. The hospital also offers 24-hour physician coverage by pediatric intensivists, neonatologists, emergency doctors, and nursing staff.

Named for the Colt's Super Bowl winning quarterback and his generous support, Peyton Manning Children's Hospital specializes in treating children with complex, chronic, or congenital conditions.

RICHARD L. ROUDEBUSH VA MEDICAL CENTER
1481 W. 10th St.
(317) 554-0181
www2.va.gov
Named for former Indiana congressman and Veterans Administration director Richard L. Roudebush, the VA Medical Center is located two miles northwest of downtown Indy. Since 1932, the center has been serving Indiana veterans with acute inpatient medical, surgical, psychiatric, neurological, and rehabilitation care, as well as both primary and specialized outpatient services. Specialized services include comprehensive cardiac care, radiation oncology treatment, and community-based extended care. Indianapolis VA Medical Center is aggressively utilizing emerging technology in the tele–home-care and tele–disease-management arenas. The medical center was selected as the site for the Veterans in Partnership VISN 11 Polytrauma Network Site and is currently planning the opening of that center to provide ongoing support to veterans from Operation Enduring Freedom/Operation Iraqi Freedom (OEF/OIF).

The more than 47,000 patients treated by the Indianapolis VA Medical Center require almost 410,000 outpatient visits and over 7,100 inpatient episodes of care yearly. The medical center conducts extensive research and training programs. With annual research support exceeding $11.8 million, staff members are conducting studies in such areas as diabetes, alcoholism, AIDS, Alzheimer's disease, pulmonary diseases, cancer, and other areas related to veterans' health. The medical center has nine sharing agreements with the Department of Defense and plays a key role in disaster preparedness as a federally designated coordinating center for National Disaster Medical System. An active TRICARE/CHAMPUS Clinic Program is also available to provide care for active-duty military service members, retirees, and their dependents.

RILEY HOSPITAL FOR CHILDREN
702 Barnhill Dr.
(317) 274-4060
www.rileychildrenshospital.com

A Clarian Health Partner and strong affiliate with the Indiana University School of Medicine, Riley Hospital for Children was named in honor of Hoosier poet James Whitcomb Riley. Caring for children and their families since 1924, Riley offers 447 beds. As Indiana's first and only comprehensive pediatric hospital, Riley Hospital has more than 245,000 inpatient and outpatient pediatric visits annually from across the state, nation, and the world. Riley Hospital's relationship with Clarian Health and its strong affiliation with the Indiana University School of Medicine—an institution that continues to advance its reputation by engaging in cutting-edge research and developing new therapies—makes it the only comprehensive pediatric clinical resource for Indiana's children and a premier source for health-related information for their parents. From simple acute routine care to the most critically ill and medically complex cases, Riley Hospital offers pediatric specialists in every field of medicine and surgery in a family-centered environment.

i *U.S.News & World Report*'s 2008 edition of "America's Best Children's Hospitals" ranked five specialty programs at Riley among the top 30 children's hospitals in the nation.

Riley Hospital is also one of the nation's largest and most comprehensive outpatient facilities for children and offers the world's largest pediatric sleep-disorders center, along with one of the nation's three largest autism-treatment centers. A national leader in providing clinical care and conducting research for children with cancer, the Riley Children's Cancer Center is the only comprehensive pediatric cancer center in Indiana. It is also Indiana's only pediatric burn center and has the state's largest and most comprehensive pediatric intensive-care unit.

ST. FRANCIS HOSPITAL–BEECH GROVE
1600 Albany St., Beech Grove
(317) 787-3311
www.stfrancishospitals.org
Founded in 1914 in Beech Grove by the Order of

the Sisters of St. Francis of Perpetual Adoration, St. Francis Hospital started with just 75 patient beds. The hospital was founded on the belief that human needs should be met in a holistic manner. As one of the largest health care systems in Indiana, St. Francis operates three main facilities in Beech Grove, Indianapolis, and Mooresville. Additional outpatient facilities are located in the Indianapolis metropolitan area.

Services at St. Francis Beech Grove include bariatric surgery, a cancer center, emergency services, an HLA-vascular biology lab, neurology, neurosurgery, occupational therapy, orthopedic surgery, an outpatient lab, physical therapy, radiology, rheumatology, speech and hearing services, stroke care, and a wound-care institute.

ST. FRANCIS HOSPITAL—INDIANAPOLIS
811 S. Emerson Ave.
(317) 865-5000
www.stfrancishospitals.org
St. Francis Hospital–Indianapolis is the newest general hospital built in the city of Indy. Opened in 1995, the hospital features state-of-the-art technology. Services include cancer care, Center of Hope for sexual-assault victims, emergency/PromptCare, a heart center, imaging, a neonatal intensive-care unit, massage therapy, neurology, neurosurgery, occupational therapy, orthopedic surgery, an outpatient lab, a pain-management clinic, pediatric specialty clinics, physical therapy, radiology, rheumatology, sleep medicine, speech and hearing care, sports medicine, vascular surgery, and women and children's services.

i In the 1980s Eli Lilly and Company of Indianapolis introduced Prozac®, the first major introduction in a new class of drugs for treatment of clinical depression.

ST. VINCENT HEART CENTER OF INDIANA
10580 N. Meridian St.
(317) 583-5000
www.theheartcenter.com
Opened in Dec 2002 as the Heart Center of Indiana, the facility was one of the nation's first freestanding heart-specialty hospitals and the first in

the Indianapolis area. Founded by some of the nation's leading cardiologists and cardiovascular surgeons from the Care Group and CorVasc, the Heart Center became part of St. Vincent Health in 2006. The mission at St. Vincent Heart Center is to provide advanced specialized cardiovascular care.

ST. VINCENT HOSPITAL & HEALTH SERVICES
2001 W. 86th St.
(317) 338-7000
www.stvincent.org
In 1878, Bishop Francis Silas Chatard—a physician before he was ordained—sought to establish a Catholic hospital in Indiana to be operated by the Daughters of Charity. Located in an unused seminary building next to St. Joseph's Church on East Vermont Street in Indianapolis, the facility was ready for the first four Daughters of Charity who arrived on April 26, 1881. They had only $34.77 among them. The bishop gave them $50 more to begin their mission of converting the abandoned mission into a hospital. Just eight years after their arrival, the sisters moved to a second home, where the mission remained for two decades. With its legal name of St. Vincent Hospital, the facility moved again to a new 250-bed hospital in 1913. Another move and expansion came in 1974 through a massive community effort.

ST. VINCENT SETON HOSPITAL
8050 Township Line Rd.
(317) 415-8500
www.seaton.stvincent.org
A long-term acute-care facility, St. Vincent Seton Hospital opened in 1996 as a healing gateway between the intensive-care unit and rehabilitation. Patients come to the hospital with multiple complications requiring an extended hospital stay of 25 days or more. Services include ventilator and individualized weaning programs, complex infusion therapy, long-term wound care, chemotherapy, respiratory therapy, telemetry, physical therapy, occupational therapy, speech therapy, and hemodynamic monitoring.

ST. VINCENT WOMEN'S HOSPITAL
8111 Township Line Rd.
(317) 415-8111
www.stvincent.org
Dealing with all aspects of women's health, St. Vincent Women's Hospital offers the state's largest newborn intensive care unit. The 75-bed unit features 14 separate suites for multiple births. Among the maternity services offered is the Maternal Fetal Medicine and Genetics Center with prenatal diagnostic testing, genetic counseling, and high-risk pregnancy management. The High Risk unit offers 26 private rooms in a homelike environment for patients needing an extended hospital stay. The Family Care Unit offers 48 private patient rooms, a nursery, lactation consultants, and a newborn portrait studio.

At the Center for Women's Health, women can receive a health-risk assessment that covers 11 key areas, including breast health, menopause, osteoporosis, cardiovascular health, sleep disorders, incontinence, gastroesophageal reflux disease, irritable bowel syndrome, depression, gynecologic health, and colorectal health. The St. Vincent Women's Health Boutique has professional certified fitters in mastectomy bras and prostheses, compression garments, and wigs. The boutique also offers maternity support products, breastfeeding accessories, personalized bra fitting, wigs, hats, scarves, and incontinence products.

WISHARD MEMORIAL HOSPITAL
1001 W. 10th St.
(317) 639-6671
www.wishard.edu
The history of Wishard Health Service can be traced back to 1855 when a smallpox epidemic prompted Indianapolis to begin building a hospital. Since that era, the institution has evolved and grown into a diverse health care system with 353 beds. Wishard provides a full range of care. Services include a Level I Trauma Center, Richard M. Fairbanks Burn Center at Wishard, outpatient surgery services, a full range of women's services, and much more. Wishard offers eight community health centers and 21 midtown community health sites and residential facilities.

In 2007 Wishard Health Services became one of the first hospitals in the country to utilize new electronic medical technology that gives primary care physicians the ability to check whether patients with certain conditions are receiving the recommended follow-up tests or treatments. The new system, created by the Indiana Health Information Exchange, provides valuable information electronically for doctors to look at their patients' medical history.

i Wishard Hospital is home to the first museum in Indiana focusing on the development of the nursing profession from 1883 to the present. The Wishard Nursing Museum is located on the second floor of the Bryce Building of Wishard Memorial Hospital and is housed in the parlor of the old Nurses' Residence. In addition to being the oldest hospital in Indiana, Wishard Hospital had the first School of Nursing in Indiana and the second school west of the Alleghenies.

SPECIAL NEEDS AND SERVICES

DAMIEN CENTER
26 N. Arsenal Ave.
(317) 632-0123
www.damien.org
Alarmed at the growing AIDS crisis, an Indianapolis Episcopalian minister, Earl Conner, established a facility to coordinate community response in 1987. Since then, the Center has provided care to thousands of people infected by HIV, as well as their friends and families. The center is named after Father Damien, a Belgian Catholic priest known for his compassionate work with lepers. The Damien Center is a nonsectarian, not-for-profit facility.

FAIRBANKS HOSPITAL INC.
8102 Clearvista Parkway
(317) 849-8222
www.fairbankscd.org
Founded in 1945 as the "Indiana Home," a 12-bed facility for alcoholic men, Fairbanks is the oldest

nonprofit addiction treatment program in Indiana. In the mid-1960s, a grant from the Cornelia Cole Fairbanks Trust Fund, as well as several community donations, made possible a new, 60-bed facility for men and women that was located on West 16th Street. This new facility helped meet the increasing demand for services. In 1980 Fairbanks expanded its care to include treatment of adolescents and added a training component and an employee-assistance program. At that time, a new facility was built at its current location on the northeast side of Indianapolis. Today, Fairbanks offers a range of care including inpatient treatment, day and evening outpatient programs, aftercare services, and residential living programs.

KINDRED HOSPITAL—INDIANAPOLIS
1700 W. 10th St.
(317) 636-4400
www.kindredhospitalindy.com
A long-term acute-care facility, Kindred Hospital is a 59-bed facility located in the heart of the Indianapolis medical community. Close to Indiana University Hospital and Methodist Hospital, Kindred is a full-service hospital with a six-bed intensive-care unit, telemetry capability in medical/surgical units, special negative-airflow isolation rooms, and dialysis service in patient rooms.

Types of patients appropriate for services at Kindred Hospital include pulmonary and cardiac disease, severe wounds, neuromuscular diseases, gastrointestinal diseases, multisystem failure, post-op complications, renal disease, and rehabilitation.

LARUE D. CARTER MEMORIAL HOSPITAL
2601 Cold Spring Rd.
(317) 941-4000
www.in.gov
A state-operated facility, LaRue D. Carter Memorial Hospital is a 159-bed psychiatric hospital. Founded in 1948, the hospital provides inpatient treatment by referral from community mental-health centers for children, adolescents, and adults or by private physician. The hospital charges on a sliding scale.

NEW HOPE
8450 N. Payne Rd., Stateroom 300
(317) 388-9600
www.stvincent.org
A not-for-profit, faith-based organization, New Hope provides support services to individuals with developmental disabilities. Founded in 1978, New Hope is a member of St. Vincent Health, the state's largest health care employer with 17 health ministries serving 45 counties in central Indiana. The ageless mission of St. Vincent de Paul remains the same—to minister to the minds, bodies, and spirits of those in need, regardless of religion. While New Hope has historically provided residential services, the need for other options has been added, such as community-based services in schools.

St. Vincent Health is dedicated to spiritually centered holistic care.

PLANNED PARENTHOOD OF CENTRAL INDIANA
200 S. Meridian St.
(317) 637-4343
www.ppin.org
Since 1932, Planned Parenthood of Central Indiana has been providing family planning and reproductive-health services to Indianapolis area residents. The organization operates clinics around the city.

REHABILITATION HOSPITAL OF INDIANA
4141 Shore Dr.
(317) 329-2000
www.rhin.com
Since opening its doors in January 1992, Rehabilitation Hospital of Indiana has become one of the largest freestanding rehabilitation hospitals in the Midwest. The hospital provides inpatient acute services, as well as outpatient and vocational-rehabilitation services for adults with spinal-cord and brain injuries, strokes, amputations, orthopedic conditions, neuromuscular diseases, burns, and related disabilities.

Rehabilitation Hospital of Indiana is a community collaboration between Clarian Health and St. Vincent Health. Built for rehabilitation, the scenic campus offers a 12,000-square-foot gymnasium with state-of-the-art equipment. The hospital also has two whirlpools and a swimming pool for rehabilitation and large rooms that don't restrict wheelchair mobility. Large bathrooms with customized showers and sinks were built especially for rehabilitation patients. Hallways and doors are wide, and nursing stations are built at wheelchair height. The hospital also offers two transitional living units—apartment-style living areas that let patients practice being at home while professional help is still readily available. Patients can test their skills and build confidence in their abilities while discovering areas where they still need improvements.

WESTVIEW HOSPITAL
3630 Guion Rd.
(317) 920-8439
www.westviewhospital.org
Located on the city's west side, Westview Hospital is the state's only osteopathic hospital. The practice of osteopathic medicine recognizes that the body is inherently capable of healing itself, and doctors of osteopathic medicine encourage and facilitate this process. Westivew has a strong focus on preventive care, as evidenced by its premier sports and fitness center.

With 116 licensed beds, Westivew is nestled on a quiet wooded campus surrounded by landscaped flower gardens. All inpatient and specialty outpatient rooms are private and have been recently renovated with flat-screen televisions. Westview Hospital offers a wide array of services, including a 24-hour emergency room, intensive acute-care nursing units, surgical services, imaging services, lab services, cancer care, cardiopulmonary rehabilitation, sleep lag, renal/dialysis services, inpatient and outpatient rehabilitation services, and geriatric psychiatric care.

i In the 1940s the Indy-based Eli Lilly and Company was among the first companies to develop a method to mass-produce penicillin, the world's first antibiotic, marking the beginning of a sustained effort to fight infectious diseases.

Immediate Care Facilities

Immediate care facilities are convenient and less costly alternatives for treatment of minor injuries or illnesses. Area immediate care facilities include the following.

IMMEDIATE CARE CENTER

In 1981, United Physician Group recognized the need for accessible, economical medical care, particularly for patients with minor accidents and illnesses not necessarily requiring the extensive services of a hospital's emergency room. The Greenwood Immediate Care Center opened in July of 1981 and was an immediate success.

Since then, additional centers have opened, serving almost 150,000 patients a year. The centers are always staffed by physicians and are open 365 days a year. No appointment is needed.

URGENT CARE
1001 N. Madison Ave., Greenwood
(317) 888-3508

URGENT CARE
650 N. Girls School Rd.
(317) 271-5080

URGENT CARE
860 E. 86th St.
(317) 580-3200

URGENT CARE
992 N. Mitthoeffer Rd.
(317) 899-5546

URGENT CARE
6620 Binford Medical Dr.
(317) 598-9918

INDY URGENT CARE
3479 W. 86th St.
(317) 471-0001

MEDCHECK
Established in 1956, Community Health Network offers several MedCheck walk-in centers for medical treatment.

MEDCHECK CARMEL
11911 N. Meridian St.
(317) 621-6700

MEDCHECK CASTLETON
8177 Clearvista Parkway
(317) 621-7800

MEDCHECK EAST
1703 N. Post Rd.
(317) 355-3200

MEDCHECK GREENWOOD
1664 W. Smith Valley Rd., Suite B, Greenwood
(317) 887-7640

EDUCATION

One of Indy's favorite sons paid his hometown a huge compliment: "That city gave me a free primary and secondary education richer and more humane than anything I would get from any of the five universities I attended," Kurt Vonnegut said. As a foreshadowing of his career to come, Vonnegut was a sometime editor of *The Daily Echo* at Shortridge High School, the nation's first and longest-running high school daily, in print from 1898 to 1981. Of course, the Indianapolis-born Vonnegut (1922–2007) went on to become the acclaimed author of award-winning novels such as *Slaughterhouse-Five* and *Cat's Cradle*.

Education has long been an important cornerstone of Indianapolis. Indiana's state constitution of 1816 was the first in the United States to provide for a system of free public schools from the elementary to the university level. However, such a plan proved far too grandiose for a pioneer society. No funding was available for such a system. Most of the voters of that era didn't favor taxation for education. Then along came a man named Caleb Mills. "A disciplined mind and cultivated heart are elements of power," Mills said. A prominent educator, Mills was determined to see free public education offered to all. He finally prevailed. In 1847 the people of Indiana voted in favor of public schools. A tax levy of 12.5 cents per $100 assessed valuation of property tax was established. In 1854 Indianapolis incorporated its school system.

Vonnegut's alma mater was the first free high school in the state. Opened in 1862, it was called Indianapolis High School and the first superintendent was Abram C. Shortridge, who made it possible for African Americans to attend public school. The school was renamed in his honor—Shortridge High School—in 1897. Shortridge eventually outgrew its downtown location on the Circle and moved to new facilities at 34th and Meridian Streets in 1927. Despite the Great Depression and other problems, Shortridge continued to maintain high standards and to offer excellent extracurricular programs. The school had a radio station, orchestra, championship sports teams, and English Department reading list that featured such classics as Ibsen, Chekhov, Poe, and Woolf. Shortridge was honored as one of the nation's top high schools in both *Time* and *Newsweek* in 1957. Racked by racial strife in the 1960s, Shortridge struggled to stay open but closed its doors in 1981. Reopened as a middle school in 1987, Shortridge was tapped in 2009 to serve as a magnet school for grades 6 through 12, with a special concentration in the study of law and government.

In 1895 the city's second high school opened as Manual Training School during a time when manual training was an innovation. The school was among the first institutions in the United States to accommodate vocational as well as academic instruction. Charles Emmerich was the school's first principal and is credited with introducing the manual arts in the fashion of German schools. In 1960 the school was renamed Emmerich Manual High School in his honor. The school relocated to its present location at 2405 Madison Ave. in 1953.

Improving the schools of Indianapolis has been an ongoing priority and a struggle, particularly in today's dire economy. Indianapolis is now home to the state's largest school district—Indianapolis Public Schools—along with an excellent system of religious and private schools and an impressive roster of colleges and universities. Some of those are spotlighted in this chapter. Like Vonnegut,

Hoosiers remain loyal to their beloved alma maters and many make it a tradition to follow their high school teams and other school activities long after their school days are past.

PUBLIC SCHOOLS

INDIANAPOLIS PUBLIC SCHOOLS (IPS)
120 E. Walnut St.
(317) 226-4400
www.ips.k12.in.us

Indianapolis Public Schools serve about 34,000 students in 49 elementary schools, 9 middle schools, 5 high schools, 3 alternative learning schools, and 1 vocational school. As in most sectors of the nation, IPS is battling serious economic concerns. In 2008 the district closed four elementary schools and four middle schools, and in 2009 it closed six elementary schools.

But all is not doom and gloom. In fact, the 2009–2010 school year started off with a nice surprise. In each of the past five years, enrollment had dropped by more than 1,000 students. Projections for the 2009–2010 year were even worse. Officials expected IPS enrollment to drop by almost 1,900 students. That didn't happen. Instead, on the first official count day in 2009, IPS tallied 33,521 students compared to 33,824 on the same day the previous year. That is a drop of 303 students, far less than expected.

With less of a decline than expected, IPS can avoid millions of dollars in cuts, along with school closings and layoffs that had already been planned for 2010. In the 2009–2010 school year, the superintendent announced plans to reduce the teaching faculty by 400 teachers and the administrative staff by 17 employees, and to eliminate 95 percent of academic coaches paid out of the general fund. The school system has started spending cash reserves to fund the budget. Although the budget is funded, it is not a balanced budget. Revenues do not equal expenses. Officials estimated that the school system would be in deficit spending for 2009–2010 and the following year. In order to correct the deficit, the system planned to reduce its general fund budget by $25 million over the last half of 2009 and the first half of 2010.

State funding is based on how many students attend a district, so the huge declines in enrollment were a real problem for IPS. Getting an attendance boost was just what IPS needed. The causes for an increase in students are not clear but may be part of a change in state law that took effect, making it easier for students to attend schools in districts where they don't live. That added at least 120 students from other districts, with many opting to attend IPS magnet schools. Two new magnet high schools—Shortridge High School with its law and public-policy program and Broad Ripple with its arts and humanities program—have proven popular with hundreds of students who might have left the district. Also about 300 more kindergarten students than usual entered IPS this year.

Indianapolis Public Schools offer numerous programs to help students succeed and a variety of tools to enhance education. Using cutting-edge technology, each IPS classroom is wired for Internet access. Parents can track a student's attendance and grades at IPS Online, a Web portal that also helps parents stay connected with teachers via e-mail. Full-day kindergarten classes are aimed at better preparing students for the rigors of academics at subsequent grade levels. All IPS elementary schools offer full-day kindergarten classes.

IPS offers more magnet programs than any other school district in Indiana. Magnet schools are just like other IPS schools—with one big difference. Magnet schools emphasize a particular area of study, giving students new insight and more opportunities to explore what interests them most. "Magnet" refers to how the schools draw students from across the normal boundaries of the school zones. Some of the studies emphasized by IPS magnet schools are business and finance; environmental studies; foreign languages; health and medical professions; humanities; math, science, and technology; performing

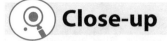

Close-up

The Man in Charge

The man in charge of Indianapolis Public Schools knows the value of education. That's obvious in his own personal life. Named superintendent of the state's largest school district, Dr. Eugene G. White was the first person in his family's history to graduate from high school. Born December 1947 in Alabama to a single 17-year-old mother, White grew up in a time of segregation and Jim Crow practices. Strong influences on the young man's life were his mother, grandmother, and athletic coaches. White excelled in high school sports—football, basketball, and baseball. A starting member of the 1966 Alabama State Championship Basketball team, White was awarded a basketball scholarship to Alabama A&M University. He graduated with academic honors and set career scoring marks at the university.

White later attended the University of Tennessee and Ball State University in Muncie, Indiana. White started his Indiana educational career in the Fort Wayne Community Schools, where he was a teacher, coach, and school administrator for 19 years, becoming the first African-American high school principal in the district. In 1990 White became the first African-American high school principal at North Central High School in Indianapolis. He served in that office until 1992, when he was appointed deputy superintendent of Indianapolis Public Schools, and he moved over to the top job in 1995. Among his many honors, White was selected as the 2009 Indiana Superintendent of the Year and was one of four finalists for the AASA National Superintendent of the Year.

and visual arts; teaching; and the science and technology of agriculture.

In addition to the neighborhood schools, IPS offers three elementary magnet choices. STRETCH is the district's program for academically talented elementary and middle school students. Forest Glen International Studies School offers programs in global studies and Spanish immersion. Indian Creek DISCOVERY Science and Technology Magnet School promotes science education.

IPS also features vocational education training that offers hands-on experiences leading to post–high school careers. The IPS alternative school programs offers more than 60 alternative programs in all middle and high schools. These programs are for students who do not thrive or succeed in traditional school settings. The first school sponsored by an NBA franchise, Pacers Academy is a secondary alternative school serving at-risk students in grades 6 through 12. Horizons is an alternative middle school program for students who are not succeeding in the traditional school setting. The KIND school also

offers alternative programs, with smaller classes and more individualized instruction for middle and high school students who have not been successful in traditional school programs. Other alternatives are offered throughout the city.

In 2007 IPS adopted strict dress codes for students district-wide that require solid-colored slacks, collared solid-color shirts, belts, and closed-toe shoes. A specific uniform is not necessary but students must adhere to the dress code, which bans T-shirts, jeans, jean skirts, jean jackets, hoodies, oversized pants or shirts, pants worn below the waist, sweatpants, jogging suits, tight dresses or tops, ruffled shirts, sunglasses, pajama tops or bottoms, heelies or wheelies (athletic shoes with skates), head rags, bandanas, sweatbands, visible underpants, "grills" or detachable gold teeth, baggy and sagging clothes, untucked shirts or blouses, flip-flops, leggings, and hats. The dress code, which is enforced by superintendent Dr. Eugene G. White, covers other bases with the sentence, "Anything else the principal or designee deems inapposite or disruptive to the educational environment will be prohibited."

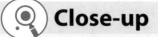

Close-up

City's First Black High School

In the 1920s a move was afoot in Indianapolis to create an all-black high school because many blacks felt out of place attending predominantly white schools. Although almost 800 black students were enrolled in Indy high schools, many athletics and other extracurricular activities were largely segregated. Some classrooms even had segregated seating.

The city already had some all-black elementary schools. In 1922 the move was made. The school board voted unanimously to create an all-black high school. Located at 1140 N. West St., the facility was to be called Thomas Jefferson High School. But that name was dropped when a petition drive requested that the school be named for Crispus Attucks, a black man who was the first American to die in the Revolutionary War.

Although controversy had swirled about the creation of the school, excitement and pride were the tone when Crispus Attucks High School opened in 1927. Black teachers and a black principal, Matthias Nolcov, were on hand when more than 1,300 students filed in that first day. Attucks was built to hold 1,000 students.

Not all black students wanted to attend the new school, however. About 18 black students returned to their regular high schools, wanting to continue to study subjects that weren't offered at Attucks, such as trigonometry and Spanish. The students were barred from their former high schools and forced to attend Attucks.

As was apparent from the first day, overcrowding quickly became a problem at Crispus Attucks High School. Enrolled climbed to nearly 3,000 in the 1940s and an adjacent school became part of the all-black facility. During the years, Attucks also became an important community center for black residents, its powerhouse sporting teams usually playing to standing-room-only crowds. On March 19, 1955, Crispus Attucks made history by becoming the nation's first all-black high school basketball team to win the coveted state championship. Led by Oscar "The Big O" Robinson, the Attucks Tigers also became the first Indianapolis team to win that title. The Tigers went on to win another state crown in 1956 and again in 1959.

Despite national recognition for educational excellence and many community supporters, Crispus Attucks was closed in 1986 in a cost-cutting measure. The school was converted to a middle school in 1986 and a magnet high school in 2009.

The Crispus Attucks Museum, located on the school campus, was given a ribbon-cutting ceremony for the opening of its renovated exhibition space in September 2009. One of the only museums of its kind in the county, Crispus Attacks Museum is devoted to the story of the school and the African-American experience. The museum has four galleries and more than 70 exhibits ranging from school history and student achievement to local, national, and international history. There are also sports trophies, banners, uniforms, photographs , memorabilia, and yearbooks from the years 1928 to 1986. For more information, call the Crispus Attucks Museum at (317) 226-2432.

Although the dress code seems to be working, several dozen students are sent home each school year and suspended for several days for violating the code.

Among its most recent successes, in 2009 IPS opened its first student-run credit union branch at Arsenal Technical High School, in partnership with Finance Center Federal Credit Union. Students work as tellers, giving them real-life work experience. Students and teachers bank at the credit union during school hours. Students are able to open checking and saving accounts and have access to the branch's ATM (with parental permission).

In 2009 students at the Center for Inquiry began studying Mandarin Chinese, joining their older peers learning the language in the International Magnet at Arsenal Technical High School.

In 2009 the IPS Science Bound Program had 57 students enrolled in Purdue University. Science Bound is a partnership with Purdue University that provides IPS students with advanced science experiences and mentorship from middle school through high school. IPS students who successfully complete the program can attend Purdue University free of charge. Thirty-two of the 2008 students in the program entered Purdue.

Through the work of the College Summit Program, Emmerich Manual High School sent nearly 50 percent more graduates to college from the Class of 2008 than the Class of 2005. Currently over 65 percent of the Class of 2009 has applied for college admission.

i In October 1843, William Willard opened a school for the deaf on the north side of Washington Street in Indianapolis. Deaf and mute himself, Willard was formerly a teacher at the Ohio School for the Deaf. The Willard School opened with 12 scholars who paid for board but got their instruction free.

PRIVATE AND PAROCHIAL SCHOOLS

ARCHDIOCESE OF INDIANAPOLIS
1400 N. Meridian St.
(800) 382-9836, ext. 1430
www.archindy.org/oce
The Archdiocese of Indianapolis has more than 15,000 students in 32 elementary schools and 7 high schools (including 3 private high schools) in the Indianapolis metropolitan area. Catholic schools in the Archdiocese of Indianapolis are all state accredited and staffed with licensed educators, and most are also accredited by the North Central Association of Colleges and Schools. Tuition is set at the parish level and varies greatly, but the average elementary school tuition is

about $3,315 and the average high school tuition is about $6,355.

BISHOP CHATARD HIGH SCHOOL
5885 Crittenden Ave.
(317) 251-1451
www.bishopchatard.org
Opened in 1961, Bishop Chatard High School is located in the Broad Ripple area and has a student body of about 670 students in grades 9 through 12. Students in the Class of 2009 scored in the top 95th percentile of Indiana students taking the ISTEP math and English exams. The average graduate rate of seniors is 99 percent. In 2008, 98 percent of seniors continued their education in college. The Class of 2008 received over $7.2 million in college scholarships and awards.

In 1997 Bishop Chatard began a $2 million renovation, including a new roof, windows, main entrance, and lobby, along with modifications in parking and landscaping. In 1999 a $1.5 million building drive was conducted to add an extension to the south end of the main building, which houses six classrooms and three suites dedicated to the fine arts, along with a new library and media center. In the fall of 2007, the school added a new activity center/auxiliary gym. Tuition is about $8,090.

BREBEUF JESUIT PREPARATORY SCHOOL
2801 W. 86th St.
(317) 872-7050
www.brebeuf.org
One of five secondary school apostolates sponsored by the Chicago Province of the Society of Jesus, Brebeuf was founded in 1962 and currently serves a coeducational student body of 822 in grades 9 through 12 and a faculty and staff of more than 100. Brebeuf serves as an interfaith high school with students from a variety of religious backgrounds. About half of the students are Roman Catholic and 19 percent represent minority populations. Brebeuf offers more than 50 activities and 29 athletic teams. The school motto is "Men and Women for Others." In April 2009 the school added the state-of-the-art Mark G. Kite Wellness Center, which offers space and

equipment to promote cardiovascular health and conditioning with a wide range of physical activities. Tuition to Brebeuf is about $12,950 plus $275 in fees. About 25 percent of all Brebeuf Jesuit students receive financial assistance.

BUREAU OF JEWISH EDUCATION
6711 Hoover Rd.
(317) 255-3124
www.bjeindy.org
Founded in 1910 by Rabbi I. E. Neustadt, the Bureau of Jewish Education has the second-oldest Hebrew school in the United States. Housed in the Smulyan-Stolkin Education Center, the bureau is the primary resource of Jewish education for all age levels and groups within the community and beyond.

CARDINAL RITTER HIGH SCHOOL
3360 W. 30th St.
(317) 924-4333
www.cardinalritter.org
Founded in 1964, Cardinal Ritter was named for Cardinal Joseph Ritter, the first archbishop to integrate Catholic schools. Located on the city's west side, Cardinal Ritter has 582 students and 42 teachers with an average class size of 22. The school features more than 100 courses, including Advanced Placement and dual-credit classes. About 95 percent of students pursue post-secondary education. Cardinal Ritter offers extra-curricular activities in fine arts, music, and theater and has 19 varsity sports. Launched in 2008, a new concept in community service is called Ritter Town, which encourages volunteer projects within the school and surrounding area. In its first year, Ritter Town participants volunteered in a neighborhood nursing home, raked leaves at more than 60 homes, and provided tutoring services. Tuition at Cardinal Ritter is about $6,600 for Catholics and $8,090 for non-Catholics.

CATHEDRAL HIGH SCHOOL
5225 E. 56th St.
(317) 542-1481
www.cathedral-irish.org
Founded as an all-boys Catholic high school on Sept. 12, 1918, by Bishop Joseph Chartrand, Cathedral now services 683 boys and 604 girls in grades 9 through 12. With 95 faculty members, the student-teacher ratio is 13 to 1. Cathedral features 11 academic departments with more than 188 course offerings. Tuition is about $10,390, with a student activity fee of $300.

COLONIAL CHRISTIAN SCHOOL
8140 Union Chapel Rd.
(317) 253-0649
www.ccsindy.org
Started in 1976 as a ministry of what was then Northeast Baptist Church, led by Pastor Wendell Heller, Colonial Christian School now has about 270 students in grades kindergarten through 12. Tuition is about $3,770 per year. In 1998 the new Heller Building was completed to help meet the growing academic needs and programs of the school.

COVENANT CHRISTIAN HIGH SCHOOL
7525 W. 21st St.
(317) 390-0202
www.covenantchristian.org
In the fall of 1995, 15 families began the push for a Christian high school on the west side of Indy. A year later, a grandfather donated $8 million to build a facility. Now Covenant Christian High School is fully accredited and has 385 students. Covenant offers 13 varsity sports teams. Boarding at the school is available for students at a cost of about $21,900.

FATHER THOMAS SCECINA MEMORIAL HIGH SCHOOL
5000 Nowland Ave.
(317) 356-6377
www.scecina.org
Named for the only priest from the local diocese killed in action during World War II, Father Thomas Scecina Memorial High School has 341 students and an average class size of 22. Opened in 1953, Scecina offers Advanced Placement classes in several subjects; 96 percent of its 2008 graduates continued on to higher education.

HASTEN HEBREW ACADEMY OF INDIANAPOLIS
6510 Hoover Rd.
(317) 257-5216
www.hhai.org

Founded in 1971, Hasten Hebrew Academy of Indianapolis serves children from 18 months old to grade eight. Hasten's dual curriculum provides students with a program in both secular and Judaic studies. Judaic studies include Hebrew language, Israeli culture, Biblical text in Torah and prophets, Jewish history, and oral law, as well as holiday customs and prayers. General studies are aligned with Indiana state standards. Extracurricular programs include sports, music, chess, Spanish, and more. The program culminates in an eighth-grade trip to Israel. Hasten has about 300 students. Tuition ranges from about $2,560 for 18-month-old children to $8,660 for students in grades one through eight.

HERITAGE CHRISTIAN SCHOOL
6401 E. 75th St.
(317) 813-3843
www.heritagechristian.net

Founded in 1965, Heritage started on land donated by Frank Best at 75th Street and Binford Boulevard. The vision of the private nondenominational school was to offer an uncompromised commitment to Jesus and the word of God in all facets of a student's education. A $13 million building campaign in 2005 brought new elementary classrooms, a playground, high school gym renovation, lobby expansion, and more. In 2007 a $3.1 building campaign added a new two-story building addition to the high school, including 12 classrooms, two science labs, a commons and administration offices. Heritage has about 1,500 students, averaging about 135 students per grade level. Tuition ranges from $3,765 for half-day preparatory kindergarten to $9,000 for grades 9 through 12.

INTERNATIONAL SCHOOL OF INDIANA
4330 N. Michigan Rd.
(317) 923-1951
www.isin.org

Opened in September 1994, the International School of Indiana emphasizes academic excellence and is founded on the belief that an introduction to a second language and exposure to different nationalities and ethnic backgrounds will better produce smarter students. As the only school in the Midwest to offer a trilingual program and an international baccalaureate program for all students, International School of Indiana strives to prepare students to live a life without borders.

JEWEL CHRISTIAN ACADEMY
5750 E. 30th St.
(317) 591-7200
www.jewelchristianacademy.org

Jewel Christian Academy was founded in 1995 when senior pastor Jeffrey Johnson Sr. had a vision to start a Christian school that was affordable for parents in the church community. Based on a Biblical foundation, Jewel offers education for kindergarten through grade 5. The school has about 170 students and about 35 faculty members. Core curriculum classes include Spanish, computer, music, art, Bible, and physical education. Jewel offers after-school clubs and activities, as well as interscholastic sports such as cross-country, volleyball, baseball, basketball, and kickball. Tuition is about $4,910.

LUMEN CHRISTI CATHOLIC SCHOOL
580 Stevens St.
(317) 632-3174
www.lumenchristischool.org

Founded in 2002 by Edie Anderson and a group of four home-schooling families who wanted a classic Catholic education for their children, Lumen Christi Catholic School serves 80 students in grades kindergarten through 12. Students attend daily Mass, which is celebrated in Latin most weekdays. The school teaches Latin as well as other academic courses. Lumen Christi is independent but operates with the permission of the Archdiocese of Indianapolis. The chief administrator is Stephen None, a former principal of Bishop Chatard High School and past superintendent of schools in the Archdiocese of Indianapolis. The school is attached to Holy Rosary Catholic Church in the site of the former Latin School. Tuition costs about $2,500 per year.

LUTHERAN HIGH SCHOOL OF INDIANAPOLIS
5555 S. Arlington Ave.
(317) 787-5474
www.lhsi.org

Founded in 1976, Lutheran High School of Indianapolis now has about 275 students in grades 9 through 12. Affiliated with the Missouri Synod of the Lutheran Church, the school holds a first-class commission from the Indiana Department of Education. Along with a core curriculum, Lutheran offers sports including baseball, basketball, cheering, football, soccer, tennis, volleyball, cross-country, golf, softball, track and field, and weightlifting. Extracurricular activities include academic competition teams, Civil Air Patrol, chamber choir, drama, forensics, men's chorus, jazz band, National Honor Society, student council, wind ensemble, women's chorus, and yearbook. Tuition is about $7,400 for church-associated students and $8,200 for nonassociated students.

i In 1903, at the end of Tudor Hall's first year, nine young women in long white dresses processed into a church, carrying 18 red roses, the senior class flower. Each spring, Park Tudor's female graduates continue this tradition at the commencement ceremony. A private school in Indianapolis, Park Tudor was created in 1970 with the merger of Park School for boys and Tudor Hall for girls.

PARK TUDOR
7200 N. College Ave.
(317) 254-2700
www.parktudor.org

Created in 1970 with the merger of Park School for boys and Tudor Hall for girls, Park Tudor is an independent private school for children age three through grade 12, with a student body of almost 1,000. The school boasts a 9-to-1 student-teacher ratio, 100 percent college-placement rate, more than $2.5 million awarded annually to Park Tudor students, and students who score consistently among the highest average SAT scores in the state.

Park Tudor offers 16 upper school and 12 middle school sports, with 80 percent of students playing on athletic teams. Tuition ranges from $13,300 per year for full-time kindergarten to $16,570 a year for grades 6 to 12. Financial aid is available

PROVIDENCE CRISTO REY HIGH SCHOOL
75 N. Belleview Place
(317) 860-1000
www.pcrhs.com

Opened in 2007, the school offers students from families with modest financial means access to a Catholic college preparatory education, integrated with real-world work experience in a shared entry-level job at one of the city's major corporations. Students earn about 75 percent of their tuition through work-study. Family contribution is based on need.

After the student's work income is deducted, each student owes about $2,250 for tuition and other school costs. However, the school realizes that for some families, even that amount might be more than they can afford. Therefore, additional financial aid is available to families who qualify for it. Located minutes from downtown, Cristo Rey was created to help central city children at risk for dropping out of high school. The majority of students are not Catholic, although the school emphasizes the tenets of Catholicism and students are required to take theology all four years. Extracurricular activities include student council, cross-country, volleyball, soccer, and men's and women's basketball. Serving grades 9 through 12, Cristo Rey has about 95 students.

RONCALLI HIGH SCHOOL
3300 Prague Rd.
(317) 787-8277
www.roncalli.org

Located on the south side of the city, Roncalli High

School was the result of a merger of two other schools—John F. Kennedy Memorial High School and Bishop Chartrand High School. When the two schools were merged in 1969, the new school was named Roncalli High School by the students, in memory of Angelo Roncalli, more widely known as Pope John XXIII. A four-year, interparochial school, Roncalli has been recognized three times as a Blue Ribbon School of Excellence by the U.S. Department of Education. Tuition is about $7,275. The student body totals about 1,120.

SYCAMORE SCHOOL
1750 W. 64th St.
(317) 202-2500
www.sycamoreschool.org
Founded in 1985 by parents who wanted an advanced curriculum for their children, Sycamore School is the only private school in the state of Indiana and one of the few schools in the nation where all academics and activities are designed for gifted children in preschool through grade eight. Instruction is differentiated and students are able to work at their own ability level, no matter how high. Classes are not only accelerated but enriched with hands-on projects, special speakers, and field trips. Instruction in art, music, Spanish, physical education, and computers is provided from early grades through middle school. Sycamore has about 450 students. Tuition is about $13,500. Financial aid is available.

TODD ACADEMY INC.
302 N. East St.
(317) 636-3100
www.toddacademy.com
Since 2002, Todd Academy has been guiding students through the Indiana University-Purdue University Indianapolis (IUPUI) Span program. The school is an early college program for grades 5 through 12. Most Todd Academy students work at least two grade levels above their age and sometimes more. No uniforms are required and the school is in the historic Lockerbie location. Tuition for a full-time student in the college preparatory program is about $8,800. Financial aid and scholarships are available.

TRADERS POINT CHRISTIAN ACADEMY
6600 S. Indianapolis Rd.
(317) 769-2450
www.tpcs.org
Started in 1976 when a nursery school opened within Traders Point Christian Church, Traders Point Christian Academy now has about 580 students age two through high school. Students in grades five through high school may compete in baseball, soccer, basketball, girl's volleyball, track, softball, tennis, golf, and cheer squad. Other activities include the student council and the yearbook committee. After-school programs such as computer, science, art, and math clubs are offered according to student interest. The average class size is 15 to 20 students, with a student-to-teacher ratio of 11 to 1. Annual tuition ranges from about $4,300 for half-day kindergarten to $9,800 for high school.

COLLEGES AND UNIVERSITIES

BALL STATE UNIVERSITY—INDIANAPOLIS CENTER
50 S. Meridian St.
(317) 822-6167
www.ssu.edu
Located in downtown Indy, this high-tech center offers access to programs from Ball State University, based in Muncie. The center emphasizes innovative digital media research being conducted by Ball State faculty, staff, and students. The center, which offers free wireless Internet access, is also home to the College of Architecture and Planning.

BUTLER UNIVERSITY
4600 Sunset Ave.
(317) 940-8000
www.butler.edu
Founded in 1855 by attorney and abolitionist Ovid Butler, Butler University occupies 290 acres in the beautiful Butler-Tarkington neighborhood. Butler emphasizes a liberal arts–based education with more than 60 majors. The job-placement rate has averaged 96 percent over the past five years, and 100 percent in education and

🔍 Close-up

How the Butler Bulldogs Got Their Name

Prior to 1919, Butler's athletic teams were known as the "Christians." However, Butler fans got tired of the nickname after numerous losses in the 1919 football season. When it was time for a game with Butler's rival, the Franklin "Baptists," *Butler Collegian* editor Alex Cavins and his staff decided the school's weekly pep session needed something to liven it up.

About the same time, the mascot of a Butler fraternity—a bulldog named Shimmy (because you couldn't shake him)—wandered into the *Collegian* office. That gave the staff an idea. In the next school paper, a huge page one cartoon by George Dickson showed Shimmy the bulldog—labeled Butler—taking a bite out of the pants seat of a figure labeled John the Baptist. The caption: "Bring on That Platter, Salome!" The reference, of course, was to the biblical story of John the Baptist losing his head and having it presented to the dancer Salome on a platter. Butler lost the game to Franklin, 14-0. But the Bulldogs name stuck.

pharmacy. Butler has 4,437 students, with 3,939 undergrads and 498 graduate students, with an average class size of 21. Butler students come from all 50 states and 60 counties. Annual tuition costs about $36,000. Butler offers more than 115 student organizations, with activities ranging from religious and spiritual to service oriented and political. The university also has 19 NCAA Division sports and dozens of club and intramural sports.

From the beginning, it was clear that athletics were going to play an important role in Butler University. When the school moved to its current location, two of the first structures completed were a 15,000-seat field house and a 36,000-seat football stadium. The football stadium, which came to be known as the Butler Bowl, was downsized to a 20,000-seat stadium in the mid-1950s and is home of the Butler football and lacrosse teams. The field house, the largest of its kind when it was completed in 1928, is a historical landmark. The Butler Fieldhouse, renamed Hinkle Fieldhouse in 1966, symbolized Indiana's "Hoosier Hysteria." Hinkle Fieldhouse became the combined home of Butler basketball and the Indiana High School state tournament. Legends of Indiana basketball, from Oscar Robertson to George McGinnis to Larry Bird, all played in the Fieldhouse at one time or another.

CHRISTIAN THEOLOGICAL SEMINARY
1000 W. 42nd St.
(317) 924-1331
www.cts.edu
A private four-year college, Christian Theological Seminary is a fully accredited ecumenical seminary related to the Christian Church (Disciples of Christ). The seminary offers eight graduate-level degree programs and has about 325 full-time students. Tuition is $490 per credit hour.

CROSSROADS BIBLE COLLEGE
601 N. Shortridge Rd.
(317) 352-8736
www.crossroads.edu
Established in 1980 as the Baptist Bible College, the institution changed its name in 2000 to Crossroads Bible College. A four-year, coeducational college, Crossroads grants degrees at the associate and bachelor level in programs such as ministry, theology studies, and religious education. The institute also offers certificate courses and vocational training in subjects including pastoral ministry, elementary education, and international ministry. Tuition at Crossroads is about $9,500 per year.

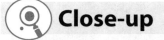

Close-up

Indiana University Dance Marathon

On April 8, 1990, an Indiana teen died shortly before he would have graduated from high school. A hemophiliac, Ryan White became infected with HIV from a contaminated blood treatment. AIDS was poorly understood at the time, and Ryan's hometown of Kokomo, Indiana, expelled him because of fear of his infection. A lengthy school battle ensued, turning a national spotlight on AIDS and helping to destigmatize the horrible disease. Ryan acted as a beacon of hope to many. He eventually left Kokomo and finished his schooling in Cicero, Indiana.

Ryan sought treatment for the disease from Riley Hospital for Children in Indianapolis. He also dreamed of going to Indiana University. On March 29, 1990, however, shortly before his senior prom, Ryan was admitted to Riley Hospital for Children with a respiratory infection. As his condition deteriorated, he was placed on a ventilator and died on Palm Sunday. Over 1,500 people—including Michael Jackson, Elton John, football star Howie Long, and First Lady Barbara Bush—attended Ryan's funeral at the Second Presbyterian Church on Meridian Street. He was buried in Cicero, near his mother's home.

Wanting to memorialize the courageous young man, a friend, Jill Stewart, started a fundraising drive at Indiana University—a Dance Marathon. In 1991 IU held its first Dance Marathon. The 36-hour event raised $11,000. The annual event has now raised over $7 million for the children at Riley Hospital. Run entirely by student volunteers, the fund-raiser culminates in the 36-hour marathon every fall. During the marathon weekend, 850 dancers choose to remain awake and standing for 36 hours in honor of the children who are unable to do that.

HARRISON COLLEGE
550 E. Washington St.
(317) 264-5656
www.harrison.edu
Originally known as Indiana Business College, the school changed its name in 2009 to Harrison College since it is no longer only a business college and is opening another campus in Columbus, Ohio. Harrison College offers more than 30 degree programs in five schools of study. Harrison's programs fall within schools of health science, veterinary, information technology, criminal justice, business, and culinary arts.

The history of the college goes back to 1902 when a former educator, Charles Cring, realized that a diversifying economy needed trained workers. The needed skills in 1902 were shorthand, typing, penmanship, English, bookkeeping, and accounting. Cring built his school based on education in those areas, helping students become marketable in the world of business. Even during the Great Depression, Cring's students thrived because employers knew they could look to the college for well-trained people to hire.

Today, Harrison has about 4,400 students throughout Indiana. Tuition runs from $4,650 a quarter for at least 17 credit hours in health care management to $4,450 for at least 17 credit hours in criminal justice and in accounting. About 93 percent of Harrison students receive some form of financial aid.

> **i** Indiana University-Purdue University Indianapolis is home to the only professional medical and dental schools in the state. Its nursing school is the largest multidiscipline nursing school in the nation.

INDIANA UNIVERSITY-PURDUE UNIVERSITY
INDIANAPOLIS
420 University Blvd.
(317) 274-5555
www.iupui.edu

The birth of Indiana University-Purdue University Indianapolis was a fast one. Established over a six-month period in 1968, IUPUI was created out of a vision of then Indianapolis mayor Richard Lugar, IU president Joseph Sutton, Purdue president Frederick Hovde, and other community leaders. In 1969 IUPUI was formed as a partnership between Indiana University and Purdue University, an effort to bring together all of the IU and PU schools in Indianapolis. By 2005 all IUPUI schools had moved to what is now the IUPUI campus, just two blocks west of the Indiana State Capitol.

IUPUI alumni account for 85 percent of Indiana's dentists, half the physicians, nearly half of the state's lawyers, more than a third of the nurses, and a larger percentage of the health and rehabilitation sciences and social work professionals. More than 30,000 students attend IUPUI, representing all 50 states and 122 countries. One out of every 10 Indianapolis residents has attended or graduated from IUPUI. The college offers 22 schools and academic units, with over 200 programs of study. Student housing has the capacity for 1,107 students in a traditional residence hall, townhomes, and the Campus Apartments on the Riverwalk. Tuition is about $218 a credit hour for Indiana residents and $665 for nonresidents.

i Indiana University at Bloomington was the first state university in the nation to grant equal privileges to women and graduate a female student.

INDIANA WESLEYAN UNIVERSITY
3777 Priority Way South Dr.
(317) 574-3980

6325 Digital Way, Suite 222
(800) 456-5327
www.indwes.edu
Indiana Wesleyan University's main campus is located in Marion, midway between Indianapolis and Fort Wayne. Established in 1920, the 300-acre campus is where 2,800 students attend IWU's traditional four-year liberal arts college and residential graduate school. In 1985 IWU

began offering programs designed for working adults. Since 1987, IWU's College of Adult and Professional Studies has established nine education centers across Indiana, including two in Indianapolis. Tuition per three-credit-hour classes costs about $535.

INTERNATIONAL BUSINESS COLLEGE
7205 Shadeland Station
(317) 813-2300
www.ibcindianapolis.edu
Founded in 1889, International Business College offers programs in business, technology, and health care. The college has about 400 students. Tuition costs about $12,440 a year, or $26,605 for students living on campus.

ITT TECHNICAL INSTITUTE
9511 Angola Court
(317) 875-8640
www.itt-tech.edu
A private college system offering technology-oriented programs, ITT Technical Institute serves about 2,500 students at its Indianapolis location. Headquartered in Carmel, Indiana, ITT operates more than 100 institutes in over 35 states. ITT has been actively involved in the higher education community since 1969. Tuition is about $425 per credit hour or about $15,600 per year for students living on campus.

IVY TECH COMMUNITY COLLEGE
50 W. Fall Creek Dr. North
(317) 921-4800
www.ivytech.edu
Ivy Tech Community College is the nation's largest statewide community college with single accreditation. It is the state's largest public post-secondary institution, serving more than 130,000 students a year. Created by the Indiana General Assembly to provide "occupational training of a practical, technical, and semi-technical nature," Ivy Tech was formerly known as Indiana Vocational Technical College. That is where the initial "I.V." came from, giving the college its name of Ivy Tech. The college was founded in 1963 and now offers more than 150 programs statewide.

Ivy Tech has 23 campuses through Indiana, and classes are offered in more than 75 communities. Tuition is about $100 per credit hour for state residents, $207 for out-of-state students.

LINCOLN COLLEGE OF TECHNOLOGY
7225 Winton Dr., No. 128
(317) 632-5553
www.lincolnedu.com
Since its founding as a post-war job-training center in 1946, Lincoln Technical Institute has been helping people get jobs in the skilled trades. Lincoln has about 1,500 students. Students receive hands-on training in fields such as computer programming, software applications, network systems, personal-computer support, and help desk analysis.

MARIAN UNIVERSITY
3200 Cold Spring Rd.
(317) 955-6000
www.marian.edu
A private four-year institution, Marian is a Catholic and Franciscan university that grew out of the vision of Sister Theresa Hackelmeier and the Sisters of St. Francis in Oldenburg, Indiana. They established a school in Oldenburg in 1851. Founded in Oldenburg in 1936, Marian College moved to Indianapolis in 1937. On July 1, 2009, Marian College became Marian University.

Marian University has more than 2,000 full- and part-time students from 20 states and 12 countries. The faculty features 81 full-time professors, with a student to faculty ratio of 17 to 1. Tuition is $25,200 for full-time nonresidential students and $32,712 for those who are residential.

MARTIN UNIVERSITY
2171 Avondale Place
(317) 543-3243
www.martin.edu
Founded by a Benedictine priest in 1977, Martin University's original mission was to serve low-income, minority, and adult learners. That goal, as envisioned by Rev. Boniface Hardin, has not changed. The average age of students at Martin continues to be about 40, although the university is enrolling a growing number of young people.

Dramatic changes have taken place over the years. More than two dozen buildings used by the university were razed to make way for parking lots, landscaping, and the new $10 million Educational Center. The building opened in 2001, along with the Peace Garden connecting it with the Bernice Fraction Performing Arts Center and the Dr. Andrew J. Brown Building.

Martin University was named in honor of Dr. Martin Luther King Jr. and St. Martin de Porres. The school offers 17 undergraduate degrees and two graduate degrees in community psychology and urban ministry studies. Classes are offered during the day as well as at night and on Saturday. Martin University has about 1,075 undergrad students and 48 graduate students. Tuition is about $14,000. More than 75 percent of Martin University students receive some form of financial aid.

UNIVERSITY OF INDIANAPOLIS
1400 E. Hanna Ave.
(317) 788-3368
www.uindy.edu
Though relatively small in size at 4,700 students, University of Indianapolis awards more doctoral degrees than all but four of the largest universities in Indiana. UIndy produces more physical therapists, occupational therapists, and clinical psychologists than any other university in the state. With a student-to-faculty ration of 12 to 1, UIndy has an average class size of 18 students.

Affiliated with the United Methodist Church, the University of Indianapolis was founded in 1902 as Indiana Central University. In 1986 the name was changed to the University of Indianapolis. The college offers 70 undergraduate academic programs, one of the widest selections of degree programs among private colleges in Indiana. Indiana's only degree in nurse midwifery—a master's program—is offered at UIndy. The cost is $375 per credit hour or $17,760 a year for tuition, room, and board.

MEDIA

Indianapolis had a newspaper before it even had roads or mail service—or even before Indiana became a state. Six months after the city of Indianapolis was founded, the *Indianapolis Gazette* began sharing news with its citizenry. Wisely, the fledging newspaper took a politically neutral stand. A year later, the *Western Censor* and *Emigrants Guide* began publishing. They took a decidedly political position, campaigning strongly against Andrew Jackson.

Since then, newspapers have come and gone. Today, the city has many publications, ranging from newspapers to business journals, alternative news, shopping circulars, and magazines. But there is only one daily newspaper—the *Indianapolis Star*.

The first radio station went on the air in the early 1920s, and Indianapolis got its own permanent station in 1924—WFRM. By the early 1940s, two other stations had hit the airwaves—WIBC and WISH. Take a look at the list below to see how many AM/FM stations are now available to listeners.

Network television began broadcasting locally in 1950. The local public TV station, WFYI, signed on in 1970 after dedicated volunteers went door to door in a fund-raising campaign. Now, through the wonders of cable and satellite, viewers can choose from a multitude of channels for round-the-clock viewing.

Following is a roundup of the city's best-known media outlets, as well as some smaller ones. Whether you're visiting Indianapolis or relocating here, you'll find the local media to be a wealth of information on the city's life.

PUBLICATIONS

INDIANAPOLIS STAR
307 N. Pennsylvania St.
(317) 633-9273
When the *Indianapolis Star* debuted on June 6, 1903, it challenged existing newspapers in the city and let the city know a new kid was on the block through a publicity stunt. Newspaper founder George F. McCulloch paid a balloonist $650 to drop red stars on the city in the days leading up to the paper's debut. More stars were dropped from the year-old Soldiers and Sailors Monument.

Slowly, the *Star* absorbed its competition. By 1948, the *Star* had become the state's largest circulation paper. The news turf was dominated by three dailies—the *Times*, the *Star* and the *News*. In 1965, the *Times*, a Scripps Howard publication, ceased publication, leaving the *News* and the *Star*

as the city's two major dailies. After the death of owner Eugene S. Pulliam in 1999, the *News* folded. In 2000 the *Indianapolis Star* became part of the Gannett Co., the nation's largest newspaper chain, leaving Indianapolis with no locally owned daily newspaper. *The Star* has a circulation of about 255,000 daily and 325,000 on Sunday.

BUSINESS LEADER
425 Vernwood Court
(317) 273-8701
www.businessleader.bz
The *Business Leader* offers a monthly business publication for Carmel, Hendricks County, and Johnson County.

INDIANAPOLIS BUSINESS JOURNAL
41 E. Washington St., Suite 200
(317) 634-6200
www.ibj.com

Established in 1980, the *Indianapolis Business Journal* is a weekly, tabloid-size business newspaper. It offers finance and business news and analysis about local business trends. Circulation is about 16,000.

i David Letterman, host of CBS's *Late Show* and the original host of NBC's *Late Night,* was born and raised in Indianapolis and began his broadcasting career there as a weatherman for WLWI-TV (now WTHR). His mother, Dorothy Mengering, who still lives in the Indianapolis area, has made frequent appearances on her son's show.

INDIANAPOLIS MONTHLY
40 Monument Circle, Suite 100
(317) 684-8320
www.indianapolismonthly.com
A monthly magazine covering many facets of the Circle City, *Indianapolis Monthly* is a popular general-interest publication.

INDIANAPOLIS RECORDER
2901 N. Tacoma Ave.
(317) 924-5143
www.indianapolisrecorder.com
Started as a two-page church bulletin in 1895 by cofounders George Stewart and Will Porter, the *Indianapolis Recorder* has grown to be one of the top African-American publications in the nation. The weekly newspaper covers local and national news.

INDIANAPOLIS WOMAN
6610 N. Shadeland Ave., Suite 100
(877) 469-6626
www.indianapoliswoman.com
Founded in 1994, *Indianapolis Woman* is a monthly magazine featuring issues of interest to women.

NUVO
3951 N. Meridian St.
(317) 254-2400
www.nuvo.net

Indy's alternative voice, *Nuvo* is published weekly with news, entertainment, investigative reporting, and opinion. It can be picked up free at numerous street-corner boxes, businesses, and restaurants.

i *The Bob and Tom Show,* a syndicated US radio program established by Bob Kevoian and Tom Griswold at radio station WFBQ in Indianapolis in 1983, has been syndicated nationally since 1995. It is still based in Indy.

RADIO

AM Radio Stations
WSYW 810—Spanish radio
WXLW 950—Indianapolis sports radio
WFNI 1070—Local affiliate for ESPN radio
WNDE 1260—Sports news and talk show station, affiliate for Fox Sports
WTLC 1310—"The Light," a contemporary gospel station, offers music and talk
WXNT 1430—Political talk
WBRI 1500—Christian radio

i The television sitcom *One Day at a Time* was set in Indianapolis. The opening credits of the show include a shot of the Pyramids, a set of three distinctive office buildings located near the northwestern edge of the city.

FM Radio Stations
WICR 88.7—Jazz
WJEL 89.3—Variety of programming from North Central High School
WBDG 90.0—Round-the-clock programs from Ben Davis High School
WFYI 90.1—Public radio
WRFT 91.5—Hit music and news from Franklin Central High School
WTTS 92.3—Home of classic rock, with hits from the '60s to today
WIBC 93.1—News, talk, top 40
WFBQ 94.7—Q95 is home to the *Bob & Tom Show* and classic rock

WFMS 95.5—County station
WHHH 96.3—Hip-hop and rhythm and blues
WLHK 97.1—Known as "Hank FM," plays country
    and talk shows
WZPL 99.5—Music and talk shows
WNOU 100.9—Hit music and talk shows
WKLU 101.9—Oldies music
WRZK 103.3—Rock
WJJK 104.5—Classic hits
WYXB 105.7—Soft rock
WEDJ 107.1—Spanish
WNTR 107.9—Contemporary and classical oldies

TELEVISION

Local Stations

Channel 4—CW
Channel 6 WRTV—ABC
Channel 8 WISH TV—CBS
Channel 13 WTHR—NBC
Channel 20 WFYI—PBS
Channel 40 WHMB—Religious
Channel 59 WXIB—Fox

ℹ️ On the classic sitcom *I Love Lucy,* Fred Mertz was originally from Indianapolis and his mother still lived there. Before moving to New York and meeting the Ricardos, he and his wife, Ethel Mertz, ran a diner in Indy.

RETIREMENT

Indianapolis doesn't have an ocean or the year-round warm weather of places that once were the dream destinations for retirees. But Indy does have a rapidly expanding senior population choosing to spend their "golden years" in the Hoosier capital city. An easy-to-navigate city with a friendly, inviting atmosphere, the nation's 12th largest city has gone through a dramatic revitalization and remarkable renaissance, making it a far different place than it was even a decade ago. Today, Indy is an appealing mix of big-city amenities and small-town charm that makes it a great place to live.

Retirement today has evolved into an interesting balance of leisure, work, volunteerism, family, and travel. People still prefer to stay in their own homes as long as they are able. The idea of remaining in familiar communities, near family and friends, has even gotten a name—"Aging in Place." As the baby-boomer generation eases into retirement, Aging in Place is expected to become even more important.

The same benefits that make Indianapolis such an attractive place for all ages—in a nutshell, a high quality of life combined with a relatively low cost of living—make it an especially desirable place for retired people. Those who have left the constraints of the work world now have even more time to enjoy Indy's thousands of acres of parks, golf courses, historic attractions, music, world-class art, smorgasbord of restaurants, fun shopping, top-notch professional sports, and much more.

A number of retirement communities offer a range of lifestyle options, from independent to assisted living. An excellent senior citizens center with convenient branches throughout the area provides opportunities for recreation, travel, education, relaxation, and even volunteerism with friends old and new. For many retired people, the issue of health care becomes increasingly important. With many respected health institutions in town, health care access is excellent in Indianapolis.

The central location near major interstates, along with an international airport, makes getting in and out of town a breeze. Of course, turning that magic retirement age also means you get a reduced cost at many attractions detailed in this book, and you now can explore all the city offers. Indianapolis is a great place to grow old and to remain young at heart.

GETTING STARTED

CICOA (CENTRAL INDIANA COUNCIL ON AGING)
4755 Kingsway Dr.
(317) 254-3660
www.cicoa.org

Indiana's largest area agency on aging, CICOA is the central clearinghouse for information and access to Indiana's agencies on aging. CICOA serves Boone, Hamilton, Hancock, Hendricks, Johnson, Marion, Morgan, and Shelby Counties,

where more than 20 percent of Indiana's population lives. Established in 1974 by an amendment to the 1965 Older Americans Act, CICOA and its network of 300 for-profit and not-for-profit providers offer a wealth of services for older adults and people with disabilities.

The organization's network of services includes adult day care, in-home care, delivering hot meals, modifying homes to meet homeowners' special needs, care-management services, home visits, neighborhood meal sites, providing caregivers with respite or supplemental services, equipping people with personal emergency-response systems, providing transportation, legal services, and being advocates on senior issues.

ℹ️ Enjoy visiting museums and helping people? All the Indianapolis museums welcome older adult volunteers. Pick out the one you want and give them a call. The Attractions chapter has a list and description of Indy museums.

OLDER ADULT SERVICE AND INFORMATION SYSTEM (OASIS)

OASIS West
6640 Parkdale Place, Suite T
(317) 291-5033

OASIS Glendale
6101 N. Keystone Ave.
(317) 253-1951

OASIS at Washington Park
10800 E. Washington St.
(317) 396-3751

OASIS South
65 Airport Parkway, Suite 109, Greenwood
(317) 888-8577
www.oasisnet.org
Serving more than 26,000 members in the Indianapolis area, OASIS is the largest, most comprehensive national not-for-profit education and volunteer service for mature adults. OASIS is dedicated to enriching lives of adults age 50 and older through lifelong learning and service. Membership is free. Members receive a complimentary course catalog with programs in the arts and humanities, health and wellness, history and science, computers, and distance learning. Regular programs are offered at the four OASIS centers in Indianapolis and at other locations throughout the community.

ℹ️ Most attractions and many restaurants in Indianapolis offer a special senior discount. Reduced prices are listed throughout this book.

UNITED SENIOR ACTION
324 Morris St., Suite 114
(800) 495-0872
www.usaindiana.org
Since 1979, United Senior Action of Indiana has been uniting older Hoosiers into a powerful voice to impact policies affecting senior citizens' lives and communities. United Senior Action is an Indiana-based organization with officers, volunteers, and operations located in Indiana.

The group works on issues such as nursing home quality and reform; alternatives to nursing homes, including home and community-based care; utility and telephone rates; prescription drug prices; and more. Members get as involved as they choose—from writing letters and participating in public meetings to walking the halls of the State Capitol. Membership dues are $15 for an individual, $20 for a couple. If your senior club is a group member of United Senior Action, dues are $8 for an individual, $10 for a couple.

SENIOR CENTERS

Senior Centers are an excellent way to find out about all the services and activities available to area seniors. With dozens of senior centers throughout the area, it isn't feasible to provide a comprehensive list or description of each. The few that have been profiled will give you an idea of what is offered. Most senior centers provide older adults with educational opportunities, health and fitness programs, social and cultural events, lunch, and assistance in a wide array of senior issues, including legal, medical, and financial problems.

THE ABBEY APARTMENTS
4012 S. Mann Rd.
(317) 821-1903
www.rhf.org
Nestled in a meadow in a country setting, the Abbey Apartments are away from traffic and congestion but close to shopping, churches, and medical facilities. One-bedroom apartments include a full kitchen, with an on-site laundry room, individual indoor mailboxes, an entry

access system, elevator, and community room. A social service coordinator is also available for assistance.

CHRISTAMORE HOUSE
502 N. Tremont St.
(317) 635-7211
www.christamorehouse.org

A United Way organization, Christamore House was founded in 1905 by two Butler University students. Its mission is to promote the general welfare of residents in the Haughville neighborhood, a west-side community near downtown Indy and the IUPUI campus. The Christamore House was built and moved to its location in 1924 and is listed on the National Register of Historic Places. The senior program engages senior citizens in social activities, health and fitness, safety and senior benefits, field trips, and recreation. A hot meal is provided daily through Second Helpings. Gleaners Food Bank provides a monthly care package for every senior enrolled.

CITIZEN'S MULTI-SERVICE
601 E. 17th St.
(317) 926-2351

COMMUNITY ALLIANCE OF FAR EASTSIDE
8902 E. 38th St.
(317) 890-3288

CONCORD CENTER
1310 S. Meridian St.
(317) 637-4376

CROOKED CREEK MULTI-SERVICE CENTER
2990 W. 71st St.
(317) 293-2600

EAGLE CREEK WORSHIP/COMMUNITY CENTER-SALVATION ARMY
4400 N. High School Rd.
(317) 299-4454

EDNA MARTIN CHRISTIAN CENTER
1970 Caroline Ave.
(317) 637-3776

FLANNER HOUSE OF INDIANAPOLIS
2424 Dr. Martin Luther King, Jr., St.
(317) 925-4231

FLETCHER PLACE COMMUNITY CENTER
1637 Prospect St.
(317) 636-3466

FOREST MANOR MULTI-SERVICE CENTER
5603 E. 38th St.
(317) 545-1204

FOUNTAIN SQUARE
1337 Shelby St.
(317) 632-0156

HAWTHORNE SOCIAL SERVICE ASSOCIATION
2440 W. Ohio St.
(317) 637-4312

HERITAGE PLACE OF INDIANAPOLIS
4550 N. Illinois St.
(317) 283-6662

INDIANAPOLIS SENIOR CENTER
416 N. New Jersey St.
(317) 263-6272

INDY YMCA
501 N. Shortridge Rd.
(317) 357-8441

JEWISH COMMUNITY CENTER
6701 Hoover Rd.
(317) 251-9467

KENNEDY KING SENIOR CENTER
601 E. 17th St.
(317) 327-7008

i If you can resist the temptation of warm cinnamon buns wafting through the air, you might like to get your exercise by mall walking. Many enclosed shopping centers open early just for walkers, and some stay open later for the same reason. Malls are popular for walking because they offer easy parking, are temperature-controlled, and have smooth floors, bathrooms, and security. Of course, you can also shop or get a snack afterwards. Check with local malls to see which offer walking clubs.

MARTIN LUTHER KING COMMUNITY CENTER
40 W. 40th St.
(317) 923-4581
www.mlk-msc.org
Founded in 1971 as the Butler Tarkington Multi-Service Center, the Martin Luther King Community Center serves people of all ages in the Metropolitan Indianapolis area. The Senior Program at the center offers activities for people 55 and older. From 9:30 a.m. to 1 p.m. Wed through Fri, participants enjoy various activities including current events, games, shopping, and presentations from guest speakers. Lunch is provided every day and seniors also enjoy field trips. Health and wellness presentations are offered as well as health fairs that provide education to keep seniors mentally and physically fit. Participants are also provided free blood pressure and cholesterol checks on a monthly basis.

MARY RIGG NEIGHBORHOOD CENTER
1920 W. Morris St.
(317) 639-6106

MID-NORTH SHEPHERD
3808 N. Meridian St.
(317) 924-0959

PERRY SENIOR CITIZENS CENTER
6901 Derbyshire Rd.
(317) 783-9231

ST. ANDREW UMC
2560 S. Villa St.
(317) 784-4662

SOUTHEAST COMMUNITY SERVICES
901 Shelby St.
(317) 236-7400

STERRETT SENIOR CENTER
8950 Otis Ave.
(317) 549-4815

UNITED NORTHWEST AREA
3006 N. Clifton St.
(317) 924-5786

RETIREMENT COMMUNITIES

Indianapolis has many housing options for seniors, including luxury retirement communities, independent living and assisted living communities, nursing homes, Alzheimer's assisted living, licensed residential homes, and government-subsidized housing. A few of the many retirement communities in the area are profiled below. Many of the agencies listed in this chapter can provide information on housing as well.

ALTENHEIM COMMUNITY
3525 E. Hanna Ave.
(317) 788-4261
www.altenheimcommunity.org
From its first location in a large Victorian mansion in downtown Indianapolis to its present site on a 32-acre scenic campus on East Hanna Avenue, Altenheim has provided care and services to families for generations. Founded by two local churches, Altenheim is the oldest not-for-profit, church-related retirement community in Indianapolis. Today, residents represent many denominations and the community is a homogenous blend of faith backgrounds.

i Downtown Indianapolis was named as one of the best "four-season downtowns" to retire to, according to the book *Retire Downtown*.

Residents can choose from two- and three-bedroom garden homes or a variety of apartment floor plans with full amenities in the independent and assisted living complex. Skilled nursing care and rehabilitation also are available in the health care center. Planned social activities are abundant, as is transportation to community events. Altenheim offers gathering places for socializing throughout the community as well as a garden walk. Two dining rooms accommodate independent living and assisted living residents. A waitstaff provides table services. Meals include cooked-to-order breakfast, lunch, and dinner, with menus offering a choice of entrées. Special diet needs are accommodated, and there are seasonal menus. Family and friends are welcome to dine with residents.

ATRIUM VILLAGE SENIOR APARTMENTS OF INDIANAPOLIS
2636 N. Mitthoeffer Rd.
(317) 899-4281
www.atriumvillage.com
Located on the east side of Indianapolis, Atrium Village Senior Apartments offers two-bedroom apartment homes, all on one floor, with a private entrance, washer and dryer connections, and central heat and air-conditioning. Homes are all electric and residents are responsible for all utilities except for trash removal.

Services include an Atrium Village shuttle bus, 24-hour emergency maintenance, an arts and crafts room, beautician and barber, a business center, cardio fitness center, courtyard, covered parking, a gazebo, television room, stocked lake for fishing, and gardening area. Membership in the Atrium Village Activity Center is included in the rent price for all residents. This includes full use of all facilities at the center and inclusion in all activity programs. Pets are welcome for an additional fee of $100, plus a $200 deposit and $20 extra per month. Rental rates start at $685 for a two-bedroom, one-and-a-half-bath apartment.

CLEARWATER COMMONS
4519 E. 82nd St.
(317) 849-2244
www.americansrcommunities.com

This north-side community offers both independent and assisted living.options. For independent residents, garden homes offer maintenance-free living with a variety of floor plans that include one or two bedrooms with attached garages, sunrooms, dens, laundry rooms, and full kitchens. Assisted living options include studio as well as one- or two-bedroom floor plans. Three meals a day are provided in a restaurant-style dining room.

The community offers a wide range of social activities as well as scheduled transportation to shopping, restaurants, and appointments. On-site amenities include a salon and wellness program. Housekeeping services are also available.

THE FORUM AT THE CROSSING
8505 Woodfield Crossing Blvd.
(317) 257-7406
www.theforumatthecrossing.com
Welcoming seniors since 1986, the Forum at the Crossing offers a convenient location on the city's north side, with easy access to shopping, banking, and medical care. A full-service, continuing-care retirement community, the Forum features independent living rental residences, enhanced services for assisted living, Alzheimer's/memory-care suites, a skilled nursing and rehabilitation center, in-house or outpatient rehabilitation services, short-term stays, hospice care, and much more. The Forum is a rental community; no endowment or buy-in is required. Amenities include restaurant-style dining with a variety of menu options, community areas with furnishings and artwork, a beauty and barber shop, gift shop and store, housekeeping, musical programs and entertainment, transportation, social and recreational activities, maintenance and security, a 24-hour emergency call response system, and paid utilities except phone.

THE HARRISON
3060 Valley Farms Rd.
(317) 291-1112
www.harrisonretirementliving.com
The Harrison offers independent living, assisted living, and temporary care. A three-story garden

atrium sets the comfortable tone with other amenities including a pool table, exercise room, fireplace in the atrium, large-screen cable television and VCR in the lounge area, waist-high gardening plots, courtyard, recreation room, four lounges, on-site free storage, bird aviary, beauty/barber shop, gift shop, convenience store, chapel, complimentary laundry facilities, and carports.

Accommodations include studio apartments and one- or two-bedroom apartments. Cable television and individual heating and cooling controls are offered. Restaurant-style dining, weekly full-service housekeeping, 24-hour emergency service, complimentary manicures, and a schedule of social, educational, and recreational activities are available. Scheduled, unlimited courtesy transportation can be arranged.

i Senior citizens ride for half price on Indy's public transit system. Nicknamed IndyGo, the bus system started in 1953 when the city's streetcar system was converted to bus routes. Today, IndyGo features more than 6,000 bus stops and 110 bus shelters around the city. The fare is 85 cents for people age 65 and older. Medicare cardholders should display their Medicare card to the IndyGo bus operator when boarding to receive half-fare benefits. Or you can show your Medicare card and for $2 buy an IndyGo Half-Fare Identification Card.

MARQUETTE MANOR
8140 Township Line Rd.
(317) 875-9700
www.marquettemanor.com
Centered on 46 wooded acres on the north side of Indianapolis, Marquette offers easy access to dining, shopping, and entertainment. A variety of living options include independent living in either an apartment or cottage, assisted living in the Pavilion, a specialized memory-care neighborhood in Reflections at the Pavilion, and skilled and supportive nursing care in a licensed, Medicare-certified health care center.

Services include a personal trainer in the new Wellness Center, housekeeping, transportation, branch bank, two hair salons, gift shop, convenience store, technology center, wireless Internet, business center, housekeeping, library, new underground parking, and 24-hour maintenance and security.

MORNINGSIDE OF COLLEGE PARK
8810 Colby Blvd.
(317) 872-4567
www.morningsideofcollegepark.com
Located just off I-465 on the northwest side of Indianapolis, MorningSide is only minutes away from a wide variety of shopping, fine restaurants, theaters, banks, and St. Vincent Hospital and Medical Center. MorningSide offers independent and assisted living apartments. Apartments feature a private patio or balcony with great views. Residents have 10 floor plans from which to choose. Each apartment offers a fully equipped kitchen and a walk-in shower and tub with shower. Garages and lake views also are available. MorningSide provides free tours and luncheons for interested retirees.

Security is emphasized at MorningSide, where the building is locked and secure and visitors may enter only through the front atrium entrance. All side doors are locked and secure. Residents have keys to side doors. The main entrance is open until 10 p.m. each day, with the building staffed 24 hours a day.

Three chef-prepared meals are served daily. The Brass Rose Restaurant offers a wide range of hot breakfast items, soups, entrees, vegetables, breads, desserts, and a full salad bar each day for lunch and dinner. Residents often bring their church friends and their family so they can host Sunday dinner just as they used to in their homes.

Residents are welcome to have pets in their apartments. Dogs must weigh less than 25 pounds and have proof of health and vaccinations. There is a pet deposit and rent premium per month to have a pet. Dogs must live on the first floor so they can easily get outside. Birds, cats, and fish can reside throughout the building.

Amenities include no buy-in endowment or entrance fee and a month-to-month lease only.

The monthly rent includes all utilities, plus free local telephone service and free basic cable-television service. State-of-the-art exercise equipment and a hot tub are available. A 24-hour emergency call program is offered, as are weekly free blood-pressure checks. Also on-site are complimentary laundry rooms, valet service, beauty salon, plant room and garden plots, elevators, individual locked mailboxes, a library, full-time social director, chapel, computer, and Internet access, Sunday services, a courtyard and gazebo, Red Hat Society chapter, and movie theater with films shown twice daily. A monthly newsletter is provided. Fees range from $500 to $1,500 per month.

WESTMINSTER VILLAGE NORTH
11050 Presbyterian Dr.
(317) 823-6841
www.westminstervillagenorth.com

Since 1972, Westminster Village North has been conservator of 57 acres of trees, parks, and pastoral serenity while creating homes for independent, assisted, and health center living. The village offers independent living in apartments and cottage homes, as well as assisted living and a licensed health center. The village also features health center memory care for people with moderate dementia. The center offers a 24-hour nursing staff along with a suite for privacy, plus gathering spaces for socializing, which are so important to those with moderate cognitive impairment.

Activities include book clubs, movies, arts and crafts groups, a state-of-the-art wellness center, wooded trails along Indian Creek, an outdoor fitness walk, billiards, dining, and travel trips.

WORSHIP

Religion has always played an important role in the lives of Hoosiers. Since the first settlers established Indianapolis in 1821, the new residents sought to nurture their faith and to shape the moral character of what would become the seat of state government in 1825. A city of churches, Indianapolis was described by historian Jacob Piatt Dunn "as unquestionably more moral and religious than the average frontier town."

As in other early settlements, the first religious meetings were held in homes and businesses. A schoolhouse built in 1821 was a frequent church meeting site. Conducted by traveling preachers, these early church meetings attracted settlers of every denomination. A popular meeting site was a wooded knoll in the center of town, what is known today as Monument Circle.

Methodists were first on the scene, organizing a class in 1821 and later erecting a brick building at the southwest corner of the Circle and Meridian Street. A multidenominational Sunday school was organized in 1823, and three years later the Indianapolis Sabbath School was founded.

Baptists established a church rather than a class in 1822, making them the first denomination to claim a real home in the state's capital city. Presbyterians started sharing a preacher with Presbyterians in nearby Bloomington in 1822 and formally became a church in 1823. After about a dozen years, a disagreement led to a division that separated American Presbyterians into a traditional or Old School church and an evangelical or New School church. In 1838, 15 members of the First Presbyterian Church withdrew to organize a Second Presbyterian Church. The new church's minister was Henry Ward Beecher.

After leaving Indianapolis in 1847, Beecher went on to become of the nation's most renowned clergymen. His sister, Harriet Beecher Stowe, wrote Uncle Tom's Cabin (1852), said to be a major impetus for the Civil War. Upon meeting the author, Abraham Lincoln allegedly remarked, "So you're the little woman who wrote the book that started this great war."

As settlers made their way to Indianapolis, they brought their own religions and beliefs. The first setters, of course, were from surrounding states. Gradually, people from the East Coast and from Europe headed to new homes in Indiana, creating a wide array of religious denominations.

A new denomination that came into existence in 1830, the Disciples of Christ, built a house of worship on Kentucky Avenue in 1836. They also opened a coeducational college known as North Western Christian University in 1855. Located at what is now 13th Street and College Avenue, the school was founded by Ovid Butler to promote that Christian movement. The school had no president, two professors, and 20 students. In two decades the college had proven so successful that it moved to a 25-acre campus and was renamed Butler University in honor of its founder. In 1922 Butler University purchased Fairview Park and in 1928 moved its campus to the current Fairview location, which consists of 31 buildings covering 290 acres. Today, Butler University is a nationally recognized comprehensive university with more than 4,000 students. Butler University's athletic teams are known as the Bulldogs. Butler's basketball arena, Hinkle Fieldhouse, was the largest basketball arena in the United States for several decades.

For a century or more, the religious center of Indianapolis was the heart of the city—in a very real sense. The Circle, the center of the city's Square Mile, was home to five churches. By 1884, Christ Church was the only one left. The others moved to new locations as the city expanded and folks left the downtown area for the suburbs.

Today, Christ Church Cathedral is a city landmark on the Circle, the oldest religious building in continuous use in Indianapolis. The building is also the city's best example of early Gothic Revival architecture. The parish of Christ Church built a simple chapel on this site in 1838, a year after the congregation was formed. Listed in the National Register of Historic Places, Christ Church Cathedral features stained glass and a bell tower.

Organized in 1836, the Bethel African Methodist Episcopal Church is the oldest continually operating African-American church in the city. The group obtained its first church building from the Episcopalians when the Christ Church congregation started the facility that would become Christ Church Cathedral.

WHERE TO FIND A PLACE TO WORSHIP

Today, the Greater Indianapolis area is home to more than 1,100 congregations covering more than 100 denominations. A good place to find information on local houses of worship is the Yellow Pages of the telephone book. Organized by denomination as well as by alphabetized listing, the Yellow Pages give locations and telephone numbers for various houses of worship. Many churches also have Web sites, which are a handy way to learn when services are held and what programs are offered.

The local daily newspaper, the *Indianapolis Star*, also offers worship listings, as does the paper's Web site—www.indystar.com.

If you are a newcomer to Indianapolis, another good place to learn about houses of worship is from your coworkers and neighbors. You might also like to look around your neighborhood to find a house of worship that is close to home and seems inviting. There is nothing wrong with "just looking" and visiting several houses of worship before you settle on the one that suits you best.

INDEX